Educational Research

Educational Research

An Integrative Introduction

Evelyn J. Sowell

Boston   Burr Ridge, IL   Dubuque, IA   Madison, WI   New York   San Francisco   St. Louis
Bangkok   Bogotá   Caracas   Lisbon   London   Madrid
Mexico City   Milan   New Delhi   Seoul   Singapore   Sydney   Taipei   Toronto

McGraw-Hill Higher Education

*A Division of The **McGraw-Hill** Companies*

EDUCATIONAL RESEARCH: AN INTEGRATIVE INTRODUCTION

Published by McGraw-Hill, an imprint of The McGraw-Hill Companies, Inc., 1221 Avenue of the Americas, New York, NY 10020. Copyright © 2001 by The McGraw-Hill Companies, Inc. All rights reserved. No part of this publication may be reproduced or distributed in any form or by any means, or stored in a database or retrieval system, without the prior written consent of The McGraw-Hill Companies, Inc., including, but not limited to, in any network or other electronic storage or transmission, or broadcast for distance learning.

Some ancillaries, including electronic and print components, may not be available to customers outside the United States.

This book is printed on acid-free paper.

2 3 4 5 6 7 8 9 0 VNH/VNH 0 9 8 7 6 5 4 3

ISBN 0-07-059817-7

Vice president and editor-in-chief: *Thalia Dorwick*
Editorial director: *Jane E. Vaicunas*
Sponsoring editor: *Beth Kaufman*
Developmental editors: *Cara Harvey/Kate Scheinman*
Marketing manager: *Daniel M. Loch*
Project manager: *Christine Walker*
Production supervisor: *Kara Kudronowicz*
Coordinator of freelance design: *David W. Hash*
Cover designer: *Jamie A. O'Neal*
Photo research coordinator: *John C. Leland*
Supplement coordinator: *Jodi K. Banowetz*
Compositor: *Shepherd, Inc.*
Typeface: *10/12 New Baskerville*
Printer: *Quebecor Printing Book Group/Fairfield, PA*

Library of Congress Cataloging-in-Publication Data

Sowell, Evelyn J.
  Educational research : an integrative introduction / Evelyn J. Sowell. — 1st. ed.
    p. cm.
  Includes bibliographical references and indexes.
  ISBN 0-07-059817-7 (alk. paper)
    1. Education—Research—Methodology. I. Title.

LB1028 .S675   2001
370'.7'2-dc21   00-055454
                                                      CIP

www.mhhe.com

About the Author

Evelyn J. Sowell, Professor of Education at Arizona State University West, received her doctorate in elementary education from Northern Illinois University. A former elementary teacher, she has authored articles, reports, and books including Curriculum: An Integrative Introduction, Second Edition (Prentice-Hall-Merrill, 2000). In addition to educational research methods, her special interests include mathematics education and curriculum education.

To Sharon, Duane, and Norm

Brief Contents

Preface xii

PART I — Introduction to Educational Research 1

CHAPTER 1 — *Overview of Research Processes and Products 2*

CHAPTER 2 — *Overview of Research Problems and Methods 14*

PART II — Research Problems, Participants, and Instrumentation 27

CHAPTER 3 — *Problem Statements and Literature Reviews 28*

CHAPTER 4 — *Participant Procedures 42*

CHAPTER 5 — *Instrumentation Procedures 59*

PART III — Methods and Results for Quantitative Studies 77

CHAPTER 6 — *Design Procedures for Experimental Research 78*

CHAPTER 7 — *Design Procedures for Descriptive Research 94*

CHAPTER 8 — *Descriptive Statistical Data Analyses and Results 107*

CHAPTER 9 — *Inferential Statistical Data Analyses and Results 126*

PART IV — Methods and Results for Qualitative Studies 141

CHAPTER 10 — *Qualitative Research Procedures and Results 142*

CHAPTER 11 — *Historical Research Procedures and Results 155*

PART V — Integration of Research Problems, Methods, and Outcomes 167

CHAPTER 12 — *Discussions of Results 168*

CHAPTER 13 — *Creation of Research Problems and Literature Reviews 179*

CHAPTER 14 — *Creation of Proposals for Research Projects 199*

Answers to Selected Exercises 217

APPENDIX A — *Research Reports 222*

APPENDIX B — *Data Collection Strategies 340*

APPENDIX C — *Inferential Statistical Tests 348*

References 356
Glossary 359
Index 367

Contents

Preface xii

PART I Introduction to Educational
Research 1

CHAPTER 1 *Overview of Research Processes
and Products 2*

The Nature of Educational Research 3
Purposeful Ethical Enterprise 3
Systematic Processes 3
Valid and Reliable Outcomes 4

Qualitative and Quantitative Inquiry Modes 5
Goals of Research 5
Plans of Attack 7
Settings for Projects 7
Roles of Researchers 8
Intended Uses of Results 8

Reports of Educational Research 8
Primary and Secondary Reports 9
Sources 11

CHAPTER 2 *Overview of Research Problems
and Methods 14*

Goals of Research and Research Problems 15
Explanation 15
Prediction 17
Control 17

Importance of Understanding Research Goals 19

Research Methods 20
Descriptive Methods 21

Experimental Methods 22
Qualitative Methods 22
Historical Methods 23

Common Elements in Research Plans 24

PART II Research Problems, Participants, and
Instrumentation 27

CHAPTER 3 *Problem Statements and Literature
Reviews 28*

Problem Statements and Goals of Research
Revisited 29
Explanation 29
Prediction 30
Control 30

Literature Reviews 31
Purpose 31
Content 32

Introductory Sections of Research Reports 36
Descriptions 36
Criteria for Evaluation 38
Applications of Criteria 38

Introduction to the Creation of Research Problems
and Literature Reviews 41

CHAPTER 4 *Participant Procedures 42*

Populations and Samples 43

Random Samples 43
Simple Random and Stratified Random Samples 44
Cluster and Multistage Samples 44

Nonrandom Samples 45
  Systematic Samples 45
  Quota Samples 45
  Purposeful Samples 45
  Convenience Samples 47
Procedures for Quantitative Studies 47
  Determination of Sample Sizes 47
  Selection Procedures 48
  Assignment Procedures 50
Procedures for Qualitative Studies 52
  Determination of Sample Sizes 52
  Selection Procedures 52
Participant Subsections of Research Reports 54
  Descriptions 54
  Criteria for Evaluation 55
  Applications of Criteria 55

CHAPTER 5 *Instrumentation Procedures 59*

Instrumentation for Research Projects 60
Procedures for Quantitative Studies 61
  Selection or Development of Strategies 61
  Suitability of Strategies for Projects 62
Procedures for Qualitative Studies 68
  Development of Strategies 68
  Suitability of Strategies for Projects 69
Instrumentation Subsections in Research
    Reports 70
  Descriptions 71
  Criteria for Evaluation 71
  Application of Criteria 72

PART III   Methods and Results for Quantitative
         Studies 77

CHAPTER 6 *Design Procedures for Experimental
         Research 78*

Treatment Procedures 79
  Major Types of Comparisons 79
  Other Comparisons 79
  Treatment Administration 81

Procedures for Data Collection
    and Handling 81
Systematic Application of Procedures 81
Designs for True Experiments 82
  Pretest and Posttest Control Group Design 82
  Posttest Only Design 83
  Factorial Designs 83
Designs for Quasi-experiments 85
Designs for Pre-experiments 86
Designs for Complex Experiments 88
Method Sections in Experimental Research
    Reports 89
  Descriptions 89
  Criteria for Evaluation 89
  Application of Criteria 90

CHAPTER 7 *Design Procedures for Descriptive
         Research 94*

Procedures for Data Collection
    and Handling 95
Systematic Application of Procedures 95
Design Procedures for Status Studies 95
  Meta-Analyses 95
  Survey Studies 97
Design Procedures for Causal Comparative
    Studies 98
Design Procedures for Correlation
    and Prediction Studies 100
  Correlation Studies 100
  Prediction Studies 101
Method Sections in Descriptive Research
    Reports 102
  Descriptions 102
  Criteria for Evaluation 103
  Applications of Criteria 103

CHAPTER 8 *Descriptive Statistical Data
         Analyses and Results 107*

Procedures for Group Data Analyses 108
  Distributions and Percentages 109

Measures of Central Tendency and Variation 109

Normal Distributions 113

Standard Scores 115

Effect Sizes 115

Procedures for Analyses of Associations among Data 116

Correlation Analyses 116

Regression Analyses 119

Results Sections of Research Reports 121

Descriptions—Part 1 122

Criteria for Evaluation 122

Application of Criteria 123

CHAPTER 9 *Inferential Statistical Data Analyses and Results 126*

Procedures for Inferential Statistical Analyses 127

Hypothesis Testing Strategies 127

Statement of Hypotheses 128

Selection of Inferential Tests 131

Selection of Significance Levels 132

Application of Tests 134

Evaluation of Test Outcomes 135

Results Sections of Research Reports 136

Descriptions—Part 2 137

Criteria for Evaluation 137

Application of Criteria 138

PART IV Methods and Results for Qualitative Studies 141

CHAPTER 10 *Qualitative Research Procedures and Results 142*

Procedures for Data Collection and Handling 143

Circumstances 143

Preparation of Data for Analyses 145

Procedures for Analyses and Interpretations 146

Assignment of Codes 147

Memos and Diagrams 149

Computer Software Programs for Analyses 150

Results and Interpretations 150

Procedures and Results Sections in Qualitative Research Reports 151

Descriptions 151

Criteria for Evaluation 151

Application of Criteria 152

CHAPTER 11 *Historical Research Procedures and Results 155*

Procedures for Data Collection 156

Location of Data Sources 156

Evaluation of Data Sources 158

Data Collection Techniques 159

Procedures for Analyses and Interpretations 160

Development of a Frame of Reference 160

Data Reduction 161

Construction of the Narrative 162

Introduction and Narrative Sections in Historical Research Reports 163

Descriptions 163

Criteria for Evaluation 164

Application of Criteria 164

PART V Integration of Research Problems, Methods, and Outcomes 167

CHAPTER 12 *Discussions of Results 168*

Outcomes of Research Projects 169

Interpretations of Results in Quantitative Reports 169

Problem Definition and Literature Review 170

Design Components 170

Conclusions 171

Recommendations 172

Discussion and Conclusion Sections of Research Reports 174

Descriptions 174

Criteria for Evaluation 174

Application of Criteria 175

Abstract Sections of Research Reports 177

CHAPTER 13 *Creation of Research Problems and Literature Reviews 179*

Initiation of a Research Project 180

Sources of Research Problems 180

Brief Literature Survey 182

Preparation of an Initial Problem Statement 183

Selection Criteria 183

Wording Strategies 184

Execution of the Literature Search 186

Databases for the Search 186

Scope of the Search 190

Search Strategies 190

Use of Search Results 192

Preparation of an Initial Draft of the Literature Review 193

Selection of the Justification 193

Support of the Justification 193

Development of the References List 194

Reconsideration and Revision of the Problem Statement 195

Revision of the Literature Review and References List 196

Content Revisions 196

Form Revisions 197

CHAPTER 14 *Creation of Proposals for Research Projects 199*

Initiation of a Research Proposal 200

Treatment Procedures in Experiments 200

Definition of Levels 200

Assignments to Participants 202

Personnel and Costs 202

Data Source Procedures 203

Participant Sources 203

Selection Strategies 203

Nonparticipant Sources 204

Costs 204

Instrumentation, Data Collection, and Handling Procedures 205

Strategies for Numerical Data 205

Strategies for Verbal Data 206

Circumstances for Data Collection 207

Personnel and Costs 207

Data Analysis Procedures 209

Strategies for Quantitative Analyses 209

Strategies for Qualitative Analyses 209

Personnel and Costs 209

Summary of the Method Section 210

Time Line 210

Budget 211

Introduction to the Project 211

Introduction 211

Purpose of the Study 212

Educational Significance 212

Definitions 212

Summary 212

Title 212

Completion of the Proposal 213

Review Board Approval 213

Answers to Selected Exercises 217

APPENDIX A *Research Reports 222*

APPENDIX B *Data Collection Strategies 340*

APPENDIX C *Inferential Statistical Tests 348*

References 356

Glossary 359

Name Index 367

Subject Index 368

Preface

Prior to engaging in any project, researchers must study the reports of other investigations in the same problem area. This study must answer questions such as these: How does a particular report contribute to knowledge in this problem area? Do the methods used provide data for solid answers to the research questions? Can the results be applied to other research settings?

Equipping students enrolled in an introductory educational research course to answer similar questions is one major purpose of this text. Assisting them in planning a project using their knowledge of research is a second purpose.

Moreover, students should be aware of qualitative as well as quantitative inquiry. Both the numbers of qualitative research reports and the journals that publish them have increased in the past decade. Consequently, reading these reports with understanding should be part of an introductory educational research course.

Qualitative inquiry is more than just a method, as described in some educational research texts. Qualitative researchers investigate questions of a different nature, reach conclusions by different means, and use outcomes differently than do their quantitative colleagues. In this text, the two inquiry modes are considered as complementary approaches for answering research questions.

✄ Themes

In *Educational Research: An Integrative Introduction,* educational research is characterized as a purposeful ethical enterprise that uses systematic processes to achieve valid and reliable solutions to educational problems. This characterization provides several themes that bind together the book's content and give it its subtitle. Throughout the chapters:

1. The goal or purpose of research is shown to prescribe the general method (e.g., experimental, historical) for obtaining the solution to an educational problem.

2. Procedures are tied to systematic processes (e.g., identify the problem, review known information in the problem area).

3. The validity and reliability of procedures are shown to be critically important in the collection, analysis, and interpretation of data.

4. Ethical considerations are tied to the selection of problems, procedures for solution, and interpretations of outcomes.

These recurring themes are intended to demystify the processes for individuals beginning their study of educational research. Content is presented incrementally, allowing readers to connect new information with knowledge they have. Frequent use of illustrations from research reports shows these themes at work in various research settings. Exercises and questions for discussion also assist readers in integrating educational research content.

Organization

The ideas highlighted in Chapters 1 and 2, which overview the domains of educational research, are elaborated in the chapters that follow. Chapters 3 through 12 use as their organizing focus the sequence of research report sections; that is, introduction including literature review and problem, method, results, and discussion.

Two final chapters, which can be studied at any point following Chapter 3, focus on the creation of problem statements and literature reviews (chapter 13) and the remainder of a project proposal (chapter 14). Use of these chapters helps readers to integrate their knowledge and skills and provides background for additional study of research methods.

Nine research reports from educational journals are located in Appendix A. These reports use the methods discussed in this text and a variety of data sources, including participants from elementary grades through university levels, as well as historical sources such as school boards minutes, newspaper advertisements, and others.

These reports furnish many of the illustrations for the content and for the exercises in this text. The decision to place these intact reports in an appendix is a deliberate strategy to help readers study research concepts within contexts.

Pedagogy

To help students understand and apply the concepts, the following pedagogical features are used in *Educational Research: An Integrative Introduction:*

- Each chapter begins with **one or two goals that establish a focus** for study.
- **Accessible and friendly writing style** is addressed to readers using technical, but simple, language.
- **Criteria for evaluation of research report sections** pull together major ideas at the end of Chapters 3–12.
- **Exercises allow readers to apply these criteria** to reports in Chapters 3–12.
- Author-prepared **critiques provide examples of how to apply these criteria.**

- **Additional exercises** assist readers in processing information within chapter sections.
- **Answers to selected exercises** provide feedback to readers.
- **Clearly written suggestions for the development of research proposals, including problems, literature reviews, method, time line, and budget sections** are invaluable guides and resources.

An Instructor's Manual to accompany *Educational Research: An Integrative Introduction* is available from the publisher. This manual provides suggestions for instruction and evaluation.

✖ Acknowledgments

I am indebted to many people for helping to make this book possible. Students at Arizona State University West used the book in various drafts. Your questions and comments helped to clarify my ideas. Bee Gallegos, ASU West librarian, contributed information about literature searches and reviewed Chapter 13. My colleagues, Ray Buss and Joe Ryan, offered helpful comments that improved this manuscript. My thanks to all of you.

The author and McGraw-Hill would like to thank the following reviewers for their helpful comments and insights during the writing of this text:

Richard L. Antes, *Indiana State University*
Francis X. Archambault, *University of Connecticut*
Karen Block, *University of Pittsburgh*
Dogoni Cisse, *Western Kentucky University*
Jan Gamratd, *The University of New Mexico*
David A. Gilman, *Indiana State University*
Warren Hodge, *University of North Florida*
Marilyn Lisowski, *Eastern Illinois University*
Joe D. Nichols, *Purdue University*
Doris Prater, *University of Houston–Clear Lake*
John R. Ray, *University of Tennessee*
Thomas R. Renckly, *Troy State University*
John Tenny, *Willamette University*
Paul Westmeyer, *The University of Texas at San Antonio*
Dale Whittington, *Cleveland State University*

I thank the authors and copyright holders who gave permission to reprint their materials. Inclusion of these materials improves the quality of learning that can take place through study of this text.

To the editorial and production staffs at The McGraw-Hill Companies, I offer my sincere thanks. Your encouragement, patience, and help with many details were vital to the completion of this book.

Finally, to my family and friends, thanks for letting me talk to you about this writing project. Your caring support was very helpful.

Introduction to Educational Research

The term *educational research* applies in many situations. For example, research refers broadly to the processes or procedures that investigators use, as well as to the products or reports that follow completion of their projects. This term also applies to specific situations. Teachers who systematically search for an increased understanding of students' academic needs may use research processes. So may administrators and staff developers who seek to improve a school's environment.

Chapter 1 introduces you to the nature of educational research, to what it is, and to what is meant when this term is used. Researchers typically adopt one of two basic approaches to research, known as quantitative or qualitative inquiry, both of which are described briefly. In this chapter you also become acquainted with several research reports that will be studied in depth during the course of reading this book.

Chapter 2 narrows the focus slightly as it overviews research problems and methods. Its main point is to show how a well-stated research problem reveals a particular goal for research. This goal, in turn, prescribes a general method of solution.

The information about research in Part I is general; that's why it is called an introduction. However, the information in Chapters 1 and 2 serves as a framework on which you can hang the additional information you encounter in later chapters. Each idea introduced in Part I is elaborated on and related to concepts in later chapters. This is a major reason for the book's subtitle, *An Integrative Introduction.*

Overview of Research Processes and Products

❖ **The Nature of Educational Research**
    Purposeful Ethical Enterprise
    Systematic Processes
    Valid and Reliable Outcomes
❖ **Quantitative and Qualitative Inquiry Modes**
    Goals of Research
    Plans of Attack

    Settings for Projects
    Roles of Researchers
    Intended Uses of Results
❖ **Reports of Educational Research**
    Primary and Secondary Reports
    Sources

The outcomes of research projects can provide major sources of information for the solution of educational problems. However, to produce viable results, researchers must pursue solutions to problems through the use of systematic procedures.

Researchers use systematic procedures in quantitative and qualitative inquiry modes based on their problem. In quantitative and qualitative inquiry, researchers attack problem solutions differently, use different research settings, take different roles for themselves, and produce results for different purposes. Nevertheless, these modes provide complementary methods for the study of educational problems.

Following the completion of projects, researchers disseminate research reports to ben-efit practitioners and other researchers who work in the problem area. Although some reports are presented as conference papers, many more are published in books and journals. Much of this textbook is dedicated to helping you understand written research reports so that you, too, may use these sources of information in your professional role.

Goals

To enable you to:

- distinguish between reports that use quantitative and qualitative inquiry modes; and
- describe the format of primary research reports.

⚔ The Nature of Educational Research

In this text, educational research is broadly conceived as the investigation of problems or questions concerned with the improvement of education. More specifically, **educational research**[1] is characterized as a purposeful ethical enterprise that uses systematic processes to obtain valid and reliable outcomes as solutions to educational problems.

Purposeful Ethical Enterprise

Potential educational research problems exist wherever people work together in teaching and learning situations. Therefore, when investigators undertake the study of these problems, they are expected to have a purpose for their project beyond the satisfaction of their own curiosities.

In some situations, researchers investigate **problems** whose answers contribute to the stores of knowledge about theory and practice. Usually cast as long-term projects, these studies benefit the education community generally. Typically, these projects are described as *basic* research because their contribution advances fundamental knowledge and theory (Patton, 1990). For example, Larson and Parker (1996)) study teachers' conceptions of classroom discussion and Wentzel (1997) studies student motivation in middle school.

Other researchers investigate problems whose answers provide insights into societal concerns. Outcomes of these studies, known as *applied* projects, may ultimately benefit many people, but the impetus for, and the direct beneficiaries of, the results are known at the outset. Gettinger's (1993) study of the effects of error correction, a method of teaching spelling, and Holmes and Keffer's (1995) report on attempts to increase verbal *Scholastic Aptitude Test (SAT)* scores are examples of applied projects.

Educational practitioners sometimes engage in applied research by undertaking *action* research projects. Their purpose is the solution of a particular problem located within a particular setting (Patton, 1990). Had Holmes and Keffer been interested in increasing the *SAT* scores of a particular group of high school students, their study would qualify as an action research project.

Regardless of its specific purpose, research should be conducted as an ethical enterprise that protects participants, whether they are children or other vulnerable populations. Those engaged in educational research are expected to evaluate their research for its ethical and scientific adequacy and conduct internal and external relations according to high ethical standards (Ethical Standards of the American Educational Research Association, 1992).

Systematic Processes

Stated explicitly in the conception of research used in this text is the idea that investigators use systematic processes that typically identify the problem,

---

[1]Boldfaced terms are defined in the Glossary.

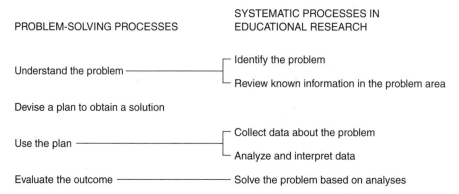

FIGURE 1.1   Relationships between problem-solving processes and systematic processes in educational research.

review the known information in the problem area, collect data about the problem, analyze and interpret data, and solve the problem based on these analyses. These processes are closely related to problem-solving processes (see Figure 1.1).

The problem, at least the problem *area*, is identified as one of the initial processes. Almost immediately, researchers search for, read, and evaluate known information about it. Of course, understanding the problem by figuring out what is known and what is unknown is a common problem-solving technique. This process often results in clarification of the research problem.

The next problem-solving step consists of making a plan for the solution of the problem. Although this process is not explicit within the systematic processes, most researchers devise a research plan as their next step. Researchers then collect and analyze data that provide answers. Note that research problems drive data collection and analysis, not vice versa (Eisenhart & Howe, 1992). Analysis includes the appropriate interpretation of data in terms of their setting and known information about the problem. In the process of drawing conclusions, researchers systematically search for patterns and convergence within their data. These processes provide a defensible solution to the problem, a process that problem solvers label as "evaluating the outcome."

The general flow of research processes is from beginning-to-end of the sequence. However, these processes may backtrack and overlap, depending on the problem and the mode of inquiry selected by researchers. Additional information about these processes follows in the Quantitative and Qualitative Inquiry Modes section.

Valid and Reliable Outcomes

If research is to improve education, outcomes must provide valid and reliable answers to questions. However, because answers to questions about people and their activities are not absolutes, research outcomes have degrees of validity and reliability.

Validity of research refers to the degree to which outcomes are accurate and grounded in data. For example, did the data collection processes provide accurate data for analyses and were the analyses suited for answering the problem? Valid outcomes result from the selection and application of procedures that produce truthful answers to research questions.

Reliability of research refers to the degree to which outcomes are dependable or trustworthy. For example, are there sufficient data to ensure their dependability? Can the data be replicated? Reliable outcomes result from consistency in the selection and application of research procedures.

As standards for evaluating research, validity and reliability can usually be traced to the degrees of systematization in the processes used by researchers. Those who painstakingly formulate and carry out research plans typically obtain outcomes having greater validity and reliability than the results obtained by individuals who proceed haphazardly.

✴ Quantitative and Qualitative Inquiry Modes

How the systematic processes are carried out is governed largely by the researchers' choice of inquiry modes. In everyday language, **quantitative inquiry** suggests investigations involving numbers. **Qualitative inquiry** involves the use of words. To some extent, these distinctions are also valid in discussions about educational research. However, qualitative inquiry can and does use numbers and quantitative inquiry also uses words. Understanding inquiry modes is more substantive than a numbers versus words distinction.

Some researchers view quantitative and qualitative inquiry as separate models, based on wholly different philosophical assumptions about how the world works, how knowledge is created, and the role of values (Lincoln & Guba, 1985; Maykut & Morehouse, 1994). Other researchers take a moderate approach, acknowledging that the two inquiry modes serve different purposes, employ different processes, and use results in different ways (Jaeger, 1988; Lancy, 1993; Newman & Benz, 1998).

While the moderate approach acknowledges differences, it allows for the possibility that the two inquiry modes provide complementary means for solving educational problems. This is the perspective of the research methods used in this text. The subsections that follow highlight the goals, planning approaches, settings, researcher roles, and intended uses of results in the two inquiry modes.

Goals of Research

Quantitative and qualitative inquiry modes can be used to investigate several types of educational problems. In the *quantitative* approach, researchers usually begin their investigation with a particular **hypothesis,** or proposed answer to a question, which the research project is to test. This hypothesis may

TABLE 1.1

What Are Variables?

Feature	Description
Definition	**Variables** are the things that educational researchers study. "A variable is a property that takes on different values. Putting it redundantly, a variable is something that varies" (Kerlinger, 1986, p. 27).
Illustrations	Consider how learning environments may differ in two elementary school classrooms. Two teachers typically structure time, space, and student interactions differently, even though they teach essentially the same content to students of approximately the same age. Students in one class may work independently most of the time, while those in the other class perform most of their activities cooperatively. "Learning environments" and "work style" are examples of variables.
General or specific designations	Variables may be identified by their general names, such as learning environment or academic performance. Other variables may be named specifically, such as independent work style or cooperative work style.
Numerical or categorical values	Researchers assign numerical or categorical values to the variations in variables. Test scores, such as 75 or 92, frequently represent values of the variable, academic achievement. Attitude toward school, if measured by rating scales, may also be represented by values such as 1 or 3. Values for these variables have been assigned numerically.
	Role-play, lecture, and discussion represent values of the variable, methods of teaching social studies. Authoritarian, democratic, and laissez-faire represent values of the variable, leadership styles. Values for these variables have been assigned categorically.

be deduced from theory or observations from the researchers' own experiences. The intent of these inquiries is to answer questions concerning relationships between (among) variables named in the hypothesis (for additional information, see Table 1.1). Some studies seek the confirmation of a relationship, but others seek knowledge about the nature of the relationships.

In the *qualitative* mode, researchers typically begin with a less clear purpose because their interest is in describing, explaining, or possibly both describing and explaining particular social phenomena found in organizations, informal gatherings, and individuals. Examples of phenomena include the interactions within teachers' lounges, peer group influences, and decision-making strategies in parent-teacher organizations. Any one of these examples suggests a **social phenomenon** that includes multiple variables of interest bound together in intricate, multifaceted relationships. Qualitative researchers seek to discover patterns of meaning in the examination of words, actions, and documents associated with social phenomena.

Plans of Attack

Quantitative inquiry proceeds through a generally deductive approach in which researchers begin with a hypothesis, as mentioned in the purpose. This hypothesis grows out of the review of known information in the problem area. Thereafter, the researchers arrange for testing the hypothesis. They collect and analyze data to reach a conclusion about the viability of the hypothesis as an answer to the research question. The processes involved are largely deductive, in that reasoning proceeds in a general-to-specific sequence.

On the other hand, *qualitative* inquiry uses a largely inductive approach. Researchers begin with an idea or an intention for their study that captures the essence of what they expect to work on in the research setting. Some researchers examine literature and then design their study, and some use the opposite sequence (Berg, 1998). Specific questions may emerge as the study proceeds. Data are gathered, analyzed, and interpreted in ongoing cycles that pose opportunities for additional questions and data gathering. Thus, processes usually proceed from specific-to-general.

Settings for Projects

Educational researchers conduct research in many settings and institutions, including schools, colleges, universities, hospitals, and prisons (Ethical Standards, 1992). For *quantitative* studies, researchers locate participants who embody the variables of concern. For example, if the study focuses on social studies problem-solving abilities, researchers seek participants who are studying or have studied social studies, rather than those in romance languages or woodworking.

Settings for *qualitative* research projects must be chosen with care because the phenomenon of interest to researchers must be present. Settings include the circumstances that involve individuals, as well as bounded groups, such as classrooms, social organizations, community groups, and school faculties. Moreover, researchers must have professional access to the people within these settings. These issues combine to make selection of sites for qualitative studies an especially important process.

Roles of Researchers

Researchers adopt different roles in quantitative and qualitative research. In the former, investigators maintain a detached position in which they interject themselves into the research situation as little as possible, to minimize any effects their presence might have on the outcomes. Frequently, individuals other than researchers, such as teachers or assistants, carry out the tasks involved in generating changes or gathering data.

The opposite situation is characteristic of *qualitative* research. Here, investigators are closely associated with the processes and participants in the study. Because their purpose is to understand social phenomena, researchers usually have opportunities not only to observe the situation, but also to converse with the participants within the setting. These investigators are likely to ask questions, record information at research sites, and discuss findings with the participants. Therefore, these researchers are involved heavily in the details of the project.

Intended Uses of Results

Quantitative researchers are typically concerned with relationships between (among) specific variables. Under some circumstances, investigators may infer that their results apply in other settings. In brief, when the participants who provide data actually represent larger groups of individuals who are not selected, then investigators may infer that results from participants are similar to those that might be obtained from the larger group. These processes, known as **generalization,** apply in limited circumstances.

On the other hand, *qualitative* researchers usually recognize the uniqueness of each project. Because the results are a product of the people involved, researchers have little expectation that the same results occur in alternate settings with other individuals. This does not mean that generalization of results is impossible; rather, it means that qualitative researchers do not expect that outcomes in one situation necessarily hold true in others.

Table 1.2 summarizes these sketches that compare quantitative and qualitative modes of inquiry. The remaining chapters support these comparisons.

Reports of Educational Research

Following the completion of research projects, investigators typically prepare reports. These reports take different forms depending on whether they are delivered orally or prepared as reading material. A report delivered at a conference attended largely by researchers and other interested educators may differ from one published in a journal. Sometimes conference reports are working papers that ultimately result in published reports.

Reports are usually written for particular audiences that influence the authors' choices of content and writing style. Graduate students prepare their reports for faculty committees. Grant recipients write reports for their funding agencies. Authors of journal reports prepare papers for the

TABLE 1.2

Comparisons of Quantitative and Qualitative Modes of Inquiry

	Quantitative Inquiry	**Qualitative Inquiry**
Goals of research	Explanation, prediction, or control of observable events that involve specific variables	Description and explanation of past and present social phenomena
Plans of attack	Generally deductive	Generally inductive
Settings for projects	Important to study; contain variables of concern and interest	Essential to study; contain phenomenon of concern and interest
Roles of researchers	Detached from study	Indispensable to study
Intended uses of results	Results sometimes generalized to other settings	Results explain phenomenon for particular settings

journal's primary readerships (e.g., educational practitioners, laypersons, researchers).

Primary and Secondary Reports

Primary research reports include theses and dissertations prepared by graduate students, as well as reports prepared by researchers for funding agencies or publications. These reports are called primary because they provide first-hand descriptions of the projects. Here, researchers systematically display the problem, its connection with the literature, the methods of solution, and the outcomes.

Research reports typically contain the following sections in this format: a **title,** an **abstract,** the **introduction, methods** or **procedures, results** or **findings, discussion, references,** and occasionally, **appendices** (see Table 1.3 for the functions of each section). This format is popular for primary research reports in many journals. Because of space limitations, graduate student reports and those prepared for funding agencies usually contain more information than do journal reports, but follow a similar format. Note, however, that content subheadings typically serve as section heads in historical and secondary reports.

Some researchers study primary reports to prepare **secondary research reports.** One major category of secondary reports consists of reviews that aggregate research findings from primary studies on a selected topic. Here, authors examine the findings from multiple reports, comment on their strengths and weaknesses, and interpret them, usually to advance or clarify a theory.

TABLE 1.3

Functions of Research Report Sections

Section	Function
Title	Communicates the focus of research reports by naming the variables or the phenomena of the project and the setting in which they were studied.
Abstract	Condenses the entire report into a few well-chosen sentences.
Introduction	Introduces the problem and the context in which it was investigated. Context consists of a critical review of literature about the problem variables or phenomena along with the researchers' justification for the study.
Method (procedures)	Describes the participants, experimental procedures (when used), data collection procedures, and sometimes plans for data analyses.
Results or Findings	Describe the outcomes of data analyses as one or more of the following: figures, tables, or verbal descriptions. May contain unfamiliar symbols that can appear threatening.
Discussion	Provides a conclusion as the solution to the problem, elaboration of results, and comments on how findings add to knowledge in problem area.
References	List complete citations for each source in the report.
Appendices	Provide additional information about instruments, participants, data collection processes, or other procedures that clarify the method section.

For example, in a review of English-as-a-second language (ESL) cognitive reading processes, Fitzgerald (1995) examined 67 primary reports of research conducted in the United States. The purposes of this review were to characterize this research and integrate the findings. The author claims that this characterization can inform educators about "several issues, such as the particular strengths and/or weaknesses of United States ESL readers, the extent to which their cognitive reading processes are similar to those of native English speakers, and helpful directions for future research" (Fitzgerald, 1995, p. 148). This review helps to clarify a theory about cognitive reading processes.

Other reviews, called *meta-analyses,* serve similar purposes. However, authors of meta-analyses statistically reanalyze data from primary reports dealing with the same general topic (e.g., use of manipulative instructional materials in mathematics, cooperative learning). Outcomes of these analyses are also reported within interpretive frameworks.

Either type of review furnishes a good starting point for beginning a study of research on a particular problem. These reviews typically contain multiple references to primary research reports that provide detailed information.

A second category of secondary research reports consists of abbreviated versions of primary reports, prepared by authors not associated with the projects. For example, the *Educational Research Newsletter*[2] provides educators, mainly classroom teachers, with research findings on numerous topics. Brief reports highlight the main ideas of several projects in nontechnical language and refer readers who want additional information to the complete reports. A monthly feature in the *Phi Delta Kappan,* entitled "Research," has a similar purpose. The feature describes one or two research reports and adds commentary.

Sources

Research reports in books and journals are available at university libraries and in many school district professional development centers. Books typically furnish reviews of research on topics within broad areas. For example, almost every subdiscipline within education has a handbook of research (e.g., *Handbook of Research on Curriculum*) that provides comprehensive overviews of the status of research on topics of common interest.

Other books, however, provide firsthand accounts of research usually directed to one major theme. For example, *Volume 7: Advances in Research on Teaching* "is devoted to research on the formation, functioning, and effects of teachers' and students' expectations in classrooms" (Brophy, 1998, p. ix). Each of the book's nine sections elaborates on this theme.

GENERAL INTEREST

    American Educational Research Journal
    Journal of Educational Psychology
    Journal of Educational Research
    Review of Educational Research

SPECIALIZED INTEREST BY CONTENT

    Counselor Education and Supervision
    Early Childhood Research Quarterly
    Educational Administration Quarterly
    For the Learning of Mathematics
    Journal of Research in Science Teaching
    Reading Research Quarterly
    Research in Middle Level Education
    Research in the Teaching of English
    Social Education

SPECIALIZED INTEREST BY METHOD

    Anthropology and Education Quarterly
    History of Education Quarterly
    International Journal of Qualitative Studies in Education
    Journal of Experimental Research

FIGURE 1.2   Examples of educational research journals.

---

[2]For more information, contact Educational Research Newsletter, Inc., P. O. Box 789, West Barnstable, MA 02668-0789.

Many educational research journals are published in the United States. In addition, an increasing number of journals published in other countries share international audiences, including readers in the United States. Professional educational organizations or colleges of education sponsor journals that publish research reports; for-profit corporations own other journals. Some journals publish research and research-related papers exclusively, but other journals publish opinion papers and other types of articles in addition to research reports.

Most educational researchers recognize the existence of several levels of journals in the United States. Some editorial advisory boards set such rigorous standards for acceptance of papers that only a few of the many reports received can be published. Other journals have less rigorous standards, but their editors deny publication of reports deemed to have major flaws.

Each subdiscipline within education has at least one journal devoted largely to the publication of research. Some journals also specialize in the publication of reports based on methods of study. Finally, a number of journals publish research on a range of topics. For example, the *Journal of Educational Psychology* publishes reports on a broad spectrum of research topics. Figure 1.2 displays a sampling of journals that publish research reports.

Appendix A contains nine primary research reports reprinted from diverse educational journals. You will see many references to these reports and will be asked to read sections from them as you study this text. These reports provide illustrations of major ideas described in the chapters. The reports are also used in exercises.

E X E R C I S E   1 . 1

This exercise provides an opportunity to acquaint you with several research reports in Appendix A and to check your understanding of the chapter goals.

1. Note the format of these reports:

   A5 Preservice and Inservice Secondary Teachers' Orientations to Content Area Reading

   A9 Reconsidering the Power of the Superintendent in the Progressive Period

   Does each report have an introduction, method, results, discussion, and reference section? Do the sections bear these labels? Explain.

2. Scan the following reports:

   A1 Effects of Error Correction on Third Graders' Spelling

   A2 What Is Classroom Discussion? A Look at Teachers' Conceptions

   One report is from a quantitative study; the other is from a qualitative project. Which is which? Explain. Check your responses with those in Answers to Selected Exercises, which follows Chapter 14.

Summary

Chapter 1 describes educational research as the application of systematic processes in the investigation of problems broadly concerned with the improvement of education. It is a purposeful ethical enterprise in which researchers identify their problem, connect it with known information in the problem area, and methodically search for its solution. Researchers aim to obtain valid and reliable outcomes largely through careful linkages among the processes.

Quantitative and qualitative modes of inquiry allow for investigation into many types of research questions. These inquiry modes vary in their purposes for research; in the importance of the setting, the researchers' roles, and the plan of attack; and in the uses of results. These inquiry modes provide complementary methods of finding solutions to educational problems.

Although some research reports are presented orally, many more are written. Primary reports are firsthand accounts of the processes and outcomes. Secondary reports, which are based on primary reports, usually include reviews or provide condensed versions of first-hand accounts. Research reports are abundant in books and journals, particularly in university libraries.

Questions for Discussion

1. Recall an experience in which you heard the term "educational research." Was its meaning in that situation similar to its meaning as used in this chapter? Explain.
2. How are the systematic processes described in Figure 1.1 related to the steps in the scientific method? In brief form, these steps include observation, question, hypothesis, method, result, and conclusion.
3. Refer again to Table 1.1. Name at least three additional variables that are likely to exist in elementary grade classrooms. As you consider these variables, do they have numerical or categorical values? Explain.
4. For the elementary grade classrooms mentioned in question 3, consider the numbers and types of possible teacher-student interactions and student-student interactions. Explain why qualitative researchers might consider these interactions as phenomena.
5. This chapter suggests that researchers adopt different roles, depending on their choice of inquiry modes. With which role would you be more comfortable? Explain.
6. Consider the difference between primary and secondary research reports. Suppose you were seeking an overview of the research on a particular research question. Which type of report would be better at providing an overview? Why?

Overview of Research Problems and Methods

❖ **Goals of Research and Research Problems**
  Explanation
  Prediction
  Control
❖ **Importance of Understanding Research Goals**

❖ **Research Methods**
  Descriptive Methods
  Experimental Methods
  Qualitative Methods
  Historical Methods
❖ **Common Elements in Research Plans**

To understand a research report, you must become aware of the researchers' goal for the project—whether it is for explanation, prediction, or control. This goal is communicated primarily through the wording of the research problem and varies according to quantitative or qualitative inquiry mode.

Understanding the goal of a research project is important because it tells the method by which researchers investigate their problem. Quantitative inquiries use descriptive or exper- imental methods, and qualitative inquiries use one or more naturalistic or historical methods.

Goals

To enable you to:

- link research questions with their respective goals; and
- link research questions with methods appropriate for their solution.

✖ Goals of Research and Research Problems

Whenever researchers investigate problems, they have a broad purpose that corresponds to one of three **goals of research:** explanation, prediction, or control (Kerlinger, 1986). Projects answer different questions, depending on which goal of research the investigators pursue. Table 2.1 displays the three goals of research alongside the research questions commonly associated with the goals.

Explanation

The general idea of explanation as including all the processes for making something clear or understandable is familiar. As a goal of research, explanation has the same meaning. **Explanation** includes grasping the nature of an idea or situation, understanding the relationships among its parts, and describing these relationships. Of course, explanation encompasses the description of events and phenomena.

Quantitative investigations have explanation as their goal whenever researchers appraise the status of variables or determine whether particular variables are associated with, or related to, other variables. Note how these conditions are embedded within the following research questions:

1. What is the status of knowledge about student learning styles?
2. Is self-concept related to public-speaking abilities among high school sophomores?

By its wording, question 1 assumes the existence of a variable known as student learning styles. This question suggests that the researchers describe

---

TABLE 2.1

Relationships among Goals of Research and Their Associated Research Questions

Goal of Research	Questions Answered
Explanation	What is the status of knowledge about a variable?
	Are two or more variables related?
	What is the nature of a phenomenon?
Prediction	Based on a known relationship between (among) variables, can one or more variables be used to predict other variables?
Control	Is the known relationship between (among) variables one of cause and effect?

and explain what is known about learning styles through a review of relevant primary research on this variable. This research provides information about what is known about student learning styles and what needs further study.

Question 2 inquires into the possibility that high school sophomores' self-concepts could be related to their public-speaking abilities. As the question is stated, two variables (self-concept and public-speaking abilities) are clearly identified and both can be measured. Data from measures of sophomores' self-concepts could be associated with data from measures of their public-speaking abilities to see if any relationship exists.

That is, are self-concept scores associated with ratings of public-speaking abilities? Are positive self-concept scores associated with good ratings of public-speaking abilities? If an association is found, researchers note its magnitude or strength, as well as its positive or negative direction. With this information they can explain the relationship between these variables.

Explanation is also the goal of researchers who use *qualitative* inquiry to study social phenomena, whether present or past. Recall that phenomena are typically not well defined because they contain several variables in complex relationships. The following questions have explanation as their goal:

3. What is meant by "learning style"?
4. Which classroom conditions promote academic success of middle school students considered to be at risk of failure?
5. Of what importance are the curriculum reform efforts of the 1960s and 1970s in the development of today's science education standards?

Question 3, which is worded slightly differently from question 1, does not carry the same presumption about the existence of "learning style" as a variable. As used in this question, learning style is a present-day phenomenon whose nature is to be investigated. Researchers expect to observe and interview several individuals to obtain firsthand information about their dispositions, attitudes, and strategies for acquiring information. These processes allow researchers to describe and explain the nature of learning style.

Question 4 calls for explorations of middle school classroom conditions, another *present*-day phenomenon, but question 5 investigates a *past* phenomenon—curriculum reform efforts of 40 years ago. Investigations to answer both questions require researchers to locate and examine relationships among many variables within the settings where the phenomena are studied. To answer question 4, researchers study the interrelationships among students, teachers, curriculum, and school environments. Within this maze of people and events, investigators attempt to discover patterns of meaning that provide explanations about conditions under which low-achieving students can succeed.

Question 5 requires that investigators study retrospectively the curriculum reform efforts in the United States in the 1960s and 1970s following the launch of Sputnik. These curricula set in motion many changes in K–12 science education. Researchers would search for patterns within the science education curriculum literature and the societal changes that prompted the reform efforts.

Prediction

As a goal of research, **prediction** estimates how particular variables are related based on what is known about the past and current relationships among the variables in *quantitative* studies. That is, prediction can serve as a goal of research only in situations in which a strong relationship is known to exist among the variables of interest.

For example, high school students frequently take the *Scholastic Aptitude Test (SAT)* or the *American College Test* (ACT) to meet college or university entrance requirements. Admissions committees use scores from these instruments as one criterion for admission because these test scores have been shown to predict college grade point averages. Associations or relationships between *SAT* or *ACT* scores and college grade point averages have been established by gathering and analyzing data from large numbers of students. Researchers have found that high school students with good test scores earn reasonably good grade point averages.

Consider the following question:

6. Does pre-algebra aptitude predict achievement in algebra I for eighth graders?

In some schools, pre-algebra is a prerequisite to algebra, especially for eighth grade students. Pre-algebra allows students the opportunity to study selected algebra concepts on an informal basis. Because the content of the two courses is related, forecasting the outcome of eighth graders' achievement in algebra I is possible if their pre-algebra aptitude is known. Because pre-algebra aptitude actually measures achievement, scores in pre-algebra can predict scores in algebra, within reason.

Control

When a relationship among variables has been shown to exist, *quantitative* researchers sometimes conduct projects to study further the nature of this relationship. Do these variables have a cause-and-effect relationship? To find out, researchers manipulate or change the values of one variable, then observe effects of this change in the related variable. The essence of **control** is the ability to direct or influence one variable to bring about change in a related variable.

The **manipulated variable** makes changes in the **responding variable** only if a true cause-and-effect relationship exists. Of course, if variables do not have a cause-and-effect relationship, the responding variable is not affected by alterations in the manipulated variable, and any changes observed are due to other causes. An example question involving control as a goal of investigation is:

7. Which of two approaches to teaching reading—literature-based or basal reader—results in better reading comprehension by upper elementary grade students?

This question begins with the assumption that approaches to teaching reading are related to, but are not the only determiners of, students' reading comprehension. The question tests the proposed cause-and-effect relationship between these variables. The approaches to teaching reading in this question are limited to two categorical values, described as literature-based teaching and basal reader teaching. The values of the variable thought to be the "cause" are usually called **treatments,** or **treatment levels.**

Note the future orientation of this question. Researchers must arrange an intervention in which manipulation of the approaches to teaching reading to upper elementary grade students takes place. Following the intervention, its effects are to be observed in the variable, reading comprehension.

In some situations, researchers suspect cause-and-effect relationships among variables, but cannot investigate them using control as a goal because of ethical considerations. Consider this question:

8. Will kindergarten students who had nursery school experience be better developed socially than kindergarten students with no nursery school experience?

At a surface level, this question is similar to question 7 because it involves school experiences and their outcomes—a presumed cause-and-effect relationship. Another look, however, shows that whether children have nursery school experiences is a parental decision, not one that can be made by researchers.

This question has a retrospective orientation. Researchers who investigate question 8 must obtain data on social development from kindergarten children who did and did not have nursery school experience. In this case, the presumed cause, nursery school experience, has taken place naturally; researchers cannot manipulate the variable of nursery school attendance. They can study the effects after the treatment occurs. What results is an explanation, but cause and effect cannot be claimed.

Although researchers might prefer to seek control as their goal, they are restricted to explaining any relationship they find between the variables. The goal of control is appropriate only when researchers are free to manipulate variables. See Table 2.2 for a summary of the research questions and their respective goals of research, as described in this section.

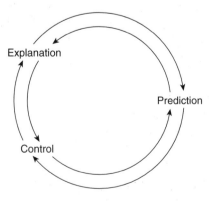

FIGURE 2.1   Relationships among goals of research.

TABLE 2.2

Research Questions Associated with Their Goals of Research

Research Question	Goal of Research
1. What is the status of knowledge about student learning styles?	Explanation
2. Is self-concept related to public-speaking abilities among high school sophomores?	Explanation
3. What is meant by "learning style"?	Explanation
4. Which classroom conditions promote academic success of middle school students considered to be at risk of failure?	Explanation
5. Of what importance are the curriculum reform efforts of the 1960s and 1970s in the development of today's science education standards?	Explanation
6. Does pre-algebra aptitude predict achievement in algebra I for eighth graders?	Prediction
7. Which of two approaches to teaching reading—literature-based or basal reader—results in better reading comprehension by upper elementary grade students?	Control
8. Will kindergarten students who had nursery school experience be better developed socially than peers with no nursery school experience?	Explanation

⚡ Importance of Understanding Research Goals

Much educational research focuses on explanation because researchers recognize the need for knowledge about phenomena or variables and their relationships. In addition, the complexities of educational settings make research that focuses on prediction or control difficult to manage. Consequently, the three goals often function as a loop or circle (see Figure 2.1), with explanation leading to prediction or control and vice versa. New research questions can be generated at any point within the loop.

Why is understanding the goals of research important? Goals prescribe the methods by which researchers investigate research questions. Naturally, outcomes depend on the questions and methods used in their solution.

EXERCISE 2.1

Check your understanding of linkages between research questions and their respective goals of research by completing this exercise. For each research question:

a. Indicate whether the question suggests quantitative or qualitative inquiry;* and
b. Identify the goal of research inferred by the question.

Explain your choices.

1. Does the length of instructional sessions in language laboratories influence high school students' vocabulary development in foreign languages?
2. Which communication patterns are effective in counseling parents of underachieving elementary school students?
3. Does a relationship exist between middle school students' flexibility-of-thinking and their problem-solving capabilities in social studies?
4. How has the passage of the Disabilities Education Act (Public Law 94-142) in 1975 affected educational opportunities for children and youth in the state of Idaho?
5. How will perceptual motor development training affect the eye-hand coordination of first graders?
6. Does knowledge of students' reading comprehension capabilities predict their success in solving mathematics word problems?

*Hint: Quantitative inquiries typically investigate variables that require numerical measurements. Qualitative inquiries explore phenomena that typically result in verbal descriptions.

Therefore, you must be aware of the underlying goal as the first step in evaluating research reports. Without this understanding, attempts to assess reports are problematic.

Research Methods

To this point, *quantitative* and *qualitative* inquiry modes have been used to describe two major approaches to research. Within each inquiry mode, however, are specific research methods. Quantitative inquiries typically use descriptive or experimental research methods. Qualitative inquiries use many methods including, but not limited to:

> semiotics, narrative, content, discourse, archival, and phonemic analysis, even statistics. They (qualitative researchers) also draw upon and utilize the approaches, methods, and techniques of ethnomethodology, phenomenology, hermeneutics, feminism, rhizomatics, deconstructionism, ethnographies, interviews, psychoanalysis, cultural studies, survey research, and participant observation, among others (Denzin & Lincoln, 1994, p. 3).

In this text, most projects that use these methods are described as qualitative studies. However, historical methods are discussed as a separate type of qualitative research.

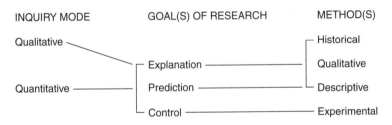

INQUIRY MODE   GOAL(S) OF RESEARCH   METHOD(S)

Qualitative ╮   ┌─ Historical

            ┌─ Explanation ──────────── Qualitative

Quantitative ──────── Prediction ──────────── Descriptive

            └─ Control ──────────────── Experimental

FIGURE 2.2   Relationships among inquiry modes, goals of research, and methods.

Figure 2.2 displays the relationships among inquiry modes, goals of research, and general methods for solution of research problems. In particular, notice that the term "qualitative" refers both to a mode of inquiry and to a general method.

Descriptive Methods

Descriptive methods require the careful collection, analysis, and interpretation of mostly quantitative data to show the status of knowledge about specific variables or to describe degrees of relationships among variables. These studies, which serve the goals of explanation and prediction, are popular.

Researchers concerned with the status of knowledge about learning styles (question 1) would likely use primary research reports prepared by other investigators as their main sources of information. Their tasks would include careful review of these reports to note their strengths and weaknesses. Then the researchers would integrate these findings.

Quantitative researchers who seek an answer to question 2, about the relationship between self-concepts and public-speaking abilities, use self-concept scores and ratings of public-speaking abilities for individual high school sophomores. Analysis should show the degree to which students' self-concept scores are associated with their public-speaking ability ratings. Analysis should also show the direction, whether positive or negative, of any association between these variables.

Researchers who study question 6 (pre-algebra aptitude as a predictor of algebra achievement) also use descriptive methods. These researchers first determine how pre-algebra aptitude scores are related to algebra I achievement scores for a given population of eighth graders. Then researchers collect algebra I achievement scores from eighth grade students who took pre-algebra aptitude tests. Using both items of data for individual students, the researchers calculate a result that shows the degree to which these scores are related. Afterward, they can predict, within reason, algebra I achievement based on pre-algebra aptitude scores within that population.

Question 8, concerned with social development of kindergartners and nursery school experience, uses descriptive methods in its solution.

Researchers measure kindergartners' social development, then determine whether the children have prior nursery school experience. Based on the two sets of information, researchers examine the social development data that distinguish the two groups of kindergartners. Thereafter, the results of these numerical analyses are interpreted and reported.

Experimental Methods

Experimental methods also require the careful collection, analysis, and interpretation of quantitative data. However, prior to data collection, participants undergo planned treatments intended to produce changes in a selected variable related to the treatments. Experimental methods are used in research projects in which control is the goal.

Research question 7 (approaches to teaching reading and reading comprehension) requires the use of experimental methodology. Typically, two groups of students are involved: one group receives literature-based reading instruction and the other, basal reader instruction. In the language of educational research, these groups receive different treatments or levels of the treatment variable, approaches to teaching.

Following a period of instruction using these respective approaches to teaching, researchers measure reading comprehension in both student groups. Data from the two groups are then compared to see if differences exist that might be attributed to the treatments.

Qualitative Methods

Qualitative methods refers to an array of strategies used by researchers to gather mostly verbal data in natural settings, usually over a relatively long time period. Researchers gather data during recurring cycles of collection, analysis, and interpretation. These strategies are intended to provide researchers with holistic perspectives about the phenomenon under investigation.

To understand and describe the meaning of learning style (question 3), the researchers select a setting in which several individuals study the same curriculum content. Data collection focuses on ways that individuals interact with content and methods of presentation. The researchers may observe the individuals' verbal and nonverbal behavior or interview students about their unique ways of learning. Afterward, investigators search for patterns and themes within their data to provide descriptions of learning styles.

Qualitative researchers undertake a challenge in a search of classroom conditions that promote academic success for underachieving students (question 4). The nature of this problem requires that researchers seek information through interactions with students, teachers, and other school and community personnel. Study and analysis of these data are expected to show linkages among the people and their circumstances that distinguish more favorable classroom conditions from less favorable conditions.

TABLE 2.3

Research Questions Associated with Their Goals of Research and Methods

Research Question	Goal of Research	Method
1. What is the status of knowledge about student learning styles?	Explanation	Descriptive
2. Is self-concept related to public-speaking abilities among high school sophomores?	Explanation	Descriptive
3. What is meant by "learning style"?	Explanation	Qualitative
4. Which classroom conditions promote academic success of middle school students considered to be at risk of failure?	Explanation	Qualitative
5. Of what importance are the curriculum reform efforts of the 1960s and 1970s in the development of today's science education standards?	Explanation	Historical
6. Does pre-algebra aptitude predict achievement in algebra I for eighth graders?	Prediction	Descriptive
7. Which of two approaches to teaching reading—literature-based or basal reader—results in better reading comprehension by upper elementary grade students?	Control	Experimental
8. Will kindergarten students who had nursery school experience be better developed socially than peers with no nursery school experience?	Explanation	Descriptive

Historical Methods

Historical methods are typically used to investigate phenomena that occurred in the past, which may be defined as yesterday or hundreds of years ago. Researchers gather data from whichever sources can be located, including archives, libraries, personal testimonies, minutes of meetings, and others. After they ensure the authenticity and credibility of their sources and content, researchers prepare a narrative detailing their analyses.

To answer question 5, for example, researchers must examine science curriculum literature and obtain information from people involved in the reform efforts, including scientists, educators, and community members. The researchers evaluate these data sources and content. As part of their activities, the researchers construct a narrative that interprets their findings.

The display of the eight research questions and their goals shown in Table 2.2 is repeated in Table 2.3. In addition, Table 2.3 records the methods for solution of the research questions. The relationships among goals of research and methods illustrated with simple research questions here are elaborated on in subsequent chapters.

E X E R C I S E   2 . 2

This exercise allows you to see if you can link research questions with appropriate methods for their solution. For each research question in Exercise 2.1, identify a method (e.g., descriptive, qualitative) appropriate for its solution. Explain your choice. (Hint: The examples in Table 2.3 may be helpful.)

⋈ Common Elements in Research Plans

The essence of research method is communicated in a **research plan** or **research design** that describes the procedures that investigators use to obtain answers to research problems. As illustrated in the previous section, the procedures vary depending on the goal of research.

Within each plan, however, researchers must include answers to questions such as these:

- Which data sources are needed? If data sources are people (participants), who are they? How are they selected? If data sources are documents or artifacts, which ones are useful and where are they located?
- Which strategies or instruments are used for data collection? Are these strategies or instruments available commercially or are they constructed by the researchers? Have these strategies or instruments provided valid and reliable data in situations similar to the current research project? Is more than one strategy or instrument used?
- Where are data to be gathered? Who collects these data? How are data handled prior to analysis?
- How are data organized and summarized? Who performs the data analyses?

The care with which researchers answer these questions is strongly related to the systematization of the research processes and the production of valid and reliable outcomes. The options from which researchers choose their answers to these questions are described in Chapters 4 through 11.

Summary

Researchers who pursue solutions to educational problems are typically guided by one of three goals of research: explanation, prediction, or control. Explanation encompasses description as well as searches for understandings about, and relationships among, variables and phenomena in social interactions. Both quantitative and qualitative researchers use explanation as their goal.

Quantitative researchers pursue prediction when they estimate the values of one variable based on known values of a related variable. Control is the goal of research in which researchers search for cause-and-effect relationships among variables.

Goals of research prescribe the methods by which researchers seek solutions to their problems. Explanation may suggest descriptive methods to quantitative researchers, or any of several naturalistic methods, including historical methods, to qualitative researchers. Prediction also suggests descriptive methods, but control requires that quantitative researchers use experimental methods.

Research plans communicate the method by which investigators solve their problems. These plans usually describe data sources, strategies or instruments for data collection, the circumstances for data collection, and intended data analyses.

Questions for Discussion

1. Many more studies in education use explanation as a goal than use control. Describe one educational problem for which you would like to have an answer. Explain why this particular problem could or could not use control as its goal of research.
2. An alternate description of the relationships among goals of research suggests that explanation, prediction, and control form a hierarchy, with control as the highest goal and explanation as the lowest. Prediction fits between the two as shown here:

Control

↑

Prediction

↑

Explanation

This hierarchy suggests top priority for research with control as its goal. This is contrary to the presentation in this chapter (see Figure 2.1). Discuss the similarities and differences of these descriptions.
3. Explain why qualitative, historical, and descriptive studies cannot have control as a goal of research.
4. Reflect on the items within a research plan or design. Explain why researchers must make systematic decisions about these items to obtain valid and reliable data.

Research Problems, Participants, and Instrumentation

Part II begins an elaboration of the definition of educational research from Chapter 1, which says "educational research is a purposeful ethical enterprise that uses systematic processes in the pursuit of valid and reliable outcomes." The notion of research as "a purposeful enterprise" is captured by the problem statement because this is where researchers say what they intend to do and why they want to do it.

The "ethical enterprise" idea is expected to be part of each research process, as well as each use of project outcomes. Educational researchers typically follow the ethical standards of a professional organization, such as the American Educational Research Association (1992).

Valid and reliable outcomes usually result from researchers' careful planning and use of the research processes. The first two of these processes, identification of the problem and review of known information in the problem area, are the topics of Chapter 3. Both processes are discussed from the research consumer's point of view. That is, you are introduced to the abilities necessary to evaluate research problems and literature reviews in research reports. Both topics are discussed further in Chapter 13 from the viewpoint of creating research problems and literature reviews.

The third systematic process, collect data about the problem, includes participants and instrumentation procedures. Whereas Chapter 4 describes participant selection and assignment procedures, Chapter 5 discusses the procedures for researchers' choices of strategies or instruments for data collection. As in Chapter 3, the abilities for evaluating these subsections of research reports are emphasized.

Both participants and instrumentation procedures are discussed further in Chapter 14 from the research producer's point of view. In that chapter, the emphasis is on planning participant and instrumentation procedures for a project of your choice.

Problem Statements and Literature Reviews

❖ **Problem Statements and Goals of Research Revisited**
    Explanation
    Prediction
    Control
❖ **Literature Reviews**
    Purpose

    Content
❖ **Introductory Sections of Research Reports**
    Descriptions
    Criteria for Evaluation
    Applications of Criteria
❖ **Introduction to the Creation of Research Problems and Literature Reviews**

Researchers typically choose problems based on their interests, experiences, or study of the literature. As a beginning activity, they read and critically evaluate the educational literature in the problem area. This study helps researchers to sharpen their problem statements, furnish tentative answers to problems, contribute to research plans, and provide contexts for discussion of the results of their own projects after their completion.

Read within its literature review, a research problem indicates the project's underlying goal, which prescribes the general method used to solve the problem. To illustrate these connections, the goals of research discussed in Chapter 2 are revisited and related to problem statements in selected research reports.

This chapter also describes the content of introductory sections of research reports and offers criteria for their evaluation. These criteria are then applied to two research reports.

Goals

To enable you to:

- evaluate the clarity of problem statements and titles in selected research reports for communicating their underlying goals of research and general research methods; and
- assess the adequacy of literature reviews in selected research reports for connecting research problems with related bodies of knowledge.

✗ Problem Statements and Goals of Research Revisited

As noted in Chapter 1, educational research is a purposeful ethical enterprise. Therefore, educational problems or questions must serve ethical purposes to be considered as research problems. Think about the following questions in terms of ethics and purpose:

1. What are the benefits for students of closed (or open) high school campuses?
2. How well do closed (or open) high school campuses promote co-curricular activities?
3. Should high school campuses be closed (or open)?

Although each question can be considered ethical, only the first two questions serve a purpose. Data that answer questions 1 and 2 could help policymakers to make decisions about the closing or opening of high school campuses. Data that answer question 3 are opinions unrelated to a particular purpose. Therefore, questions 1 and 2 are researchable, but question 3 is not.

Problem statements in research reports differ in form and are sometimes more complex than the simple research questions mentioned previously. Some problem statements have special wording to show their location, but others do not. Of the reports in Appendix A, for example, one problem statement mentions "purpose," and four use "question(s)" to signal their beginning. The remaining reports have problem statements, but do not signal their locations with key terms.

As an alternate form of research problem, a hypothesis is a conjecture or a prediction about the solution to a problem. Quantitative investigators create **research hypotheses** as tentative answers to problems, based on literature reviews and their expertise in the problem area. On occasion, a hypothesis is substituted for the problem statement in a report.

In this section, problem statements from research reports illustrate how the goals of research may be expressed for projects. To increase your understanding, read the problem statements within their literature reviews for these reports located in Appendix A. These problem statements are located within the introduction to the report, ahead of the Method section.

Explanation

In the following research question, the researchers seek explanations about secondary teachers' orientations to content area reading and instruction. Orientations are the relationships between teachers' theoretical beliefs and their teaching practices. In this particular quantitative project, the researchers want to know if the naturally occurring condition of being a preservice or an inservice teacher could be related to particular orientations to reading.

> In the present study we attempted to determine the beliefs and decisions of preservice and inservice secondary teachers regarding content area reading and instruction. (Konopak, Readence, & Wilson, 1994, p. 221)

The researchers might wish to manipulate the status of teachers as preservice or inservice, but this is impossible. Therefore, they must be content to explain any relationships they find between teacher status and their reading orientations through descriptive methods. See this problem statement in the introduction to A5.

Here is a problem statement from qualitative research that uses explanation as the goal of research:

> . . . this study demonstrates that similar conditions indeed existed in America during the first half of the nineteenth century. The data support the thesis that by 1840, the subjects of natural philosophy, chemistry, and astronomy had become more prevalent in American schools for middle- and upper-class girls than in comparable institutions for boys (Tolley, 1996, p. 129).

The "similar conditions" refer to a report, which stated that the British government of the 1860s found that boys' education centered around Latin and Greek and that girls took many science courses in secondary schools. Tolley's (1996) problem statement begins with the words, "The data support. . . ." Her historical study is intended to find if comparable conditions existed in American schools during that same period. See the first four paragraphs of A8.

Prediction

The statement that follows is from a study in which the researcher plans to test a prediction. Note the wording of this specific question:

> To what extent do adolescents' perceptions of caring teachers predict efforts to achieve positive social and academic outcomes at school? (Wentzel, 1997, p. 411)

This project statement assumes that adolescents' perceptions of caring teachers are related to these students' efforts to achieve positive social and academic outcomes. The researcher plans to use the first variable to predict the second related variable (see the introduction to A7). This report uses descriptive methods.

Control

The next statement comes from a project in which a researcher sought information about a possible cause-and-effect relationship between variables. Gettinger (1993) wants to know if manipulating methods of teaching spelling will bring changes in spelling performance. If this relationship can be shown to exist, the researcher will be able to control or influence changes in spelling performance.

> I predicted that students who received the error-correction intervention would evidence higher spelling accuracy than would students who received no additional modification beyond their standard spelling practice, or whose practice was optimized by dividing their words into smaller, daily chunks (Gettinger, 1993, p. 40).

This hypothesis conjectures that teaching spelling using error-correction strategies enables students to perform better in spelling than students taught with other strategies. In this report, the hypothesis serves the same function as a problem statement by naming the variables, suggesting their relationship, and communicating the underlying goal of research (see the introduction to this report in A1).

Literature Reviews

Literature reviews provide the contexts for understanding research problems. Here, researchers organize and integrate the findings related to problem variables or phenomena into a discussion that shows both what is known and what is unknown about the problem area.

Purpose

The overarching purpose of a literature review is to connect the researchers' problem with knowledge in the problem area. Ordinarily, researchers undertake literature reviews as one of the first major systematic processes. Researchers use the information to focus research questions, suggest procedures, and provide background for the interpretation of results.

Through study of others' work in the problem area, researchers may specifically identify their own research problem. For example, literature reviews help researchers establish meanings for variables and phenomena and find out what is known about the relationship between variables. This information is useful in wording problems and hypotheses.

Reviewing literature can provide suggestions to researchers about procedures. In which populations of participants have the variables or phenomena been studied? Which additional populations should be studied? Which instruments or strategies have been used for data gathering? Can improvements be made in the quality of data through modifying the instruments or the collection procedures? How were data analyzed in previous studies? Should alternate analyses be tried? Where treatments are used, literature reviews may suggest modifications in the levels of treatment.

Following the completion of a project, researchers interpret their results in terms of the literature review. In other words, they report the extent to which their project filled gaps in knowledge, how design modifications worked in their study, and sometimes how their results differed from those in previous studies in the problem area.

Content

Literature reviews include the results of searching and sorting the literature, combining and interpreting findings to make a particular point, and using these interpretations to explain what is known about the problem area. Literature reviews deserve careful study because they set the stage for understanding research reports.

Organization

Literature reviews can be organized in several ways. Typically, however, general material is discussed first and information directly related to the problem is discussed last (Martin, 1980). For example, at the beginning of a review, researchers may provide a brief history of major events in the problem area or discuss its background. They usually reserve information about their specific project, including the justification or need for the study, for the end of the review. In between these points, of course, researchers build a case or an argument that justifies their study.

Lengthy reviews may be subdivided by headings for the major points. In a report on the relations of perceived pedagogical caring and student motivation, Wentzel (1997) subdivides the literature review as follows:

- Teachers as providers of care and support; and
- Characteristics of pedagogical caring.

Within each subsection, she discusses research pertinent to these variables. Although the review contains 12 paragraphs, these subdivisions focus readers' attention on the major points (see the beginning section of A7).

In addition to preparing an overall organization, researchers are expected to organize the literature review internally. For example, several studies may share similar findings. Instead of discussing each study separately, researchers typically weave the findings together and point out their similarities and differences. Researchers are expected to show how all information contributes to the review and to omit references that do not contribute to an understanding of the problem context.

Explanations and Critiques

Much of any literature review explains research findings. For example, Wentzel (1997) *explains* the relationship between the literature and the problem area in one of the first sentences:

> Of interest for the present research is that recent studies have linked interpersonal relationships between teachers and students to motivational outcomes (e.g., Birch & Ladd, 1996; Pianta, 1992; Wentzel & Asher, 1995). (p. 411)

Within the same paragraph, she supports this statement and *explains* it with a research finding:

> The quality of students' relationships with peers also has been linked to academic performance (see Parker & Asher, 1987) (p. 173).

Other literature review statements *critique* or evaluate research findings. In the following excerpt, notice that the first sentence describes what research has shown about the importance of caring teachers. The second sentence indicates that no one has begun research on the effects of caring teachers on student motivation, an important antecedent to academic success:

> According to Noddings (1992), the academic objectives of schools cannot be met unless teachers provide students with a caring and supportive classroom environment (see also Noblit, 1993). However, even the most basic questions concerning the influence of caring on student motivation have not been addressed empirically. (p. 411)

With these statements, Wentzel points to deficiencies in existing research. Statements such as these point toward the researchers' justification for their project.

Justifications for Projects

Following their careful study of the literature, researchers must be able to say why their study should be done. They typically choose a need or **justification for the project** to serve as the organizing principle for the literature review. Said another way, the literature review is arranged to support the justification for the project. Common justifications (Martin, 1980) include these four:

1. There is little or no existing research in a particular problem area.

   This self-explanatory justification is used occasionally by researchers who are among the first to investigate a topic in educational research. Gierl and Bisanz (1995), who carried out a study of anxieties and attitudes, used this justification for a study in mathematics in grades 3 and 6. In their introduction, these authors indicate that researchers have speculated that mathematics anxiety starts early in children's school experience and contributes to negative outcomes, including lower mathematics performance. The justification for their study states that "very little research has been conducted on the development of mathematics anxiety in young children" (p. 139). This statement is supported by references to two major reviews, which showed no studies involving children under age 11.

2. Some research exists, but it is insufficient to be considered reliable as a solution to the research problem.

   Researchers who replicate studies to verify their conclusions use this justification, which is also self-explanatory. New studies, for example, may use different participants, alternate data collection approaches, or variations in levels of treatment. The intent of these projects is to strengthen existing knowledge in a problem area. This is a popular justification.

   Knowles (1993) conducted a qualitative inquiry into the part that schools play in the development of children's perceptions of international conflict. The justification reported in this study was an explicit request for research using qualitative inquiry to supplement the knowledge obtained by quantitative studies on this topic.

3. There is a lot of research, but the findings are conflicting or contradictory. Researchers seek information that clarifies the findings for their particular setting.

Within educational theory and practice are problems that have been studied many times. However, the efficacy of direct instruction versus child-centered instruction continues and exemplifies the type of study that might use this justification.

4. Two or more theories explain the same phenomenon, but each predicts different outcomes of a common action. Researchers conduct research to find out which theoretical orientation to follow.

In their literature review, Petersen, Johnson, and Johnson (1991) describe two theories concerning status, or social rankings, in which it is better to be in a high state rather than a low state. In expectation states theory, status of individuals is considered a predictor in how groups operate. In contrast, social interdependence theory predicts that status is irrelevant in group operations. Obviously, the outcomes of these two theories differ. In the cited study, the investigators tested the two theories' opposing predictions. Specifically, they placed participants in cooperative structures and varied the groups in terms of gender majorities to see the effects of status on group operations.

By their nature, problem statements suggest a need for the study, but a full-blown primary justification is also expected in the literature review. Table 3.1 summarizes the major purposes of different types of statements in literature reviews.

TABLE 3.1

Purposes of Literature Review Statements

Statement Type	Purpose
Explanation	Describes the nature of phenomena or variables *or* discusses possible relationship among variables
Critique	Describes strengths and weaknesses in existing research
Justification	Provides the rationale for conducting a research project based on one of the following: • Need for an answer in situations in which little or no research exists • Need for reliable answers to questions based on additional research • Need for clarification in cases of conflicting or contradictory findings • Need to know which theory to follow; previous research predicts different outcomes of a common action

Analysis of a Literature Review

Let's examine the report, Preservice and Inservice Secondary Teachers' Orientations Toward Content Area Reading (Konopak, Readence, & Wilson, 1994) to see the organization of its literature review and examples of these statement types. First, read the introduction to this report in A5, which encompasses all the information from the beginning to Method.

The review begins with general information about teacher belief and practice relationships, then progresses toward discussion of beliefs and practices in secondary teachers' content area reading. Table 3.2 contains summaries of each of the eight paragraphs in this review.

This review contains a wealth of explanation about the nature of the variable, teachers' orientations toward content area reading. The second paragraph is devoted to a discussion of teachers' beliefs and decision making as critical components in teachers' orientations. The third and fourth

---

TABLE 3.2

Paragraph Summaries of the Literature Review of Preservice and Inservice Secondary Teachers' Orientations Toward Content Area Reading

1. Introduces belief and practice relationships as the domain of this research project

2. Indicates that current research on teaching focuses on teachers' beliefs, decision making, and interactions with students; teachers' beliefs about teaching and learning especially important

3. Puts teacher beliefs about teaching and learning into the context of reading education; specifically discusses research related to the effects of teachers' beliefs on instruction

4. Discusses research suggesting that factors outside the teacher influence instruction

5. Begins discussion of Kinser's research aimed at finding how experience affects teacher beliefs and consistency between beliefs and instructional choices

6. Explains the results of Kinser's research with elementary teachers

7. Explains and briefly interprets the outcomes of Kinser's research

8. Discusses purpose of current project, ties it to Kinser's research, and provides the justification for study

---

(Konopak, Readence, & Wilson, 1994). See A5.

paragraphs provide further explanations by reviewing research from two points of view on relationships between beliefs and instructional choices.

Their inclusion of these paragraphs provides evidence that Konopak, Readence, and Wilson evaluated the research in the problem area. Had the paragraphs been omitted, you as a reader might wonder why these investigators chose their project.

In fact, Konopak and her colleagues indicate that their project with secondary teachers extends Kinser's work with elementary teachers. This justification acknowledges that although some research exists, it is insufficient to be considered reliable as a solution to the research problem.

E X E R C I S E   3 . 1

The ability to distinguish among types of statements in literature reviews is a prerequisite for evaluating these report sections, the topic of Exercise 3.2. The following exercise allows you to see how well you recognize the statement types.

Read the opening section from beginning to Study Design of this report:

A6 The Impact of Personal, Professional and Organizational Characteristics on Administrator Burnout

Read statements 1–4 as they appear in the report. Decide the purpose for each statement, whether for explanation, critique, or justification. Give reasons for your choice.

1. "Since 1980, over 90 studies have explored the causes, responses, and consequences of administrator stress and burnout." (p. 146)

2. "Much yet remains unknown about the associations, relationships, and influences of stress . . . personality, gender, and age." (p. 146)

3. "There is a growing body of evidence which links the effects of burnout on job satisfaction, . . . and personal characteristics such as age and gender (Blix *et al.*, 1994; Dey, 1994)." (p. 146)

4. "Such an understanding should increase present knowledge to present facets of administration which need closer attention . . . by administrators." (p. 147)

⚔ Introductory Sections of Research Reports

Previous sections describe the actions of researchers in revising problems and literature reviews. Using this information as a background, this section describes introductions to research reports, provides criteria for their evaluation, and applies these criteria to two research reports.

Descriptions

Beginning sections of research reports include titles, abstracts, and introductions. The following descriptions apply specifically to journal reports, but are similar for theses, dissertations, and reports for funded projects.

Titles

Because the title is probably the first thing read, it is an important part of the study. Titles communicate the project goal by naming the phenomena or major variables and their relationships. Studies involving explanation may use words such as "relationship between (variable *p*) and (variable *q*)" or comparable wording. Studies whose goal is control sometimes use words such as "effects of (variable *x*) on (variable *y*) . . ." to signal that a possible cause-and-effect relationship was investigated. Of course, clue words are not completely reliable because some titles are worded loosely.

Titles may also communicate the scope or range of interests in the study. Were the participants toddlers, teenagers, or adults? Was the setting in counseling, teaching, staff development, or administration? Was subject matter in a particular curriculum area emphasized? Scope information enables you to locate reports to meet specific needs.

Abstracts

Following the title, almost all research reports contain an abstract that highlights major points of the report. Brief information should be included about the problem, procedures, results, and conclusions. (Abstracts that omit pertinent information about any of these items are incomplete and should be called summaries.) Abstracts provide additional information beyond the title to help potential readers decide whether to read the complete report. An abstract can also serve as an advance organizer for reading the report.

Research Problems and Literature Reviews

Most journal reports begin with an unlabeled introductory section that contains a review of literature and a problem statement. Historical studies are an exception because the literature review is typically included within the report. (Chapter 11 provides additional information.)

In many cases, journal reports are tailored to satisfy publication guidelines concerning length, with the result that literature reviews may be condensed. However, authors of research reports, other than those in journals, usually do not have space limitations and may devote an entire chapter to literature review.

The problem statement is often presented near the end of the introduction. The problem of a descriptive or experimental study may be presented as one or more of the following: purpose, research question, or research hypothesis. Qualitative projects usually have a purpose or problem statement. If qualitative researchers develop hypotheses, these will usually be included in the results, rather than in the introduction.

Regardless of its location, the problem provides critical information for understanding the report. Careful reading of the problem within its context reveals the underlying goal of the research. Clear knowledge of the researchers' intentions is necessary to evaluate the remainder of the report accurately.

Authors of journal reports use whatever amount of space the guidelines permit to present their literature review. They define the justification for the project and organize the findings from the review to support that need. Well-prepared reviews create a context for understanding the problem of the study.

Criteria for Evaluation

The following criteria for evaluating problems, titles, and literature reviews are based on information presented in this chapter. (Abstracts will be reconsidered in Chapter 12 after all report sections have been discussed.) Consistent application of these criteria can increase your understanding of introductory sections of research reports.

1. The "problem" must communicate the underlying goal of the project.

    Research problems may be presented in one or more forms as questions, purposes, statements, or hypotheses. Regardless of the form, the problem should provide a clear understanding of the underlying goal of research, when read in the context of the literature review. The problem should identify the phenomenon or variable(s) of interest and any relationship sought among variables. You should be able to identify whether a descriptive, experimental, qualitative, or historical method will be used to solve the problem based on the goal of research.

2. The report title presents an abbreviated form of the research problem. Therefore, it should also name the phenomenon or variables and communicate the goal of research.

    Although a well-designed title is short, it should indicate the scope or range of interests included in the project. The wording is extremely important because titles are sometimes the only part of a report that is read. Unless the title suggests that the report is useful, would-be readers may not actually read it.

3. The literature review should connect the research problem to existing knowledge in the problem area.

    Researchers are obligated to provide a context for their problem that clarifies their goal of research. Unless there's a link to existing knowledge, a research study is not likely to make a significant contribution to education.

4. Researchers should supply a reasonable justification for their project that is substantiated by their literature review.

    This justification describes how the proposed study is expected to contribute to existing knowledge.

Applications of Criteria

To illustrate the use of these criteria, this subsection provides an evaluation of the introductory sections of two research reports. These critiques discuss problem statements, literature reviews, and titles. Read Exercise 3.2 for the questions on which the critiques are based, and the introductory sections of A1 and A2.

Effects of Error Correction on Third Graders' Spelling

This report (A1) investigates the effects of three approaches to teaching spelling on spelling performance. Read in the report context, Gettinger (1993) wants to test a possible cause-and-effect relationship between these variables. The researcher pursues the goal of control; notice the reference to a "controlled investigation." Gettinger uses experimental methods with the methods of teaching spelling as the manipulated variable and spelling performance as the responding variable.

The title clearly communicates the goal and scope of the study as encompassing third graders' spelling and a method of instruction. The words "effects of . . ." are used here correctly and capture well the essence of this study.

The literature review does an excellent job of connecting the problem to knowledge about teaching spelling. The opening paragraph introduces several positions regarding spelling instruction, the importance of corrective feedback as a common element in effective spelling instruction, and the idea of conducting spelling research among different populations.

The next several paragraphs elaborate on the meaning of error correction strategies and describe their use with learning disabled children, including the conditions under which students are successful. Gettinger then presents two explanations about why the corrected-test approach "works" with learning disabled students and suggests that children in regular classrooms may have similar spelling difficulties. In the sixth paragraph, Gettinger asserts that teachers do not use valid techniques even when they know them, choosing instead to use procedures based primarily on commercially prepared materials.

As the climax to the review, Gettinger cites the need for studies of spelling instruction involving corrected-test procedures in regular classroom spelling instruction. This is a way of saying that some research exists, but that it has not been applied in enough situations to be considered reliable as a solution to the research problem. Because the reported study is expected to address this difficulty, Gettinger builds a strong justification for this study. The research hypothesis, which informs readers about the purpose of the study, is a natural outgrowth of this review.

What Is Classroom Discussion? A Look at Teachers' Conceptions

This report (see A2) investigates the phenomenon of teachers' conceptions of discussions in high school social studies classes. Larson and Parker (1996) sought answers to major questions about characteristics of classroom discussions, teachers' beliefs about the purpose of classroom discussions, whether teachers have more than one notion of discussions, and possible reasons for their conceptions. The researchers clearly state their intent to begin an explanatory theory of teachers' conceptions of classroom discussions. This study uses qualitative methods.

The title communicates the project goal well by naming the social phenomenon, classroom discussion, and asking what it is. However, adding the words "high school social studies teachers'" conceptions would provide a better notion of the scope than does the current title.

The researchers connect their problem to the body of knowledge concerning classroom discussions well in a terse literature review. First, they describe researchers' purposes of classroom discussions, then make the point that classroom discussions might be used as laboratories to prepare students for living in democratic societies (one purpose for discussions). The final, brief section describes conceptions of classroom discussion and pushes for including teachers' conceptions.

The primary justification for this study is that some research exists, but it is insufficient to be considered reliable as a solution to the problem. Larson and Parker make a good case for this justification by showing that theoretical knowledge about classroom discussion is the work of researchers, who have not considered teachers' knowledge on the topic. Their plan is to build a theory of teachers' conceptions of discussion, grounded in information obtained directly from teachers.

E X E R C I S E   3 . 2

A clear understanding of the introductory section of a research report furnishes a good foundation for understanding the remainder of the report. This exercise allows you to self-assess your understanding.

Scan the introduction of each report. Then, study the problem statement in whichever form it is expressed. Read the literature review and title carefully.

A3 A Phenomenological Study with Youth Gang Members: Results and Implications for School Counselors

A4 A Computerized Method to Teach Latin and Greek Root Words: Effect on Verbal SAT Scores

Answer questions 1–4 for each report. Save your responses for use in subsequent exercises.

1. Identify the variables or phenomenon of interest in this research project. Discuss any relationship(s) sought among these variables. Identify and discuss the underlying goal of research and the method used for solution of this problem.

2. How well does the title communicate this project's goal of research? Does the title indicate the scope of the study? Explain.

3. How well connected is the problem to existing knowledge, as determined by the literature review? Explain.

4. Describe the primary justification for this study. Do the researchers make a good case for this justification? Explain.

✷ Introduction to the Creation of Research Problems and Literature Reviews

At this point, explore Chapter 13, Creation of Research Problems and Literature Reviews, especially if you expect to create a research proposal or complete a research project during the course of using this text. That chapter extends and applies the information discussed here.

Summary

The goals of research are revisited in a discussion of problem statements from research reports. Research hypotheses are described as an occasional substitute for the problem statement in reports.

As part of the review processes, researchers explain findings from related work. They also discuss the strengths and weaknesses of the related research. Through completion of these processes, the researchers are able to show how their project fills a gap in existing knowledge.

Introductory report sections include titles, abstracts, literature reviews, and research problems or hypotheses. Each subsection contributes specialized information that is important in understanding the report. Criteria for judging introductory sections are described and applied to two research reports.

Questions for Discussion

1. Many educators have important questions about their professional endeavors for which they would like answers.
   a. Identify a work-related question whose answer is important to you.
   b. Does this question suggest a quantitative or a qualitative inquiry? Explain.
2. Describe the common features among research problems, hypotheses, and titles. Describe how each item differs from the others.
3. Rethink the discussion of explanations and critique statements as the content of literature reviews. Explain how these types of statements may be related.
4. Explain how you, as a *reader* of research, could be affected by a poorly prepared literature review. How might you be affected as a *researcher*?

Participant Procedures

❖ **Populations and Samples**

❖ **Random Samples**

   Simple Random and Stratified Random Samples

   Cluster and Multistage Samples

❖ **Nonrandom Samples**

   Systematic Samples

   Quota Samples

   Purposeful Samples

   Convenience Samples

❖ **Procedures for Quantitative Studies**

   Determination of Sample Sizes

   Selection Procedures

   Assignment Procedures

❖ **Procedures for Qualitative Studies**

   Determination of Sample Sizes

   Selection Procedures

❖ **Participant Subsections of Research Reports**

   Descriptions

   Criteria for Evaluation

   Applications of Criteria

After researchers review the literature about a problem of their interest, they plan the procedures for obtaining a solution. A primary component of any research plan or design is the data source. For historical researchers, major data sources include documents and artifacts. However, data sources are mainly people or participants in plans that use descriptive, experimental, or qualitative methods.

Participant procedures vary within and between quantitative and qualitative projects because researchers answer different research questions and use results differently. Descriptions of populations and samples as well as random and nonrandom samples furnish background for the discussions of procedures for quantitative and qualitative studies.

The last section of this chapter describes the content of participant subsections in research reports and criteria for evaluation of these subsections. Finally, these criteria are applied to two research reports.

Goal

To enable you to:

- evaluate the participant procedures in selected research reports for the production of valid and reliable data for analysis.

⚹ Populations and Samples

A **population** refers to a group that has one or more characteristics in common, such as middle school students, first-born children, freshmen at State University, or teachers in Pinnacle School District. Notice that population sizes can differ radically. The number of freshmen at State University is likely to be greater than the number of teachers in a school district. Also, note that these populations are named by a single common characteristic. People within each named group may vary on other characteristics such as languages spoken, understanding of mathematics, or hobbies.

Using every member of a population in a research study is not usually practical, unless that population is very small. Therefore, it's often important to distinguish between a target population and one that is accessible. A **target population** consists of all the people with a common characteristic to whom investigators plan to generalize their results. This might be 15-year-olds living in rural areas, all fourth graders in the United States, or preschoolers in privately operated nursery schools. The opportunity to gather data from all the people in these populations is usually not feasible.

Consequently, researchers delineate a population within the target population to which they have access. Participants are selected from this group, called an **accessible population.** This group may be the 15-year-olds in a particular school district, fourth graders within one state, or preschoolers in two private nursery schools. Accordingly, accessible populations typically have fewer members than do target populations and may differ from target populations on some characteristics.

Accessible populations may be too large for research purposes. That is, attempts to provide experimental treatments or to gather data from all the people included in these populations would be expensive and time consuming, and could be impossible. Therefore, researchers use subsets, or **samples,** of an accessible population. Multiple samples may be drawn from populations using the random or nonrandom selection strategies described in the next section.

Because accessible populations may differ from target populations, samples may share more characteristics with the accessible population than with the target population. Figure 4.1 displays the relationships among populations and samples.

⚹ Random Samples

Random samples allow for the possibility that every member of the population could be among those selected. Use of these selection procedures tends to provide samples representative of the population from which the samples were drawn and are free of researcher bias. Researchers who use random samples are able to estimate the probability that results obtained from their samples are also found within the population.

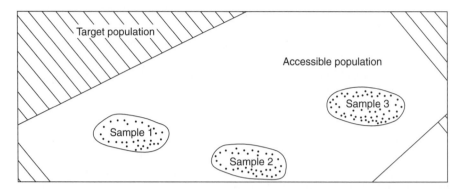

FIGURE 4.1   Relationships among target population, accessible population, and samples.

Simple Random and Stratified Random Samples

Simple random and stratified random sampling strategies use random selection mechanisms to eliminate possible subjective bias by the researchers in the selection processes. "Random selection mechanisms include either using a lottery procedure with well-mixed numbers, extracting a set of numbers from a listing of random numbers, or using a computer program to generate a random list of units from an automated listing" (Henry, 1990, p. 26).

As used here, "random" does *not* mean haphazard. Rather, it means that very careful, specific procedures are used to ensure that selection of any one unit for the sample is independent of the selection of any other unit.

In *simple random sampling*, everyone in the accessible population has an equal chance of being selected. There are no favorites, no teachers' pets or researchers' offspring, except by chance selection. Because the participants are selected at random, the choice of one individual does not influence the selection of any other individual. By using simple random sampling, researchers try to ensure that only chance prevents the sample from being an accurate representation of the accessible population.

Stratified random sampling, a variation of simple random sampling, allows researchers to ensure that the sample is representative of the accessible population on the basis of identified characteristics such as grade level, gender, reading comprehension level, or primary language. Researchers who use stratified sampling assign every member of the accessible population to a stratum, or group, according to one (or more) identified characteristic(s). Then they select a simple random sample representative of the accessible population by strata.

Cluster and Multistage Samples

Cluster sampling, another variation of simple random sampling, replaces individuals as the unit for selection with groups such as all the teachers in a department, all classrooms of a given grade, or all schools in a district. Researchers assign every member of the accessible population to a group or cluster. Next, the investigators select clusters at random and include all members of the selected clusters in the sample.

When the accessible population is large, random selection of clusters, rather than individuals, may be the strategy of choice because it is both time and resource efficient. However, use of clusters can increase the possibility of samples atypical of the population because clusters can be internally biased by factors such as ethnicity, gender, or age.

Multistage sampling can help overcome this shortcoming. First, clusters are selected, then individuals are selected from the clusters by simple random sampling. As an example, in multistage sampling, researchers first randomly select departments (i.e., clusters) then randomly select individual teachers within the chosen departments as the sample. This method of sampling is an efficient method to obtain samples representative of a large population.

�֍ Nonrandom Samples

Nonrandom samples are selected on the basis of investigators' judgments about achieving particular research objectives (Henry, 1990). The populations associated with nonrandom samples are usually ambiguous or unknown. Therefore, inferences are questionable that results obtained from these samples are true for any particular population.

Systematic Samples

In *systematic sampling,* researchers either assemble or list all the members of the accessible population. Then they select the first individual by a random method and the remaining participants from the population at predetermined intervals (e.g., every 11th, 34th person). Both decisions involve use of mathematical procedures.

Quota Samples

Quota sampling involves selection of participants according to diverse, but known and easily identifiable, characteristics of the population. For example, the target population may be subdivided into groups by gender or by ethnicity. In using this strategy, researchers ensure that samples reflect proportions according to the characteristics deemed important. Quota samples result in miniature approximations of their populations with respect to the selected characteristics (Henry, 1990), but these samples are not selected at random.

Purposeful Samples

Purposeful, or purposive, **samples** are composed of individuals or groups that provide information "about issues of central importance to the purpose of the research" (Patton, 1990, p. 169). To claim that a sample is purposeful, researchers present evidence showing that data collected from selected participants are particularly relevant as answers to the research questions. In the descriptions that follow, notice the logic used to claim that samples are purposeful. These samples are particularly useful in qualitative research.

Typical case sampling applies in situations in which researchers select samples believed to represent the norm. Of course, this type of sampling requires that researchers be knowledgeable about a population so they can rule out unique or special cases in favor of typical cases.

Used in quantitative research, typical case sampling has shortcomings because the cases selected as typical can differ on important variables that adversely influence project results. However, qualitative researchers may choose typical case sampling to describe and illustrate what is typical to those who are unfamiliar with the phenomenon. As Patton (1990) says, "(t)he sample is illustrative not definitive" (p. 173).

Extreme or *deviant case sampling* focuses on cases that are unusual or special (e.g., outstanding successes, notable failures). Researchers who use this strategy think about cases that provide the most and best information for answering their questions, then select among them for study. Knowledge from unusual cases can sometimes provide help in understanding typical cases.

Intensity sampling uses similar logic. However, researchers select information-rich cases that show the phenomenon of interest intensely, but not at the extremes of the previous discussion. For example, researchers who study the nature of creativity might find that cases classified as extreme would have little value in helping to understand "ordinary" people. They might then settle for sampling cases in which individuals were more creative than "ordinary" people; these could be considered as cases of intensity sampling. This requires that researchers predetermine the nature of the variations in the phenomenon under study, prior to sampling intense examples.

Maximum variation sampling is used when researchers wish to locate and describe the central themes or principal outcomes that describe the range of participant variations. In small samples, heterogeneity can be a problem, but maximum variation sampling uses it to advantage. For example, researchers studying creativity might create a small sample of information-rich cases that range from few visible signs of creativity to many signs of creativity. By studying the common patterns that emerge from this sample, the researchers may be able to capture the core aspects of creativity.

Homogeneous sampling is the opposite of maximum variation sampling. Here, researchers intend to describe one subgroup in depth, a task that can be accomplished when the people have similar backgrounds and experiences. To continue with the example on creativity, researchers who use homogeneous sampling might bring together individuals who share musical creativity. These individuals could provide data to researchers, based on similarities in their backgrounds and interests.

Convenience Samples

Convenience sampling, probably the most popular sampling strategy, occurs whenever researchers select participants based on their availability. This approach is used when educators carry out research projects in their own classrooms or those of colleagues. This is also the sampling strategy used when volunteer participants provide data or when researchers gather data from whomever is available (e.g., answers the telephone, logs onto the Internet, walks through the hall). The common denominator among these situations is that the people chosen to participate in the research project are available.

✄ Procedures for Quantitative Studies

Chapter 1 indicates that researchers engaged in quantitative inquiry usually intend to apply their results to groups other than those from whom data are gathered. To do this requires careful attention to the determination of the sample size and the procedures for selection and assignment of participants.

Determination of Sample Sizes

Researchers typically base decisions about sample sizes on one of these rationales: requirements for inferential statistical data analyses, requirements of a statistical power analysis, or availability of participants in a particular setting. The first two rationales are similar to each other but are quite different from the third.

Researchers who plan to use inferential statistical data analysis are aware that larger samples are more likely to provide statistically significant results than are smaller samples. The minimum requirements are roughly 15 or more participants per group. Additional information about these analyses is provided in Chapter 9.

Completion of a statistical power analysis is a mathematically based approach to determining the sample size required to obtain statistical significance at a level of significance predetermined by the researchers (Cohen, 1988). Consequently, this method is a refinement of the previous rationale.

Other researchers base their decisions about sample size on the number of participants available in a particular setting. This approach offers the advantage of a known number of participants, but its disadvantage is that these individuals may or may not be representative of any larger group to which the researchers may want to apply their results.

In general, a population that is relatively homogeneous with respect to the variables of concern can be represented by a smaller sample than a varied population with respect to the variables under study. Small samples from heterogeneous populations are likely to contain wide variations. However, a sample must represent a population in order for the results to generalize to that population.

The number of participants selected for a project affects validity of the data. With too few participants, data may be inaccurate or invalid. That is, the variations detected in the data may not show the full range that would be noted if more participants had been used.

Researchers also risk inconsistent or unreliable data if these come from small numbers of participants. To illustrate, data collected in small samples from the same population may show considerable variations due to fluctuations within the samples, rather than real variations within the data. For example, asking two samples, each having 5 fourth graders, to name their favorite school subject may show more variations than asking the same question of 30 fourth graders. The differences may be due to fluctuations within the samples rather than real variations among the students.

Selection Procedures

Selection procedures include the processes by which researchers identify a population of potential participants, determine the number of participants needed, and select a sample. Although random samples are used in some cases, nonrandom samples are the norm.

Random samples are distinguished by clear references to the populations and the method by which the samples are selected. Coutts (1996), for example, used simple random sampling in a project to determine how school principals used computers. He began the procedures subsection with this statement: "From a list of approximately 3,500 school principals, 1,000 were randomly selected to participate in the study" (p. 8). This sentence identifies both the population and the sampling strategy as simple random sampling.

Participants selected through a random selection procedure are usually representative of the population from which they are drawn. This is the chief advantage of random samples. Results from these participants are potentially generalizable to the population they represent.

Unfortunately, researchers may find that the identification of a precise population is difficult. Without knowledge of the population, of course, random samples are not possible. Also, researchers who want to use school students as participants may be unable to select them at random. Imagine the effects on students' learning if they are pulled from regular instructional activities to participate in research projects unrelated to the regular instruction. At least partly because of these disadvantages, relatively few researchers use random sampling strategies.

Nonrandom sampling strategies, such as systematic, quota, or purposeful selections, are useful in projects with specialized groups, such as gifted students or administrators in private schools. Ordinarily, the populations of these individuals are relatively small compared to populations of students or administrators in general. Nonrandom sampling strategies enable researchers to obtain results for these particular samples. However, generalization of results should be limited because researchers cannot take into account all the variables that affect the results.

Convenience samples are typically unclear about which population the participants represent and the method by which they were selected. Therefore, these samples cannot be considered as random. For example, Wentzel (1997) says only that "[e]ighth grade students ($N = 375$) from a sixth- through eighth-grade suburban middle school in a mid-Atlantic state participated in the study" (pp. 412–413) (see A7, Participants subsection of Method). There's no mention of either a population or a sampling strategy. In this case, the participants are probably a convenience sample.

Some researchers name their participants as volunteers, also an indicator of a convenience sample. Holmes and Keffer (1995) sought individuals from college-preparatory-level English classes as participants in their study to improve *Scholastic Aptitude Test* scores. All the participants were volunteers (see A4, Method section).

As these descriptions show, participants selected by convenience are chosen on the basis of their availability, typically without reference to a defined population. Consequently, researchers may be unable to manage certain variables that affect the project outcomes; generalization should not be attempted. See Table 4.1 for a summary of this discussion of random and nonrandom sampling strategies.

TABLE 4.1

Comparisons of Random and Nonrandom Sampling Strategies for Quantitative Research

Sampling Strategy	Advantages	Disadvantages
Random (i.e., simple random, stratified random, cluster, multistage)	Participants are generally representative of the population from which they came.	Researchers may have difficulty in the identification of a precise population; schools may be unwilling to allow random sampling because of possible disruptions to students' learning.
Nonrandom (i.e., systematic, quota, purposeful)	Participants selected through use of these strategies can provide data pertinent to particular research populations and settings.	Researchers cannot take into account some variables that can affect the results; results from participants should not be generalized.
Nonrandom (i.e., convenience)	Participants are usually easily available to the researchers.	Participants may not represent the population to which the researchers wish to generalize their results; researchers cannot take into account some variables that can affect the results.

Assignment Procedures

Recall that in experimental projects, researchers plan to manipulate at least one variable by administering various levels of the treatment to participant groups to detect possible changes in a responding variable. **Assignment procedures** refer to the processes by which participants are designated to receive particular treatments. Assignments can be made to individuals or to intact groups, either by random or nonrandom assignment.

Random assignment employs a nonbiased strategy, such as a coin flip or a tossed die, to determine which participants or participant group receive(s) a particular treatment. Of course, researchers use random assignment to avoid creation of bias among the groups with respect to treatments. Researchers may also place participants or groups in treatments by **nonrandom assignment** methods. These assignments, which are arbitrary, do not involve coin flips or other nonbiased strategies. The importance of random assignment of participants to treatments is elaborated on in Chapter 6, Design Procedures for Experimental Research.

Despite the advantage of random assignment, its actual use in school research is difficult, except for assignment of treatments to groups. School officials are reluctant to allow individual students to miss classroom instruction to participate in research efforts. One way of avoiding this problem, of course, is to use the entire student group as participants whenever possible.

To illustrate, an experiment was used to evaluate the effectiveness of a conflict resolution program taught within different contexts in a rural Canadian school (Stevahn, Johnson, Johnson, & Real, 1996). The entire population of seventh and eighth grade students ($N = 111$) was randomly assigned to one of four conditions. The first group received conflict resolution training as part of an English literature unit in a cooperative learning context. The second group studied the same unit using a cooperative learning context, but had no conflict resolution training. The third group, which was taught the same unit with conflict resolution training, worked in an individualistic learning context. The fourth group was also taught the same unit without conflict resolution training, but in an individualistic learning context (see Figure 4.2).

EXERCISE   4.1

The ability to distinguish between strategies in descriptions of sampling procedures is necessary to evaluate participant subsections of research reports, the topic of Exercise 4.3. The following exercise provides you with feedback on your ability to make these distinctions.

For each situation in questions 1–3, describe the probable accessible population. Is the selection strategy, as described, random or nonrandom? Explain.

1. A research group decides to investigate possible relationships between flexibility-of-thinking and problem-solving capabilities in social studies of students in a large, urban middle school. In this school, 40% of the student body is Chicano, 45% is Anglo, and 15% is Black. The researchers randomly select one-eighth of the total students in each ethnic group as their sample.

2. Mr. Charles, a high school foreign language teacher, wants to vary the length of instructional sessions in language laboratories to see if this change helps students improve their vocabularies. With the approval of his department chair, he agrees to use long sessions with three classes that meet during morning hours and use short sessions with three classes that meet during afternoon hours.

3. One hundred first-grade students, who exhibit varying degrees of eye-hand coordination, are enrolled at Briarwood Elementary School. The first-grade reading teachers and the physical education teacher have ideas about how to improve children's abilities in this area, but they want to try their ideas on a limited basis. The teachers listed the names of all children, mixed names together in a container, and drew 15 names of children to receive the initial training.

By using all the seventh and eighth grade students, the researchers were able to assign treatments on a random basis to individual participants. These procedures reduce potential biases that could contaminate the experiment. Intact groups of students can also be assigned to treatments by random procedures, but variations within groups may make them less free of bias than assignments of individuals by random methods.

In descriptive studies, participants are *not* assigned to groups. In many projects, all participant data are collected and kept intact. In Wentzel's (1997) study, data from 375 eighth-graders in a middle school were collected and kept together for analysis by the researcher (see A7, Method section).

In other descriptive studies, data from participants are grouped according to naturally occurring characteristics among the participants. For example, Konopak, Readence, and Wilson (1994) used preservice and inservice secondary teachers (a naturally occurring characterization) enrolled in education courses. All these teachers provided data in university classrooms,

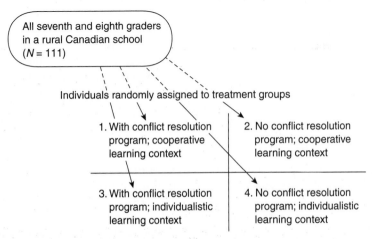

FIGURE 4.2   Examples of randomly assigned groups.
Based on Stevahn et al. (1996)

presumably as part of regular classes. However, data from preservice teachers were kept separate from inservice teachers' data because the groups were to be compared (see A5, Method section). Here, too, the unit of concern is the group, whether preservice or inservice teachers.

❄ Procedures for Qualitative Studies

Previous discussion shows that qualitative researchers explore, describe, and study social phenomena involving people or cases of interest. The nature of qualitative inquiries necessitates that researchers select their settings carefully. Because settings are typically unique, most qualitative researchers do not intend to generalize their findings to other situations.

Patton (1990) claims that much of the validity of qualitative research resides in the researchers' skill and competence. Consequently, researchers' special attention to the selection of settings and participants adds to confidence in the accuracy of project outcomes.

Determination of Sample Sizes

Sample sizes may be smaller in qualitative inquiries than in quantitative studies. Although single cases provide the information-richness needed for some studies, other studies require multiple participants.

The factors that affect sample size in quantitative studies are largely unimportant in qualitative studies because the data gathered are of a different type and serve a different purpose. However, the number of participants chosen must be adequate to provide reliable, consistent data.

> *There are no rules for sample size in qualitative inquiry.* Sample size depends on what you want to know, the purpose of the inquiry, what's at stake, what will be useful, what will have credibility, and what can be done with available time and resources (Patton, 1990, p. 184).

Patton (1990) recommends that researchers specify minimum samples, subject to change as the study unfolds. These samples should have a strong rationale based on the study's purpose and the interests of those involved. Built into the specifications for the sample are criteria by which changes can be made. These comments call for balance among several important considerations that qualitative researchers make as part of participant selection.

Selection Procedures

Researchers investigate their phenomena in one or more research settings. Ideally, qualitative researchers use purposeful sampling strategies because these provide rich data for answering their research questions. For example, Larson and Parker (1996) report the use of a purposive or purposeful sample of three high school social studies teachers. They chose teachers from the same school, who taught the same subject matter to the same students.

TABLE 4.2

Comparisons of Purposeful and Convenience Sampling Strategies for Qualitative Research

Sampling Strategy	Advantages	Disadvantages
Purposeful (i.e., extreme or deviant case, intensity, maximum variation, homogeneous, typical case)	Participants or cases provide information-rich data fitted to specific research purposes.	Location of participants or cases requires researchers' expertise, time, and effort.
Convenience	Participants or cases are easily available to the researchers.	Participants or cases may vary in the richness of information they provide about the phenomenon or variables under study.

All these teachers used discussion frequently and all were effective and thoughtful, according to their principal. The reasons that Larson and Parker provide for selecting these particular teachers suggest that this may be a homogeneous sample (see the data source subsection of A2).

Choosing a purposeful sample requires expertise, effort, and time. Therefore, researchers who use purposeful samples include descriptions of their activities to locate information-rich data sources, thereby substantiating their claim.

Although purposeful samples are desirable, convenience sampling is "probably the most common sampling strategy—and the least desirable" (Patton, 1990, p. 180). Participants selected with this strategy may or may not provide rich data about the phenomenon or variables of the project, but convenience samples are easy to access and inexpensive to use. Table 4.2 compares the advantages and disadvantages of purposeful and convenience sampling strategies for qualitative research.

EXERCISE   4.2

The ability to distinguish between strategies in descriptions of sampling procedures is required to evaluate participant subsections of research reports, the topic of Exercise 4.3. The following exercise provides you with feedback on your ability to make these distinctions.

For each situation in questions 1 and 2, tell whether the selection strategy, as described, is purposeful or convenience. Explain.

Adobe Middle School serves a large urban population that includes many students who are considered at risk of failure. Here, teachers serve on teams according to their special qualifications as teachers of language arts, mathematics, science, social studies, and the fine arts.

1. Ms. Bordeaux, a university graduate student, wants to increase her understanding and ability to work with students such as those at Adobe. She made the appropriate arrangements with school officials to observe several classes, where she noted student and teacher interactions. She found that these interactions were qualitatively different depending on the teacher and subject matter. Some students functioned well with some teachers and subject matter, but not well with others. After several observations, Ms. Bordeaux sought and received permission to study further the interactions in one classroom where the interactions were positive and in one classroom where they were negative.

2. Mr. Clay, a colleague of Ms. Bordeaux, is also interested in at-risk middle school students. He, too, received permission to study teacher-student interactions at Adobe Middle School. However, the principal, who seems to know the teachers and students well, identified a teacher who teaches at-risk students and suggested to Mr. Clay that he begin his study in that teacher's classroom.

✴ Participant Subsections of Research Reports

Following an introductory section in research reports is the method section that describes procedures concerned with participants, instrumentation, and data collection and handling, and treatments (in experiments). Through their descriptions, researchers provide information that enables readers to assess the validity and reliability of data collected by their use.

Decisions about participant selection are critical in research plans. Perhaps this is one reason why method sections usually start with descriptions of participant procedures. The following discussion also provides criteria for the evaluation of participant procedures and applies these criteria to two research reports.

Descriptions

Participants in a research project may be called "subjects," "participants," "sample," or "data source." In the subsection with one of these names, researchers describe the individuals from whom data were taken, as well as any larger groups these individuals represent.

Information such as the number of participants and their ages, grade levels, or both are nearly always given. Additional information about participants' reading abilities, cultural backgrounds, subject matter areas, and other descriptive information may also be included. This information is extremely important in determining the information richness of data for qualitative projects.

In quantitative studies, if participants are a sample that represents a population, report authors describe both the population and sampling procedures. Failure to mention a population and sampling procedures probably means that participants are a convenience sample.

In qualitative studies, researchers describe the participants and their setting. Sample sizes in qualitative studies may be smaller than those in quantitative studies. When researchers consider their sample as purposeful, they typically describe the particular information-rich cases they chose and outline the logic of their choice. Absence of this information probably means that the researchers used a convenience sample.

Criteria for Evaluation

You should be aware of criteria for evaluation of participant procedures because of their role in determining which data are used for answering the research questions. The following criteria are based on information presented in this chapter:

1. The relationship between the variables or phenomenon named in the research problem and the participants identified in the report should be evident.

   Researchers should provide information about the participants or cases that describes their ages, grade levels, language abilities, or experiences pertinent to the project.

2. Researchers should describe their strategies for the selection of participants or cases.

   The report should indicate whether the participants represent a particular population. If they do, both the population and the methods for selection of the participants should be described. When the sampling strategy is purposeful, the logic for this designation should be clear.

3. Data collected from these participants or cases should be valid for analysis.

   In quantitative studies, the number of participants selected should ensure that the full range of variations of the variables could be obtained. In qualitative studies, researchers should describe their participants or cases in terms of information-richness. As a reader, you should be convinced that the participants could provide accurate data about the phenomenon or variables.

4. Data collected from these participants or cases should be reliable for analysis.

   In quantitative research, the number of participants furnishes one index of reliability. Data from many participants is more reliable than data from few participants. In qualitative research, the information richness of the cases provides an indication of the consistency among the data.

Applications of Criteria

These criteria are applied to the participant subsections of two research reports. See Exercise 4.3 for the questions on which the critiques are based. Refer to these questions and the research reports as you read this section.

Effects of Error Correction on Third Graders' Spelling

In this experiment, spelling performance is the responding variable on which the researcher must gather data. Third grade students in regular classrooms are the data source for this project.

These students are expected to perform in spelling as part of the regular school curriculum. Three classroom-size groups totaling 65 students can provide data about the full range of variations within spelling performance for primary grade children, but only those enrolled in selected white, middle class suburban schools. Because no selection strategy is mentioned, convenience sampling is the probable method of participant selection. Data from these students should not be considered necessarily similar to data from any larger group. However, the numbers of participants is adequate for showing consistency among the data.

What Is Classroom Discussion? A Look at Teachers' Conceptions

The phenomenon on which this report centers is teachers' conceptions of classroom discussion. Data were gathered from three social studies teachers who were experienced in the use of classroom discussions.

The selected teachers taught similar subject matter in the same school and were mid-career social studies teachers who had been nominated by their principal. The researchers report having used a purposive (i.e., purposeful) sample. Given the richness of this information, it is likely that data are consistent.

E X E R C I S E   4 . 3

For each report, study the research problem or question within its literature review. Then study its participants-subjects-sample-data source subsection.

   A3 A Phenomenological Study with Youth Gang Members: Results and Implications for School Counselors

   A4 A Computerized Method to Teach Latin and Greek Root Words: Effect on Verbal SAT Scores

Answer these questions for each report.

   1. Identify the variables or phenomena named in the research question(s) on which the researchers must gather data. Are participants the data source for each variable or phenomenon? Continue with question 2 only if you answered "Yes" to this question.

   2. To estimate the validity of data provided by the participant procedures, answer these questions:
      a. (For quantitative reports)
         • Describe the relationships between participants identified in the report and the variables named in the research questions.
         • Is the number of participants selected sufficient to provide data about the full range of variations within these variables? Explain.

- Does the selection strategy used suggest that data from the participants are likely to be similar to data from any larger group that these participants represent? Explain.
  b. (For qualitative reports)
    - Describe the relationships between participants or cases identified in the report and the phenomenon or variables named in the research questions.
    - Based on this description, how information-rich are these cases?
    - Does the selection strategy used suggest that these cases are a purposeful sample? Explain.

3. To estimate the reliability of data provided by the participant procedures, answer these questions:
   a. (For quantitative reports) Discuss whether the numbers of participants are adequate for providing consistency among the data.
   b. (For qualitative reports) Discuss whether the information-richness of the cases is adequate for providing consistency among the data.

Summary

Samples or subsets of populations are the usual data sources in quantitative and qualitative research projects. Random samples are those in which every member of the population has an opportunity to be selected. Nonrandom samples are selected by researchers to achieve particular objectives.

Quantitative researchers choose samples whose sizes permit sampling the complete range of variations in the variables of interest. Their methods include random and nonrandom selection procedures. When participants are selected by a random sampling strategy, the results can be generalized to the population from which the participants were drawn. Large numbers of quantitative reports use convenience sampling, a nonrandom selection strategy.

Qualitative researchers may use purposeful samples that provide data relevant to a particular purpose. These are preferred over convenience samples in which researchers choose cases based on availability. Qualitative researchers usually use relatively small sample sizes, compared to those in quantitative projects.

Researchers describe participants in the participants, subjects, sample, or data source subsection of the method section. When researchers use selection strategies other than convenience sampling, they usually describe their procedures in detail. Knowledge of participant selection procedures is necessary for understanding the source of project data and the individuals affected by the results of the study.

Based on chapter content, criteria for the evaluation of participant subsections are described. These criteria are used for evaluating participant subsections in a quantitative and a qualitative report.

Questions for Discussion

1. Discuss ways in which accessible populations differ from target populations.
2. Explain how "random sampling" differs from "random assignment."
3. Explain why assignment procedures are necessary in experiments but unnecessary in descriptive and qualitative projects.
4. Explain how information-richness contributes to the validity and reliability of data gathered in qualitative studies.

Instrumentation Procedures

❖ **Instrumentation for Research Projects**
❖ **Procedures for Quantitative Studies**
   Selection or Development of Strategies
   Suitability of Strategies for Projects
❖ **Procedures for Qualitative Studies**
   Development of Strategies

Suitability of Strategies for Projects
❖ **Instrumentation Subsections in Research Reports**
   Descriptions
   Criteria for Evaluation
   Applications of Criteria

Researchers sometimes prepare their data collection procedures along with participant procedures. Obviously, the number of participants affects the choices of strategies for data collection, and vice versa. The preparations for data collection, called **instrumentation,** involve decisions about which data are necessary to answer research questions and the instruments or strategies by which data are to be gathered. These topics are the major focus of this chapter.

Researchers also decide the frequency of collections, as well as the identity of data collectors, in advance of actual collections, but typically communicate these decisions as data collection procedures. These and additional procedures are described in subsequent chapters.

For historical researchers, instrumentation is a matter of deciding which data answer their questions. Instruments for data collection are unnecessary because historians locate direct data sources (e.g., documents, artifacts, oral histories) to answer their questions.

Instrumentation in quantitative projects differs from that in qualitative studies largely because of differences in the purposes of research. Recall that quantitative researchers study variables and their relationships, but that qualitative researchers investigate social phenomena. Gathering data about variables, which are measurable, is different from collecting perceptions and gauging patterns of meaning in words, actions, and documents. Instrumentation procedures for the different modes of inquiry are described in separate chapter sections. The final section describes instrumentation subsections of reports, criteria for evaluation of these subsections, and applications of criteria in two research reports.

Goal

To enable you to:

- evaluate the choices of data collection instruments or strategies in selected research reports for the production of valid and reliable data for analysis.

❈ Instrumentation for Research Projects

Before researchers decide how to collect data, they must first decide which data provide answers to their questions. What is the nature of these data? Are they numerical or verbal, or are both types needed? Answers to these questions trigger additional questions about collection methods and personnel. Researchers answer the questions differently, depending on their orientation toward quantitative or qualitative inquiry.

In quantitative inquiry, researchers study variables and their relationships. Therefore, data are collected on each variable, with the exception of manipulated variables in experiments, usually through measurement. (Procedures for using manipulated variables are described in Chapter 6.) The data gathered are primarily numerical, but may be supplemented by verbal information. Researchers tend to use strategies such as multiple choice tests, rating strategies, and others that provide quantifiable data.

On the other hand, qualitative researchers study interactions among people, documents, and artifacts concerned with social phenomena within particular settings, typically by gathering verbal descriptions. These researchers use observation notes, open-ended questionnaires, and other strategies that provide verbal data. Historical researchers usually make copious notes while studying documents and artifacts related to particular questions. In both methods, investigators may also gather numerical data, but these are usually the exception.

Other instrumentation decisions relate to the frequency with which data are to be collected, who gathers them, and how they are gathered. Some studies, especially descriptive research projects, utilize a single data collection. However, experimental researchers may gather data, provide treatment or intervention, and then gather data a second time. Experimental research designs can also use more than two data collections.

In quantitative inquiry, researchers are usually detached from the setting to minimize the introduction of unwanted variations into the research setting. One way to do this is to allow individuals known to the participants, such as teachers, to gather data. At times, researchers use other assistants to collect data. Additional information on these topics is included in Chapters 6 and 7.

In contrast, both qualitative and historical researchers usually gather all the data for their projects, usually over the period of the research. Researchers may sometimes use existing instruments or may develop strategies for their particular projects. The researchers *themselves* are referred to as instruments because their judgments are involved, not only in deciding which data are important, but also in determining how these data will be recorded and used to answer research questions. Table 5.1 compares selected aspects of instrumentation for quantitative and qualitative research projects.

TABLE 5.1

Comparisons of Instrumentation in Quantitative and Qualitative Inquiry Modes

	Quantitative Inquiry	Qualitative Inquiry
Nature of data required by research questions	Primarily numerical data, supplemented with verbal data	Primarily verbal data, supplemented with numerical data
Examples of strategies	Multiple choice tests, rating scales, closed-ended interviews[1]	Open-ended questionnaires, observation notes[1]
Number of collections	Varies, but is defined by research plan[2]	Continuous throughout project[3]
Collectors	Researchers, assistants, teachers[2]	Researchers[3]

[1]See elaboration of these strategies in Appendix B.
[2]See elaboration of these topics in Chapters 6 and 7.
[3]See elaboration of these topics in Chapter 10.

✴ Procedures for Quantitative Studies

Quantitative researchers either select or develop strategies for their particular project. Regardless of how the strategies originate, they must satisfy several standards to be considered suitable for the project. Strategies must:

- provide the type(s) of data required by the research questions;
- yield valid and reliable measures of variables;
- fit with the participant procedures; and
- provide data at the level of measurement required for analysis.

Selection or Development of Strategies

Researchers may select commercially published instruments for data collection. Technical manuals for commercially published instruments provide researchers with information about an instrument's purpose as well as its validity and reliability of measurement, topics discussed in the next section. Researchers also consult reference works, such as *The Mental Measurements Yearbook* (Buros, 1999) and *Tests in Print V* (Murphy, 1999), for critiques of commercially prepared instruments.

For example, Holmes and Keffer (1995) used the *Scholastic Aptitude Test* (*SAT*) to gather data about improvements in verbal ability (see A4). The

SAT is a commercially published instrument, first used in the 1920s to predict student success in college. Instruments such as the *SAT* serve particular purposes and undergo extensive trials in which their developers collect evidence about validity and reliability of measurement.

When commercially published instruments are not available, investigators sometimes select instruments that were used in other research projects. As an example, Wentzel (1997) chose the Teacher Social and Academic Support subscales of the *Classroom Life Measure,* which was administered in an earlier study of cooperative learning. She used this instrument to measure middle school students' perceptions of teachers' caring (see A7, the Measures of Perceived Caring From Teachers subsection).

In other projects, researchers design their own strategies because existing instruments are either unavailable or inappropriate for their research purpose. Strategies may include, but are not limited to, tests, rating procedures, ranking procedures, questionnaires, and closed-ended response interviews. Each strategy is described in Appendix B.

Suitability of Strategies for Projects

Regardless of the origin of data collection strategies, researchers should determine that they meet defined standards before using them to collect data. The suitability of strategies is unique to each project.

Type(s) of Data

Research questions in quantitative projects investigate variables whose values are usually described numerically. Where needed, verbal descriptions may be coded or summarized as supplemental data to answer research questions. Researchers must be sure to collect all the data, regardless of type, necessary for answering their questions.

Validity of Measurement

Validity of measurement refers to the truthfulness of data from an instrument. Evidence of truthfulness of data is frequently gathered as content, criterion-related, or construct validity. **Content validity** concerns how well an instrument measures the content domain, usually gauged by the content objectives. Achievement tests, for example, should have content validity. If a social studies unit has six major objectives, a test purporting to measure achievement should measure all of the objectives to show content validity.

Similarly, a mathematics computation test has content validity for applications of arithmetic algorithms because this is the domain of computation. However, a computation test does not have content validity for mathematics achievement because it fails to adequately measure important mathematics content domains, such as reasoning and problem solving.

Criterion-related validity refers to the degree to which two or more instruments measure the same variable. To establish this type of validity, developers compare measures from two instruments that purportedly measure the same variable. For example, results from a new district-level test can be compared with results of an established state-level test on the same content. The degree to which the results correspond indicates the degree of criterion-related validity. This particular example illustrates concurrent criterion-related validity because this comparison concerns test results obtained at about the same time.

As described here, an analysis for criterion-related validity involves correlating, or associating mathematically, two or more measurements from the same individual. For example, each student's district test score may be paired with his or her state test score, then subjected to mathematical procedures that produce a coefficient showing the degree of association.

Usually noted by r, coefficients may range from +1.0 to 0 to −1.0. Positive coefficients indicate relationships in which an increase in one score is related to an increase in the second. Negative coefficients indicate relationships in which an increase in one score is related to a decrease in the second.

Coefficients close to one denote greater validity than values close to zero. Instruments with $r = .80$ have greater validity than those with $r = .50$ because variations in the first set of measurements show more joint variations between the two measures than those in the second set of measurements.

Criterion-related validity is also important in prediction. To illustrate, consider that teachers who seek certification as foreign language teachers are required to speak and read a particular language, and, in some states must pass speaking-reading tests in the foreign language. The results of the speaking-reading tests should be comparable to the results of the actual speaking-reading abilities needed for teaching the foreign language. The degree to which these results actually correspond is a measure of predictive criterion-related validity, because the test results are compared with those needed in future use of this information on the job.

An instrument has **construct validity** to the degree that it measures a variable as the literature describes it. Constructs include variables such as motivation, aggression, test anxiety, or eye-hand coordination. Eye-hand coordination, for example, describes the generalized ability of joint hand action with eye movements. Examples include positioning a tennis racket (or baseball bat, fielder's glove, or hand) so that it comes in contact with an oncoming ball.

An instrument for measuring eye-hand coordination would be performance-based. That is, participants would be required to demonstrate eye-hand coordination in the presence of an evaluator who rated the degree to which the participants perform the eye-hand coordination tasks. The specific items included in the instrument would depend on the participants—their ages, ability levels, and other factors. See Table 5.2 for a summary of information about types of measurement validity.

TABLE 5.2

Evidence Required by Different Types of Measurement Validity

Type of Evidence	Question Answered by the Evidence
Content	Does the instrument measure content that is representative of the domain?
Criterion-related • Concurrent • Predictive	Are scores from two instruments related. . . . . . . if both scores are obtained at about the same time? . . . if one score is obtained now and the second score is obtained later?
Construct	Does the instrument measure the concept as the literature describes it?

EXERCISE 5.1

To decide which variables in research problems should be measured is an important part of evaluating instrumentation in reports of quantitative research. To decide which types of measurement validity should be present is also important. Both abilities are needed in Exercise 5.4. The following exercises allow you to check your abilities in these areas.

For each situation questions 1 and 2, answer these questions:

a. Name the variable(s) for which measures are needed.

b. Identify at least one strategy for measuring each variable (see Appendix B for suggestions).

c. Which type of measurement validity should the strategy (identified in b) have? Explain.

1. A research group decides to investigate possible relationships between flexibility-of-thinking and problem-solving capabilities in social studies of students in a large middle school.

2. Mr. Charles, a high school foreign language teacher, wants to vary the length of instructional sessions in language laboratories to see if longer or shorter amounts of instruction help students improve their oral vocabularies.

Reliability of Measurement

Reliability of measurement describes the consistency or dependability of the data from an instrument. Researchers require instruments whose measurements are internally consistent or dependable from one collection date to another, as well as from one form of an instrument to another.

Evidence of reliability for many instruments, especially tests, is gathered as measures of internal consistency, stability, or equivalence. *Internal consis-*

tency is a measure of the similarity of performance across items. Item diffi-culty influences consistency. To ensure consistency, less-difficult questions must be mixed with more-difficult questions throughout the instrument. This quality is especially important in projects in which participants have lim-ited amounts of time for completion of the tasks. Researchers who use the in-struments to gather data will want to know how well participants perform on both easy and difficult tasks.

Internal consistency is estimated by using split-half, Kuder-Richardson, or Cronbach alpha procedures. Other terms mentioned in research reports include Kuder-Richardson (KR) formulas or Spearman Brown coefficients. A large correlation coefficient, usually $r = .70$ or better, from any of these methods suggests that items are internally consistent.

Data gathered by alternative methods, such as performance ratings, must also be reliable. If a single individual makes all the ratings, he or she must be consistent from one case to the next. If multi-person panels evaluate performances, they must also be consistent among themselves. Individuals must show *intrarater* or *intrascorer* reliability; panels must show *interrater* or *interscorer* reliability.

To attain consistency in scoring or rating, individuals or panels may un-dergo training, which includes practice in rating or scoring performances. Individual or panel ratings are correlated, just as test scores are, to provide measures of reliability.

Test-retest procedures provide information about consistency or de-pendability of data from an instrument over time—a measure of *stability*. A group of individuals responds to an instrument and, after a predetermined time period, responds to the same items a second time. The two sets of scores are correlated to estimate the stability of the scores.

Parallel or alternate forms procedures provide information about con-sistency or dependability of data obtained from two or more forms of the same instrument—a measure of *equivalence*. A group of individuals completes an instrument at one sitting, then completes a second instrument similar in construction, length, difficulty, and so on. When the two sets of scores are correlated, the result is a measure of how well the forms of the instruments measure the same aspects of behavior. See Table 5.3 for a summary of types of measurement reliability.

Some mismatches are to be expected in measurements due to built-in weaknesses in the instrument such as too few items, poorly worded directions for administration, poor scoring procedures, or inconsistent content within the instruments. Eliminating all these weaknesses is impossible, but minimiz-ing them improves test reliability.

Evidence of validity and reliability of measurement may be available for commercially published instruments or for those used previously in research projects. Researchers consider this evidence prior to selecting these instru-ments for their own projects. However, researchers must gather validity and reliability evidence through trial studies for any strategies they develop. In trial studies, also known as baseline or pilot studies, researchers gather data from participants who are similar to those from whom they expect to gather

TABLE 5.3

Evidence Required by Different Types of Measurement Reliability

Type of Evidence	Question Answered by the Evidence
Internal consistency	Is item difficulty distributed throughout the instrument?
Stability	Are scores obtained from an instrument now related to scores obtained from the same instrument at a later time?
Equivalence	Are scores from an instrument related to scores from a parallel or alternate form of the instrument?

data in the project. The results from the trial studies are analyzed mathematically and expressed as correlation coefficients.

Fit with Participant Procedures

Researchers should also ensure the reliability of instrumentation procedures by aligning them with participant procedures. Gathering self-report data with a written instrument, for example, is more sensible than holding interviews with 100 participants. The content and sequence of questions are uniform in a written instrument, but interviewers can deviate both in content and sequence. These deviations could allow data to be less reliable than they would be through the use of a written instrument.

Levels of Measurement

In simple terms, *measurement* means that researchers assign numbers to variables according to rules (Kerlinger, 1986). Depending on the nature of their variations, variables yield data at different **levels of measurement:** nominal, ordinal, interval, and ratio.

- **Nominal measurement,** the lowest level of measurement, uses numbers that do not have numerical meanings—they cannot be ordered or added. These are categorical labels, given so that distinctions can be made between the values of the variable. Assigning labels to participants as preservice or inservice teachers (Konopak, Readence, & Wilson, 1994) and designating classes as A, B, and C (Gettinger, 1993) are examples of nominal measures.
- **Ordinal measurement** applies to measures in which assigned numbers or labels have rank values, which means they can be ordered. Examples include designations of graduates as first in class,

second in class, and so on. Grades such as above average, average, and below average are also ordinal measures.

- **Interval measurement** refers to measures in which the numbers assigned can be ranked and are considered as having equal intervals, which can be added and subtracted. Examples include scores on the *Scholastic Aptitude Test* as used in Holmes and Keffer's (1995) study. Teachers' global ratings of students' spelling performance in Gettinger's (1993) report are also examples. In those ratings, the interval from 1 (far below average) to 2 (below average) is considered as equal to the interval from 2 (below average) to 3 (average).
- **Ratio measurement,** the highest level of measurement, refers to measures in which the numbers assigned are considered as having equal intervals and a zero that has meaning. Variables involving dollars or class attendance provide examples of ratio measurement in educational research.

Nominal and ordinal data allow researchers to sort and rank information, respectively. These operations are low level compared with the sophisticated mathematical analyses possible with interval and ratio data. Largely because of this advantage, quantitative researchers typically prefer to use data of at least interval level, especially for measures of responding variables. Therefore, in addition to the other suitability standards, researchers must also be sure that the strategies selected for data collection yield data at the levels appropriate for their anticipated analyses. Data analyses for quantitative studies are the topics of Chapters 8 and 9.

E X E R C I S E   5 . 2

The levels of measurement of the data provided by instruments or strategies are a concern in the selection or development of data collection instruments or strategies. Use of this knowledge is important in the discussion of data analysis procedures in Chapters 8 and 9.

Identify the level of measurement associated with each of these measures. Explain your choice.

1. Ratings, such as strongly agree, agree, etc.
2. Male-female designations
3. Student identification numbers
4. Grades, such as excellent, very good, etc.
5. Years of formal schooling

✷ Procedures for Qualitative Studies

For historical researchers, instrumentation is a matter of deciding which data answer their questions. Their chief concern then becomes the location of data sources (e.g., documents, artifacts). These processes are described in Chapter 11.

Qualitative researchers typically develop strategies tailored for data collection in the unique settings in which their projects take place. It's not unusual for these researchers to use several strategies for data gathering, and all must be suited to the project. Strategies should:

- provide the type(s) of data required by the research questions;
- provide for collection of sufficient data to answer the research questions accurately;
- provide for checks on the consistency of the data; and
- fit with the setting (e.g., participants, researchers' access).

Development of Strategies

Wolcott (1992) proposes that the range of data-gathering techniques in qualitative research contains watching, asking, and reviewing. Stated another way, these activities are "experiencing, with emphasis on sensory data, particularly watching and listening; enquiring, in which the researcher's role becomes more intrusive than that of a 'mere observer'; and examining, in which the researcher makes use of materials prepared by others" (Wolcott, 1992, p. 19).

Depending on which strategies they choose, researchers assign themselves to particular roles, categorized by the degree to which they engage in interactions with participants and the degree of participants' awareness that they are being studied. These roles form a continuum that includes complete participant, participant-as-observer, observer-as-participant, and complete observer (Gold, 1958; LeCompte & Preissle, 1993).

- As a **complete participant,** a researcher is considered as an insider within the participant group and is not known as a researcher. Adoption of this role can involve a researcher in pretense to the point of discomfort because the pretended role requires sensitivity to mannerisms and social cues foreign to the researcher's self (Gold, 1958).
- As a **participant-as-observer,** the group knows the researcher's role. The researcher is counted as a friend and pseudomember of the group. In this role, the researcher may develop relationships with participants that turn into regular friendships (Gold, 1958; LeCompte & Preissle, 1993).
- As an **observer-as-participant,** the researcher is known in that role and has limited contact with members of the group. As Gold (1958) points out, this role is used in studies involving one-visit interviews in which researchers are not likely to develop relationships with

participants. However, misunderstandings can arise because the investigator's contact with participants is so brief.

- As a **complete observer,** the researcher is behind a one-way mirror or in a largely unseen role that permits unnoticed observation or eavesdropping of participants. Because the researcher does not interact with participants, this role is usually not the dominant one. Typically, researchers use this role at the beginning of an investigation to obtain initial information, but then they adopt different roles to gather additional data (Gold, 1958).

The research questions should guide the choices of researcher roles and strategies. If questions call for identification or exploration of a phenomenon, researchers must gather several types of data that require interactions with participants within the setting. On the other hand, if the task is simply to verify or refine a phenomenon, researchers may gather data through unobtrusive, neutral methods involving little participant contact (LeCompte & Preissle, 1993).

Researchers who interact with participants may use any of a full range of data collection techniques as long as the number of participants is considered. Interviews, which can be tailored to particular settings, can consist of standardized open-ended questions, interview guides, or informal conversations. Researchers also use existing documents, artifacts, open-ended questionnaires, or any combination of these strategies.

In studies in which researchers require less contact with participants, direct observation or audio- or videotaping of activities within the setting is an option. These researchers may also use documents and artifacts as data sources. These strategies are described in Appendix B. For additional information about data collection methods, see Marshall and Rossman (1999), particularly Chapter 4.

Suitability of Strategies for Projects

Qualitative researchers usually develop data collection strategies unique to their research questions and setting. These strategies should satisfy defined standards of suitability to ensure that data are valid and reliable.

Type(s) of Data Required by Research Questions

Most qualitative research data consist of verbal descriptions that answer questions about phenomena. On some occasions, however, qualitative researchers require quantifiable information to support their descriptions. The strategies developed for the project should support collection of whichever data answer the questions.

Sufficient Data for Accuracy

Qualitative researchers typically gather, analyze, and interpret data in recurring cycles throughout the duration of the project. Ideally, these cycles should continue until the data repeat themselves (Lincoln & Guba, 1985). Otherwise, the data collected and used may be insufficient to answer the research questions accurately.

Checks on Data Consistency

Qualitative researchers often use more than one data collection strategy or collector as part of processes called **triangulation.** By using two or more strategies to obtain data, researchers can check their consistency or reliability. In similar manner, data obtained by two or more collectors offer the same opportunity for checking data consistency.

Fit with the Setting

Researchers should align their data collection strategies with the setting and their access to it. This means acknowledging the participants—their ages, the numbers of them, their activities, and other matters—as well as the researchers' professional access to the participants.

Although a researcher might prefer the role of complete participant, the circumstances of the setting could dictate a different role. Researchers must negotiate their role(s) with the officials in charge of field settings prior to actual data collection.

E X E R C I S E   5 . 3

To understand how researcher's roles and data collection strategies work together is an important factor in the evaluation of instrumentation in qualitative research. Both abilities are needed in Exercise 5.4. The following exercises allow you to check your understanding.

For each situation in questions 1 and 2, name an appropriate role for the researcher. Then describe at least one strategy for data collection. Explain.

1. Ms. Bordeaux wants to gather data on the quality of group interactions during cooperative learning activities as the interactions occur normally in a middle school classroom.

2. She also wants to check the accuracy of the collected data through verbal exchanges with selected students in the classroom where initial data were gathered.

✖ Instrumentation Subsections in Research Reports

Instrumentation procedures are described in the method section of reports, usually following the participant procedures. The close proximity between descriptions of these procedures in research reports supports the idea that researchers select or develop their data collection strategies in conjunction with the design of participant procedures.

Descriptions

Some reports contain a subsection dedicated to instrumentation. In other reports, instrumentation is communicated within the context of data collection procedures. In these cases, you must sort through quantities of information to decide which data were to be collected and the strategies used.

In quantitative studies, the titles of commercially published instruments may appear, along with information about validity and reliability of *measurement*. Instruments may be compared with other published instruments in terms of purpose, amount of time required for completion, and other matters. References to split-half, Kuder-Richardson (KR), Cronbach alpha (α), and Spearman Brown coefficients are common. These, of course, describe procedures by which the reliability of measurement was estimated.

When they devise unique data collection strategies, some quantitative researchers describe their strategies in detail. These researchers often conduct pilot studies, also known as baseline or test studies. Here they administer their instruments to participants similar to those in their project and use the results to generate evidence of the instruments' validity and reliability of measurement.

In reports of qualitative projects, some researchers describe their planned data collection procedures in detail, but others provide minimal description. In reading qualitative reports, look for evidences of triangulation (e.g., multiple data collectors and collection methods). Look specifically for information about the validity and reliability of data collection procedures for qualitative projects.

Criteria for Evaluation

You should be aware of criteria for the evaluation of instrumentation because these procedures play a major role in determining which data are available for answering the research questions. The following criteria are based on information presented in this chapter:

1. Researchers should specify their data collection strategies for each phenomenon or variable, except for manipulated variables in experiments.
2. Data gathered with these collection strategies should be valid for analysis.

The type(s) of data collected should match the requirements of data necessary to answer the research questions. When variables are to be measured, researchers should provide evidence of the validity of measurement of data from the collection strategies. When verbal data are collected in qualitative studies, researchers should gather data over a time period sufficiently long to ensure their accuracy.

3. Data gathered with these collection strategies should be reliable for analysis.

In quantitative studies, researchers should provide evidence of the reliability of measurement of data from the collection strategies. Instrumentation procedures should fit appropriately with participant procedures. Said another way, the numbers and characteristics of participants should affect the choices of strategies for data collection.

Qualitative researchers are expected to gather data using more than one collector or strategy as a check on different perspectives of the phenomenon or variables. If data from different sources are consistent, they can be considered as reliable. The collection strategies should be aligned with the setting, including the numbers of participants and the role(s) adopted by the researchers.

Applications of Criteria

These criteria are applied to the Instrumentation subsections of two research reports. See Exercise 5.4 for the questions on which the critiques are based. Refer to these questions and the research reports as you read this section.

Effects of Error Correction on Third Graders' Spelling

The measured variable in this project was spelling performance, the responding variable. Three strategies used for data collection included weekly dictation spelling tests, accuracy in spelling words in dictated stories, and teacher ratings. These strategies provide the numerical data required to answer the researcher's question.

The trials-to-criterion and orthographic ratings mentioned in the report provide additional data about the experimental group, but these data are unrelated to the test of the researcher's hypothesis. (A brief discussion of the results of these strategies is included in Chapter 12.)

Weekly dictation spelling tests have built-in content validity because the words used in spelling instruction are the words tested. The dictated story strategy also has built-in content validity for the same reason. Participants were expected to spell certain words from the spelling lists that were incorporated into a dictated story. All the spelling words came from an organized spelling curriculum.

Gettinger asked participants' teachers to rate their students' spelling globally during the baseline (trial) phase of the study. Teacher ratings of students correlated strongly with students' spelling accuracy in lists and stories, a case of criterion-related validity. The data collected in this project using these three strategies are valid for answering the researcher's question.

The data that result from use of these strategies are generally reliable. Gettinger established test-retest reliability for weekly dictation spelling tests and teacher ratings at acceptable levels during the baseline period of this study. The use of dictated stories probably also gives reliable data although there is no mention of reliability evidence for this strategy. It is reasonable to believe that the participants wrote dictated stories during the baseline period.

These instrument selection or development procedures fit well with the participant procedures. These procedures can be applied with the classroom size groups of 20–25 participants.

What Is Classroom Discussion? A Look at Teachers' Conceptions

Larson and Parker (1996) used an interview schedule, a think-aloud task, and observations of classroom teaching to collect data from teachers about their conceptions of discussion. These data collection strategies are well suited for providing data about this phenomenon because the verbal data generated fit the requirements for answering the researchers' question.

This report does not mention the amount of time over which data were gathered. Although actual questions are not provided, the analysis subsection clarifies how the interviews and think-aloud tasks generated data. These descriptions suggest that the researchers probably obtained sufficient data to answer their questions accurately. Because the report contains so little information about classroom observations, the part that these played in furnishing data is questionable.

Three methods of collecting data, each of which provides a different perspective about classroom discussion, were used in this study. The full description of how two methods were used suggests that the researchers checked and found their data to be consistent. How classroom observation data were used would probably offer additional evidence of reliability.

These data collection strategies are aligned well with the setting. Based on the descriptions, the researcher(s) probably adopted the role of participant-as-observer and worked with the participants individually. This approach offered maximum opportunities to obtain these teachers' ideas about classroom discussion.

E X E R C I S E   5 . 4

For each report, study the research problem or question. Then study the instrumentation subsection.

> A3 A Phenomenological Study with Youth Gang Members: Results and Implications for School Counselors
>
> A5 Preservice and Inservice Secondary Teachers' Orientations Toward Content Area Reading

Answer the following questions for each report:

1. Identify the variables or phenomena named in the research question(s) on which the researchers must gather data. Specify the instruments or strategies used to collect data for each variable or phenomenon.

2. To estimate the validity of data provided by the instrumentation strategies, answer these questions: (For quantitative reports)
   - Discuss the type(s) of data provided by the instruments or strategies identified in question 1 compared with the type(s) of data required for answering the research questions.

- Discuss the evidence presented for the validity of measurement for data from each instrument or strategy.
  a. (For qualitative reports)
     - Discuss the type(s) of data provided by the instruments or strategies identified in question 1 compared with the type(s) of data required for answering the research questions.
     - Discuss whether the time period over which data were collected is long enough to gather sufficient data to answer the research question(s) accurately.
3. To estimate the reliability of data provided by the instrumentation strategies, answer these questions:
   a. (For quantitative reports)
      - Discuss the evidence presented for the reliability of measurement for data from each instrument or strategy.
      - Discuss the degree of fit between instrument selection or development procedures and participant procedures.
   b. (For qualitative reports)
      - Discuss the procedures used to check data consistency.
      - Discuss the alignment of data collection strategies with the setting.

Summary

Instrumentation includes the researchers' preparations for data collection, including decisions about what data are needed to answer their research questions, the number of collections, the instruments or strategies by which data are collected, and the data collectors. These preparations differ according to mode of inquiry.

Quantitative researchers collect mostly numerical data one or more times during a project. They select or develop instruments or strategies for their project, and provide evidence of their validity and reliability of measurement. These strategies should fit with the participant procedures and provide data at a level of measurement compatible with the researchers' intended data analysis procedures.

Qualitative researchers collect mostly verbal data throughout the duration of their projects in recurring collection and analysis cycles. They usually develop instruments or strategies uniquely fitted to their setting and to the role(s) they wish to take in data collection. These researchers rely on gathering large quantities of data to ensure accuracy and on the use of multiple collectors or strategies to ensure consistency among the data.

The method section of research reports describes instrumentation procedures in a separate subsection or as part of data collection. These descriptions should be read carefully to determine whether the data produced by the instruments or strategies are valid and reliable for analysis. Criteria for evaluating instrument selection or development were outlined and applied to two research reports.

Questions for Discussion

1. Some quantitative researchers use instruments developed by researchers for other projects. Discuss at least two precautions investigators should take before using these instruments.
2. Explain why triangulation is considered to be more important in qualitative research than it is in quantitative inquiries.
3. The instrumentation sections of some research reports contain details, but are sparse in other reports. Discuss the implications for readers of these two situations.

Methods and Results for Quantitative Studies

At this point, the discussion of research processes divides according to mode of inquiry. Part III focuses on methods and results for quantitative studies. Comparable topics for qualitative studies are discussed in part IV.

Chapters 6 and 7 discuss the design procedures for experimental and descriptive studies, respectively. Designs encompass all the processes, including the participant and instrumentation procedures discussed previously. Additional processes include data collection and handling in all studies and treatment procedures for experiments. The sequences in which researchers apply these procedures vary according to the goal and purpose of their projects and, thus, give rise to various designs.

The fourth systematic process is analyze and interpret the data. For quantitative research, this typically means collection of numerical data, from which investigators deduce answers to their research questions. The descriptive statistical data analyses, such as those described in Chapter 8, furnish the tools by which researchers obtain their answers or results for the project participants.

Many researchers want to see if these results hold true for a population. They subject the participant results to inferential statistical data analyses, as described in Chapter 9. The results of analysis procedures for participants and populations are briefly explained in these chapters, but are described in detail in Chapter 12.

If you are preparing a proposal for a quantitative project, Chapter 14 provides additional information about design procedures from the perspective of the producer of research. The emphasis is on planning data collection and analysis procedures for a project of your choice.

Design Procedures for Experimental Research

❖ **Treatment Procedures**

    Major Types of Comparisons

    Other Comparisons

    Treatment Administration

❖ **Procedures for Data Collection and Handling**

❖ **Systematic Application of Procedures**

❖ **Designs for True Experiments**

    Pretest and Posttest Control Group Design

    Posttest Only Design

    Factorial Designs

❖ **Designs for Quasi-experiments**

❖ **Designs for Pre-experiments**

❖ **Designs for Complex Experiments**

❖ **Method Sections in Experimental Research Reports**

    Descriptions

    Criteria for Evaluation

    Application of Criteria

Using control as their goal, experimental researchers devise research designs that incorporate the participant selection and assignment procedures and the instrument or strategy choice procedures discussed in Chapters 4 and 5. The remainder of the procedures consists of those associated with treatment levels and data collection and handling, which are topics discussed here, plus data analysis procedures, which are discussed in Chapters 8 and 9.

First, general information about treatment procedures and procedures for collection and handling of data is described. Next is a discussion about the importance of systematic application of procedures in research designs to assist researchers in managing variance associated with measures of the responding variable. These procedures differ in the designs for experimental research.

True and quasi-experiments, two major groups of experimental designs, allow researchers to account for **variance,** or variability of scores, better than do pre-experiments, a third group of designs. Consequently, the data from the former designs are considered more valid and reliable than are data from the latter.

The final chapter section describes the content of method sections in experimental research reports, with brief reviews of participant and instrument or strategy choices from previous chapters. Criteria for evaluation of method sections of experimental reports are discussed and applied.

Goal

To enable you to:

- evaluate research design procedures in selected experimental research reports for the production of valid and reliable data for analysis.

⚹ Treatment Procedures

Experimenters design their procedures to accomplish comparisons of several types. Whereas some comparisons are simple, others are complex. Researchers must also describe the administration and circumstances of applying the treatments.

Major Types of Comparisons

Researchers operationally define the manipulated variable, or "cause" in their research question, as levels of treatment. Next, they apply these treatment levels to participant group(s) and measure the responses as the "effect." Three major types of comparisons are illustrated:

- Before- and after-treatment performances for one group

Suppose researchers want to see if using a literature-based approach to reading instruction improves elementary students' comprehension. They measure the students' comprehension, administer the literature-based instructional intervention, and then re-measure students' comprehension. Investigators compare the before-treatment and after-treatment scores.

- Performance of one group that receives treatment with performance of a second group that receives no treatment

In this case, researchers use two groups, administer the literature-based reading instruction to one group, and do not administer this instruction to the second group. Afterward, they measure reading comprehension in both groups and compare group after-treatment scores.

- Performances of two or more groups that receive different levels of treatment

Here, researchers use two groups. They administer the literature-based reading instruction to one group, and administer a different reading instruction, perhaps a basal reader approach, to the second group for the same length of time. Then they measure students' reading comprehension abilities and compare the after-treatment scores of the two groups. To expect differences in measures of the responding variable requires that participant groups experience genuinely different levels of treatment (Charters & Jones, 1973; Hall & Loucks, 1974).

Other Comparisons

To this point, the discussion of experimental research has focused on the relationship between one manipulated and one responding variable. In some comparisons, the cause-and-effect relationships between more than one manipulated variable, responding variable, or both may be tested. See the discussion of factorial designs in the design sections that follow.

Researchers must also account for the possibility that variables in the research setting, other than the manipulated variable, effect changes in the responding variable. Called **extraneous variables,** some of these variables can be included in the design.

Naturally occurring variables, such as age and gender, cannot be manipulated, but they might affect a responding variable. However, researchers can account for the effects of these variables in at least two ways. In the example reading experiment, researchers who believe that either age or gender affects reading comprehension could choose to limit participation in the experiment to individuals of one age or one gender. This action removes from consideration the effects of this extraneous variable on the responding variable.

Or, the researchers could select participants of more than one age (or gender) and identify them by their age (or gender) during the collection of reading comprehension data. They would use data analysis procedures that account for possible contributions of age (or gender) to changes in the responding variable. The variables of age and gender are **attribute** or **assigned** variables; their values are naturally occurring.

Several functions of variables in experimental research are displayed in Table 6.1. Manipulated and attribute variables are types of **independent variables;** responding variables are **dependent variables.**

TABLE 6.1

Functions of Variables in Experimental Research

Variable	Description	Examples
Independent	Generally considered as variables that receive much attention from researchers; includes manipulated and attribute variables	See examples of manipulated and attribute variables below
• Manipulated (or **experimental** or **active**)	Researchers change the values of these variables; the presumed "cause" in a cause-and-effect relationship	Variable is method of teaching reading; values include literature-based, basal reader, and phonics approaches
• Attribute (or assigned)	Values are naturally occurring; cannot be manipulated; cannot be presumed as "causes"	Variables that can affect reading comprehension: Age—6, 9, 15 years; Gender—male, female; Grade level—first, fourth, tenth grades
Dependent • Responding	Variables are associated with independent variables; also known as responding variables; the presumed "effect" in a cause-and-effect relationship	Variables that potentially respond to changes by method of teaching reading; include comprehension, word fluency, and decoding abilities

Treatment Administration

Researchers sometimes administer treatments. In other cases, teachers or assistants participate as treatment administrators. They may have to attend training sessions to become thoroughly familiar with the materials and equipment they are to use.

Treatment should be administered over a time period long enough for changes to occur in the responding variable. The length of time needed depends on the variables involved and the change expected.

✖ Procedures for Data Collection and Handling

Data collection procedures require researchers' decisions about the circumstances, the frequency, the schedule, and the collectors, including their expertise. Because participants are usually grouped for treatments, they are likely to provide data within groups as well. Data are usually collected in settings familiar to participants, such as where they live, work, or play. In school-based projects, teachers are frequently data collectors, but whoever collects data must have the necessary expertise to handle the collection tasks well.

Data collection procedures in experiments are commonly referred to as pretests if they are made prior to treatment, or as posttests if made after treatment. The term "test" refers to any method of data collection and is not restricted to actual tests. Some experimental research designs require more than two data collections. See the Designs for Quasi-Experiments section, time series design.

The raw data provided by participants typically undergo several procedures, called **data handling procedures,** to prepare them for analysis. In some cases, the instruments require scoring either manually or by computers. Other procedures involve checking the completeness of data for all participants, handling missing data, and sorting data by groups. Sometimes data are transformed from one level of measurement to another (e.g., from interval to ordinal measures). Handling also involves entering data into computer files for analysis.

✖ Systematic Application of Procedures

All of the procedures in quantitative projects must be carried out systematically to produce valid and reliable data for analysis. These procedures include participant selection and assignment, choice of instruments or strategies for collection of data, the administration of treatment, data collection, and data handling procedures.

Research plans or designs for experiments call for procedures to be applied in various sequences in true, quasi-, and pre-experiments. These different experimental designs exist because they assist researchers in managing variance, or variability of the scores associated with the responding variable. Although experimenters deliberately introduce some variance into projects by the manipulation of variables, undesirable variance, or **error variance,** comes from undetermined sources. Management of variance, then, involves eliminating as much error variance as possible.

Experimenters use randomization procedures to distribute error variance equally across groups. The random selection of participants from a population helps to ensure the comparability of participant groups in terms of naturally occurring variables. The assignment of individuals or groups to treatments by random methods helps to eliminate potential researcher biases.

In an experiment, including certain attribute variables that can effect changes in the responding variable further ensures that the effects noted are the result of the manipulated variable(s) rather than those of extraneous variables. These actions are part of the researchers' goal of control. Note how these ideas are incorporated in the descriptions of designs in the sections that follow.

Designs for true and quasi-experiments generate data that are more valid and reliable than are data from pre-experimental designs. The major reason for this difference is that researchers are able to account for variance better in true and quasi-experiments than in pre-experiments. For additional information about accounting for variance, see the discussion of threats to validity in experiments in Campbell and Stanley, 1979.

⚔ Designs for True Experiments

True experiments are used to test the effects of an independent variable on a related dependent variable. Minimum requirements include an independent variable with at least two treatment levels to which participants must be randomly assigned. The random assignment of participants to treatment levels creates unbiased comparisons.

Pretest and Posttest Control Group Design

The sequence of procedures can vary in true experiments. The *pretest and posttest control group design* uses participants who are randomly assigned to one of two levels of treatment. One level is usually the special intervention that is being tested. The other level may be either a second special intervention, called a comparison, or the usual treatment, called a control.

All participants provide data on the pretest prior to undergoing the treatments. (Pretest is the shorthand way of referring to the data collection strategy chosen by the researchers.) After treatments are completed, all participants provide data a second time on the posttest. The use of pretests allows researchers to observe changes over the period of the intervention, or experiment (see Figure 6.1a).

To illustrate, suppose a swim coach wants data to help him decide whether adoption of a new technique for swimmers will improve their speed. The coach-researcher collects data on participants' times for swimming a series of laps as a pretest. Then he randomly assigns half the swimmers to instruction with the new technique (NT), and the remaining swimmers continue using the traditional technique (TT). After a period of intervention, swimmers in both groups are timed on laps identical with the first series. The data from the two groups are analyzed to see if the performance of NT swimmers improved to a greater extent than of the TT swimmers.

Posttest Only Design

Figure 6.1b displays a sequence for the procedures in a *true experiment posttest-only design*. First, participants are assigned randomly to treatment and control groups. Following the intervention, both groups take a posttest. The data are analyzed to see if the two groups performed differently.

To use this design, the coach-researcher could simply randomly assign swimmers to NT and TT groups. Following this intervention, both groups are timed on a series of laps as a posttest. The researcher can tell which of the two groups has the better performance but he does not have information about improvement in performance.

Factorial Designs

A third variation on the true experiment involves the use of more than two groups of participants. **Factorial designs** require at least two independent variables, called factors, and at least one dependent variable. Use of these designs is better than two experiments because researchers can determine if the independent variables interact to produce changes in the dependent variable that are different from the total effects in two simple experiments.

(a) Pretest and posttest control group design

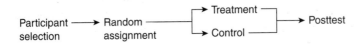

(b) Posttest only, control group design

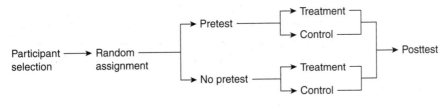

(c) Solomon four-group design

FIGURE 6.1   Procedures in true experiments.

One popular factorial design is the *Solomon four-group design*, in which participants are randomly assigned to different levels of treatment, half each to treatment and to control. The treatment and control groups are each subdivided into two groups, making a total of four groups. In each pair of treatment and control groups, one group takes a pretest and the other group does not (Solomon, 1949) (see Figure 6.1c). This design combines the advantages of pretest-posttest and posttest only designs, but as is true of all factorial designs, many participants are required to fill the groups.

Use of pretests is not a requirement in factorial designs. Suppose the swim coach mentioned earlier wishes to study not only the new technique, but also the effectiveness of sessions of different lengths. A *true experiment factorial design* with technique and session length as the factors allows the coach to study these variables simultaneously.

If the coach-researcher chooses two values for each factor, four groups of participants are required. Each value of technique (i.e., new or traditional) must be paired with a value of session length (i.e., long or short) (see Figure 6.2).

Use of this particular 2 by 2 factorial design permits the swim coach to answer these questions:

1. Does the type of technique interact with session length to affect the speed of swimmers? (Compare groups A with B with C with D.)
2. Does the type of technique (new versus traditional) affect the speed of swimmers? (Compare groups A and C with groups B and D.)
3. Does session length (long versus short) affect the speed of swimmers? (Compare groups A and B with groups C and D.)

Questions 2 and 3 could be answered if the swim coach conducts two simple experiments, but question 1 can be answered only by using a true factorial design.

In carrying out the procedures, the coach selects a sample and randomly assigns each participant to a group. This example, which uses a true experimental factorial design with two independent manipulable variables, allows participants to be assigned randomly.

True experiments in school settings are unusual unless researchers use the entire population. Stevahn et. al (1996) evaluated the effectiveness of a conflict resolution program in a rural Canadian school using a true factorial

SESSION LENGTH

TYPE OF TECHNIQUE	A—Long, new technique	C—Short, new technique
	B—Long, traditional technique	D—Short, traditional technique

FIGURE 6.2   Groups for a true experiment 2 by 2 factorial design.

experimental design. In this project, the entire population of two grades was assigned individually at random to one of four groups. By using the entire population of students, the researchers averted difficulties associated with failure to include students in the experiment (see Figure 4.2).

⚓ Designs for Quasi-Experiments

In some schools, students cannot be randomly assigned as individuals to treatment groups because this disrupts schedules and learning opportunities. However, all the students within any one classroom can be randomly assigned as an intact group to serve as a treatment or control group; hence the term **quasi-experiment.**

The disadvantage of considering the classroom as the unit of concern, of course, is that students within any one classroom may vary widely with respect to the variables of concern. Variations within one classroom may or may not be comparable to the variations within the classroom used as a comparison. These variations may affect the results because they are not subject to control by the researchers.

The *nonequivalent control group design* uses procedures that are similar to those in the pretest and posttest true experiment. In this quasi-experiment, however, intact classrooms of participants, rather than individuals, are assigned at random to treatment and control groups (see Figure 6.3a).

Quasi-experiments also use time series and counterbalanced designs. A *time series design,* depicted in Figure 6.3b, shows that a single group of participants engages in a series of measures that is interrupted periodically by a treatment or intervention. Researchers who use this design note patterns in the data taken before treatment and compare them with patterns taken after treatment. Although the diagram shows two tests prior to a treatment,

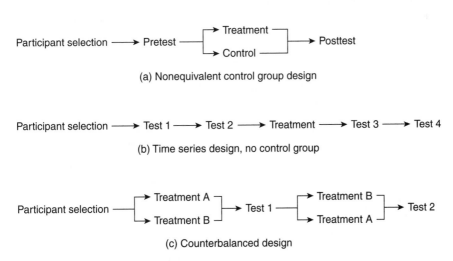

FIGURE 6.3   Procedures in quasi-experiments.

researchers can plan any number of tests and any number of treatments in a time series design.

In *counterbalanced designs,* two groups of participants take both treatments in opposite order, but a data collection point separates the treatments (see Figure 6.3c). This design allows researchers to gather data from all the participants concerning both treatments. The analysis procedures permit the researchers to evaluate effects of both treatments on the responding variable.

However, this design is not appropriate in situations in which the effects of one treatment can contaminate the effects of the other treatment. For example, in learning mathematics, children typically follow concrete to pictorial to abstract sequences of activities. This means that hands-on manipulations of objects precede the use of diagrams and pictures of objects for learning. Use of concrete and pictorial instruction is inappropriate in a counterbalanced design because participants who engage in concrete activities during the first cycle could have an unfair advantage over participants who engage in pictorial activities in their first cycle.

Both time series and counterbalanced designs are also called **repeated measures** designs. This term describes projects in which data are collected from the same participants more than once. Usually researchers use repeated measures designs to find whether participants make measurable gains in projects that compare before-treatment data to after-treatment data.

Recall that independent variables are not always manipulable; some are attribute or assigned variables. If one of the independent variables is gender or age, for example, researchers may find it impossible to assign participants to groups randomly. In these cases, researchers first subdivide the sample into groups according to the values of the attribute variable. Then they randomly assign participants within these groups according to the values of the manipulable variable. Use of these procedures results in a *quasi-experiment factorial design.*

Factorial designs can be more complex than the 2 by 2 factorial design described in Figure 6.2. If the swim coach has both male and female swim-

SESSION LENGTH

TYPE OF TECHNIQUE AND GENDER	A—Long, new technique, males	E—Short, new technique, males
	B—Long, new technique, females	F—Short, new technique, females
	C—Long, traditional technique, males	G—Short, traditional technique, males
	D—Long, traditional technique, females	H—Short, traditional technique, females

FIGURE 6.4   Groups for a quasi-experiment 2 by 2 by 2 factorial design.

mers, for instance, he may also check whether the participants' gender interacts with the new technique and the session length. The design becomes 2 by 2 by 2 (two techniques, two session lengths, two genders) and requires eight groups (see Figure 6.4). The use of factorial designs provides one way to answer complex research questions.

⚒ Designs for Pre-Experiments

As the name indicates, a **pre-experiment** should probably not be called an experiment, except for the manipulation of the independent variable. The data obtained from pre-experimental designs are questionable for the reasons mentioned in the following discussion.

Figure 6.5 shows three designs for pre-experiments, none of which uses randomization and only one of which has a control group. The first design is called a *one-shot case study* in which a participant group undergoes a treatment, then takes a posttest (Figure 6.5a). Data from these design procedures have little validity because there is no basis for determining the extent to which the treatment affected the dependent variable.

The second design is similar to the first; the only difference is that the group takes a pretest before undergoing treatment (Figure 6.5b). Pretests allow researchers to compare before-treatment scores with after-treatment scores.

At first glance, the *static group comparison design* shown in Figure 6.5c is similar to the posttest only true experiment. What makes it different, of course, is that the treatment and control groups are not randomly assigned. Because the pre-experiment groups may be dissimilar prior to the intervention, any number of explanations can account for differences in data collected as part of this design.

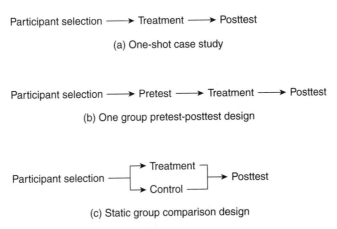

FIGURE 6.5   Procedures in pre-experiments.

EXERCISE 6.1

The ability to recognize the type of experiment by reading descriptions of design procedures is helpful in evaluating the validity and reliability of data. Check your ability here in preparation for Exercise 6.2.

Name the research design described by the procedures. Explain your choice. When possible, suggest modifications in design procedures that could possibly increase the validity and reliability of data.

1. The director of speech therapy in a large school system is faced with a shortage of therapists. In this system, students usually have individual therapy sessions, but the number of students who need therapy has risen sharply. In an effort to handle all these students, a research project is begun to see if small-group therapy is as effective as individual therapy, and if student age has an effect on progress in therapy. From the 600 students who need therapy, the director randomly selects a sample of 150. These students are separated into two groups by their median age, with those above the median designated as older students and those below the median as younger students. Half the students in each of these two groups are randomly assigned to receive group therapy. The remaining half is assigned to individual therapy. The therapists who work with students will keep weekly performance logs of student progress in speech therapy.
2. Mr. Ballou is a middle school art teacher who uses basically the same teaching method and content in each of six class sections. He plans a research project to evaluate the effects of a change in teaching method on students' attitudes toward art. He decides that the three morning classes will continue with the teaching method he uses. However, the three afternoon classes will have free choice of several art projects, which they pursue at their own pace. At the end of the grading period, he administers an art attitude scale to students in all six class sections.
3. Students enroll in Introduction to Psychology at a state university through computer registration, which results in their random assignment to class sections. Instructors in the psychology department want to find out whether videotaped lectures are as effective in terms of student achievement as live lectures. Half the classes are randomly assigned to watch videotaped lectures, while the remaining half attend live lectures. At the end of the semester, their scores on a comprehensive final exam measure of achievement are compared.

Designs for Complex Experiments

The designs described thus far have a single dependent variable. However, experimental researchers do undertake projects in which they seek data on more than one *dependent* variable using complex experiments.

An example of the design complexity is illustrated by a study of the effects of cooperative learning on the perceived status of male and female pupils (Petersen, Johnson, & Johnson, 1991). In this study, the researchers used two independent variables: a manipulated variable, with values of cooperative and individualized learning; and an assigned variable, with three gender groupings—equal numbers of males and females, a female majority, and a male majority. The *four dependent* variables were achievement, verbal interaction, perceived leadership, and perceived change in status. It's easy to see that this design involves testing many hypotheses.

✖ Method Sections in Experimental Research Reports

This section describes the method sections of experimental research reports, with special emphasis on treatment levels and data collection and handling. Participant selection and instrument choice procedures are the topics of Chapters 4 and 5. Criteria for the evaluation of method sections are discussed and applied to an experimental research report.

Descriptions

Reports of experimental studies sometimes have more than one subsection related to procedures; at least one of these describes treatment procedures. Here, researchers describe the treatments, or interventions, for all groups, their duration, and the expertise of the administrators.

Researchers usually detail the experiences provided to the experimental group, including frequency of treatments and duration. If teachers serve as treatment administrators, they may undergo specialized training to increase their expertise. However, the same reports are sometimes lax in their descriptions of control or comparison group experiences. References to "usual activities" are insufficient, because these can vary widely from one classroom to the next one. Failure to provide complete information about the comparison groups asks readers to accept blindly that participant groups experienced different treatment levels.

Data collection and handling procedures are also described in procedures subsections and may be intertwined with treatment descriptions. The circumstances in which data were collected, the schedule, and number of collections are necessary for an understanding of the design procedures. The amount of detail that researchers provide varies from one report to another.

Criteria for Evaluation

Readers of experimental research reports should be aware of several criteria related to the content of method sections. The following criteria are based on information presented in this chapter, plus material from Chapters 4 and 5 on participant and instrument or strategy choices, respectively.

1. The design used for the project should be clearly identifiable. The procedures should be suitable for providing data to answer the research questions.

The number of independent and dependent variables should be obvious, as a signal about the complexity of the design. Whether treatment is assigned at random to individuals or groups is also important because this distinction marks the difference between true and quasi-experiments.

Once the design is identified, consider its fit with the researchers' questions. The design should enable the researchers to obtain valid and reliable data for answering their research questions.

2. Data gathered through the use of these design procedures should be valid.

Researchers should provide sufficient information about treatment procedures for all groups to clarify how the groups differed in levels of treatment. Researchers should also describe who administered treatment, their preparation for this role and the duration and sequence of treatment procedures for all groups.

Researchers should also describe the data collection and handling procedures in detail. The description should include circumstances in which data were collected, the frequency of collection, the identity of the data collectors, and their expertise for the job. The data handling procedures should describe briefly the end-of-collection activities about scoring procedures, checks for data completion, and missing data procedures.

Next, the overall validity of the data from the design procedures should be evaluated. This includes the participant, the instrument or strategy for data collection choices, the treatment, and data collection and handling procedures.

3. Data gathered through the use of these design procedures should be reliable.

Both the treatment and data collection and handling procedures should be consistent with participant procedures and the instrument or strategy choices. All participants should be assigned to treatments, preferably by random methods. The data collection and handling procedures should be natural extensions of the instrumentation procedures.

Researchers should describe all design procedures clearly. Independent researchers should be able to use the procedures with similar populations and expect similar results.

Application of Criteria

These criteria are applied to the Method sections of an experimental research report. See Exercise 6.2 for the questions on which the critique is based. Refer to these questions and the research report as you read this section.

Effects of Error Correction on Third Graders' Spelling

This report (A1) uses a nonequivalent control group quasi-experimental design in which treatment levels were assigned at random to three intact classroom groups. The error correction classroom received the experimental treatment, the reduced number of spelling words classroom served as a modified control group, and the standard classroom was the control group. Both the pretest and the posttest consisted of the weekly tests, dictated stories, and teacher ratings taken at the end of the baseline and intervention periods, respectively. This design is well suited for answering the researcher's questions, particularly because Gettinger wished to test the effectiveness of error correction in regular classrooms, rather than in special education classrooms.

Three regular third grade teachers taught spelling, each using a different instructional approach to his or her students. Gettinger describes each treatment level in enough detail to ensure that these treatments are different. Regular preparation and experience would enable teachers of the standard condition and the reduced number class to administer these treatments without additional training. However, there's no information about the preparation of the teacher who used error correction, a small detail. The treatments lasted for 6 weeks and were preceded by 6 weeks of similar treatments during the baseline period. This treatment period duration should be long enough for changes in spelling performance to be noticed. These procedures probably provide valid data, despite the missing detail about error correction for the treatment giver.

The classroom teachers collected data at regular intervals. Spelling tests were given weekly; dictated stories that used spelling words were given at the end of each 6-week unit; and teacher ratings were made at regular 3-week intervals. The description of data collection procedures suggests that these either were, or became, routine so that participants had little reason to be apprehensive about data collection.

Students scored their classmates' weekly dictation spelling tests using their standard procedures. When tests were re-scored by the researcher, student-scoring procedures were found to be accurate. No information about the scoring of dictated stories or other data handling procedures was included. The data collection procedures probably produce valid data.

Previous critiques in Chapters 4 and 5 noted that the participant and instrument choice procedures provide largely valid data. However, because the participants are probably a convenience sample, these data are not necessarily representative of other third graders and there was a minor question about the reliability of measurement of the data collection strategy for dictated stories. Overall, these design procedures probably provide valid data for analysis.

Both the treatment and data collection and most handling procedures are clearly described. Details are missing about scoring dictated stories, otherwise independent researchers could also use these data handling procedures. Independent researchers could use these procedures and expect to obtain similar results.

Previous critiques noted that the participant and instrument choice procedures provide largely reliable data. Of all the measures, only the dictated stories data collection strategy fails to provide information about reliability. The design procedures are clearly described and should provide generally reliable data for analysis.

E X E R C I S E   6 . 2

The method section of a report provides you with important information about procedures used in the project. This knowledge is useful in evaluating the validity and reliability of the collected data. Use this exercise to self-assess your understanding.

Study the problem and the method section for this report:

A4 A Computerized Method to Teach Latin and Greek Root Words: Effect on Verbal SAT Scores

Answer these questions:

1. Identify the design used for this project. Comment on the appropriateness of this design for providing data to answer the research question(s).

2. To estimate the validity of data provided by the design procedures, answer the following questions:
   a. Discuss the likelihood that data from the treatment procedures are valid. For example, do the descriptions indicate that the groups actually received different levels of treatment? Do the treatments last long enough to have an effect? Do the treatment administrators appear to be well prepared?
   b. Discuss the likelihood that data from the collection and handling procedures are valid. For example, consider the data collection procedures, including the circumstances in which data were collected, the frequency of collection, and the probable expertise of the collectors. Consider the data handling procedures.
   c. Consider the validity of the data provided by all design procedures. In addition to your answers to questions 2a and 2b, include the contributions of participant and instrument or strategy choices. (See Exercise 4.3, question 2a and Exercise 5.4, question 2a.) On an overall basis, can these data be considered valid? Explain.

3. To estimate the reliability of data provided by the design procedures, answer the following questions:
   a. How clearly described are the treatment procedures? The data collection and handling procedures? Could independent researchers use these procedures and expect to obtain similar results?
   b. Consider all the design procedures and the reliability of the data they provide. In addition to your answer to question 3a, include the contributions of participant and instrument or strategy choices. (See Exercise 4.3, question 3a and Exercise 5.4, question 3a.) On an overall basis, can these data be considered reliable? Explain.

Summary

Several types of comparisons are described as part of treatment procedures. These may involve manipulated or attribute variables, or both. These procedures, as well as all other procedures, including data collection and handling, should be applied systematically in experimental research to reduce error variance. The control of extraneous variables and the use of randomization procedures help these efforts.

Designs that account for variance well provide valid and reliable data for analysis. In particular, true and quasi-experiments do a better job of accounting for variance than do pre-experiments. Designs for factorial and complex experiments allow researchers to pursue answers to complex research questions.

Procedures for research reports are described in method sections. Here, researchers should provide complete descriptions of all treatment levels and all data collection and handling procedures. Combining the assessments of participant, instrument or strategy choice, treatment, and data collection and handing design procedures enables readers to gauge the validity and reliability of data produced in a project. Criteria for making these judgments were stated and applied to a research report.

Questions for Discussion

1. Explain how the effects of the randomization procedures suggested in this chapter are similar to the effects of sample selection using random procedures, which were described in Chapter 4.
2. Describe the advantages of factorial designs over single independent variable designs. Speculate about reasons why factorial designs are not used more frequently.
3. This chapter emphasized the point that researchers should describe treatment activities in *all* groups involved in experiments. Explain why this is important.
4. Suppose you are a graduate student who is expected to complete an experimental research project. What arguments, if any, could you make to your adviser for the design of a pre-experiment?

Design Procedures for Descriptive Research

❖ **Procedures for Data Collection and Handling**

❖ **Systematic Application of Procedures**

❖ **Design Procedures for Status Studies**

 Meta-Analyses

 Survey Studies

❖ **Design Procedures for Causal Comparative Studies**

❖ **Design Procedures for Correlation and Prediction Studies**

Correlation Designs

Prediction Designs

❖ **Method Sections in Descriptive Research Reports**

Descriptions

Criteria for Evaluation

Application of Criteria

After quantitative investigators decide on a problem and examine the literature about the problem area, they locate research settings, select participants, and choose instruments or strategies for data collection. Then, if the study has explanation or prediction as its goal, researchers plan the data collection and handling procedures for descriptive research. They also plan their data analysis procedures as described in Chapters 8 and 9.

Researchers who use descriptive methods also try to account for variance, insofar as possible. Options are typically limited to systematic applications of carefully designed procedures. The use of adequate numbers of participants in random samples for survey, correlation, and prediction studies increases the likelihood that researchers gather data showing the full range of variations in variables.

Research plans or designs for descriptive studies are simple, but they have different configurations depending on the purpose of the research, the number and nature of the variables under study, and the frequency of data collections. This chapter describes the procedures for data collection and handling and integrates them with participant and instrument or strategy choices for data collection described in previous chapters.

The final section discusses the method sections of descriptive research reports. Criteria for the evaluation of method sections encompass content from this and previous chapters on participant selection and instrument or strategy choices. Finally, these criteria are applied to a report.

Goal

To enable you to:

- evaluate the design procedures in selected reports of descriptive research for the production of valid and reliable data for analysis.

✖ Procedures for Data Collection and Handling

Decisions about the circumstances, frequency, schedule, and expertise of data collectors and handlers are important in descriptive research. Many of the procedures are similar to those for experimental research. However, descriptive researchers do not refer to pre- or posttests as a part of designs because treatments are not part of these designs.

For some descriptive research projects, the necessary data can be collected at one sitting. In other projects, however, data collections may be separated by defined time intervals that allow participants to achieve the changes the project is designed to monitor. Researchers who conduct survey research typically use interviews, questionnaires, or both to obtain data. Special concerns about these procedures are described in the Design Procedures for Status Studies section.

In some causal comparative designs, researchers may choose to collect data about an extraneous variable related to other variables in the project. The researchers use data analysis procedures that allow them to account for possible joint relationships with other project variables. Design procedures for causal comparative studies are discussed in a section with this name.

✖ Systematic Application of Procedures

All of the procedures in descriptive projects should be carried out systematically. This includes participant selection, choices of instruments or strategies, data collection, and handling procedures. Haphazard applications or failure to apply the procedures systematically typically results in unreliable data and increased variance.

Designs for descriptive studies enable researchers to pursue explanation and prediction as goals and to serve several different purposes. Table 7.1 provides an overview of descriptive designs. In all studies, analyses require valid and reliable data.

✖ Design Procedures for Status Studies

Status studies use descriptive methods to obtain data about the condition or standing of variables. These studies focus on explanation as the goal of research. As discussed in this chapter, status studies include meta-analyses and survey studies.

Meta-Analyses

Although **meta-analyses** were introduced in Chapter 1 as secondary research reports, they also merit discussion here as a descriptive research design. Researchers who undertake meta-analyses first prepare a problem statement about a topic or variable on which sizable numbers of primary reports exist. These reports investigate the same question, involve similar variables, and may be published or unpublished (e.g., dissertations, conference presentations).

TABLE 7.1

Designs for Descriptive Research with their Goals of Research and Major Purposes

Goal of Research	Design Name	Major Purpose
Explanation	Status studies • Meta-analyses • Survey studies	To assess the standing or condition of variables or topics
Explanation	Causal comparative studies	To investigate potential cause-and-effect relationships that occur naturally without manipulation of variables
Explanation	Correlation studies	To determine the magnitude and direction of associations or relationships among variables
Prediction	Prediction studies	To use associations among variables as the basis for the prediction of unknown variables based on the known variables

The researchers develop criteria to use in decisions about which reports to include in their project. Criteria may include minimum numbers of participants, dates, or types of treatments. Next, the investigators locate reports on the topic or variable and apply these criteria. For reports that meet the criteria for inclusion, the researchers classify, code, and measure the study findings. Measuring the findings for each report typically involves the calculation of one or more effect sizes. These provide a measure common to all the reports and become the data for analysis. Additional information about effect size is described in Chapter 8.

Meta-analyses provide status concerning variables in the form of the researchers' interpretations of their analyses of multiple studies on the variable. Rosenshine and Meister (1994) reviewed 19 studies in which reciprocal teaching was researched. (Reciprocal teaching is an instructional approach that helps students develop cognitive strategies in reading.) In their discussion section, the researchers summarize results in 13 different categories. The brief summary paragraphs are then expanded to full-blown discussions about many features of reciprocal teaching. Readers who study this meta-analysis can learn a great deal about reciprocal teaching.

Since the development of meta-analytic methods in the late 1970s, meta-analyses have been completed on many topics, including the relationship of class size to classroom processes (Glass & Smith, 1979), the effects of ability grouping (Noland & Taylor, 1986) and the effectiveness of computer-based instruction (Kulik & Kulik, 1991). Researchers using meta-analyses anticipate that better answers to important problems can be obtained by combining the results of many studies than by using simple inquiries.

Survey Studies

Designs for **survey studies** allow researchers to systematically collect and analyze data about variables and topics of interest for a variety of audiences. The design procedures require participant selection, instrument or strategy choices, and data collection and handling.

Survey studies may gather information from a population, called a *census,* or from samples, called *sample surveys.* A census might be used by researchers in a school district who seek responses from every household on matters such as curriculum, school policies, or school tax issues. In many cases, the population is so large that costs and time constraints prohibit attempts to collect data from all the members.

Large numbers of survey studies are *sample surveys* in which participants are part of a population. If the samples are random, the results of the survey can be generalized to the population represented by the samples. For non-random samples, of course, the results are true for the participants, but not necessarily for anyone else.

Each year, Phi Delta Kappa and the Gallup organization poll randomly selected citizens of the United States about a variety of questions related to education. This poll asks questions in diverse categories about attitudes toward public schools, school choice, problems facing the public schools, improvement strategies, standards, instructional issues, and others (Rose & Gallup, 1999). Although the questions change slightly from year to year, the responses provide information that helps with decision making about educational issues.

Sample surveys can be classified further as longitudinal or cross sectional. *Longitudinal studies* involve at least two data collection points at specified intervals over a time span. Random samples of participants are selected so that results can be applied to a defined population. As an example, researchers who study personality development might gather data from a specific group of individuals on a yearly basis throughout the group's formative years.

In contrast to these studies are *cross-sectional studies,* in which data are collected only once from random samples who are *representative* of the population. To continue the example about personality development, a cross-sectional study requires data from representative 5-year-olds, 6-year-olds, and so on. The sample sizes should be large to include all variations of the variable of interest to the researchers.

Survey studies typically use questionnaires or interviews for data collection. Questionnaires may be administered in person, by computer, or by mail. Interviews are administered in person or by telephone. See Appendix B for additional information about these data collection strategies.

Surveys typically include large numbers of participants, especially when face-to-face data collection is *not* involved. Researchers who use these strategies (e.g., mail or telephone surveys) must make special efforts to obtain data from almost all the participants through follow-up collections because data from nonresponders may differ from data provided by the responders. After survey researchers exhaust the possibilities for data collection, they work out evidence to show that the data are unbiased. Researchers organize their data around the questions and pursue a cumulative analysis that describes the status of the topic or variable.

❊ Design Procedures for Causal Comparative Studies

Designs for **causal comparative studies** permit researchers to study naturally occurring, cause-and-effect relationships through comparisons of data from participant groups who exhibit the variables of interest. Sometimes referred to as *ex post facto* studies, these studies are retrospective analyses made possible by gathering and analyzing data on variables. These projects have explanation as their goal of research.

Although no variables are manipulated, the variables of interest are frequently called independent and dependent variables and are sometimes treated as if they have a cause-and-effect relationship. Causal comparative designs furnish approaches for study of variables that cannot be manipulated ethically. Examples of such variables include anger, depression, and aggression.

A causal comparative design is chosen, for example, when researchers want to study the possible influences of aggression on task performance. Researchers locate a population in which several levels of aggression are known to exist and then select a sample of participants. The researchers collect data from all participants on measures of aggression and task performance, perhaps in the same sitting.

Once they have collected their data, researchers decide how many levels of aggression they wish to study. For this illustration, suppose the researchers want two groups. They could place the participants' aggression scores in order from highest to lowest, then locate the middle score of the list. All those participants whose measures are above the middle score are designated as "more aggressive," and those below it, "less aggressive."

Next, the researchers compare task performance scores in each group to see if placement by aggression levels appears to influence task performance. Consider these three possibilities that could emerge from the study:

- Participants labeled as more aggressive have lower task performance scores than those labeled as less aggressive.
- Participants labeled as more aggressive have higher task performance scores than those labeled as less aggressive.
- No discernible pattern shows in the task performance scores of participants labeled as more aggressive or less aggressive.

Each statement suggests a possible relationship between the two variables, but none says that aggression is the cause of task performance. Researchers cannot establish cause-and-effect relationships using descriptive methods.

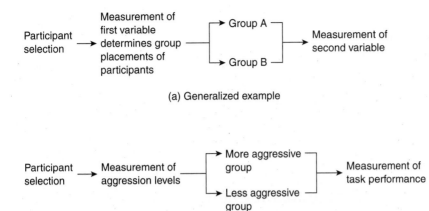

(a) Generalized example

(b) Example for aggression and task performance

FIGURE 7.1   Procedures in causal comparative designs.

Figure 7.1 displays a sequence for the application of the procedures in causal comparative designs. The generalized sequence is displayed in Figure 7.1a, and the example about aggression and task performance is shown in Figure 7.1b.

When none of the variables of interest can be manipulated, researchers may use a factorial causal comparative design. This design is appropriate, for example, if researchers want to know whether aggression interacts with age or gender to potentially influence task performance. Neither aggression nor age nor gender is subject to manipulation by researchers. However, researchers can place participants into age, gender, or age and gender groups according to their aggression scores. If there are two age groups and two levels of aggression, participants fit into one of four groups shown in Figure 7.2.

Use of this design allows the researchers to answer these questions:

1. Do aggression levels interact with age to influence task performance? (Compare groups A with B with C with D.)
2. Does aggression level influence task performance? (Compare groups A and C with groups B and D.)
3. Does age level influence task performance? (Compare groups A and B with groups C and D.)

Including the age factor strengthens the design by controlling a variable that might otherwise produce unwanted variance. Use of causal comparative factorial designs permit the simultaneous study of two (or more) variables as they influence a third variable.

AGE LEVELS

AGGRESSION LEVELS	A—Younger, more aggressive	C—Older, more aggressive
	B—Younger, less aggressive	D—Older, less aggressive

FIGURE 7.2   Groups for a causal comparative 2 by 2 factorial design.

✖ Design Procedures for Correlation and Prediction Studies

Correlation and prediction studies enable researchers to examine associations or relationships among variables and to potentially use these associations for prediction purposes. The designs appear simple because their procedures consist of participant selection and data collection and handling. Nevertheless, the details of these procedures require painstaking care to provide valid and reliable data for analysis.

Correlation Studies

Correlation designs are used to test hypotheses about the magnitude and direction of possible relationships between (among) variables. These studies provide explanations about associations among data taken on two or more variables.

The procedures are simple. Researchers sample a population for participants who embody the variables of interest. Next, they collect data on two or more variables from each participant. These data are subjected to mathematical procedures to evaluate the degree of their joint variations or relationship.

For example, Wentzel (1997) wanted to know the relation of perceptions of caring teachers to young adolescents' motivation to achieve academic and social outcomes (see A7). From each participant in the sample of middle school students, she obtained data on several variables that included scores on measures of perceived caring from teachers and academic effort. The scores on the measure of perceived caring from teachers represent variations in this variable just as the student responses to the questions about academic effort show variations.

One question to be answered by an analysis of these scores is, Do students who perceive their teacher as caring also put forth academic effort? A modified statement of this same question is, To what extent do the variations in the perceptions of teacher caring scores map onto the variations in academic effort? If this map of scores shows that variations in one variable correspond well to variations in the other variable, then the two variables are said to be associated.

To the degree that the sets of scores overlap as shown by the mapping, the variations in the first variable can be explained by the variations in the second variable. Of course, if the mapping shows little correspondence between the two sets of scores, then these variables are not associated. The variations in the first variable are independent of variations in the second and cannot be used to explain variations in the second variable. Either of these findings provides information about the *magnitude* of the relationship of the variables.

The *direction* of the relationship will be positive if the map shows that high scores on one variable correspond to high scores on the other variable. The relationship will be negative if high scores on one variable correspond to low scores on the other variable. Neither direction is necessarily better than the other.

Prediction Studies

Prediction designs are used to see if known relationships among variables can be used for prediction purposes. Researchers begin with variables known to be strongly correlated. One or more **predictor variables** in this set of variables is (are) used to make predictions about other variables in the same set, called **criterion variables.**

Prediction designs are also simple. Depending on the nature of the variables, data collection for the predictor variables may be separated from data collection on the criterion variables by a time interval. In other situations, data collections for predictor variables are simultaneous with those for criterion variables.

A further look at Wentzel's (1997) problem statement shows that she wanted to find if knowledge of students' perceptions of caring teachers could predict their efforts to achieve positive and academic outcomes at school (see A7). In this project, the researcher collected data about several variables and, for some variables, there were measures from two different years of schooling. Of most concern for this discussion are perceptions of caring as the predictor variable and social goals and academic effort as the criterion variables. All variables were measured with more than one instrument.

One question to be answered by an analysis of these scores is, Given that perceptions of teacher caring are correlated with academic effort, can these perceptions of teacher caring be used to predict academic effort? The analysis consists of using each predictor variable, on an individual basis, to see how well it predicts the criterion variable. Then various combinations of all the predictor variables are systematically tried to see how well they predict the criterion variable. As was true in correlation, application of the prediction processes provides information about the amount of variance that can be explained by the combinations of variables. Of course, increases in variance that can be explained increase the likelihood that the predictor variables actually predict the criterion variables.

E X E R C I S E   7 . 1

The ability to relate research problems or questions to designs for descriptive research is necessary for completion of Exercise 7.2. Try this exercise as a check on your ability.

Suggest a design appropriate for the investigation of each of these research questions. Explain your choice.

1. Will beginning kindergarten students who had previous nursery school experience be better developed socially than kindergarten students with no prior nursery school experience?

2. Are the abilities of middle school students to suggest alternative solutions to social problems influenced by their intellectual developmental levels?

3. What is the optimal age at which children are ready for formal schooling?

4. Does pre-algebra aptitude predict success in algebra I for eighth graders?

5. Is self-concept related to public-speaking abilities among high school sophomores?

⋈ Method Sections in Descriptive Research Reports

Participants and instrumentation subsections of method sections were described in Chapters 4 and 5, respectively. The following discussion describes the content in the remainder of the method sections. Specifically, this section describes data collection and handling procedures, provides criteria for evaluation of method sections, and applies these criteria to a descriptive research report.

Descriptions

In procedures subsections, researchers describe the circumstances in which participants provided data, whether in regularly scheduled classes or in settings especially arranged for this purpose. Usually researchers indicate the identity of the data collectors, whether they were teachers, assistants, researchers, or others. Such information is important because participants may provide information to known individuals differently than they do to strangers. Participants may also give information in a familiar setting differently than they do in unfamiliar locations.

Frequently researchers indicate the amount of time required for data collection and a schedule. Many descriptive projects have a single collection. However, requirements for extensive amounts of data may require more than one sitting. Longitudinal surveys and some prediction designs require data collected at different time intervals, which also necessitates more than one sitting.

On completion of data collection, researchers see that data are prepared for analyses. The preparation may include the scoring of inventories or tests, development of coding categories for open-ended questionnaires, or similar procedures with outcomes from other instruments. Investigators sometimes describe these data handling techniques, if they are used. Researchers may describe their data analyses plans, but usually this information is included in the results section.

Criteria for Evaluation

As readers of descriptive research reports, you should be aware of criteria for evaluation of method sections. The following criteria are based on information presented in this chapter, plus Chapters 4 and 5 on participant and instrument or strategy choices, respectively.

1. The goal of research and design used for the project should be clearly identifiable. The procedures should be suitable for providing data to answer the research questions.

   The problem statement should provide a strong indication of whether the research has explanation or prediction as its goal. A quick scan of the method section should indicate which design was used. Once the design has been identified, consider its fit with the researchers' questions. These elements must be matched if the design procedures are to provide valid and reliable data for answering these questions.

2. Data gathered through the use of these design procedures should be valid.

   Researchers should provide full information about data collection and handling, including the circumstances in which data are collected, the frequency of collection, the identity of the data collectors, and their expertise. The data handling procedures should describe briefly the end-of-collection activities about scoring procedures, checks for completion, and missing data procedures. The overall validity of the data from the design procedures should be evaluated. This includes the participant, instrument or strategy choices, data collection, and data handling procedures.

3. Data gathered through the use of the design procedures should be reliable.

   The data collection and handling procedures should be consistent with participant and instrument or strategy choices procedures. Each set of procedures should fit with the others.

   Researchers should describe all design procedures clearly. Independent researchers should be able to use the procedures with similar populations and achieve similar results.

Application of Criteria

These criteria are applied to the method sections of a descriptive research report. See Exercise 7.2 for the questions on which the critique is based. Refer to these questions and the research report as you read this section.

The Impact of Personal, Professional, and Organizational Characteristics on Administrator Burnout

The goal of research for this study (A6) is prediction and it uses a prediction design. Notice the information that begins the third paragraph about this study as an extension of earlier correlation studies. Gmelch and Gates (1998) wish to locate personal, professional, and organizational variables that predict administrator stress and burnout. This design is appropriate for answering this question.

The data were collected by mailed questionnaires to school administrators. The response rate was only 74% and the rate for usable questionnaires was 66%. In effect, this means that about one-third of the expected data were missing, an unusually high percentage, especially when there's no mention of any follow-up effort by the researchers to obtain additional data. No information is given about data handling procedures. The absence of information about follow-up data collection and handling procedures makes the validity of these data questionable.

All participants were practicing school administrators, which indicates that they are a good source of data about the project variables. The original number of 1,000 participants in the four categories is sufficient to provide data about the full range of variations in the project variables. However, the population these participants represent is unclear. This makes it impossible to say whether these data are representative of those that might be gathered from other groups of administrators.

This project used the Administrator Work Inventory (AWI), composed of questions from six existing instruments. There's no information about the validity or reliability of measurement of data from the AWI, even though the data appear to be the data needed to answer questions about administrator burnout. The data collected in this study cannot be deemed valid because of concerns about follow-up data collection procedures, missing data, and lack of clear validity of measurement information about the instruments used.

Information about data collection and handling procedures is scant; it's doubtful that independent researchers could use them. Use of a mailed questionnaire fits as a strategy for data collection from large numbers of participants, but lack of information about follow-up collections and validity-reliability of measurement raises questions about the reliability of these data.

E X E R C I S E   7 . 2

The method section of a report provides you with important information about procedures used in the project. This knowledge is useful in evaluating the validity and reliability of the collected data. Use this exercise to self-assess your understanding.

Study the problem and the method section for this report:

A5 Preservice and Inservice Secondary Teachers' Orientations toward Content Area Reading

Answer these questions:

1. Identify the goal of research and the design used for this project. Comment on the appropriateness of this design for providing data to answer the research question(s).

2. To estimate the validity of data provided by the design procedures, answer the following questions:
   a. Discuss the likelihood that data from the collection and handling procedures are valid. For example, consider the data collection procedures, including the circumstances in which data were collected, the frequency of collection, and the probable expertise of the collectors. Consider the data handling procedures.
   b. Consider the validity of the data provided by all design procedures. In addition to your answers to question 2a, include the contributions of procedures for participant and instrument or strategy choices (see Exercise 4.3, question 2a; and Exercise 5.4, question 2a). On an overall basis, can these data be considered valid? Explain.

3. To estimate the reliability of data provided by the design procedures, answer the following questions:

   a. How clearly described are the data collection and handling procedures? Could independent researchers use these procedures and expect to obtain similar results? Explain.
   b. Consider all the design procedures and the reliability of the data they provide. In addition to your answer to question 3a, include the contributions of procedures for participant and instrument or strategy choices (see Exercise 4.3, question 3a; and Exercise 5.4, question 3a). On an overall basis, can these data be considered reliable? Explain.

Summary

Descriptive research serves the goal of explanation through status, causal comparative, and correlation studies. Prediction studies enable researchers to seek the goal of prediction. Designs for these studies are deceptively simple because they include participant selection, instrument or strategy choices, data collection, and handling.

Status studies have the assessment of the standing or condition of variables as their major purpose. Meta-analyses use the findings of primary research reports, all on the same topic or variable as their data. Through reanalysis of the findings, meta-analysts provide status information about the topic or variable. Survey studies serve the same function but require researchers to collect and analyze data firsthand. Researchers who conduct survey research must be especially careful to explain missing data because these could jeopardize the validity and reliability of the data in the analysis.

Causal comparative studies allow researchers to explore naturally occurring, cause-and-effect relationships among variables. Researchers look at manifestations of events that have already occurred to explain observed differences in the variables between groups.

In correlation studies, researchers first look for associations among variables. If variables are highly correlated, then investigators may try to learn whether known variables can be used to predict unknown variables from the group of correlated variables.

Method sections of descriptive research reports contain information about all the design procedures. These procedures should convince you as a reader of the validity and reliability of data obtained by the use of these procedures. Criteria developed for evaluating descriptive research were applied to one research report.

Questions for Discussion

1. Explain how experimental researchers might use the results of descriptive research advantageously.
2. Describe some commonalities and differences between these pairs of designs:
   a. longitudinal and cross-sectional surveys
   b. correlation and causal comparative designs
3. As discussed in this chapter, causal comparative studies involve participant groups. On the other hand, surveys, correlation, and prediction studies make no mention of groups. Explain.

Descriptive Statistical Data Analyses and Results

❖ **Procedures for Group Data Analyses**

Distributions and Percentages

Measures of Central Tendency and Variation

Normal Distributions

Standard Scores

Effect Sizes

❖ **Procedures for Analyses of Associations Among Data**

Correlation Analyses

Regression Analysis

❖ **Results Sections of Research Reports**

Descriptions—Part 1

Criteria for Evaluation

Application of Criteria

Following data collection and handling, the researchers' next step is analysis of these data, the fourth systematic process. In quantitative projects, researchers typically collect large amounts of numerical data that must be reduced to a few understandable pieces of information known as *results* or *findings*. Data reduction takes place during the application of the analysis procedures. The **descriptive statistics** that emerge from analyses are then tied to the project variables to provide answers to the researchers' questions for the participants.

Descriptive analysis procedures serve two major purposes: (1) to analyze data that describe the status of variables or that compare groups; and (2) to analyze associations among data. Researchers choose between these purposes based on their research problem and goal of research. Sections of this chapter describe briefly the analysis procedures for each purpose.

The final chapter section describes the content of results sections as they pertain to descriptive statistics, criteria for the evaluation of results sections, and their application to a research report. Chapter 9 extends the discussion of results.

Goal

To enable you to:

- evaluate descriptive data analysis procedures in selected research reports for the production of valid and reliable results for project participants.

ꕤ Procedures for Group Data Analyses

As described in the design procedures in Chapters 6 and 7, data may be collected from one or more groups of participants. In these cases, data are first aggregated by group(s), then reduced to summaries, which can be used to describe status or make comparisons. The statistical procedures that accomplish these tasks must be appropriate for the data according to their levels of measurement (i.e., nominal, ordinal, interval, ratio). Measurement levels are described in Chapter 5.

Figure 8.1 provides an overview of descriptive statistics that researchers may calculate for their group data. They choose statistics appropriate for their research problem and the measurement level of their data. This figure can help guide your reading of this section.

With scores from a distribution, researchers calculate ⟶ Descriptive statistical summaries for groups, including:

Measures of central tendency	their corresponding measures of variation
• Mean (*M*) or ($\overline{X}$)	• Standard deviation (*sd*)
• Median (*Mdn*)	• Quartile deviation
• Mode	• Range

Using *M* and *sd*, researchers calculate ⟶ Standard scores

Using *M* and *sd* mainly, researchers calculate ⟶ Effect sizes

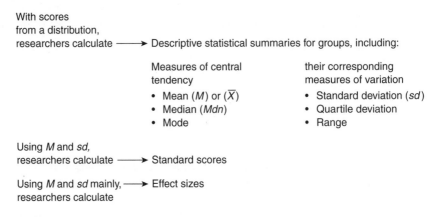

FIGURE 8.1 Overview of descriptive statistics for group data.

The descriptive statistics frequently associated with data analyses for the designs described in Chapters 6 and 7 are displayed in Table 8.1. When these statistics are connected appropriately with project variables, they furnish answers to the research questions *for the participants.*

Distributions and Percentages

Suppose that researchers who study the effects of different lengths of instructional sessions in foreign language laboratories collect data on vocabulary development from high school students. Figure 8.2a shows a **distribution** of students' scores from one level of treatment, according to the number of points earned by each of 28 people. This distribution, hereafter called Distribution A, shows that two people scored 100 points, three scored 98 points, and so on.

The researchers could convert the number of score points to a percentage or a proportion of the whole. In Distribution A, for example, three of 28 students earned the grade 89. These three students represent 10.7% of the total class. Of course, percentages can be figured for each of the other scores

---

TABLE 8.1

Descriptive Statistics Commonly Associated with Methods and Designs

Method	Design	Descriptive Statistics
Descriptive	Survey studies	Percentages, measures of central tendency and variation
Descriptive	Meta-analyses	Effect sizes
Descriptive	Causal comparative studies	Measures of central tendency and variation, percentages, standard scores
Experimental	True-, quasi-, and pre-experiments	Measures of central tendency and variation, standard scores, effect sizes

---

as well. Percentages provide rough indicators of the performance levels within the group.

Although data shown in Distribution A are of interval level, nominal or ordinal data can also be expressed as percentages. For example, Konopak, Readence, and Wilson (1994) gathered nominal level data from preservice and inservice teachers about their orientations to reading. The percentages of teachers in the two groups who held each of the three orientations shown here are taken from Table 1 of the Results section of A5.

	Text-based	Reader-based	Inter-active
Preservice	2	28	70
Inservice	0	57	43

Comparisons of the percentages answer the question about differences between teacher groups on how reading takes place. These percentages also show that preservice teachers heavily favored the interactive orientation over the two alternate orientations and that inservice teachers were divided between a reader-based and an interactive orientation. These statements answer the researchers' questions.

Another way of thinking about frequency distributions is to convert them to bar graphs, called *histograms,* or line graphs, called *frequency polygons.* These graphs transform numerical information into pictorial displays. In both cases, the scores or measures are located along the horizontal axis and the frequency of scores or measurements is indicated on the vertical axis. Figure 8.2b communicates the same information as the tally marks in Figure 8.2a. Discussion of frequency polygons continues in the Normal Distributions section.

Measures of Central Tendency and Variation

In projects in which researchers compare group performances, they usually reduce the data gathered from each group to two summaries. One summary

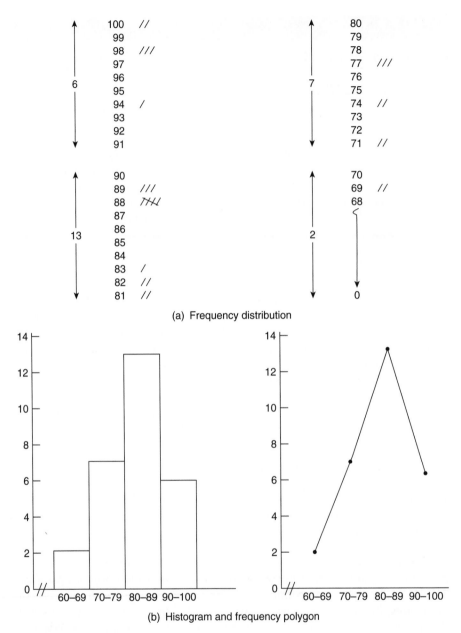

(a) Frequency distribution

(b) Histogram and frequency polygon

FIGURE 8.2   Distribution A—foreign language vocabulary development scores.

is typically a measure of central tendency and the other, a measure of variation.

Central Tendency

Look again at the tallies for Distribution A in Figure 8.2. Thirteen of the 28 total scores fall between 81 and 90, suggesting that a *single* number representative or typical of all 28 data points lies within this interval. In fact, three different measures within this interval show the bunching of scores, or their **central tendency.** These measures, called *modes, medians,* and *means,* serve as locations for the distribution. That is, these measures locate this particular distribution with respect to possible distributions that could be constructed with 28 data points on a measurement scale of 0 to 100.

Five students scored 88 points, making this score the one that occurred most frequently, an example of the modal score, or **mode.** Had five students scored any other number of points, a second mode would exist, and Distribution A would be a bimodal distribution.

A second way of locating a typical score is to use the middle score of the distribution. Called the **median** and abbreviated as *Mdn,* this score is the midpoint of the distribution. In Distribution A, the median is a score of 83.5.[1] Calculating the median is complicated if no score falls precisely in the middle of the distribution, or if more than one score exists at the middle point. Introductory statistics texts provide information about calculating medians.

A third way of finding a measure of central tendency is to total the number of score points and divide the sum by the number of students to obtain an average. The total number of score points for this class is 2363; dividing this total by 28 gives an average score of 84.4. In statistical language, this is an arithmetic mean, usually called a *mean score.* A **mean,** symbolized by *X* or *M,* is the measure of central tendency obtained by summing a set of scores and dividing that sum by the number of scores.

Which of these methods is best for obtaining a measure of central tendency? The answer depends on the situation. A mode provides a rough idea of that measure, but the mean provides a precise measure, with medians intermediate between means and modes. Because modes are obtained by counting, they are the least stable of the measures. In Distribution A, for example, two additional scores in some instances would result in three additional modes (i.e., 98, 89, and 77).

A median is more stable than a mode because ranking the scores is required to find the middle score. Medians are useful because extremely high or extremely low scores do not influence them. For example, suppose that Distribution B is exactly the same as Distribution A, with one exception. In Distribution B, one score of 69 is now 5. Although the medians remain equal, the means are not equal because they take into account every score, including extreme scores. Compare the measures of central tendency for the two distributions:

---

[1]In this case, the median is the upper real limit of the class interval in which the frequency is *N*/2 or 14.

	Mean	Median
Distribution A	84.4	83.5
Distribution B	82.1	83.5

If researchers have interval data, they almost invariably calculate means as the preferred measure of central tendency because of its precision. (Modes and medians can also be used with interval data, but they are not as precise as means.) With data at ordinal level, the appropriate measure of central tendency is the median because ranks are used in its determination. If data are nominal, only modes can be described.

Variation

Each measure of central tendency has a corresponding measure of **variation,** which provides an index of the amount of dispersion among the scores. The smaller the number, the closer the scores tend to cluster around the measure of central tendency. In general, data from participants who are homogeneous with respect to the measured variable tend to have smaller measures of variation than data from participants who are heterogeneous with respect to that variable.

The least precise measure of variation is the **range,** or difference between the top and bottom scores. For Distribution A, the range is 100 minus 69, or 31 points. The range, used with a mode, communicates overall information. For example, the modal age of participants is 7.3 years; the range is 5.1 to 12.3 years.

The quartile deviation, a measure of variation used with medians, is rarely included in research reports. Based on the division of the distribution into four equal-sized groups, the three points that separate the distribution into four groups are called *quartiles.*

Standard deviations, the most commonly used measures of variation and abbreviated as *sd*, describe dispersion of scores with respect to means. Standard deviations are calculated using formulas that take into account differences between individual scores and the mean. Each difference is squared, and the squared differences are added together and divided by the number of scores, resulting in an important statistic known as the *variance.* A standard deviation is the square root of a variance. When standard deviations are small, scores cluster around means. However, when standard deviations are large, scores are scattered farther from means.

In Distribution A in Figure 8.2, the sum of the squared differences from the mean is 2478.9. Dividing this sum by 28 (the number of scores) gives 88.5 for the variance. The square root of 88.5 is 9.4, the standard deviation for the distribution. Therefore, scores in this distribution are clustered fairly closely around the mean.

Again, consider Distribution B, in which the lowest score is 5 points. Here the mean is 82.1, which is not greatly different from the mean of Distribution A at 84.4. However, the sum of the squared differences from the mean is now 8465.5 and the variance is 302.3. The square root of this variance provides a standard deviation of 17.4.

	Mean	**Standard Deviation**
Distribution A	84.4	9.4
Distribution B	82.2	17.4

The standard deviation of Distribution B is almost twice the size of the standard deviation of Distribution A. This indicates that scores in Distribution B are less closely clustered around the mean than they are in Distribution A. The low score of 5 in Distribution B is the primary reason for the large standard deviation.

Standard deviations permit comparisons of the distances of various scores from the mean. The score of 94 in Distribution A is about one standard deviation above the mean of 84.4 (94 minus 84.4 = 9.6). A score of 71 is about one-and-a-half standard deviations below the mean (84.4 minus 71 = 13.4).

To illustrate how means and standard deviations are used to provide answers to researchers' questions, consider the following information from Gettinger's (1993) report on error correction and spelling performance. See A1, Results section, Table 1. The descriptive statistics include the following:

	Class A	**Class B**	**Class C**
Baseline	10.3	10.8	9.9
(3.6)	(4.3)	(3.9)	
Intervention	10.7	10.6	13.9
(3.3)	(3.8)	(4.2)	

Numbers without parentheses are mean numbers of words spelled correctly by each of three groups of students. Numbers inside parentheses are their corresponding standard deviations. Note that standard deviations in all six cases are comparable, which suggests that these data are fairly homogeneous. However, comparisons of means at baseline with their respective means at intervention by classes show that Classes A and C improved, but that Class B did not.

Also, comparison of the intervention means shows that Class C has a higher mean than either Class A or Class B. These comparisons are related to the project variables in the Results section and provide answers to the researcher's question for the participants. This discussion continues in the Applications of Criteria section.

Normal Distributions

A **normal distribution,** graphed as a frequency polygon, forms a bell-shaped curve. It results whenever most of the scores fall close to the mean and there are relatively few high or low scores at the extremes. The curve is symmetrical; folding it superimposes one half onto the other. See Figure 8.3a for two diagrams of normal distributions.

In a normal distribution, the mean, median, and mode all have the same value. The extreme ends of the curve approach zero frequency, but they do not meet the baseline. In graphs A and B in Figure 8.3a the curves are symmetrical, even though the two examples are not identical. In example B,

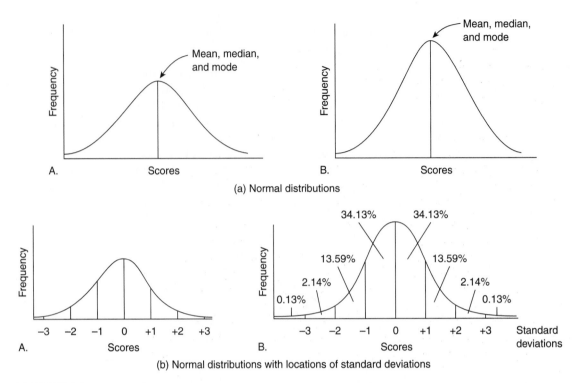

FIGURE 8.3   Normal distributions.

scores are clustered more closely around the mean than they are in example A. This explains why the height of the curve in B is taller than it is in A.

Many physical and educational variables are considered to be normally distributed, depending on the number of cases. For example, a graph of the working vocabulary sizes of all 15-year-olds in a town or a large high school would probably form a normal curve. In the same way, other characteristics such as height, achievement, and creativity are thought to be normally distributed throughout large populations.

Figure 8.3b shows the graphs of curves A and B, again marked with the locations of one, two, and three standard deviations from the mean. Note that the distance along the horizontal axis of the graph is the same for each standard deviation unit. Example B also shows the percentage of scores that fall under the portions of the curve separated by the standard deviations. In any normal distribution, about 68% of the scores fall within one standard deviation of the mean. The 34% below the mean are added to the 34% above the mean.

Standard Scores

Raw scores from participants are sometimes translated into standard scores to provide comparisons. A **standard score** expresses the distance of a raw score from the mean of the distribution in standard deviation units. For example, if the mean of a normally distributed set of measures is 60 and the standard deviation is 10, a score of 95 is three-and-a-half standard deviation units above the mean and is expressed as +3.5 or $(95 - 60)/10$.

A score of 40 is two standard deviation units below the mean of 60 and is expressed as –2. A minus sign means the score is below the mean, and a plus sign, above the mean. Subtracting –2 from 3.5 shows a difference of five-and-one-half standard deviations. Therefore, the difference between 95 and 40 is quite large.

Using positive or negative numbers as standard scores is sometimes inconvenient. In these cases, a designated number such as 100 or 500 may represent the mean, and the standard deviation is also assigned a fixed-point value. As an example, *Graduate Record Examination* (GRE) scores for Verbal, Mathematics, and Aptitude performances have an assigned mean of 500 each and a standard deviation of 100. Because these are standard scores, researchers can compare performances for individuals or groups on GRE scores across the three dimensions.

Effect Sizes

Often used in meta-analyses, an **effect size** provides a common measure of differences between two groups across a variety of research settings. The calculation of effect sizes typically makes use of means and standard deviations and is a measure of difference in terms of standard deviation units. For example, an estimated effect size for experiments is calculated by subtracting the mean of the control group from the mean of the treated group and dividing by the standard deviation of the control group.

In Gettinger's (1993) study, the error correction group achieved a mean score of 13.9 words spelled correctly and the standard (control) group achieved a mean score of only 10.7 words and had a standard deviation of 3.3. Therefore, the estimated effect size is 0.97. This positive effect size indicates that the error correction group outperformed the standard group by 0.97 of a standard deviation.

Although there are no defined rules about their magnitude, an effect size close to 1.0 is considered important. In this case, an effect size of 0.97 shows that error correction is a powerful treatment.

When the reduced number treatment group ($M = 10.6$) is compared to the standard group ($M = 10.7$), the effect size is –0.03 and is negligible. This small effect size confirms that the reduced number group actually serves as a second control group.

EXERCISE   8.1

A sound understanding of the meanings for measures of central tendency and variation, normal distributions, and standard scores can help you to interpret statistical analyses found in research reports. This ability is necessary for evaluation of data from selective descriptive data analysis procedures.

Answer the following questions:

1. Situation: Mr. B teaches reading to upper grade elementary students using a literature-based approach. Ms. X teaches reading in the same grade, but uses a basal reader approach. Each teacher administers an exam to measure reading comprehension. In Mr. B's class, the mean score is 88 and the standard deviation is 4. In Ms. X's class, the mean score is 76 and the standard deviation is 6. Assume that the reading comprehension scores reflect a normal distribution in each classroom.
   a. In which class, Mr. B's or Ms. X's, are scores more homogeneous? Explain.
   b. About what percent of the students in Mr. B's class scored between 84 and 92 points? Explain.
   c. About what percent of the students in Ms. X's class scored between 64 and 70 points? Explain.
   d. Both Juanita, a student in Mr. B's class, and Bill, a student in Ms. X's class, earn scores of 86 points. Do these scores reflect comparable performances for Juanita and Bill? Why or why not?

2. Suppose that raw scores are translated to standard scores in a distribution for which the mean is 50 and the standard deviation is 8. Explain how far apart in standard deviation units these standard scores are:
   a. 42 and 58
   b. 52 and 75

❈ Procedures for Analyses of Associations among Data

In some projects, researchers collect two or more items of data from each participant. Designs for correlation studies require analyses that provide the degree and magnitude of possible associations among these data. Designs for prediction studies take advantage of known associations between (among) variables to determine if one variable can predict the other. These analyses result in coefficients of correlation and regression, respectively.

Correlation Analyses

Educational research questions are often concerned with relationships among behaviors, performances, or capabilities demonstrated by students, teachers, counselors, administrators, and other school personnel. For example, researchers may seek an understanding of the relationships between students' flexibility-of-thinking and problem-solving abilities, teachers' work patterns and their principal's leadership style, or test scores and scores on the same test given 3 weeks later. Each research question lends itself to data analysis using correlation techniques.

Suppose a researcher measured middle school students' flexibility-of-thinking and also measured their problem-solving capabilities on hypothetical instruments in which scores range from 40 to 100. Here is a partial set of results:

Student	Flexibility-of-Thinking Scores	Problem-Solving Scores
Chang	65	86
Jill	58	78
Clarice	55	70
Sam	52	60

Chang and Jill, who have good flexibility-of-thinking scores, also have high problem-solving scores. Clarice's flexibility-of-thinking score is lower than Chang's or Jill's. Sam, whose flexibility-of-thinking score is low, also has the poorest problem-solving performance. In fact, these data show a one-to-one correspondence between flexibility-of-thinking scores and problem-solving scores. Another way of stating this idea is to note that the order of the flexibility-of-thinking scores exactly matches the order of problem-solving scores from high to low.

Spotting relationships among data is not usually this easy. However, one way to approximate the relationship between variables is to make a scatterplot. In Figure 8.4a, notice that flexibility-of-thinking scores are plotted on the horizontal axis and problem-solving scores on the vertical axis. A plot (or dot) shows Chang's position at the intersection of 65 on the horizontal axis (flexibility-of-thinking scores) and 86 on the vertical axis (problem-solving scores). Other plots show positions for Jill, Clarice, and Sam.

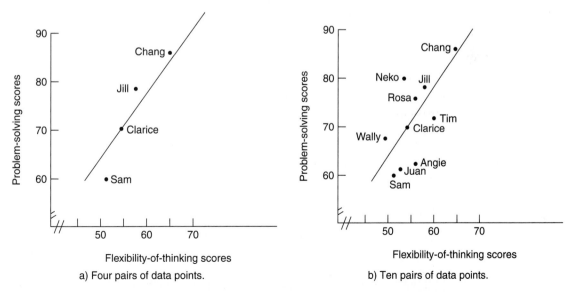

a) Four pairs of data points.   b) Ten pairs of data points.

FIGURE 8.4   Correlation between flexibility of thinking scores and problem-solving scores.

Including data for other students complicates the scatterplot, but shows how the variables of flexibility-of-thinking and problem-solving abilities are related among this group of students (see Figure 8.4b). Some students with poorer flexibility-of-thinking scores showed better problem-solving abilities than classmates with better flexibility-of-thinking ability. For examples, see the scores for Wally and Neko. In other cases, some students with good flexibility-of-thinking scores showed poorer problem solving-abilities than others with better flexibility-of-thinking scores. See, for example, the scores for Angie and Tim. Despite these exceptions, problem-solving scores tend to increase as flexibility-of-thinking scores increase.

A best-fitting straight line drawn through the points shows that plots tend to cluster around the line. Based on these data, flexibility-of-thinking shows a linear relationship with problem-solving performance. This is an example of a positive relationship between two variables, because as one variable increases, the other variable also increases.

However, not all relationships are positive, nor are they all linear. Suppose researchers investigated the relationship between lengths of time allowed for typing a set of words and typing accuracy. The results might be similar to those shown in Figure 8.5.

Frequency of typing mistakes is plotted on the vertical axis and the number of minutes allowed for typing is plotted horizontally. These plots suggest that as the amount of time increases, the number of mistakes decreases. The major difference between this diagram and the diagram in Figure 8.4b is the direction of the plots. Figure 8.5 shows a negative, or inverse, correlation between mistakes in typing and time.

Although diagrams such as these are helpful, this information is usually communicated with numbers. Researchers use computer statistical programs

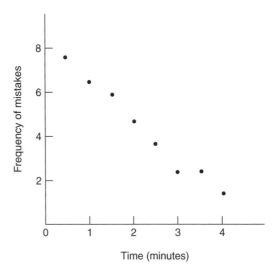

FIGURE 8.5   Typical correlation between mistakes and time.

to calculate the amount and type of correlation. The results of these calculations are decimal numbers called *correlation coefficients* that range from +1.00 to –1.00.

Correlation coefficients are index numbers that provide information about strength (the closer to 1, the greater the strength) and direction (positive or negative) of the relationship between variables. (This concept was introduced in Chapter 5 in the discussion of criterion-related measurement validity.)

The decimal number in a correlation coefficient is neither a regular number nor a percentage. A correlation coefficient of .54 should not be interpreted as twice as much as a coefficient of .27. Nor does a correlation coefficient of .54 mean 54 percent. What a coefficient *does* tell is the amount of variation shared by the two variables used in its calculation.

A popular correlation coefficient is the Pearson product moment coefficient, symbolized by r. Suppose that creativity and reading comprehension scores are subjected to a correlation procedure that results in $r = .54$. Squaring this r-value (.54 × .54) produces $r^2 = .29$. This squared correlation coefficient means that about 29 % of the variations in creativity can be associated with variations in reading comprehension. Given this percentage of covariation, or variance common to these variables, means that 71 % of the variation in reading comprehension and creativity is not accounted for by their association.

Wentzel's (1997) report provides examples of correlation coefficients (see A7, Results section). This study sought information about adolescents' perceptions of caring teachers in relation to a number of variables. In Table 1, numbers along both axes identify the variables. The fourth line shows this information:

T2 Perceived teacher caring .39***	.45***	.36***

The numbers are coefficients that show magnitude and direction of the correlation between perceived teacher caring and prosocial goal pursuit, responsibility goal pursuit, and academic effort, respectively. These coefficients are interpreted by squaring them to estimate the covariations explained by these relationships. (Meanings for asterisks are explained in Chapter 9.)

To this point, discussion of correlation has focused on use of the Pearson r correlation coefficient. To use this procedure requires that both data items be of interval measure. If the data are of ordinal measure, Spearman rank (rho) and Kendall rank (τ) correlation procedures should be used. If the data are of nominal measure, tetrachoric (r^t), contingency (C), and phi (ϕ) correlation procedures should be used. If one datum is interval and the other nominal, biserial (r_{bis}) or point-biserial (r_{pbis}) correlation procedures should be applied. These coefficients are interpreted in the same way as rs.

Regression Analysis

A chief use of correlation is in prediction studies, which rely on regression analyses. Once researchers establish that at least a moderate amount of covariation exists between variables, they may predict values of one variable for members of that population when values of the related variable are known.

The *r* in the correlation coefficient stands for *regression* (Kerlinger, 1986), a phenomenon that occurs among correlated variables. To illustrate, suppose a large group of students takes a test and later takes an equivalent form of the test. Students are expected generally to have comparable scores. However, students who score extremely high on the first test typically tend to score not quite so high on the second test, while those who score extremely low on the first test tend to score not quite so low on the second exam. Scores on the two forms of the test are correlated, but the second set of scores is closer to the average score of the group than is the first set. This phenomenon is an example of regression toward the mean.

Now apply this idea to the example on flexibility-of-thinking and problem solving. If additional measures of these variables are taken from students in this class, Chang is likely to demonstrate good scores on both measures and Sam is likely to continue to rank near the bottom of the class on the measures. On the other hand, Chang could move down in rankings among students and Sam could move up in the rankings, depending on the day and the circumstances in which the measures are taken. However, their overall rankings are likely to stay about the same. This can also be said for other students at the extremes.

Look again at Figure 8.4b and notice the line that represents the best fit for the data points. Suppose there are additional students in this class whose data were not shown in this scatterplot. Using this line, called the *regression line,* as a very rough guide permits the estimation of problem-solving scores if flexibility-of-thinking scores are known, or vice versa. For example, if Nell's flexibility-of-thinking score is 63, her problem-solving score is estimated to be between 84 and 87, as read from Figure 8.4b.

It is also possible to reverse the process and estimate flexibility-of-thinking based on a known problem-solving score. For example, if Jed's problem solving score is 68, his flexibility-of-thinking score is about 55. These predictions, a simple form of **regression analysis,** are for students in this same class. (In making these estimates, the known variable is called the *predictor* variable; the unknown variable is named the *criterion.*) Because the same observed relationship might not hold in other classrooms, estimates for students outside this group are not warranted.

Notice the emphasis on estimation because that's all that is available. No one can know how well students will solve problems until they are asked to do so. The estimate is rough and cannot predict exactly the degree of problem-solving ability or flexibility-of-thinking. This example of regression, or prediction, is deliberately simple to communicate the idea. Regression analyses are carried out with computer programs just as most correlation measures are calculated using computer programs.

Prediction studies typically use many more participants than are mentioned in the illustration. Some samples contain hundreds of people who represent still larger populations. Regardless of size, however, variables found to be correlated within a sample are probably correlated in the population if the sample is representative of the population.

Typically studies use several predictor and criterion variables. Regression analysis in these studies is called **multiple regression,** or **stepwise regression,** and the outcomes are R-values, whose meanings are interpreted the same way as those for r-values. Researchers usually use computer programs to make these analyses.

To conduct a regression analysis, the predictor variable that is most highly correlated with the criterion variable is entered first, followed by the predictor that is next most highly correlated, and so on. The analysis tries to find the best sequence for entering the predictor variables into the analysis. "Best" is determined by the amount of variance that each predictor variable explains. Of course, the larger the amount of variance that can be explained, the better the prediction.

E X E R C I S E   8 . 2

A sound understanding of correlation and regression analyses can help you to interpret statistical analyses within research reports. This ability is necessary for the evaluation of data from selected descriptive data analysis procedures.

Answer the following questions:

1. Use Figure 8.4b. Suppose that Maria is also a member of this group of students. Estimate her problem-solving score, if her flexibility-of-thinking score is 52. Explain.

2. Identify the level of measurement (e.g., nominal) suggested by the measures named in the following situations. Then identify an appropriate correlation coefficient for measuring the association between the variables.
   a. A high school psychologist gathers and studies data concerning grade point average and gender for members of the freshmen class.
   b. For a study in elementary school, an educational researcher obtains measures of attitude toward school and measures of attitude toward mathematics from each of 100 students. Both sets of attitudes are measured on Likert scales.

✕ Results Sections of Research Reports

In some reports, researchers describe data analysis plans in the method or procedures section. Particularly in journal reports, researchers may say little about their plans, but they report results of data analyses in a section called results or findings. Researchers occasionally combine data analyses results with a discussion of them in a report section titled results and discussion.

This is the first of two descriptions of results sections; the second is in Chapter 9. Here, the description is limited to descriptive statistical procedures and results for participants, the topic of Chapter 8. Also included are criteria for evaluating results and an application of the criteria to a research report.

Descriptions—Part 1

Results sections usually contain two types of information: (1) tables or figures that describe the results or findings of data analyses in graphic form; and (2) verbal descriptions that highlight the major results. You should read all titles and legends associated with graphic portrayals of results. Also, note whether graphic and verbal forms of results agree.

Be aware that results sections usually contain information about inferential statistics, which are discussed in Chapter 9. For now, skip references to "p," "F," or other symbols *not* discussed in this chapter. Concentrate on the measures of correlation, regression, central tendency, and variation.

Correlation and regression coefficients (rs and Rs) are common in studies in which researchers seek information about strength and direction of associations among variables. Measures of central tendency (X or M, Mdn, mode) and variation (sd and range) are found frequently in reports in which data gathered from groups of participants are compared (see Table 8.1).

The report should connect the statistical results with the variables of the study as answers to the researchers' questions. As a reader, make your own estimate about the degrees of association or regression by examining both the magnitude and direction of the coefficients. Estimate the magnitude of differences between (among) the groups by comparing their frequencies, proportions, or measures of central tendency and relate these differences to the variables. These estimates provide answers to the researchers' questions for the project participants.

Criteria for Evaluation

As readers of descriptive and experimental research reports, you should be aware of criteria for the evaluation of results sections. These criteria are based on information presented here and in previous chapters.

1. The data subjected to descriptive statistical data analysis procedures must be valid and reliable.

Data obtained from other procedures, including participant selection, choices of instruments or strategies, collection strategies, and handling procedures must be valid and reliable as a condition for analysis. Only if these conditions are met can researchers expect to obtain valid and reliable results.

2. The descriptive statistical data analysis procedures used should be appropriate for the problem and design to produce valid results for the project participants.

Look to see if the data analyses conform to expectations. That is, for any correlation or regression design, look for correlation, regression, or both types of coefficients. For experiments, causal comparative studies, and survey studies, look for one or more of these: percentages, measures of central tendency, variation, and standard scores. These descriptive statistics should be connected with appropriate variables to provide answers to the research questions for the participants.

3. The descriptive statistical data analysis procedures should fit with other design procedures to produce reliable results for project participants.

Data analysis procedures should be consistent with other procedures. For example, data analyses should account for all participants and statistical procedures should be appropriate for the level of measurement. Researchers should strive to describe their data analysis procedures so clearly that independent researchers could use them with similar populations and expect similar results.

Application of Criteria

To illustrate these points, this section provides an evaluation of the descriptive statistical analyses in Effects of Error Correction on Third Graders' Spelling (Gettinger, 1993). This review discusses the extent to which this report meets the criteria for results sections. Take time to read Exercise 8.3 to see the questions to which this review provides answers. Refer to these questions and the research project (A1) as you read this section.

Effects of Error Correction on Third Graders' Spelling

The goal of research is control and the design is a quasi-experiment. This goal and design require analyses of group data to answer the researcher's question.

As indicated in previous chapters, the data used in the analysis procedures can be considered generally valid and reliable. Table 1 presents means and standard deviations for three measures: spelling accuracy on weekly tests, spelling accuracy on dictated stories, and teacher ratings for each of the three classes (groups) of students. These data summaries of the dependent variable allow for comparisons among three groups.

The results of descriptive statistical analyses answer the research question for the participants well. Recall Gettinger's hypothesis that students who receive error-correction intervention would have higher spelling accuracy than students having no modification beyond standard spelling practice or students whose practice was changed to smaller daily chunks.

At the end of the intervention phase, mean scores of students in the error-correction class (experimental condition) are higher than those of students in either of the other conditions on three measures: weekly tests, dictated stories, and teacher ratings. In other words, a mean score of 13.9 (experimental group) is greater than 10.7 (standard group) or 10.6 (reduced number group). The standard deviations in these groups are comparable—4.2, 3.8, and 3.3, but the experimental group shows greater variation from the mean than do the remaining groups. Students in the experimental group consistently outperformed students in the two comparison groups on each of three measures of spelling accuracy.

Table 2 provides examples of means and ranges for the measures of trials-to-criterion taken from the experimental class. In the context of this report, students in the experimental class required fewer trials to reach 100%

spelling accuracy, but these data are not directly related to the test of the study's hypothesis.

Overall, the descriptive statistical procedures are well described. An independent researcher could probably use these procedures with a similar population and achieve similar results.

EXERCISE 8.3

This exercise allows you to see how well you can evaluate descriptive data analysis procedures for the production of valid and reliable results for participants.

Study the problem, method, and results sections for these research reports:

A4 A Computerized Method to Teach Latin and Greek Root Words: Effect on Verbal SAT Scores

A5 Preservice and Inservice Secondary Teachers' Orientations toward Content Area Reading

Then answer these questions for each report:

1. Identify the goal of research and the design used for this project. Does this goal and design require an analysis of group data or an analysis of associations among data?

2. Can the data used in the analysis procedures be considered valid (see Exercise 6.2, question 2c or Exercise 7.2, question 2b)? Explain.

   Can the data be considered reliable (see Exercise 6.2, question 3b or Exercise 7.2, question 3b)? Explain.

3. To estimate the validity of the results, answer these questions:
   • Identify the descriptive statistics (e.g., means, correlation coefficients) named in the results section.
   • Are these the descriptive statistics required by the project goal and design?
   • Are these statistics connected with the appropriate variables to answer the research questions for the participants? Explain.

4. To estimate the reliability of the results, answer this question:
   • Overall, are the descriptive data analysis procedures described clearly enough that independent researchers could use them and expect similar results in similar research situations? Explain.

Summary

Researchers organize and examine participant data to provide answers to their research questions for those who took part in the study. The choices of data analysis procedures depend on their goal of research and design. For example, they may summarize their data by calculating percentages, measures of central tendency and variation, standard scores, or effect sizes.

In other instances, researchers subject their data to correlation procedures that provide indexes of the strength and direction of the association between the variables. Correlated variables—those that share much covariation—can be used for predictions within the population in which the correlation exists.

Descriptions of results sections, criteria for their evaluation, and an application of the criteria to one report are described in the final section. In particular, the criteria check on the validity and reliability of the results of descriptive statistical data analysis.

Questions for Discussion

1. Researchers usually do not portray distributions as histograms or frequency polygons. Describe pro and con arguments for this practice.
2. Explain why means and standard deviations are almost always presented in close proximity, whether in tables or in word form in research reports.
3. Given the discussion of the procedures for descriptive statistics, name advantages to researchers of using interval level data, rather than ordinal or nominal level data.
4. Explain why a correlation coefficient among variables must be moderately large in order to proceed with a prediction study.

C H A P T E R   **9**

Inferential Statistical Data Analyses and Results

❖ **Procedures for Inferential Statistical Analyses**

❖ **Hypothesis Testing Strategies**

   Statement of Hypotheses

   Selection of Inferential Tests

   Selection of Significance Levels

   Application of Tests

Evaluation of Test Outcomes

❖ **Results Sections of Research Reports**

   Descriptions—Part 2

   Criteria for Evaluation

   Application of Criteria

Inferential statistical data analyses provide researchers with the capability of answering the question, "What is the mathematical probability that a particular research outcome will occur by chance within a specified population?" To answer this question, researchers examine the results obtained from participants to see if these can be inferred to be true of the population from which participants were drawn.

However, in order to answer the question, the participants must *be* a random sample representative of a defined population. From Chapter 4 recall that random samples are those that allow for the possibility that every member of the population could be included in the sample.

To increase your understanding of data analysis procedures, a section of this chapter

on hypothesis testing strategies describes conceptually the major activities involved in making statistical inferences. Actual calculations are beyond the scope of this text.

The final chapter section continues the description of results sections that began in Chapter 8 as they pertain to inferential statistics. Criteria for evaluation of results sections and their application to a research report complete this chapter.

Goal

To enable you to:

- evaluate the inferential statistical data analysis procedures in selected research reports for the production of valid and reliable results for a population.

⚹ Procedures for Inferential Statistical Analyses

Researchers answer their questions for the participants of a study with the descriptive statistics described in Chapter 8. However, investigators usually want to know whether their results are meaningful in a broader frame of reference. Findings based on participant data generalize, or apply, to other settings only under particular circumstances.

Inferential statistics help researchers make decisions about whether results obtained from a sample can be generalized to the population from which the sample was drawn. In pursuing an inferential statistical analysis, researchers seek an answer to this question: Is the association among variables (or the difference between groups) observed in the sample real, or did it occur because of chance variations or fluctuations in the population? The association among variables (or difference between groups) mentioned in this question uses descriptive statistics obtained from participants.

Inferential statistics use logic based on mathematical probability, *which operates indirectly*. In brief, researchers state a no association (or no difference) hypothesis as an answer to the question about the reality of the association or difference. This hypothesis embodies the idea that whatever association among variables (or difference between groups) is observed in the sample is due to chance. Moreover, most researchers state their hypothesis this way with the express purpose of attempting to reject it. Of course, if they can reject this hypothesis, then an alternative hypothesis must explain the situation. Figure 9.1 provides an overview of the processes involved in inferential statistical analyses.

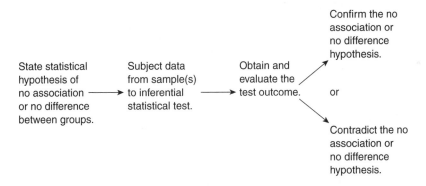

FIGURE 9.1   Overview of inferential statistical analyses.

⚹ Hypothesis Testing Strategies

Five processes are involved in hypothesis testing. Described here in order, the first three processes can occur almost simultaneously, and all must be completed prior to application of the inferential test mentioned in the fourth process.

1. State the null hypothesis and its alternative in terms of population parameters.
2. Select an appropriate inferential test and specify the sample size.
3. Identify the level of significance.
4. Use data from the sample (descriptive statistics) in the mathematical formula for the inferential test.
5. Evaluate the test outcome (Hays, 1994; Hinkle, Wiersma, & Jurs, 1994).

Statement of Hypotheses

Researchers typically cast their speculations about answers to their research questions as research hypotheses. Here are two examples:

1. Among high school sophomores, self-concept is related to public-speaking abilities.
2. Upper elementary grade students who receive literature-based reading instruction perform differently on measures of reading comprehension than their peers who receive basal reader instruction.

Research hypotheses, such as these, are not testable with statistical procedures; they must first be converted into statistical hypotheses.

Statistical hypotheses include the null hypothesis and its alternative. A **null hypothesis,** also known as the *no association/no difference hypothesis,* implies that any observed association between variables or difference between groups is due to random or chance variations in the population. This hypothesis is rejected only if findings are so unusual that they would be *un*likely to occur as the result of random variations in the population. Of course, researchers typically prefer to reject the null hypothesis.

Nonetheless, a null hypothesis is the most accurate statement about the variables, if an anticipated *research* hypothesis is *not* true. That is, there *is* no association between the variables (or difference between the groups) within the population under study if the null hypothesis is true.

An **alternative hypothesis** is a statistical hypothesis derived from the research hypothesis that states the situation *opposite* the null hypothesis. The alternative hypothesis provides the viable test outcome whenever the null hypothesis can be rejected. Therefore, the null and alternative hypotheses together must account for all the possibilities of associations among the variables or differences between groups under study in the population.

Figure 9.2 displays the relationships among research and statistical hypotheses. Note that researchers typically develop research hypotheses based on their review of literature in combination with their judgment. Research hypotheses typically give rise to alternative statistical hypotheses, and null hypotheses are based on the negation of alternative hypotheses.

Statistical hypotheses are usually written with symbols that stand for certain terms and phrases. However, this section uses words to assist you with understanding the meanings of the different types of hypotheses. Statistical hypotheses mention a descriptive statistic (e.g., means, differences in means, correlation coefficient) to be included in the test.

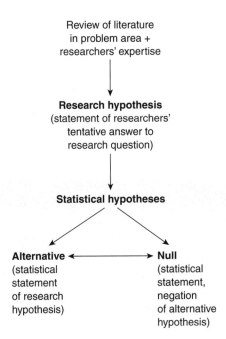

FIGURE 9.2   Relationships among different forms of hypotheses.

The remainder of this subsection describes different types of hypotheses (i.e., research, alternate, null) and their relationships. A number followed by an "r" designates a research hypothesis. Alternative hypotheses have an "a," and null hypotheses, an "n." Examples are provided for associations among variables and for differences in measures for a two-group study. Hypotheses for other research projects use similar forms.

Associations among Variables

Suppose high school teacher-researchers in communication arts are interested in improving students' oral communication. They might investigate a possible relationship between students' self-concepts and public-speaking abilities. For example, they could speculate that an association exists, such as the one shown in this research hypothesis:

1r. Among high school sophomores, self-concept is related to public-speaking abilities.

This research hypothesis can be restated as an alternative statistical hypothesis to communicate the same idea:

1a. The correlation coefficient of self-concept scores and ratings of public-speaking abilities among high school sophomores is *not* zero.

This hypothesis describes the project outcome that researchers expect. To make this hypothesis viable, however, the results must show that the following *null* hypothesis should be rejected:

1n. The correlation coefficient of self-concept scores and public-speaking ability ratings in the population *is* zero.

Differences in Measures for Two Groups

Reading teachers observe that some elementary students have better reading comprehension than their peers, but they may not know the reasons for the differences. 2r is a research hypothesis for projects in which investigators prepare and carry out a research plan to check the effect of method of instruction on comprehension:

2r. Upper elementary grade students who receive literature-based reading instruction perform differently on measures of reading comprehension than their peers who receive basal reader instruction.

Note that this research hypothesis is nondirectional and is preferred unless researchers have good reason to state a directional hypothesis. To test this hypothesis, researchers establish alternative and null hypotheses as follows:

2a. The difference between the mean score of reading comprehension of upper elementary grade students in literature-based instruction and the mean score of their peers in basal reader instruction *is not zero.*

2n. The difference between the mean score of reading comprehension of upper elementary grade students in literature-based instruction and the mean score of their peers in basal reader instruction *is zero.*

An equivalent statement to 2n is: The mean score of reading comprehension by upper elementary grade students who receive literature-based instruction is *equal to* the mean score of reading comprehension by peers who receive basal reader instruction.

If null hypothesis (2n) is rejected, the alternative hypothesis (2a) is viable. In this case, the researchers know that a difference exists, but do not necessarily know the nature of that difference. They would need additional research to establish reasons for the rejection.

E X E R C I S E   9 . 1

The ability to recognize and to state hypotheses in their research, alternative, and null forms is the beginning step in understanding how hypothesis testing strategies work. This exercise allows you to self-assess your understanding.

1. Code hypotheses as follows: A = alternative, N = null, R = research. Explain.
   a. The mean times (in numbers of seconds to the nearest tenth) posted by swimmers who had instruction using new techniques is equal to the mean times (also in numbers of seconds to the nearest tenth) posted by swimmers who continued instruction with traditional techniques.
   b. Teachers with training in questioning techniques use longer wait times than teachers without such training.

2. Write the null hypothesis for the following alternative hypothesis:
   The correlation coefficient of middle school students' flexibility-of-thinking scores and their problem-solving scores in social studies is not zero.

Selection of Inferential Tests

To determine whether a null hypothesis is true, researchers must test it with an inferential statistical test, categorized as either *parametric* or *nonparametric*. **Parameters** are population characteristics. Therefore, researchers choose **parametric tests** if data from participants in a random sample satisfy the following conditions:

- The data represent a normal distribution; this suggests samples of at least 30 or more participants.
- The variance is homogeneous.
- Data are either interval or ratio level of measurement.
- Data are independent; that is, no datum influences any other datum.

Even when data do not conform to all these standards, parametric tests may sometimes be used. For example, unless very small samples are involved, the assumption of a normal distribution is not of major importance. Furthermore, if all groups in the study contain equal numbers of participants, the assumption of homogeneous variance does not have to be met.

When these four conditions cannot be met or safely discounted, **nonparametric tests** should be used. These tests are designed for use with nominal or ordinal measurements. They make no assumptions about the distribution or variations within the population. Even with interval data, researchers may use nonparametric tests if the distribution is not normal or if the variance is not homogeneous.

Parametric and nonparametric tests differ in their capacity to test hypotheses. Generally, parametric tests are more powerful than their nonparametric counterparts. This means that parametric tests are more likely than nonparametric tests to detect the presence of the hypothesized association among variables or the difference between group measures, if it actually exists. Therefore, researchers try to use parametric tests whenever possible.

Appendix C describes several popular inferential statistical tests whose names you are likely to see in research reports. These include *t*-test, analysis of variance (ANOVA), multiple regression, and chi-square. Look in Appendix C for the names of inferential tests to find additional information about these and other tests.

Use of an inferential statistical test is an application of a mathematical procedure to compare the particular descriptive statistic mentioned in the null hypothesis with a theoretical sampling distribution for the selected inferential test. The descriptive statistic may be a correlation coefficient, the difference between means, or another statistic. Theoretical sampling distributions provide the frequencies with which sample statistics are expected to occur, given a particular sample size.

Theoretical sampling distributions consist of **critical values** that tell the probability of the occurrence of a statistically significant result in a sample of a given size. Introductory statistics texts contain tables of critical values of F for use with analysis of variance, t for t-tests, chi-square (χ^2), and others.

Recall that a statistically significant result occurs rarely. As an example, the critical value of t is equal to 2.845 for a sample size of 21. This critical value has the probability of occurring by chance only once in 100 samples of this size. t is a sampling distribution used in conjunction with the inferential statistical test known as the t-test. This particular inferential test would be appropriate for testing null hypothesis 2n, concerning the means of two groups of students who receive different approaches to reading instruction.

Researchers select the inferential tests appropriate for testing their null hypotheses. For example, selection of a test for hypothesis 1n (i.e., the correlation between self-concept scores and ratings of public-speaking abilities) requires knowledge of which correlation coefficient was computed for participant data. Direct comparison of a correlation coefficient with critical values for the particular correlation (e.g., r and rho) is the inferential statistical test. Other coefficients must be tested with inferential statistical test procedures.

E X E R C I S E   9 . 2

The ability to select an appropriate inferential statistical test for testing hypotheses is helpful in the evaluation of inferential statistical data analyses. This exercise provides an opportunity for you to check your own ability.

For purposes of testing null hypotheses 1 and 2, assume that the participant group(s) is (are) drawn from well-defined populations using random sampling procedures. Answer the following questions for each hypothesis:

   a. Identify the descriptive statistics to be tested.
   b. Can a parametric test be used? Explain.
   c. Identify an inferential test to be used (see Appendix C).

   1. The mean times (in numbers of seconds to the nearest tenth) posted by swimmers who had instruction with new techniques is equal to the mean times (also in numbers of seconds to the nearest tenth) posted by swimmers who continued instruction with traditional techniques.

   2. The correlation coefficient for keyboarding mistakes and minutes allowed for keyboarding is zero.

Selection of Significance Levels

Along with selection of an inferential statistical test, researchers also identify a probability level, known as a **level of significance,** which shows the risk they are willing to take in making incorrect decisions about the results of their statistical tests of inference. Because inferential statistics are probability-based, making correct decisions every time is impossible. Remember that unless the test result occurs rarely (say, 5 times or less in 100), it is of little consequence. A result that takes place more often is probably due to random fluctuations in sampling.

The level of significance is important at the time researchers make decisions about test results. When the results of statistical testing are complete, researchers inspect the computer printouts and make one of four possible decisions about the hypothesis. Two decisions will be correct choices, but the other two will be errors, commonly known as Type I and Type II errors.

As an example, if researchers test hypothesis 2n, they would make correct decisions if they rejected the null hypothesis when it is false or if they retained the null hypothesis when it is true. Said another way, the researchers would be correct if they *rejected* the null hypothesis when the results are due to differences in the reading interventions. They would also be correct if they *retained* or kept the null hypothesis when the results are due to chance fluctuations in sampling (that is, no real differences exist between the means).

However, the researchers would make a Type I error if they rejected the null hypothesis when it is true or a Type II error if they retained the null hypothesis when it is false. Said another way, a **Type I error** means that the results of the study are actually due to chance or random fluctuations in the sample, but the data analysis shows the results to be statistically significant.

In the ongoing example about reading instruction, researchers make a Type I error if they infer that one approach to reading instruction is superior to the other, when this result is untrue. Should educators decide to act on the basis of this erroneous information, their action would be futile and could waste time, money, and effort. In subsequent research projects that involved these reading instruction approaches, researchers would obtain similar results only by chance.

A **Type II error** means that the results of the study do not appear to be statistically significant based on the results of data analysis, but they really are. For example, in the experiment comparing reading instruction approaches, researchers make a Type II error if they infer that the two approaches give similar results, when one method is actually superior to the other. Educators who might act on the basis of this misinformation lose an opportunity to effect change, based on sound research findings. See Figure 9.3 for a summary of this discussion about decisions and errors.

Researchers have some control over both types of errors, largely through choice of the level of significance (called the *alpha level,* and written α), the number of participants, and the power of the statistical test. Type I errors are controlled by the choice of the level of significance, denoted by p (probability level). Setting the level of significance at $p = .05$ means that researchers take the risk of making a mistake 5 times in 100. A $p = .01$ level is more stringent; these researchers are willing to risk an erroneous decision only 1 time in 100.

A few researchers take greater risks than these by setting alpha at $p = .10$ or higher. However, if significant results are obtained at higher probability levels, investigators expect to replicate the project using progressively more stringent alpha levels. A stringent alpha level reduces the power of the

Researchers make correct decisions if they:

- reject the null hypothesis when it is false.
- retain the null hypothesis when it is true.

Researchers make errors if they:

- reject the null hypothesis when it is true (Type I).
- retain the null hypothesis when it is false (Type II).

FIGURE 9.3   Summary of decision possibilities in inferential statistical tests.

statistical test, which diminishes the possibility of rejecting a false null hypothesis.

Type II errors are less controllable than are Type I errors. The probability of making a Type II error (called the *beta level*, and written β) is equal to one minus the power of the statistical test, expressed as a decimal fraction. To illustrate, if the power of the test is .80, the probability of a Type II error is .20, or one minus .80. The power of the test depends on the alpha level, whether the test is parametric or nonparametric, the number of participants, and the magnitude of the association or difference.

Researchers can manipulate some of these factors. For example, increasing the number of participants means more power for the test. However, researchers must carefully consider the consequences of selecting both an alpha level and the number of participants. By doing so, they guard against making both types of errors.

Unfortunately, there is no way to avoid all risks of errors. Actions to minimize risks of making one type of error increase the probability of making the other type of error. Researchers try to strike a balance between the risks.

Application of Tests

In most cases, researchers use computer programs to handle the actual calculations in statistical tests. Using data from participants, data processing operations typically permit calculation of both descriptive and inferential statistics within the same program.

The results of the inferential tests are numbers accompanied by symbols associated with particular statistical tests. For example, the result of a *t*-test is a *t* value. *F* values are the symbols for the results from analysis of variance.

Many statistical software packages are available for these purposes. The *Handbook of Statistical Procedures and Their Computer Applications to Education and the Behavioral Sciences* (Freed, Ryan, & Hess, 1991) describes 97 statistical procedures in 9 general categories, available for data analyses. Section C of this handbook provides detailed information on using Statistical Analysis System (SAS), SYSTAT, SPSS-X, and Minitab to apply statistical tests.

Evaluation of Test Outcomes

Computer programs make calculation of statistical tests relatively easy. They usually also provide the probability levels at which results of the data analyses are likely to occur by chance. To evaluate the test outcomes, researchers compare the probability level they preselected with the p values in the printout.

Results are considered **statistically significant** if p values in the printout match, or are less than the preselected p values. Probability values greater than the preselected values mean those results are not statistically significant.

Comparison of p values on computer printouts replaces the practice researchers used in the past. Previously, researchers compared their calculated test statistics (e.g., t, F values), with a table of critical values. Investigators considered a test outcome to be statistically significant if the calculated test statistic was as large or larger than the critical value, at the specified probability level. Calculated statistics that were not as large as the critical values, of course, were deemed statistically nonsignificant.

In cases in which there is statistical significance, researchers reject the null hypothesis in favor of the alternative. Where there is not statistical significance, researchers retain the null hypothesis as the best description of the association between variables or difference between groups.

Although Gettinger (1993) does not discuss null hypotheses, a number of statistical results in her study provide examples of the information about statistical significance of results. Here is one result from the first paragraph of the Results section in A1:

> . . An analysis of variance (ANOVA) on Unit 2 (i.e., during treatment implementation) . . . did reveal a significant difference among classes, $F(2, 62) = 4.90$, $p < .05$, for Unit 2. . . . Children in Class C, on average, obtained significantly higher weekly spelling test scores during the intervention . . . than did children in the other two classes (p. 42).

This statement says that students in the experimental class (Class C) outperformed students in the other two classes following the intervention. Notice that information is given in two ways. The first part of the statement presents statistical information, and the second part states the same information with words (see A1).

Look closer at the statistical information. Analysis of variance was applied to the means of the three classes. The result of this mathematical procedure was a calculated F value of 4.90. This value was compared with a table of critical values for F at the predetermined level of significance, $p = .05$, at the appropriate sample size.

The test outcome (F value of 4.90) is rare; it could be expected to occur due to chance fluctuations less than 5 times in 100. The inference is that the differences among means are due to something other than chance. Gettinger suggests that the methods of spelling instruction are responsible. When she says that this result is significant, she means that it is statistically significant.

Notice further in Table 1 that means of the groups were compared on spelling accuracy in dictated stories after the generalization unit. Means of 20.1, 20.5, and 24.8 were compared, resulting in an F value of 2.36, which carries no asterisk. This F value is not statistically significant; differences among these mean scores can be attributed to chance variations.

E X E R C I S E   9 . 3

The ability to explain the meanings of results of inferential data analysis procedures is an important part of being able to evaluate them. This exercise asks you to explain several items of information in a prediction study.

Scan this report from its beginning to the discussion section:

A6 The Impact of Personal, Professional and Organizational Characteristics on Administrator Burnout

As you read this report, substitute these terms: "criterion" and "predictor" variables for "independent" and "dependent" variables. Answer the following questions:

1. A large section of results describes the outcomes of correlation analyses.
   a. Briefly explain why the results of correlation analyses would be reported in a prediction study.
   b. Explain what this phrase from the first paragraph in the correlation analysis subsection means: "The strongest correlations, and significant at $p = 0.001$, are found between the burnout dimension of emotional exhaustion and level of stress ($r = 0.57$) . . . ."

2. A second large section of results describes the outcomes of multiple regression analysis.
   a. Explain briefly why multiple regression analysis would be reported in a prediction study.
   b. Note the total R^2 of .47 in Table II under the *emotional exhaustion* heading. Explain what this statement means.
   c. Note the seven variables listed under the *emotional exhaustion* heading. Is importance attached to the sequence in which these variables are listed? Explain.

Once they evaluate their test outcomes, quantitative researchers have additional work involved with interpretation or explanation of the results. Chapter 12 describes these processes.

⋊ Results Sections of Research Reports

This section extends the discussion of results sections begun in Chapter 8 to include information about the inferential statistical data analyses and their outcomes. Also included are criteria for evaluation of results sections and the critique of a research report.

Descriptions—Part 2

Typically inferential statistical tests and the outcomes of their application are described in the Results or Findings sections of research reports alongside the descriptive statistical information. Results are incorporated in tables or figures and in text, depending on the report. Major findings are usually presented in more than one form (i.e., figures or text) because researchers recognize that readers have different preferences about reading research findings.

Inferential statistics are often signaled by mention of the parametric or nonparametric test name or by symbols for test results (e.g., F, t, r). Along with these symbols are related p values, sometimes noted by superscripts, as well as symbols such as "n.s." for nonsignificant, or statistical nonsignificance.

In other instances, researchers signal statistical significance through the use of asterisks and footnotes. Chapter 8 referred to a line from Wentzel's (1997) Table 1 as follows:

T2 Perceived teacher caring .39*** .45*** .36***

Below the table, Wentzel notes that a triple asterisk means $p < .001$. Any correlation coefficient in this table with a triple asterisk is statistically significant. These values would be likely to occur by chance alone less than one time in 1,000 (see A7, Results section).

Study of research reports both in this text and elsewhere shows that participants are frequently *not* random samples. Chapter 4 pointed out that the absence of information about sampling procedures and failure to describe a population suggest that participants are convenience samples. When samples are not random, references to a population are ambiguous at best. Therefore, these results of inferential statistical tests are less meaningful than if a random sample is studied.

Criteria for Evaluation

As readers of descriptive and experimental research reports, you should be aware of criteria for the evaluation of results sections. These criteria are based on information presented in this and previous chapters:

1. Descriptive statistics related to project variables must be available for use in inferential data analysis.

    These statistics include correlation coefficients, measures of central tendency, measures of variation, and others.

2. The inferential statistical data analysis procedures used should be appropriate for the design to produce valid results for a population.

    Descriptive statistics used in the inferential test must come from random samples. (If these statistics come from nonrandom samples, the population to which they can be generalized is ambiguous and renders the results less meaningful.) The inferential statistical test selected should be appropriate for evaluating the null hypothesis.

3. The inferential statistical data analysis procedures should fit with other design procedures to produce reliable results for a population.

These data analysis procedures should be consistent with other procedures. The inferential statistical test selected should conform to the requirements for parametric or nonparametric tests.

Researchers should strive to describe their data analysis procedures clearly enough that independent researchers could use them with similar populations and expect similar results.

Application of Criteria

To illustrate these points, this section evaluates the inferential statistical data analyses in Effects of Error Correction on Third Graders' Spelling. The critique discusses the inferential statistical procedures and results. Refer to Exercise 9.4 and the research report as you read this section.

Effects of Error Correction in Third Graders' Spelling

Mean scores and standard deviations are available for each measure of the dependent variable including weekly tests, dictated stories, and teacher ratings. These measures are available for each of the three treatment levels at each of three time intervals—prior to intervention, at the end of intervention, and 6 weeks after the end of intervention.

Analysis of variance (ANOVA) is used to determine if statistically significant differences could be detected among the mean scores of three classes of third graders who had undergone different treatment conditions. ANOVA was performed on the mean scores of weekly tests, dictated stories, and teacher ratings. Moreover, ANOVA was calculated for nine sets of data because data were collected at the end of three phases of this experiment on three measures. Analysis of variance is the procedure of choice for testing the statistical significance of differences among means of three groups as outlined in the researcher's hypothesis located near the end of the report Introduction.

No post hoc, or follow-up, tests were made in this project despite the finding of statistically significant F-values. In each case, experimental group means were consistently higher than means of the remaining groups. The researcher deduced that the source of significant F-values was the mean of the experimental group.

This report is unclear about the population that the three third grade classes represent, other than the fact that they were part of a white, middle-class, suburban school district. In addition, the researcher provides no indication that the classes represent a random sample.

```
E  X  E  R  C  I  S  E        9 . 4
```

This exercise allows you to see how well you can evaluate the inferential data analysis procedures for the production of valid and reliable results for a population.

Study the problem, method, and the complete results sections for these research reports:

A4 A Computerized Method to Teach Latin and Greek Root Words: Effect on Verbal SAT

A5 Preservice and Inservice Secondary Teachers' Orientations toward Content Area Reading

Then answer these questions for each report:

1. Identify the descriptive statistics that are available for use in inferential statistical tests. Note their relationships to project variables.

2. To estimate the validity of the results for the population, answer the following question:
   Identify the inferential test(s) used. Is (are) the test(s) appropriate for use with the available descriptive statistics? Can test outcomes be inferred or generalized to a well-defined population? If no, explain and do *not* continue to question 3. If yes, briefly describe the results for the population using the project variables. Continue with question 3.

3. To estimate the reliability of the results for the population, answer the following question:
   Overall, are the inferential data analysis procedures described clearly enough that independent researchers could use them and expect similar results in similar research situations? Explain.

Summary

Inferential statistical tests permit researchers to determine the probability that the results obtained from their random sample are true of the population. Inferential statistics require the formation of statistical hypotheses, which then can be tested using mathematical probability. The logic of these procedures is indirect. A null hypothesis of no association or no difference in means is formulated along with an alternative that negates the null. If the null hypothesis is retained, the alternative hypothesis is discarded. However, if the null hypothesis is rejected, the alternative hypothesis states the test result.

Application of the inferential test subjects descriptive statistics from random samples to mathematical procedures. The test outcome is evaluated against outcomes of these same procedures carried out with theoretical sampling distributions. This comparison shows the probability of the test outcome due to chance fluctuations in the population.

Outcomes that occur rarely are considered statistically significant and are noted typically as having probabilities of occurring in the population 1 (or 5) time(s) in 100 by chance. In these cases, null hypotheses are rejected in favor of alternates. If, however, the test outcome could have occurred due to chance fluctuations in the population, then the null hypothesis is retained. These results are not statistically significant.

Descriptions of results sections, criteria for their evaluation, and application of the criteria to one project are described in the final section. The critique of an experimental research report shows that inferential statistics were calculated, even though the report gives no indication that the sample is a random one.

Questions for Discussion

1. Discuss the relationship of descriptive statistics to inferential statistics.
2. Elaborate on the meaning of this statement: "The null hypothesis is the most accurate statement about the project variables if an anticipated research hypothesis is not true."
3. Research projects sometimes compare groups that receive different treatments. In some cases, the null hypothesis of no difference among the groups is rejected. Is it then appropriate to say that these comparison groups represent different populations? Explain.
4. Explain how levels of significance relate to Type I errors.

Methods and Results for Qualitative Studies

The procedures and results for qualitative and historical studies are emphasized in Chapters 10 and 11, respectively. Researchers not only design procedures in qualitative and historical projects, but they are also heavily involved in carrying them out.

The procedures encompass all the processes, including the participant and instrumentation procedures discussed in Chapters 4 and 5. Unlike their quantitative counterparts, qualitative and historical researchers begin analyses almost as soon as data become available. On the basis of initial analyses, they typically gather additional data and continue the collection and analysis processes through several cycles.

Researchers usually gather large quantities of verbal data that must be reduced in volume to obtain their meaning. These processes are both time consuming and labor intensive. Data collection, analysis, and interpretation continue through the duration of the project, with new cycles serving to refine the previous cycles.

Results of data analyses and their interpretations are intertwined in qualitative and historical inquiries; both types of outcomes are described in these chapters. Conclusions and recommendations based on these outcomes, however, are discussed in Chapter 12.

The discussions of procedures for qualitative research in part IV highlight basic ideas but are not intended to be complete discussions. Additional study of these procedures is necessary prior to your actual engagement in a qualitative research project.

Despite the limitations, you have information to prepare a preliminary proposal for a qualitative or historical study. This will help you gain insights into how the procedures work together. Study the pertinent sections of Chapter 14 for this purpose.

Qualitative Research Procedures and Results

❖ **Procedures for Data Collection and Handling**
   Circumstances
   Preparation of Data for Analyses
❖ **Procedures for Analyses and Interpretations**
   Assignment of Codes
   Memos and Diagrams

Computer Software Programs for Analyses
Results and Interpretations
❖ **Procedures and Results Sections**
   Descriptions
   Criteria for Evaluation
   Application of Criteria

Qualitative researchers have as their goal the description and explanation of present-day phenomena. These researchers usually collect data using strategies selected especially for the project and suited to the setting. Data collection, handling, and analysis are labor-intensive processes that require significant amounts of researchers' expertise.

In this chapter these procedures are described separately for clarity, but in actual practice, they take place in ongoing cycles. The final chapter section describes procedures and results sections in reports of qualitative studies, criteria for their evaluation, and an application of these criteria to one report.

Goals

To enable you to:

- evaluate the collection procedures in selected qualitative research reports for the production of valid and reliable data for analyses; and
- evaluate the clarity of results and interpretations in selected qualitative research reports.

❧ Procedures for Data Collection and Handling

Researchers invest themselves in collecting and handling data by determining which data are selected for collection as well as how they will be handled once they are gathered. Therefore, knowledge of the circumstances in which data are collected and an understanding of how the researchers prepared them for analyses are necessary to determine their validity and reliability.

Circumstances

Researchers collect data in field settings where their participants live, work, or play. Collection tasks include observing participant activities, asking interview questions, administering open-ended questionnaires, and locating documents and artifacts.

Researchers tailor-make their collection tasks to provide data to answer their questions and to fit the setting. They frequently use more than one collection strategy and may begin with one that is minimally intrusive, such as observation, and later use interviews, which can be very intrusive.

For example, Lightfoot (1984) describes the data collection methods she uses in the preparation of verbal portraits of high schools. Her intent is to capture the essence of six high schools through descriptions of their personnel, the character of interactions among their people, their hopes and dreams, and their weaknesses.

Lightfoot spent several days at each school making observations, interviewing school personnel, and examining published and unpublished school documents. The documents included newspapers, yearbooks, student literary and poetry collections, catalogs, attendance reports, records of college attendance rates, departmental evaluations, and others. With such a wide range of strategies, Lightfoot was able to obtain a variety of data to make insightful portraits of several types of high schools.

Professional Access

Before any data collection takes place, however, researchers must negotiate for permission to do so with the persons in charge of the institutions or settings where they want to collect data. These individuals may include principals, teachers, governing boards, or other supervisors.

In some cases, permission is granted without hesitation. In other cases, permission is difficult or impossible to obtain. Peshkin (1986) recounts his attempts to collect data in Christian schools. As a cross-cultural studies researcher, he sought entry to such schools for a pilot study. He says: "We were allowed entry to one (Christian school), only to be asked later to leave; allowed entry to another for 'two weeks only, that's all, no bargaining'; and absolutely refused entry to a third" (p. 12). Following these initial refusals, Peshkin spent three semesters on the campus of a Christian school.

As part of gaining access, researchers also negotiate whichever role(s) they wish to assume. Simply observing situations is quite different from interacting with participants in a field setting. Therefore, the roles that researchers plan to assume require specific permission for a particular type of access to participants.

Collection Procedures

Once researchers decide on strategies and roles for data collection, they continue planning the procedures. This includes a variety of tasks such as scheduling time spent in the field setting, securing the cooperation of fellow data collectors, and deciding which documents or artifacts are useful, and locating them.

Structuring questions for interviews or questionnaires or those to be answered by the examination of documents or artifacts is a part of many collection procedures in qualitative studies. Researchers who use interviews plan the details surrounding the actual question-asking session by answering questions such as the following:

- How much rapport should exist between participants and researcher prior to an interview?
- In what locations and on what schedules are participants comfortable answering questions?
- Will the presence of a video camera or a tape recorder negatively influence the interview?

Making arrangements for the taping of observations or interviews is typically part of data collection procedures. When interviews or observations cannot be taped, researchers jot notes about participant responses, the circumstances, and activities. Jotted notes consist of words, phrases, and sketches that trigger the researchers' memories for writing complete notes. Jotted notes must be written as field notes soon after researchers leave the setting and participants.

Field notes capture as much of the actual verbal and nonverbal communication as possible. For each entry, the notes are organized chronologically by date, time, and place. These notes provide detailed descriptions that use specific language for what was heard or said, including verbatim communications among participants and with researchers, whenever possible. Field notes often include maps, diagrams, or pictures of the field site to aid researchers in organizing events.

The example of field notes shown in Figure 10.1 is from a project in which special and general education elementary teachers seek to develop and implement a co-teaching program. The intent of the study is to identify the issues that teachers face as well as the strategies they use to address them (K. Harris, personal communication, 1999). Notice particularly the explicit language of these notes. For meanings of the codes, see the Procedures for Analyses and Interpretations section.

As part of the collection processes, researchers must be concerned about the validity of their data. Some researchers record sessions at field sites on video- or audiotapes. Preserving the information in either form allows the researchers to review the data for accuracy.

Context: Co-teaching: special educator (Theresa) and 4th grade elementary educator (Judy) in Judy's classroom

Date: October 12, 1999   Time: 10:15–11:45 AM

Field Notes	**Code**
Judy's room has a lot of stimulation, e.g., mobiles, bulletin boards, etc. The students' desks are arranged in groups of about five.	0 It Tech In
They were doing this lesson via co-teaching. They were finishing a Judy Blume story. They were then going to create a character web. Theresa introduced the activity to the entire class. Then, the entire class split into two groups. Theresa had one group and Judy had the other group. There were about 10–11 students in each group. Both groups seemed to be doing the same activity. It seemed in this particular situation Theresa had the special education students in her group. The students were given roles based on the story. They were to finish reading the story together, taking on the different roles of the characters in the story. The student would read what his/her character said in the story.	0 It Tech Co
When the students were split into groups, I first observed Theresa's group. Theresa had to explain about quotation marks and how one knows who is talking.	0 It Tech In
The two groups worked in the same room, reading aloud. The students didn't always control their voices and sometimes that got to be a problem. Theresa dealt with this issue by sitting next to two of the students and using physical prompts to get them to attend and to lower their voices. Judy sent one of the students in her group out of the room when he talked out.	0 It Tech Man

FIGURE 10.1   Example of coded field notes.

From K. Harris, personal communication, 1999. Reprinted by permission.

Qualitative researchers must collect data over a time span sufficient to assure their accuracy. Some qualitative researchers maintain that they should continue data collection until the data become repetitive; that is, until the data no longer present new information (Lincoln & Guba, 1985). Only in these circumstances will the researchers have sufficient information about the phenomenon to assure accuracy.

Sometimes two or more collectors gather information simultaneously. In other situations, researchers gather data using more than one collection strategy. Either of these procedures allows researchers to check the consistency of the data.

Preparation of Data for Analyses

Preparation of data for analysis, or handling procedures, involves at least two important tasks: the transformation of raw participant data into forms for analysis and the establishment of systems for organizing and storing data. Both are labor-intensive processes that require the researchers' expertise.

Transformation of Raw Data to Forms for Analyses

Interviews and audio- or videotapes must be transcribed carefully to preserve all verbal information, and as much nonverbal information as can be retrieved. Transcription typically involves careful processing into computer files. Each transcription also identifies all personnel by name and position title, date, and the place where data were gathered.

Responses to open-ended questionnaires or other instruments completed by participants may also be entered into computer files. These, too, contain names of personnel with their titles, dates, and the places where data were collected.

Researchers may use general word-processing programs or special computer software programs that assist with analyses. Software programs typically function either as text retrievers or as text database managers (Tesch, 1990). Additional information about these programs follows in the next major section.

Organization and Storage of Data

Qualitative research typically generates large quantities of data that must be organized and stored for easy retrieval. Although most data are computer stored, backup copies of computer files, hard copies of original data, working drafts of analyses, artifacts, and other documents must have a physical storage location accessible to all the researchers. Once analyses begin, coding keys and indexes to all the materials must be prepared and kept current. As these comments suggest, the complexity of qualitative research requires a well-developed master plan for the organization and storage of data for easy, flexible use by all the project researchers (Huberman & Miles, 1994).

✖ Procedures for Analyses and Interpretations

Data from a single qualitative project typically fill several hundreds of pages of notes. Obviously, researchers must reduce this volume drastically to discern meanings within the data. The foundation of data analysis and interpretation is the extraction of meaning from verbal data through gradual, carefully designed winnowing and meaning-making processes. Eventually, interrelated themes, concepts, or patterns suggested by convergences within the data emerge.

Depending on the project and the amount of available data, researchers sometimes read and reread their observations or other records until they deduce their meaning. This appears to be the method that Lightfoot (1984) uses in constructing school portraits. In *The Good High School,* Lightfoot (1984) says that she:

> read her daily records and summaries several times over, often making notes and offering tentative hypotheses and interpretations. When there were apparent contradictions, I would search for the roots of the dissonance. When I began to find persistent repetitions and elaborations of similar ideas, I would underscore them and find traces of the central themes in other contexts. Slowly the skeleton of the story would begin to emerge, filled in over time by detailed evidence, subtle description, and multiple perspectives (p. 17).

Projects differ in the amount and type of data required for answering the research questions. This also means that analysis procedures differ as well. From the many methods that exist, researchers use one or more methods compatible with their particular orientation to qualitative research. Computer programs can assist with many routine tasks, but researchers must decide which programs to use and what the outcomes from computer analyses mean. Analysis procedures are typically time consuming for researchers.

This section describes a generalized method for analyzing qualitative data, drawn largely from Strauss and Corbin (1998); see also Marshall and Rossman (1999). This method employs cycles of data collection, analysis, and interpretation that provide researchers with opportunities to compare data more or less continuously. These procedures give the method its name, **constant comparative,** or *iterative.*

In brief, researchers collect and analyze data in ongoing, meaning-making processes. Figure 10.2 provides an overview of the major processes and products in this method of data analysis. The processes include data collection followed by a series of coding procedures, each serving a particular function. Note the loop among the processes that suggests the ongoing nature of data collection and analysis procedures. The products resulting from the processes represent progressively reduced volumes of data. That is, large volumes of notes and documents shrink to a few well-chosen paragraphs.

Assignment of Codes

As labels for assigning units of meaning to qualitative data, "codes usually are attached to 'chunks' of varying size—words, phrases, sentences, or whole paragraphs, connected or unconnected to a specific setting. They can take the form of a straightforward category label or a more complex one (e.g., a metaphor)" (Miles & Huberman, 1994, p. 56). The importance of any code is its meaning, which researchers ascribe to the code.

Codes are valuable because researchers can use them to retrieve and organize the "chunks" they represent. This allows researchers to locate, separate, and regroup chunks that relate to particular research questions or themes, whenever necessary (Miles & Huberman, 1994).

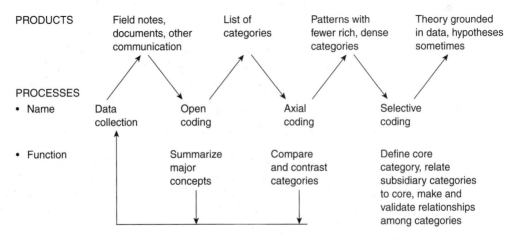

FIGURE 10.2   Products and processes in the constant comparative method of data analysis.

Prior to the start of the actual coding processes, some researchers develop a set of codes based on their knowledge of the phenomenon, the research questions, or the literature. Other researchers allow the codes to emerge as they study the data. Either approach is viable.

In the constant comparative analysis, researchers begin coding by carefully and slowly reading their qualitative notes. In their first pass through the data, researchers attempt to label each discrete incident, idea, or event. In this process, called *open coding*, researchers are free to use whichever labels the data suggest are appropriate, and to revise the labels when they reread the data. However, the same label must be assigned to similar phenomena. Open coding breaks data apart and allows researchers to compare phenomena for similarities and differences.

As an illustration of coding, see Figure 10.1, a field notes excerpt from a study of co-teaching by special education teachers and general education teachers. The researcher intends to identify the issues the teachers face and the strategies they use. In the code section, note the first code, "O," which means that the source was an observation. The second code, "It," names the individual teacher (i.e., Theresa) whose perspective is described. "Tech," the third code, refers to techniques as the issue of concern.

In the fourth position, the codes refer to the techniques that the teachers employ to address the issues. "In" refers to instruction, "Co" to co-teaching, and "Man" to management. According to Harris (personal communication, 1999), these codes emerged from study of the data.

After open coding is complete, researchers study the labels and group those with common features into categories. All assigned codes must cohere around the themes embodied within categories. Researchers reexamine any codes that do not fit readily into categories and reconceptualize the categories to include all the codes.

Next, the researchers list the categories, an action that summarizes the major concepts. These categories become the data for subsequent coding processes. Use of these processes, of course, reduces the quantity of data. During the coding processes, researchers also write notes and draw diagrams (see the memos and diagrams subsection) concerning their insights about the meanings of the data.

In the second data pass, researchers study the categories generated previously. Here, in *axial coding*, researchers reconnect the data by intensively studying the categories to answer these questions:

- What are the conditions that give rise to the category?
- What is the context in which the category is embedded?
- What are the strategies by which the category is handled, managed, or carried out?
- What are the consequences of these strategies?

To answer these questions, researchers compare and contrast the categories. Inductive and deductive thinking strategies help researchers subdivide the categories, a requirement in sorting answers to the important questions. This second round of coding produces fewer, but richer and denser, categories that have more explanatory power than those obtained in open coding. The new categories reveal patterns in the data. Again, researchers use memos and diagrams to aid in their analyses.

In some qualitative projects, researchers conclude analysis procedures at this point. They use the patterns from these analyses to generate answers to their research questions. Typically, these projects are those in which the researchers explain the status of a phenomenon.

For developing grounded theory, however, researchers continue the analysis. They form linkages among the subcategories that must conform to a defined pattern of relationships. In addition, the investigators perform another round of coding, called *selective coding,* at a higher, more abstract level of analysis.

Researchers study the rich, dense categories obtained in previous analyses to determine a core category, a central phenomenon into which all the other categories can be integrated (Strauss & Corbin, 1998). This means that the core category must be large and abstract to encompass all the other categories. For example, in the Larson and Parker (1996) study of classroom discussion, core categories include recitation, teacher-directed conversation, open-ended conversation, posing challenging questions, and application (see A2, Findings and Hypotheses).

Once the researchers identify a core category, they relate the supporting categories to it. Investigators must be able to validate the existence of core and support category relationships with data because these processes make possible the idea of hypotheses grounded in the data. Said another way, the data must support the relationships purported to exist among the categories. If these relationships cannot be shown to exist, researchers then re-examine the data for relationships other than the one they considered first.

Memos and Diagrams

During the time that researchers engage in coding, they observe and study the meanings and relationships among their data. As insights occur, they write memos that suggest possible relationships or produce diagrams that link ideas suggested by the data. Researchers may stop the coding processes in order to write memos (addressed to themselves) or make drawings because they don't want to lose their insights about what the data mean. These communications are working documents; their purpose is to assist in the researchers' meaning-making processes.

Open coding helps researchers to summarize the major concepts or themes embodied in the notes, documents, or other verbal communications. Therefore, memos prepared as part of these operations can help researchers keep track of the diversity of concepts uncovered within the data.

During axial coding, researchers work toward insights into possible connections among the concepts. Memos and diagrams created at this analysis stage typically reflect efforts to pull together information from several locations within the data.

Computer Software Programs for Analyses

In recent years, qualitative researchers have come to rely on computer assistance for certain aspects of analysis. Text retrieval programs enable researchers to search documents for specific words, count the frequency with which the words appear, and create alphabetic lists with information about where words appear in documents (Tesch, 1990).

Text database manager programs help researchers to format the database into fields into which researchers can enter the natural units of their data, such as individual utterances or actions. Each set of data is considered as one record in the database. Thereafter, researchers can assign key word codes to data units within the records of that database. This capability allows the researchers to locate specific items within their data quickly (Tesch, 1990).

Other more sophisticated software programs help researchers to code text, then retrieve and display the coded information. Examples of these programs include HyperQual, NUDIST, QUALPRO, and The Ethnograph. HyperRESEARCH and NUDIST programs not only serve these functions, but also allow researchers to make connections among codes, devise new classifications and categories, and produce a conceptual structure to fit the data (Parker, 1996).

Results and Interpretations

The patterns generated during axial coding may furnish the results for answering research questions concerned with explanations or development of concepts. The patterns that result from convergence within the data suggest explanations about the intricacies and subtleties of relationships.

In projects in which researchers develop grounded theory, they develop hypotheses based on the core categories as answers to the questions of the study. These hypotheses are held tentatively until researchers can gather and analyze additional rounds of data that confirm or refute them.

As an example, Larson and Parker (1996) present their findings as hypotheses. Their teacher-generated data support the existence of five conceptions of classroom discussion that these researchers construe as hypotheses (see A2, Findings and Hypotheses).

Some qualitative researchers share their project results with participants from whom they gathered data to obtain comments. The project is said to be member valid if the participants concur with the researchers' work. There are limitations, of course, because participants may not recognize their own ideas when shared from the researchers' perspective. This is a good way of establishing validity or credibility.

Researchers typically discuss or explain their results. They recount decisions made in the course of collection and analyses that led them to their results. These interpretations, of course, are provided to help you understand how they arrived at the results.

Recall that researchers state or infer in their literature review that a project is intended to fulfill a certain need or justification. At the point of interpreting their results, most researchers describe the contribution of their project toward meeting that need.

✷ Procedures and Results Sections in Qualitative Research Reports

Procedures or methods sections of qualitative studies contain descriptions of participants and instrument and strategy choices, as described in Chapters 4 and 5, respectively. These sections also describe all the remaining procedures, and results are usually presented separately. This chapter section describes the methods and results sections of reports of qualitative research projects, provides criteria for their evaluation, and applies these criteria to a qualitative report.

Descriptions

Within methods sections, researchers typically describe the setting and the data collection, handling, and analysis activities. Some reports contain a bare minimum of information, but others contain details. When researchers include details, of course, you have much more information on which to evaluate procedures.

Results sections contain the findings and interpretations that answer the research question. Because most data in qualitative studies are verbal, results sections consist largely of verbal descriptions of outcomes. Frequently, researchers include verbatim participant responses to augment their interpretations.

In projects in which the intent of researchers is to generate grounded theory, results sections typically contain the hypotheses that emerge from the researchers' data analysis and interpretation. Researchers consider these hypotheses as tentative explanations to be subjected to testing and refinement.

Criteria for Evaluation

Understanding the data collection, handling, and analysis procedures is key to understanding the results in qualitative research reports. Use the following criteria, based on information in this chapter, to guide your study of procedures and results or findings sections:

1. The circumstances under which data are collected should be described in detail. These descriptions should provide evidence of the validity and reliability of the collected data.

    Researchers should describe the circumstances surrounding data collection by including information about the period of time over which data were collected, the identity of the collectors, and their relationship to the project.

2. Research questions should be answered clearly, and the results should be interpreted carefully.

The results or outcomes should provide unambiguous answers to all research questions. Use of member checks helps to validate the project.

Researchers assist readers in understanding their results by providing explanations and discussions of their decisions during data collection, handling, and analysis. These interpretations should also explain how the project contributed toward the fulfillment of its stated need or justification.

Application of Criteria

This section provides an evaluation of the Analysis and Analysis Illustration subsections of the Method section, as well as the Findings and Hypotheses section of the report, "What is Classroom Discussion? A Look at Teachers' Conceptions" (Larson & Parker, 1996). Refer to Exercise 10.1 for the questions and to A2 as the basis for this review.

What Is Classroom Discussion? A Look at Teachers' Conceptions

The topic of this investigation is teachers' conceptions of classroom discussion, which these researchers investigate to establish an explanatory theory.

Details of data collection procedures are not described in this report. In the subsections, Analysis and Analysis Illustration, the researchers describe the sequence, provide brief accounts of collection activities, and list the types of data gathered during individual interviews and think-aloud tasks. The report simply indicates that classroom observations were made of each teacher leading a discussion, but little is said about these data.

Apparently all data were collected by the researchers (whether one or both is not clear), but the report contains little or no information about the circumstances, the amount of time, or data handling procedures. The Analysis Illustration describes the generation of one conception of classroom discussion and clarifies the collection and analysis procedures for interview and think-aloud data. Careful reading of these sections reveals few references to classroom observations.

Also, by collecting data through interactions with participants, the researchers demonstrate their intent to obtain valid data that explore teachers' conceptions of classroom discussion. This report does not tell how much time the researchers spent with the participants, nor whether the participants reviewed the data. Had these factors been included, readers would have a better understanding of the validity of data from these procedures.

The researchers' general question was specified as four related questions about the defining characteristics, purposes, conceptions, and influences on teachers' conceptions of discussions in high school social studies classes. The findings and interpretations, presented as hypotheses, about five conceptions of classroom discussion, answer the questions well. Answers to each related question can be located easily in the narrative.

The researchers interpret their results through extended discussions of five conceptions of discussion. Each is well defined in terms of teacher-student roles and the purposes served. Verbatim comments from the teacher participants clarify the differences among the conceptions. This study fills its stated justification of building a theory of teachers' conceptions of classroom discussion.

E X E R C I S E   1 0 . 1

This exercise allows you to see how well you can evaluate the data collection, analysis, and interpretation procedures for the production of valid and reliable results in a qualitative study.

Study both the methods and results sections for this report:

A3 A Phenomenological Study with Youth Gang Members: Results and Implications for School Counselors

Answer these questions:

1. Identify the phenomenon or topic of this investigation. What reason do the researchers give for undertaking this project?

2. To estimate the validity of data provided by the procedures, answer the following question:
   Did the researchers collect data over a period long enough to ensure their accuracy?

3. To estimate the reliability of data provided by the procedures, answer the following questions:
   Were data collected using more than one strategy or collector?
   Did researchers check for consistency between (among) the strategies or collectors?

4. Do the results clearly answer the research question(s)? Explain.
   Are the results interpreted clearly?
   In particular, did this project fulfill its stated justification? Explain.

Summary

Qualitative researchers study present-day phenomena that involve multiple variables in complex relationships. Typically they gather mostly verbal data to answer their questions using strategies especially designed for the setting. In roles they negotiate for themselves with school officials, these researchers tune to the subtleties within the research setting as they gather data.

Data collection, handling, and analysis are cyclic operations that require the researchers' expertise and time. As soon as data are gathered, they are prepared for analysis. Constant comparative, a popular method of data analysis, involves initial coding of data to derive categories. Researchers then study the categories through a second type of coding to locate patterns. These patterns become the results for projects in which the intent is the explanation of a phenomenon. If researchers wish to generate theory, they subject the patterns to further coding and meaning making.

The final section, which describes procedures and results sections of qualitative reports, suggests that their content varies, according to the authors' preferences. Despite the variations, qualitative reports should conform to certain criteria, which are applied to one qualitative report.

Questions for Discussion

1. Explain how viewing, talking, and taking notes in qualitative research situations differ from these same activities in nonresearch situations.
2. What purpose is served by collecting large quantities of data in qualitative research, especially when the researchers begin almost immediately to reduce the volume of data?
3. This chapter describes the processes for data reduction and meaning-making used in qualitative research. How similar are these processes to those used by students who prepare an outline for a literature review for a research project? Explain.

Historical Research Procedures and Results

❖ **Procedures for Data Collection**

Location of Data Sources

Evaluation of Data Sources

Data Collection Techniques

❖ **Procedures for Analyses and Interpretations**

Development of a Frame of Reference

Data Reduction

Construction of the Narrative

❖ **Introduction and Narrative Sections in Historical Research Reports**

Description

Criteria for Evaluation

Application of Criteria

Historical researchers study events, institutions, people, movements, or organizations that existed in the past, defined as beginning yesterday. Careful consideration of their work can keep present-day educators from becoming lost, by locating us in time and helping us understand the past (Genz, 1993).

The goal of historical research is to describe and explain past phenomena through careful analysis and evaluation of evidence. Rury's (1993) description of the major steps in historical research, which emphasizes their recursive, nonlinear nature, furnishes the outline for the discussions of procedures in this chapter. Historians first develop a clear idea about the phenomenon that ultimately becomes the problem for their investigation. They may begin by reading the work of other historians on the selected topic, but then seek out firsthand accounts for further study.

Researchers evaluate the authenticity and credibility of these sources, then proceed to gather and analyze data to solve their problem. They incorporate the results and interpretations of their analyses into narratives that become research reports. These processes, which require much thoughtful study and consideration, are described briefly in the first two sections.

The final chapter section describes introductions and narratives of historical reports and provides criteria for the evaluation of selected procedures used in their generation. These criteria are applied to a report.

Goals

To enable you to:

- evaluate the collection procedures in selected historical research reports for the production of valid and reliable data; and
- evaluate the clarity of results and interpretations in selected historical research reports.

✂ Procedures for Data Collection

Before historical researchers begin formal data collection, they read the work of other scholars about the phenomenon they plan to study. This reading assists the researchers in putting the phenomenon into a context and may suggest methods of investigation and potential data sources. The reading typically gives rise to guide questions that help researchers to define the domain of their problem (Thomas, 1998).

Prior to actual data collection, historians must locate, classify, and evaluate their data sources. Main data sources for historical research include documents, artifacts, and oral histories.

Location of Data Sources

Data sources used by historical researchers are typically housed in libraries or archives on university campuses, government or school board offices, private businesses, or historical societies. For example, Thomas and Moran (1992), who study the career of Ernest Clark Hartwell, searched records at the Buffalo and Erie County Historical Society and the Buffalo School Board, where Hartwell served as school superintendent. (In A9, see the footnotes, including notes 54, 60, and 72.) In addition, they use the Walter P. Reuther Archives of Labor and Urban Affairs at Wayne State University. (In A9, see the footnotes, including notes 14, 17, and 30.)

Historical researchers also use less conventional sources. As an example, Zimmerman (1994) uses the files of the Scientific Temperance Federation and the minutes of the Woman's Christian Temperance Union (WCTU) for a report on teacher professionalism during the period 1882–1904. His report contains multiple references to both data sources within the footnotes.

Hartsook (1998) describes archives and special collections, such as those named in the previous examples, as unique resources. Researchers can determine the holdings in these collections through the use of special reference tools such as the National Union Catalog of Manuscripts Collections, an online system. Two additional search tools include the Research Libraries Information Network and the On Line Union Catalog, known as OCLC (from Ohio Computer Library Catalog, its previous name).

Data from **primary sources** provide firsthand or eyewitness accounts for text that comes into being at the time that events occur. **Secondary sources** are accounts made by someone other than an eyewitness and usually come into being at later times. For example, John Dewey's publications are primary sources of information about his contributions to education. However, analyses of Dewey's writings or encyclopedia articles about his contributions are secondary sources because they incorporate their authors' interpretations of Dewey's work.

Additional examples of primary sources include minutes of meetings, unedited videotapes, and objects from earlier times such as pictures or coins, tax records, private memoranda, and personal letters. Official or authorized accounts of governmental agencies, businesses, and fraternal organizations are also usually considered as primary sources.

TABLE 11.1

Uses of Primary and Secondary Sources by Historical Researchers

Type of Source	Typical Content	Uses
Primary	Facts, which can be incomplete, plus analyses and interpretations of the author who witnessed the event	Provide the data used by researchers to answer their questions
Secondary	Facts, which can be incomplete, plus analyses and interpretations made by individuals who were not eyewitnesses	Provide context information about the phenomenon; suggest potential data sources; suggest methods of investigation

Distinctions between primary and secondary sources are important in historical research. Investigators usually study secondary sources for context information, but they use primary sources for data to answer their research questions. Primary sources reflect facts and the interpretations of the authors who witnessed the phenomenon. Data from primary sources are considered as having greater validity than data from secondary sources, which may incorporate several sets of interpretations. See Table 11.1 for a summary of information about primary and secondary data sources.

Historians typically expect to make their own interpretations of data from firsthand accounts, but these sources are not always available. Faced with this situation, historians sometimes quote facts from another historian's work and then provide their own interpretations.

E X E R C I S E   11.1

As a discerning reader of historical research, you should be aware of the degree to which the report is based on primary sources. This exercise assists you in making distinctions between primary and secondary sources.

Listed in items 1–3 are footnotes from "Science for Ladies, Classics for Gentlemen: A Comparative Analysis of Scientific Subjects in the Curricula of Boys' and Girls' Secondary Schools in the United States, 1794–1850" (see A8).

Decide whether the source appears to be a primary or secondary source. Explain.

1. (In footnote 8) John Ludlow, *Address Delivered at the Opening of the New Female Academy in Albany,* May 12, 1834 (Albany, N.Y., 1834), 7.

2. (In footnote 8) J. L. Comstock, *Elements of Chemistry* . . . (New York, 1839), preface.

3. (In footnote 9) Joan N. Burstyn and Thalia M. Mulvihill, "The History of Women's Education: North America," in *The International Encyclopedia of Education,* ed. Torsten Husen and T. Neville Postlethwaite (Oxford, Eng., 1994), 1: 6761–6765.

Evaluation of Data Sources

After researchers obtain access to data sources, they scrutinize the sources to assure their authenticity and credibility. The validity of the research project depends, in large measure, on the rigor of these evaluations.

External Criticism

The test for authenticity, known as **external criticism,** questions whether the source is an original, a forgery, or a variation of the original. Historians ask questions about the author, the date, and the circumstances surrounding each potential source. In many cases, citations on the documents answer these questions. Also, if the document is where it is expected to be—in the records of the government bureau or the school business office, for example—its presence there "creates a presumption of its genuineness" (Gottschalk, 1969, p. 123).

Although forged documents may be rare, educational historians do encounter variant sources because accounts of the same phenomenon differ, depending on the source. For example, reports from government offices may use dates and word choices different from those reported in newspapers and magazines meant for the general public. Two or more oral testimonies may be genuine, even though the details vary. Drafts of unpublished documents, which may or may not be dated, can result in nonidentical versions. In situations such as these, historians must satisfy themselves that sources are authentic before using them (Gottschalk, 1969).

Internal Criticism

Data sources are also subjected to **internal criticism,** in which researchers question the credibility of the content. To have credibility means that the content "is as close to what actually happened as we can learn from a critical examination of the best available sources" (Gottschalk, 1969, p. 139).

In tests for credibility, researchers resolve questions about the accuracy of statements within documents and the trustworthiness of the content in witnesses' testimonies. To achieve full credibility, the content must come from a primary witness who was able and willing to tell the truth, whose word was accurately reported in terms of details, and whose word can be independently corroborated (Gottschalk, 1969).

Researchers implement their evaluations by answering questions about the author of a document or the interviewee in an oral history. Was this individual an actual eyewitness or is the information reported secondhand? What are the literal meanings as well as the connotations of the content? Does the content fit the context in which it was produced? Can details mentioned in the context be verified? Based on their answers to these questions, researchers decide on the credibility of the source content.

Historians typically register their criticisms of data sources within footnotes or within the report narrative. Figure 11.1 contains an example of a

[19]Historian Christie Farnham argues that Latin appears more frequently in southern girls' schools than in northern institutions. See Farnham, *The Education of the Southern Belle,* 28–32. However, the sources examined for this study do not support Farnham's thesis. Newspaper advertisements published in North Carolina and Virginia reveal that relatively few girls' schools in these two southern states offered Latin. During the decade from 1810 to 1830, only seven (19 percent) of a sample of thirty-six North Carolina girls' schools included Latin in their advertised courses of study. . . .

FIGURE 11.1   Example of the results of internal criticism.

From "Science for Ladies, Classics for Gentlemen: A Comparative Analysis of Scientific Subjects in the Curricula of Boys' and Girls' Secondary Schools in the United States, 1794–1850," by K. Tolley, 1996, *History of Education Quarterly, 36,* p. 137. Copyright 1996. Reprinted by permission.

researcher's internal criticism. Here Tolley (1996) points out inconsistencies between her own findings and those of another researcher (see A8 for the complete report).

Historical researchers usually prefer to use more than one source as a check on data consistency. If they find only one pertinent source, researchers must decide whether to use it. Failure to use the source may weaken the project, but using a lone source may compromise the reliability of the results.

Data Collection Techniques

Historical researchers traditionally rely on systematic, careful notetaking as their primary method of data collection. However, the notes are more than just information. As part of data collection, researchers "discern how a particular author approaches, frames, and interprets the topic; the sources used by the author; and how the work being examined differs from others in regard to these matters" (Brundage, 1997, p. 453).

Notetaking is not a passive, mechanical process. Historians, like other qualitative researchers, should make notes of their own thoughts and reflections as they seek answers to their questions through study of the data sources. These insights are useful in the preparation of the narrative. It's especially important to keep track of thoughts about possible themes or major ideas, as well as notes about ideas that require further thought (Brundage, 1997).

Of course, researchers record particular data related to their topic, usually in paraphrase, along with precise references for the sources. Tracking references and putting them in the form required by the final report, as part of notetaking, is especially critical both for content accuracy and for time conservation.

Whether handwritten or word-processed, notes must be recorded in a form that permits them to be sorted. In the process of constructing a narrative, researchers classify notes several times to view their data from different perspectives. For example, researchers may sort their notes by date, topic, subtopic, or source. Barzun and Graff (1992) offer practical suggestions about these processes.

✷ Procedures for Analyses and Interpretations

Details of the procedures for analyses and interpretations are unique to individual researchers. However, all researchers typically develop a frame of reference for their project. Next, they reduce large quantities of verbal data, and sometimes numerical data, to themes and supporting details that answer their questions. As the final part of the analyses, researchers construct a narrative that contains their results and interpretations.

Development of a Frame of Reference

After study of their data, historical researchers develop a frame of reference for their project. This includes the perspective, from which they will prepare their narrative and the type of analysis they expect to make.

Point of View

Researchers usually consider their data from different perspectives and decide on one that provides the **point of view** for the development of their narrative. The particular point of view is what provides a narrative with its distinctive interpretation.

In a report on mental testing, Ackerman (1995) adopts as his point of view that 1940s and 1950s educators in the United States favored the use of mental tests because of their potential to expand educational opportunities for lower-class children. Ackerman's narrative describes the work of both proponents and critics of mental testing and carefully interprets their activities in terms of relevant social, political, and cultural forces.

Type of Analysis

Researchers also decide which of several types of analyses to use in the narrative. These analyses include descriptive narratives, interpretive analyses, and comparative analyses (McMillan & Schumacher, 1997).

A **descriptive narrative** reports a single historical educational event, such as the establishment of an institution or a biography. Smitherman (1999) describes the major activities of the Conference on College Composition and Communication (CCCC), which show the efforts of this group in assisting teachers and the public to value language diversity. With a long activist history, the CCCC advocates, for example, that all Americans become bi- or multi-lingual as preparation for citizenship in a global, multicultural society. This report synthesizes more than two decades of work by the CCCC.

An **interpretive analysis** describes a phenomenon and discusses it within the context of the period. Zimmerman's (1994) report, "The Dilemma of Miss Jolly: Scientific Temperance and Teacher Professionalism, 1882–1904" illustrates this type of analysis. During the late 1800s, parents pressed teachers to stifle Scientific Temperance Instruction, but Women's Christian Temperance Union members encouraged teachers to teach children the physiological effects of alcohol and other narcotics. Teachers were caught in a dilemma that Zimmerman interprets within the educational, social, and cultural contexts of the period.

A **comparative analysis** compares one phenomenon with other phenomena within the same or earlier time frames by highlighting the contexts. In "A Historical Comparison of Public Singing by American Men and Women," Gates (1989) compares public singing activities of men and women in early eighteenth century Boston with similar activities in the 1980s. His analyses show that men dominated in public singing in the earlier period, so much so that women and children had to be actively recruited to music literacy for religious reasons. Both men and women participated in public singing until the 1930s.

By the 1980s, however, men's participation had declined and women predominated in public singing. Because women's participation also showed decline, Gates expresses concern that public singing by either group could die by the turn of the century. (To date, public singing by both genders continues.) In his comparison, Gates shows that changes in public singing participation accompany shifts in social values.

Data Reduction

Historians' methods of data reduction are similar in many ways to the strategies used by other qualitative researchers. They must reduce large volumes of verbal data to many fewer words as answers to their questions. In some cases, historians must also analyze quantitative data.

Data Analyses

Historians subject their notes to intensive scrutiny. They sort and study their notes by topics, dates, or other classification methods as they search for themes. Once the themes emerge, they locate the supporting details. As a validity check, researchers must ensure that there are sufficient data to formulate and support the themes.

In addition to large amounts of verbal data, researchers sometimes gather numerical data. Analyses, which usually involve relatively simple descriptive statistics, complement the qualitative evidence presented in a historical project (Floud, 1979).

To illustrate, Tolley (1996) compiles data from newspaper advertisements about school science curricula in the 1800s. Based on the compiled data, she calculates the percentages of girls' and boys' schools that advertised or offered natural philosophy, astronomy, chemistry, botany, mineralogy, and natural history and then placed these percentages in tables. For the institutions within this sample, girls' schools differ from boys' schools in their advertisements and offerings of science curricula (in A8, see Tables 2–4). These quantitative data analyses support Tolley's qualitative evidence about the same points.

Quantitative data analyses are not limited to frequencies and percentages. Analyses can and do use any of the descriptive statistics, such as measures of central tendency and correlation procedures.

Results and Interpretations

The researchers answer their questions with facts, inferences, and generalizations based on primary source data. They interpret or explain these results in terms of relevant social, cultural, or educational contexts. As a rule, historians weave their results and interpretations around defined themes within the narrative.

For example, Ackerman (1995) explores mental testing in the 1940s and 1950s, when educators thought "that mental tests could further the schooling of lower-class children" (p. 280). His narrative develops around two main themes: the use of mental testing could assist in relieving the harmful effects of racial, ethnic, and class-based discrimination, and higher education enrollments could be expanded by using ability and aptitude tests to identify persons who could benefit from college education.

One result says, "the commissioners (members of President Truman's Commission on Higher Education) endorsed a vast expansion of higher education" (Ackerman, 1995, p. 284). Ackerman interprets this result by explaining that the commissioners saw the need for a much larger percentage of people to receive postsecondary education to "meet the requirements of international citizenship and a postindustrial economy" (Ackerman, 1995, p. 284). These are only two examples of many results and interpretations in this report.

Construction of the Narrative

Historians present their results and interpretations within narratives that evolve through several drafts (Barzun & Graff, 1992; Gottschalk, 1969). Gottschalk's (1969) discussion is the basis for most of the information in this section. Historians usually begin with tentative plans about the beginning, middle, and end of the report, but may change their plans during the creation of the first draft.

The historians' objective for the first draft is to include everything relevant to the problem, including arguments with other authors on the topic. This draft is constructed with notes and sources close at hand because accuracy is a major concern. Because the intent of the initial draft is to include all pertinent content, it may resemble "a lifeless juxtaposition of notes" (Gottschalk, 1969, p. 187) with little or no literary polish. Some historians omit references in the first draft.

The content of this draft furnishes answers in the form of results and interpretations to the researchers' questions. Although not required, historians typically arrange events chronologically and use themes as the framework for a narrative that tells their story.

After checking the first draft for errors in content inclusiveness, historians next work on the logical structure of the narrative. The first major task is to delete passages and phrases that contribute little or no meaning to the narrative. The second task is to reorder, as needed, the passages that survive deletion. Also in this second draft, history writers add missing information and correct content or grammar mistakes. References not already included are inserted in the second draft.

Historians typically prepare a third, and sometimes a fourth, draft to clarify and polish the narrative. Gottschalk (1969) suggests that the final draft should contain "only the simplest, most vigorous, least expendable words—. . . that have survived your (the historian's) deliberate efforts since the first draft to cut away, simplify, clarify, polish, and make precise" (p. 201). Allowing time to elapse between creation of the drafts usually enables researchers to spot things that need correction.

The narrative typically culminates in a short section that contains a summary, the project's conclusion, and recommendations. These elements are discussed in Chapter 12.

⚔ Introduction and Narrative Sections in Historical Research Reports

As the previous sections show, a major task of a historical investigation is the preparation of a narrative that details and interprets the findings. Because of their length, historical research reports look different from those that use other methods. This section describes the introduction and narrative sections of historical reports, provides criteria for the evaluation of selected procedures and results, and shows how to apply these criteria.

Description

Reports of historical research typically do *not* reflect the usual report sections (e.g., method, results). Instead, reports contain a title, a brief introduction, a relatively long narrative, and a short final section. In some journals, asterisks subdivide report sections. Reports in other journals are subdivided with section names that refer to content divisions rather than to method, results, and discussion.

Titles and introductions serve their usual functions, with some exceptions. Along with problem statements, titles help you to identify historical reports as descriptive narratives, interpretive analyses, or comparative analyses. Recognizing the type of report can assist you in understanding its purpose.

Unlike reports using other methods, the introduction of a historical project does not contain a lengthy literature review because the review is incorporated within the narrative. The introduction contains the problem or research question, the need for the study, and the historian's point of view.

The main part of a historical report is the narrative, which tells the historians' story. This section contains facts and interpretations carefully arranged to explicate the themes that result from study of the data. References to data sources abound in this section and may be shown as on-page footnotes or notes at the end of the report. Wherever the references are located, read them carefully because they provide much of the researchers' criticisms of data sources.

Criteria for Evaluation

You should be aware of the following criteria, based on information presented in this chapter, as you read historical research reports:

1. The researchers' point of view should be clear within the narrative.

    The researchers' point of view serves as the organizing focus for the narrative. Therefore, presentation of this information early in the report enables you to understand the narrative.

2. Primary sources should be the main data sources for answering the researchers' questions. Evidence of researcher critiques of data sources should be present in the report. Both are necessary to provide valid data.

    Because primary sources are firsthand accounts, they are preferred over secondary sources as the bases for answering historical research questions. Researchers should identify references clearly so that readers can be aware of primary sources. The results of researchers' criticisms of data sources should be communicated either in footnotes or text.

3. Evidence of data consistency should be presented.

    The chief method of showing consistency is to gather similar data from several sources. Historical researchers often list more than one reference for ideas included in their narrative.

4. Questions should be answered clearly within the narrative. These results should be interpreted carefully.

    Historians report their results and interpretations as verbal information that you must track through the length of the narrative. The use of themes as organizing threads should be used to assist the tracking processes. In addition, historians should include only data pertinent to the problem and use precise language to communicate results and interpretations.

Application of Criteria

To illustrate the use of these criteria, this section provides an evaluation of Tolley's (1996) report, Science for Ladies, Classics for Gentlemen: A Comparative Analysis of Scientific Subjects in the Curricula of Boys' and Girls' Secondary Schools in the United States, 1794–1850. Read Exercise 11.2 to see the questions to which this review provides answers. Refer to these questions and A8 as you read this section.

Science for Ladies, Classics for Gentlemen

This study compares the curricula of boys' and girls' secondary schools in the first half of the nineteenth century in terms of their emphases in science. Tolley undertook this project to show that current thinking that science education originated in the mid 1800s is incorrect. She takes the position that opportunities for girls were available much earlier.

Many cited sources appear to be secondary sources, but this report also uses several primary data sources. See, for example, footnote 8 references to Ludlow and Comstock and footnote 11 references to the *Columbian Centinel* and the *Richmond Enquirer*. The researcher subjects both primary and secondary data sources to extensive criticisms, perhaps because several sources are secondary. In several instances (e.g., footnotes 18 and 39), Tolley quotes facts from firsthand accounts to increase the credibility of the secondary sources.

Footnote 3 is one of several that contains source criticisms. The text also contains criticisms in comments such as, "Although advertisements are unreliable as a means of evaluating either the content or method of the actual instruction delivered in educational institutions, as marketing tools, these sources illuminate . . ." (Tolley, 1996, p. 134).

In most footnotes, Tolley cites more than one source. The multiple sources of information suggest that the data are reliable.

Tolley first analyzes the content of girls' and boys' school curricula in the late 1700s, then repeats the analyses for the early 1800s. The results show that while boys studied classics, girls studied the sciences, based on evidence in courses of study and results of examinations. Next, Tolley explains why the curricula were different by describing six major societal cultural forces that compelled the differences.

The results and interpretations provide a well-documented answer to the question. There is no doubt that middle- and upper class girls' schools afforded ample opportunities for science study long before the mid 1850s.

EXERCISE 11.2

This exercise allows you to see how well you can evaluate the procedures for the production of valid and reliable results in a historical study.

Scan the following report:

A9 Reconsidering the Power of the Superintendent in the Progressive Period

Then read the introduction and narrative sections carefully. Answer these questions:

1. Identify the phenomenon or topic of this investigation. What reason do the researchers give for undertaking this project? Describe the point of view assumed by the researchers.

2. To estimate the validity of data provided by the procedures, answer the following questions:
   Are primary sources the main data sources?
   Do the researchers communicate the results of their critiques of data sources? Explain.

3. To estimate the reliability of data provided by the procedures, answer the following questions:
   Do the researchers usually indicate more than one reference as a check on data consistency? If not, do they offer other indicators of data consistency?

4. Do the results clearly answer the research question(s)? Are the results clearly interpreted? Explain.

Summary

Research into the past depends on researchers' abilities to find records of events, people, and organizations. Most records are documents, but oral histories and artifacts are also useful in helping historians to understand phenomena. Eyewitness accounts, or primary sources, are preferred over second-hand accounts as sources of data for historical research because the former contains only one author's interpretations.

In undertaking historical research, investigators develop a problem for study, then locate sources such as libraries, archives, or museums that furnish data for its solution. After finding the sources, historians subject them to intense scrutiny to check their authenticity and credibility. In large measure, the thoroughness of these criticisms determines the validity of the research.

A major task of historians is to prepare a narrative about the phenomenon. Using carefully made notes from the data sources, history writers decide on a point of view from which to tell their story. Thereafter, the processes require weaving together the results and interpretations into a coherent presentation. Preparation of the narrative usually requires several drafts.

Because the objective of this method is development of a narrative, these reports do not usually contain the familiar research sections. Published reports of historical research are typically lengthy and well referenced. Readers of these reports should note the extent to which researchers use primary sources, communicate criticisms of their data sources, and craft their narrative. The care with which the researchers complete these tasks affects the quality of the results and interpretations.

Questions for Discussion

1. Genz (1993) refers to an old European folk saying: "No one is lost until they do not know where they have been." Comment on the possible connections among this statement, historical research in education, and current educational reform efforts.
2. Explain how the systematic processes described in Figure 1.1 relate to the major steps in historical research.
3. Since the Public Broadcasting System showed Ken Burns' film, *The Civil War,* in 1989, individuals have commented that viewing this film improved their understanding of that war. Explain how the artifacts used in this film, or in another documentary, help historians tell a story.
4. Should readers expect to find similar information in two or more interpretive analyses on the same topic? Explain.

Integration of Research Problems, Methods, and Outcomes

As the title indicates, research problems and methods must be integrated to obtain the valid and reliable outcomes required by the definition of educational research used in this text. Outcomes include the interpretations of results that qualitative and historical researchers make in conjunction with their data analyses, discussed in Chapters 10 and 11.

In quantitative projects, however, researchers gather and analyze their data to obtain results prior to making any interpretations. Interpretations of results for *quantitative* studies are discussed in Chapter 12.

In both types of inquiry, researchers use their results and interpretations to reach a conclusion and form recommendations, two additional types of research outcomes discussed in Chapter 12. The conclusion, of course, provides a solution to the research problem, and recommendations are suggestions for uses of the research outcomes.

For example, the recommendation from a project can furnish an idea for a new research problem and start a new cycle. Chapter 13 describes the nonlinear, messy processes for creating a research problem and a literature review. You are encouraged to choose a variable or phenomenon of your interest and apply the processes. Undertaking this project can help you to integrate all your research consumer abilities.

Chapter 14 outlines the processes for creating a research proposal. This chapter discusses how to begin the plans for the investigation of the problem that you described in Chapter 13. This proposal may lack details, especially if the problem calls for qualitative or historical methods, because these methods are less clearly defined than are those for quantitative projects. However, the preparation of this proposal enables you to see the complexity of planning procedures that must work together.

Discussions of Results

❖ **Outcomes of Research Projects**

❖ **Interpretations of Results in Quantitative Reports**

   Problem Definition and Literature Review

   Design Components

❖ **Conclusions**

❖ **Recommendations**

❖ **Discussion and Conclusion Sections of Research Reports**

   Descriptions

   Criteria for Evaluation

   Application of Criteria

❖ **Abstract Sections of Research Reports**

Two final systematic research processes, the interpretation of data and the solution to the problem based on data analyses, are the emphases of this chapter. Quantitative researchers interpret their results, draw conclusions, and make recommendations as part of these processes. However, qualitative researchers interpret results as part of analysis, as indicated in Chapters 10 and 11. The conclusions and recommendations for qualitative and historical reports are discussed here.

As described in Chapter 1, research can improve education only if outcomes are valid and reliable. That is, inaccurate or inconsistent outcomes do little to advance the solutions to educational problems. Consequently, this chapter discusses the meanings of valid and reliable outcomes as end products of research processes, as well as the interrelationships among the outcomes.

Goal

To enable you to:

- evaluate the outcomes of selected research reports as valid and reliable solutions to research problems.

⚒ Outcomes of Research Projects

Upon completion of data analyses, researchers interpret their results, draw conclusions, and offer recommendations based on their project. Typically they also generate one or more reports that share information about their project. Investigators are required to prepare reports for their funding agencies and may make additional reports to other audiences as well.

In generating these contributions, researchers are expected to observe the ethical considerations required by the Ethical Standards of the American Educational Research Association (1992). These standards caution researchers to "communicate their findings and the practical significance of their research in clear, straightforward, and appropriate language to relevant research populations, institutional representatives, and other stakeholders" (Ethical Standards, 1992, p. 24).

All reports should contain valid and reliable outcomes, which are obtained when researchers carefully and thoughtfully interpret results obtained from valid and reliable data analyses. Figure 12.1 displays the relationships among major research processes.

Recall that the research problem located within the literature review is the basis for researchers' choices of procedures. Using these procedures produces results that are processed further through interpretation. Whereas some interpretations provide useful information in and of themselves, other interpretations lead to the project conclusion, recommendations, or both. Each broad class of research outcomes is described in this chapter.

⚒ Interpretations of Results in Quantitative Reports

Researchers' **interpretations** encompass explanations of the results related to the problem as well as to design procedures (i.e., participants, instrument or strategy choices, procedures for data collection and handling, treatments in experiments, and data analyses) used in its solution. Researchers are obliged to explain any effects of departures from their planned procedures. For example, unforeseen changes within research settings or deviations from planned data analysis procedures can lead to unexpected results.

Prior to making interpretations, researchers should review the consistency between (among) procedures in the project. First, the research

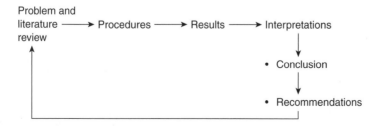

FIGURE 12.1   Relationship among research processes.

method should be appropriate for answering the researchers' question. In addition, the participant selection and assignment procedures should be consistent with instrumentation and all should be consistent with data collection, handling, and analysis. In whatever interpretations they make, researchers should maintain consistency among the procedures used in generating results. The degree to which this consistency exists is a measure of the reliability of research.

Researchers are expected to describe their procedures clearly. The extent to which outside researchers could use similar procedures with similar participants and obtain similar results is an indicator of the reliability of research outcomes.

Problem Definition and Literature Review

Recall that researchers begin their projects with an idea they wish to investigate, then they review the related literature to further define the problem. In their report introductions, researchers build a case for doing their own project based on deficits reflected in the literature about the problem. On completion of the project, researchers typically relate their findings to those in the studies mentioned in their literature review. Comparisons between results from the current study and those of other studies in the field are interpretations commonly found in quantitative studies.

To illustrate, in their discussion section, Holmes and Keffer (1995) use as a benchmark for judging the results of their study, the outcome of Becker's project that measured *Scholastic Aptitude Test* scores (see the Discussion section in A4). In addition, Holmes and Keffer reprise major arguments from their literature review concerned with design flaws, to discuss the contribution their study makes to ways of increasing *SAT* scores among high school students. This section of their Discussion section answers the inferred justification for their study, which is to provide additional research for a reliable solution to a problem.

Wentzel (1997) studies the role of perceived caring by teachers on middle school students' motivation. As her project justification, Wentzel reports that the most basic questions about this topic have not been researched. The results of Wentzel's study not only show that caring teachers influence students' motivation, but also reveal information about students' perceptions of caring.

These examples illustrate how researchers explain their results after they have reflected on them, especially as the results relate to their literature reviews. Individual researchers use their own unique interpretive processes to arrive at the statements reported in discussion sections.

Design Components

On completion of a project, researchers often reflect on their design and ask how their choices of procedures relate to results. To illustrate, Holmes and Keffer (1995) maintain that use of the Solomon four-group research design boosts the credibility of their results. Because this design is a true experiment, the results are more credible than they might be from other designs. The researchers wisely point out, however, that because participants were volunteers, the results cannot be generalized to a known population.

Wentzel (1997) clearly recognizes the limits of descriptive methods in her interpretations. She indicates that her work shows the existence of the relationships among variables, but that "the processes that underlie significant relations between perceptions of caring teachers and students' motivation are not well understood" (p. 417). She acknowledges that until experimental interventions can show cause-and-effect relations, results from descriptive research must be used cautiously.

In a separate interpretation, Wentzel (1997) acknowledges that her study contributes to the knowledge suggesting that students' perceptions of supportive, caring relationships with teachers are important regardless of students' race or family background. However, a different research effort found results similar to Wentzel's findings for white, middle class children, but not for Hispanic and African American youth. Wentzel interprets this difference as a suggestion for additional research with minority populations.

Illustrations such as these show how researchers interpret their results. Investigators draw on the literature or on any of the design procedures to explain and interpret their results.

⚔ Conclusions

Conclusions describe the researchers' solutions to research problems. In quantitative inquiries, the conclusion tells whether the research hypothesis was supported or how well a theory or part of a theory stood the test of an investigation. In qualitative inquiries, the conclusion answers the research questions, which in some cases emerge as hypotheses that are grounded in the results. Of course, researchers typically expect to continue study of these hypotheses.

In the process of drawing conclusions, researchers look for interpretations of results that converge and point toward the same outcome. In experiments, for example, researchers systematically evaluate reasons for changes in the dependent variable, other than those made by the independent variable. They attempt to rule out alternative explanations, leaving only the independent variable(s) as likely reasons for observed changes.

For example, Holmes and Keffer (1995) seek to find whether a short-term, computerized program of study of Latin terms could positively affect *Scholastic Aptitude Testing (SAT)* verbal scores. Their report (see A4) does not describe directly how the researchers ruled out alternative explanations. However, several alternative explanations were ruled out when the researchers decided to use the Solomon four-group design. They can conclude with some confidence that treatment had a positive effect. Groups of high school students who had this treatment earned higher *SAT* scores—40 points on average—than groups without the treatment.

In descriptive and qualitative studies, of course, the process of drawing conclusions is different because no manipulations are involved. Researchers must note how data align themselves and use these alignments to develop conclusions. Wentzel (1997) aligns her data through regression analyses. She notes that the variable of teacher caring contributes most to the regression equation and enters this variable following the motivation and beliefs variables. The pattern of the results is the same for prosocial goal pursuit, responsibility goal pursuit, and academic effort. This convergence in the data, no doubt, helps her to reach a conclusion.

Qualitative researchers begin work on drawing conclusions from the beginning of data analysis through "noting regularities, patterns, explanations, possible configurations, causal flows, and propositions" (Miles & Huberman, 1994, p. 11). Although vague at the beginning, conclusions become clearer and grounded as analysis proceeds. In addition, conclusions are verified as the analysis processes continue. Verification may involve activities such as researchers' revisits to research settings to check data, conversations with colleagues about outcomes, or even attempts to replicate a result in another data set (Miles & Huberman, 1994). All these activities, of course, contribute to valid project outcomes.

Once researchers form and verify a conclusion, it should be placed in perspective. In projects using random samples of participants, researchers may be able to generalize outcomes to the population from which samples were drawn, applicable in some quantitative inquiries. However, in many quantitative and almost all qualitative inquiries, participants do not represent a particular population. Therefore, these conclusions should not be generalized. Taking these precautions also contributes to the validity of research outcomes.

❧ Recommendations

Recommendations constitute a third form of research outcome, offered when researchers find that results warrant them. To be useful, recommendations must be focused; blanket recommendations calling for additional research are not helpful. Recommendations grow out of interpretations based on convergent results.

Recommendations to researchers are suggestions that might, if used in research, produce favorable results or add to the body of knowledge about the topic. Suggestions include the design of projects using qualitative rather than quantitative inquiry (or vice versa), selection of participants from populations other than those in the project, alterations in treatment, or alternative instruments for data collection.

Wentzel (1997) suggests several recommendations to researchers. She indicates that future research identify "additional student characteristics that predispose students to perceive teachers as caring or uncaring" (p. 417). She issues a general recommendation "for continued work. . .., especially with respect to ways in which students come to understand and appreciate what teachers do" (p. 418).

Recommendations to practitioners provide suggestions to teachers, administrators, and other school personnel about potentially beneficial alterations in school practice, based on the outcomes of research projects. Typically these recommendations emerge in studies that use school settings. Examples include recommendations about time schedules, instructional procedures, ways of handling student behavior problems, and others.

Holmes and Keffer (1995) found that computerized methods improved the English skills of students across a range of grade levels by increasing their knowledge of Latin and Greek root words. They suggest that because video games motivate students, practitioners might use them to improve students' verbal skills (see A4, Discussion section).

In her discussion of error correction in spelling, Gettinger (1993) found that participants who used the student-controlled activities outperformed participants in the comparison group. Based on this result and other research, Gettinger recommends the use of student-controlled interventions in academic areas other than spelling (see A1, Discussion section).

Read in the context of their respective reports, both these recommendations are clearly related to the results and their interpretations. Were practitioners to heed such recommendations, certain school problems could be solved.

E X E R C I S E   1 2 . 1

The ability to distinguish among interpretations, conclusions, and recommendations is a prerequisite to evaluating these outcomes. This exercise provides a self-assessment of this ability.

Study the complete report, but focus on the discussion and conclusion sections:

A6 The Impact of Personal, Professional and Organizational Characteristics on Administrator Burnout

Decide whether the quoted statements are interpretations, conclusions, or recommendations. Explain.

1. "It has been argued by others that unless burnout is tested as a multidimensional construct, little progress will be made in determining its linkages to other variables. . . This assertion was confirmed by the correlation analysis. . ." (p. 154).

2. "Administrator preparation programmes and on-the-job training should emphasize basic administrative survival skills such as effective time management, principled negotiation and mediation training, and programmes to develop self-awareness and understanding of the emotional intensity of administration" (p. 155).

3. "Only the burnout dimension of emotional exhaustion was explained by a significant per cent of variance, most of which related to task-based stress" (p. 157).

4. "Therefore, different strategies must be taken for separate dimensions of burnout in order to pave a more manageable road currently travelled by educational administrators" (p. 157).

✖ Discussion and Conclusion Sections of Research Reports

This section describes discussion and conclusion sections of research reports and supplies criteria for the evaluation of these sections. The criteria are applied to quantitative, qualitative, and historical reports.

Descriptions

In quantitative reports, discussion sections may stand alone or be combined with results or findings sections as the final part of the report text. The form of discussion sections is decidedly less prescribed than that of other report sections. Regardless of form, these sections typically contain the project conclusion, interpretations of the results, and recommendations.

A conclusion is expected, but beyond that, researchers exercise professional latitude in the content selected for discussion sections. For example, some discussion sections contain extensive interpretations, but others are limited. Some reports have recommendations, but others do not. These discrepancies sometimes result from space requirements that limit the length of discussion sections. In other reports, researchers simply make fewer interpretations and recommendations.

In qualitative and historical studies, the final section is often called conclusion(s). The content of these sections varies. Some reports offer a short summary of the findings, but others provide interpretations. Generally, a conclusion is stated clearly. If recommendations are included, these are part of the final section.

Criteria for Evaluation

The criteria that follow are based on information presented in this chapter and draw on earlier chapters as well.

Interpretations in Quantitative Studies

1. Important results should be explained. In particular, researchers should indicate whether their project meets its stated justification.

The researchers' interpretations should help readers understand the results of the project. Although some readers are capable of making their own interpretations, all readers can benefit from the researchers' views of the processes as they unravel the meaning of the research results. Because researchers have firsthand knowledge of the procedures, they may view results differently than do readers who were not part of the process.

2. The interpretations of results should be consistent with other research procedures.

Researchers' explanations of results must be consistent with data collection and analysis procedures to ensure research reliability. Consistency builds confidence in research outcomes.

Conclusions and Recommendations in All Projects

3. The conclusion should accurately represent the results.

Researchers should devise possible conclusions, based on patterns and convergences within the results. Before stating them as final, the researchers should attempt to verify these statements as the best answers to their questions. These actions increase the validity of the outcomes.

4. The conclusion should state a clear solution to the researchers' problem in terms of the project variables or phenomena. The conclusion should be limited appropriately.

The conclusion should be stated in terms of the project variables or phenomena and it should be limited to the group or population for whom it is appropriate as a matter of research validity.

5. Project results should support recommendations, if these are made.

Recommendations to researchers or practitioners must be based on the results. Moreover, recommendations should be sufficiently specific to allow others to act on them.

Application of Criteria

These criteria are applied to the final sections of three research reports. See Exercise 12.2 for the questions on which the critiques are based. Refer to these questions and the research reports as you read this section.

Effects of Error Correction on Third Graders' Spelling

Gettinger's (1993) interpretations of results cover several major points. Recall that this study was undertaken to see if error correction might benefit students in regular classrooms as it had been shown to benefit learning-disabled children. As an interpretation, the researcher shows the usefulness of the intervention in regular classrooms, and thereby fulfills the project's justification.

Gettinger discusses two aspects of the error correction treatment that she believes are related to the positive outcome. She attributes success to the fact that experimental students were largely in control of their treatment; they implemented and monitored the procedure with little teacher involvement. A second reason for success is believed to be that children tested each other on spelling words, a cooperative learning technique. In both these explanations, Gettinger relates her study findings to research by others.

Gettinger also discusses uses of the trials-to-criterion data and the orthographic quality ratings to provide diagnostic and remedial information. She ties the findings of her project to those of other researchers in the problem area, which advances knowledge of the effects of error correction.

Within this project, data collection, analysis, and interpretations appear to be consistent, and the procedures for gathering and handling data seem to have been carefully controlled to minimize error variance. The descriptive statistical data analyses are necessary and helpful, but the inferential statistical analyses seem superfluous. Interpretations are clear and helpful in understanding the results.

Recall that this project (A1) tested the effects of an error-correction intervention against two comparison interventions on third grade children's spelling accuracy. The first sentence in the Discussion section states clearly that spelling test performance was better in the classroom where students used error correction than it was in either of the two comparison classrooms.

This conclusion appears to be warranted based on the results of the three spelling units—baseline, intervention, and generalization. Students in the three classrooms had comparable performance before intervention, but following intervention and generalization, the experimental group outperformed both comparison groups on the weekly tests. Gettinger (1993) does not generalize findings from this study to other settings, a wise decision because the population is not identified clearly.

Gettinger offers at least one recommendation to classroom teachers that seems logical and appropriate, based on the outcomes of this project. She says:

> The results indicate that students may benefit from having their Monday-to-Friday study time, including spontaneous writing, more structured to achieve maximum performance in spelling (p. 45).

What Is Classroom Discussion? A Look at Teachers' Conceptions

Larson and Parker's (1996) report (A2) is intended to build the first layer of an explanatory theory of teachers' conceptions of discussion. The Findings section contains the five conceptions as the actual conclusions to this study. In the Conclusion, however, the authors point out that "(f)ive conceptions were developed, along with three influences" (p. 126). This conclusion is warranted and is duly limited to the first layer of an explanatory theory.

Larson and Parker recommend that researchers produce companion studies in other subject areas and settings on the topic of classroom discussion. They comment on their own intention to carry the research further in alternate settings. Both recommendations are appropriate, especially because the researchers stated at the outset that they were beginning development of a theory.

Science for Ladies, Classics for Gentlemen

Tolley's (1996) report (A8) is designed to compare science curricula in boys' and girls' schools in the first half of the nineteenth century. The conclusion for this study says "that increasingly toward the middle decades of the nineteenth century, a young woman's education included the study of the sciences" (Tolley, 1996, p. 153). This clearly stated conclusion is warranted based on the evidence gathered from newspaper advertisements, textbooks from the era, and published accounts of examination results.

The conclusion, as cited at the end of the report, is not limited. However, a statement at the beginning of the report makes clear that the schools in question are American schools for middle and upper class girls and comparable institutions for boys. Read in the context of the study, the conclusion is limited. This study contains no recommendations.

E X E R C I S E   1 2 . 2

This exercise provides a self-assessment of your ability to evaluate the outcomes of qualitative and quantitative projects in terms of their validity and reliability. Study the complete report, including discussion and conclusion sections:

A3 A Phenomenological Study with Youth Gang Members: Results and Implications for School Counselors

A5 Preservice and Inservice Secondary Teachers' Orientations Toward Content Area Reading

A9 Reconsidering the Power of the Superintendent in the Progressive Period

For *quantitative* reports, answer these questions about interpretations:

1. Discuss the extent to which quantitative researchers interpret important project results. In particular, comment on interpretations about fulfillment of the project's justification.

2. Comment on the degree of consistency among data collection, analysis, and interpretation procedures.

For *all* reports, answer these questions about the conclusion and recommendations:

3. Identify the conclusion of the study. Is it warranted based on the results of the study?

4. Does the conclusion state a clear solution to the researchers' problem in terms of the project variables or phenomena? Is the conclusion appropriately limited? Explain.

5. Do the researchers offer recommendations? To whom are they directed? Cite a recommendation and comment on whether it is based on the project results.

❖ Abstract Sections of Research Reports

Research reports frequently contain abstracts, usually located immediately following report titles. Although they are frequently limited to 200 words, well-prepared abstracts provide brief information about the purpose, the procedures, the results, and the conclusion as essential information about the project. In some reports, abstracts are complete and in others, information may be missing.

Of the five reports in Appendix A with abstracts, most contain all the essential information. However, Holmes and Keffer (1995) provide only the problem and procedures, but not results or conclusions (see A4). Within the remaining four reports, notice that the authors report their conclusions in different ways. Whereas Gettinger's (1993) and Wentzel's (1997) conclusion statements in A5 and A9, respectively, are forthright, those of Konopak, Readence, and Wilson (A5) and Thomas and Moran (A9) are less clear.

Abstracts provide overviews or advance organizers for reading the reports. By reading abstracts, you can probably decide whether reading the complete report is worthwhile. This is an efficient use of time, especially whenever you work on a literature review.

Summary

At the culmination of research projects, quantitative investigators mull over their results. They interpret their results in terms of the problem and the procedures and, based on their interpretations, typically form a conclusion. As one interpretation, researchers provide an indication of whether their study fulfills its stated justification.

Qualitative researchers typically work on conclusion making and verification throughout the data analysis processes. These researchers look for patterns and convergences in findings as the basis for drawing conclusions. In many studies, researchers of both inquiry modes also offer recommendations to practitioners or to other investigators if their project outcomes merit them.

Conclusions, interpretations, and recommendations are usually found in discussion sections of quantitative research reports. Conclusions and recommendations may be located in the conclusion section of qualitative studies, and the form of this section is not standardized. Criteria for evaluation of discussion and conclusion sections are devised and applied to three research reports.

Questions for Discussion

1. Explain how conclusions differ from findings or results, and from interpretations.
2. Explain how conclusions relate to problem statements, to hypotheses in quantitative studies, and to hypotheses in qualitative studies.
3. What is the purpose of interpreting findings in terms of the literature? Explain.
4. Professors Johns and Crim carried out an experiment, including data analyses, using plans they made at the outset. They made additional results when their planned data analyses did not turn out as expected. Should the second set of analyses be included in the results section along with the planned analyses, placed in the discussion section, or does it matter? Explain.
5. Describe possible reasons why some research reports contain no recommendations.

Creation of Research Problems and Literature Reviews

❖ **Initiation of a Research Project**

Sources of Research Problems

Brief Literature Survey

❖ **Preparation of an Initial Problem Statement**

Selection Criteria

Wording Strategies

❖ **Execution of the Literature Search**

Databases for the Search

Scope of the Search

Search Strategies

Use of Search Results

❖ **Preparation of an Initial Draft of the Literature Review**

Selection of the Justification

Support of the Justification

Development of the References List

❖ **Reconsideration and Revision of the Problem Statement**

Revision of the Literature Review and References List

Content Revisions

Form Revisions

This chapter describes the recursive subtasks associated with the creation of research problems and literature reviews. The literature review informs the formulation of the problem and vice versa; neither of these can be considered complete until both are finished.

A sequence, suggested for the completion of these subtasks, is portrayed in Figure 13.1. It begins with consideration of potential sources of research problems and moves by stages through the revision of the literature review. You may use this sequence or develop one of your own, but be sure to include all the subtasks in any sequence that you choose.

This chapter extends and elaborates on the topics of Chapter 3, which describes research problems and literature reviews. You will also find that Chapters 4 through 12 are useful, whether you have completed their study or if you return to read them. These chapters help you read critically the research literature required for creating a literature review.

Goals

To enable you to:

- develop a problem statement for a research project of your choice; and
- prepare a literature review related to this problem.

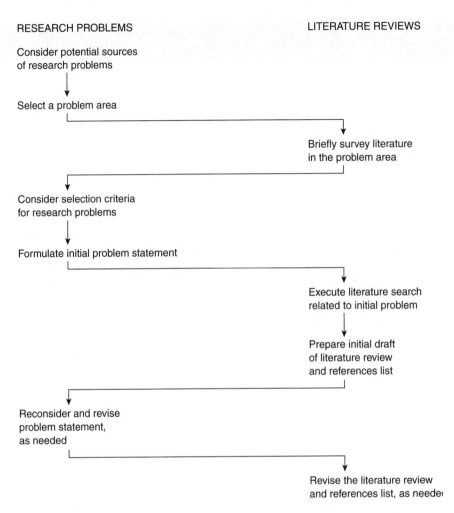

FIGURE 13.1   Suggested sequence of subtasks for the creation of research problems and literature reviews.

⚡ Initiation of a Research Project

Research problems do not necessarily begin as the well-stated forms of those included in research reports. Initial problem statements may consist of little more than vague ideas about variables or phenomena. Researchers, especially beginners, usually identify a problem *area* of interest, then read literature in this area before formally stating their problem.

Sources of Research Problems

Research problems typically emerge from the experiences of educational practitioners or researchers, from educational literature, or from a combination of these. These sources can suggest broad areas of interest in which you design a research problem.

Experiences

Your own experiences as a practitioner may furnish several problem areas. Have you or your colleagues made comments similar to these?

> "I just don't understand why students can't remember what they've been taught." (teachers)
>
> "Teachers X and Y aren't teaching as well this year as they did in the past. I would like for them to improve their teaching." (administrators)
>
> "Students seem to have so many problems these days. I wonder why so many referrals mention 'acting out behaviors.'" (counselors)

These statements probably represent the state of mind of educators at the moment they are making them. However, if the same individuals repeat these remarks, they probably would like to have answers. Statements such as these suggest problem areas for research.

Persistent questions about your own job responsibilities may provide concerns from which your research problem can come. This is a good source because you are probably willing to spend long hours working on a problem for which you want an answer. If you must devise a problem for a research project, think about your experiences. Identify a few concerns that persist day after day as you carry out your position responsibilities.

If you anticipate pursuing a qualitative inquiry, think about a particular setting. Which interactions, communications, or activities are of high interest to you? What do you want to learn about these phenomena? Experiences are one readily available source of research problems.

Educational Literature

As described in Chapter 12, the discussion sections of research reports offer suggestions for additional research. For example, Larson and Parker (1996) investigated conceptions of classroom discussion as used by high school social studies teachers. In the final section of their report, they say that "[c]ompanion studies are needed, of course, in other subject areas and settings" (p. 126) (see A2, Conclusion section). Researchers interested in classroom discussions may accept this challenge to create additional investigations about teachers' conceptions of classroom discussion.

Wentzel (1997) studied the role of perceived pedagogical caring on student motivation in middle school. In the discussion section, she calls for focused investigations about the continuity of caregiving across home and school contexts with respect to the internalization of students' goals and values. She also suggests need for research on students' characteristics that predispose them to perceive teachers as caring or uncaring (see A7, Discussion section). Both suggestions could furnish research problems.

Literature reviews published in journals, yearbooks of professional societies, and handbooks are also good sources of research problems. For example, the seventh volume in a series, *Advances in Research on Teaching*, was published in 1998. This volume, subtitled *Expectations in the Classroom,* contains eight papers plus an introduction and a review of the papers. The authors not only review the research in a subarea of expectations theory, but also discuss results of their own research. In each paper, the researchers suggest additional areas in which research is needed.

To illustrate, Jussim, Smith, Madon, and Palumbo (1998) review the research on teacher expectations and cite more than 150 references. In a subsection entitled "Un(der)-explored Process Issues," the authors discuss the power of setting high goals. They say:

> . . . whether high expectations often lead teachers to explicitly set higher goals for students is not known. But even if teachers do not set explicit goals for individual students, they may sometimes explicitly convey high expectations—which may have an effect much like setting high goals. However, both the extent to which teachers do this, and its effect on students, are currently unknown. (p. 37)

In this statement are at least two major research questions that researchers may address.

Brief Literature Survey

Once you have identified a problem area, read the abstract and scan a published literature review or two in that problem area. At the outset, these reviews may appear to be overwhelming. Most are long, are packed with references, and are written at a fairly abstract level. Despite these characteristics, study of their major points can help you understand the problem area. That's why it's important to scan these reviews before reading them in detail. To prepare a literature review for your project requires that you know the boundaries of the problem domain about which you are inquiring.

In the previous section, an example mentions that teachers sometimes wonder aloud why their students don't remember what they were taught. Semb and Ellis (1994) published a literature review entitled, "Knowledge Taught in Schools: What is Remembered?" in which they discuss six variables that affect long-term retention. These variables include the content and tasks to be learned, the retention interval, conditions of retrieval, degree of original learning, instructional strategies, and individual differences. Reading the 12-page subsection of their review provides a survey of knowledge about retention. The authors discuss and put into an interpretive framework the findings of more than 60 primary reports about the topic.

Research reviews are published in many sources including journals, handbooks, and yearbooks of professional societies. *Review of Educational Research,* published quarterly by the American Educational Research Association, for example, contains comprehensive reviews on four or five major topics in each issue. Consult the library reference department for assistance in locating research reviews.

E X E R C I S E   1 3 . 1

With this exercise you start work on the development of a problem statement and litera-ture review. Exercises 13.2 and 13.3 build on your responses.

1. This chapter section suggests that your experiences, or the literature, or a combination of the two, are prime sources of research problems. Sort through these options and locate one or two ideas about problems of interest to you. Identify these potential problems in writing.

2. Next, locate and read a literature review on the topics of these problems. Use the *Thesaurus of ERIC Descriptors* to see how the topics are defined. Identify three or four major points about what the literature review says about the topic. Reflect on these problems and the brief literature review as you continue study of Chapter 13.

✄ Preparation of an Initial Problem Statement

The preparation of an initial problem statement involves two closely related tasks that may actually take place simultaneously. The tasks are described sep-arately here to provide clarity about what's involved in each one.

First, you must be aware of important criteria for judging whether a problem is viable as the focus of your research effort. The second task in-volves wording the initial problem statement so that it is neither too broad nor too narrow for use in locating related literature.

Selection Criteria

As you begin to think about an initial problem statement, be aware of several important criteria that direct your choice. These include your interest in a particular problem, the ease with which you can manage the problem, and the educational significance of the problem. Of course, any problem that you pursue must serve an ethical purpose. Solving the problem should serve a purpose beyond the satisfaction of your curiosity.

The extent of your *interest* in a particular problem is an especially im-portant criterion because the project may require work over several months. As time passes, work on the research proposal or the project itself can be-come tedious, but the tedium is lessened if you are sincerely interested in the problem. Your personal interest is extremely important in the problem-selection process.

The selected problem should be one that you can *manage*. This means that you have or can arrange to obtain:

• the expertise necessary to handle the complexities of various tasks associated with data collection and analyses;

- the time necessary to handle a multitude of details; and
- the funds needed for copies of search materials, transportation to the research setting, printing, and other expenses.

Figure out if you can manage the problem before you make a large commitment of time and effort to it.

Any problem worth pursuing should have **educational significance.** That is, the project should have merit beyond its completion. Who, besides you, will be interested in the outcomes of your intended project? Are the outcomes likely to change instructional practices, counseling approaches, administrative policies, and so on? With whom will you share the results? Does the literature suggest that an answer to this problem is important?

Decisions about educational significance involve subjective judgments that may be difficult for you to make alone. If you are working with an adviser or a committee, talk with these individuals about the potential worth of your proposed problem. If you are working independently, talk about the intended problem with a trusted colleague. Use the questions in the preceding paragraph as points of discussion.

The three criteria were discussed in a sequence, suggesting an order in which you consider them. If you find that you have little interest in a problem, choose one in which you do have interest. If the chosen problem is not one you can manage comfortably, either modify it to make it manageable or choose a new problem. Finally, be sure the problem is one that has educational significance. Only when you are well satisfied that all three criteria are met should you proceed with the project.

Wording Strategies

Sometimes an initial problem may be so broadly or narrowly stated as to be unworkable. In these cases, brainstorming your ideas about the problem either independently or with an interested colleague may help to produce a problem better suited to investigation.

Suppose this is the initial problem statement: *How can I help students remember what they are taught?* This problem refers broadly to student retention of information and to teacher strategies for helping students remember content. But both qualitative and quantitative inquiries require problems with more direction than shows in this one. As written, the problem is so broadly stated that it's vague.

A strategy for rewording this problem might use either a concept map or a listing process. Figure 13.2 shows a simple concept map about student retention of information. Note the mixture of ideas and connections within this map. Although a listing process may generate similar ideas, their connections are typically less visible than those shown in concept maps.

A *qualitative* researcher may take this map and generate a series of open-ended research questions. For example:

- How do students' attitudes toward the content to be learned affect their retention?

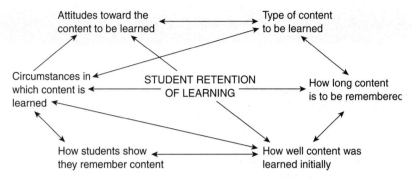

FIGURE 13.2   Sample concept map of ideas related to "student retention of learning."

- What circumstances allow for optimal initial learning of the content?
- How is optimal initial learning related to retention?

To answer these questions, the researcher will probably gather verbal data through firsthand experiences with students.

A *quantitative* researcher may use the map to specify variables and relationships to be tested. This researcher might ask:

- Do students remember facts longer than they remember concepts?
- Do students remember content learned through role-play longer than they remember content learned in lectures?

Or the researcher might test this hypothesis:

- Students remember content they learned well initially longer than they remember content that they did not learn well initially.

In these cases, the researcher will probably gather numerical data.

On other occasions, a problem statement may be so narrowly conceived that the researcher would have difficulty locating literature on the topic. In the previous section, a counselor mentioned that descriptions of students' problems referred to "acting-out behaviors."

Although such behaviors manifest themselves in many ways, as stated, this problem is narrow in its conception. By using brainstorming, this researcher may generate additional information about the behaviors and ways of helping students moderate their "acting out."

A concept map about "acting out" might show connections with repressed anger, academic failures, tantrums, depression, detached and uncaring family relationships, emotional disturbances, aggression, or other factors. Counselors usually attempt to help students learn to use words rather than behaviors to express themselves. In a word, counselors seek to help students use adaptive behavior. Following a brainstorming experience, the researcher may decide to focus the research question on the broader concepts of emotional disturbances, aggression, and adaptive behavior.

❖ Execution of the Literature Search

Searches of educational literature usually take advantage of databases accessible through university libraries, educational resource centers, other professional development facilities, and some public libraries. These searches can be conducted manually in some locations, but most are conducted electronically. Electronic searches can also be conducted at remote locations (e.g., homes, offices, schools). Contact a library reference department for assistance in accessing databases either manually or electronically.

Databases for the Search

The volume of educational literature continues to increase daily. To make this information available to educators and interested laypersons, most of the literature is now indexed in one or more databases, with the Educational Resources Information Center (ERIC) as the largest one. In 1999, ERIC contained "more than 980,000 bibliographic records of journal articles, research reports, curriculum and teaching guides, conference papers, and books" (Education Information Resources Center, [ERIC] 1999, p. 3). Furthermore, about 30,000 new records are added each year.

The ERIC database records information about documents and journal articles. The more than 410,000 document resumes referenced as ED listings in the database include research and technical reports, conference papers and speeches, project and program descriptions, opinion papers and essays, and teaching guides. These resumes are published monthly in *Resources in Education (RIE),* and are available online and in CD-ROM versions of the ERIC database (ERIC, 1999). Figure 13.3 shows a typical ERIC document resume. Notice the quantity of information provided by the resume.

Journal articles, referenced as EJ listings, include more than 565,000 entries. More than 900 journals are referenced, with all entries indexed from some journals and selected entries from other journals. Resumes for journals are published monthly in *Current Index to Journals in Education (CIJE),* also available online and in CD-ROM versions of the ERIC database (ERIC, 1999). Figure 13.4 shows a typical ERIC journal resume, which also provides large amounts of information. Discussion of the resumes continues in the subsections that follow.

A second education database, *Education Abstracts Full Text,* provides citations, abstracts, and full text for some articles from periodicals, books, and yearbooks. This database offers abstracts that are longer than ERIC listings, but it is limited in the quantity of listings.

Education Index, a companion to *Readers' Guide to Periodical Literature,* carries citations for most educational literature, including some journals not indexed by ERIC. However, this database does not include abstracts. In hard copy, *Education Index* dates from 1929; the electronic version became available in 1983.

PsycINFO, Social Science Citation Index, and *Social Work Abstracts* are major social sciences databases that sometimes provide access to information to

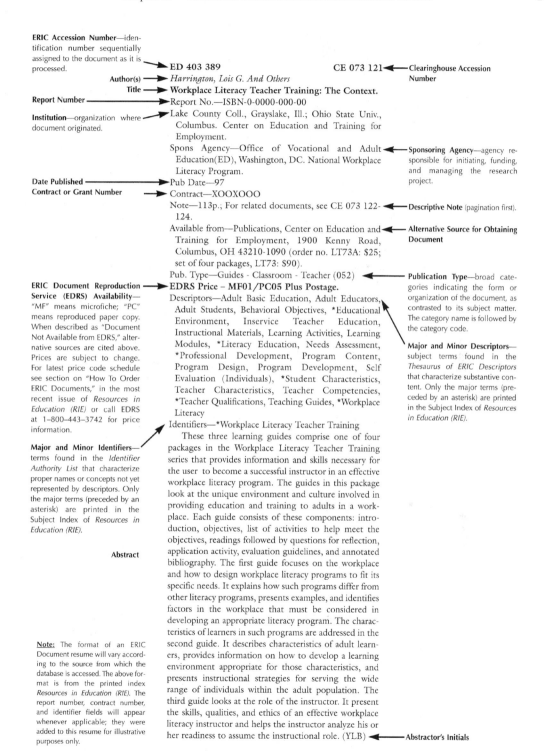

ERIC Accession Number—identification number sequentially assigned to the document as it is processed.

ED 403 389   CE 073 121 — **Clearinghouse Accession Number**

Author(s) — *Harrington, Lois G. And Others*

Title — **Workplace Literacy Teacher Training: The Context.**

Report Number — Report No.—ISBN-0-0000-000-00

Institution—organization where document originated. — Lake County Coll., Grayslake, Ill.; Ohio State Univ., Columbus. Center on Education and Training for Employment.

Spons Agency—Office of Vocational and Adult Education(ED), Washington, DC. National Workplace Literacy Program. — **Sponsoring Agency**—agency responsible for initiating, funding, and managing the research project.

Date Published — Pub Date—97

Contract or Grant Number — Contract—XOOXOOO

Note—113p.; For related documents, see CE 073 122-124. — **Descriptive Note** (pagination first).

Available from—Publications, Center on Education and Training for Employment, 1900 Kenny Road, Columbus, OH 43210-1090 (order no. LT73A: $25; set of four packages, LT73: $90). — **Alternative Source for Obtaining Document**

Pub. Type—Guides - Classroom - Teacher (052) — **Publication Type**—broad categories indicating the form or organization of the document, as contrasted to its subject matter. The category name is followed by the category code.

ERIC Document Reproduction Service (EDRS) Availability—"MF" means microfiche; "PC" means reproduced paper copy. When described as "Document Not Available from EDRS," alternative sources are cited above. Prices are subject to change. For latest price code schedule see section on "How To Order ERIC Documents," in the most recent issue of *Resources in Education (RIE)* or call EDRS at 1–800–443–3742 for price information. — **EDRS Price – MF01/PC05 Plus Postage.**

Descriptors—Adult Basic Education, Adult Educators, Adult Students, Behavioral Objectives, *Educational Environment, Inservice Teacher Education, Instructional Materials, Learning Activities, Learning Modules, *Literacy Education, Needs Assessment, *Professional Development, Program Content, Program Design, Program Development, Self Evaluation (Individuals), *Student Characteristics, Teacher Characteristics, Teacher Competencies, *Teacher Qualifications, Teaching Guides, *Workplace Literacy

Major and Minor Descriptors—subject terms found in the *Thesaurus of ERIC Descriptors* that characterize substantive content. Only the major terms (preceded by an asterisk) are printed in the Subject Index of *Resources in Education (RIE).*

Identifiers—*Workplace Literacy Teacher Training

Major and Minor Identifiers—terms found in the *Identifier Authority List* that characterize proper names or concepts not yet represented by descriptors. Only the major terms (preceded by an asterisk) are printed in the Subject Index of *Resources in Education (RIE).*

Abstract

These three learning guides comprise one of four packages in the Workplace Literacy Teacher Training series that provides information and skills necessary for the user to become a successful instructor in an effective workplace literacy program. The guides in this package look at the unique environment and culture involved in providing education and training to adults in a workplace. Each guide consists of these components: introduction, objectives, list of activities to help meet the objectives, readings followed by questions for reflection, application activity, evaluation guidelines, and annotated bibliography. The first guide focuses on the workplace and how to design workplace literacy programs to fit its specific needs. It explains how such programs differ from other literacy programs, presents examples, and identifies factors in the workplace that must be considered in developing an appropriate literacy program. The characteristics of learners in such programs are addressed in the second guide. It describes characteristics of adult learners, provides information on how to develop a learning environment appropriate for those characteristics, and presents instructional strategies for serving the wide range of individuals within the adult population. The third guide looks at the role of the instructor. It present the skills, qualities, and ethics of an effective workplace literacy instructor and helps the instructor analyze his or her readiness to assume the instructional role. (YLB) — **Abstractor's Initials**

Note: The format of an ERIC Document resume will vary according to the source from which the database is accessed. The above format is from the printed index *Resources in Education (RIE).* The report number, contract number, and identifier fields will appear whenever applicable; they were added to this resume for illustrative purposes only.

FIGURE 13.3   Sample ERIC document resume.

From *All About ERIC,* National Library of Education, Office of Educational Research and Development, U. S. Department of Education, 1999, p. 4.

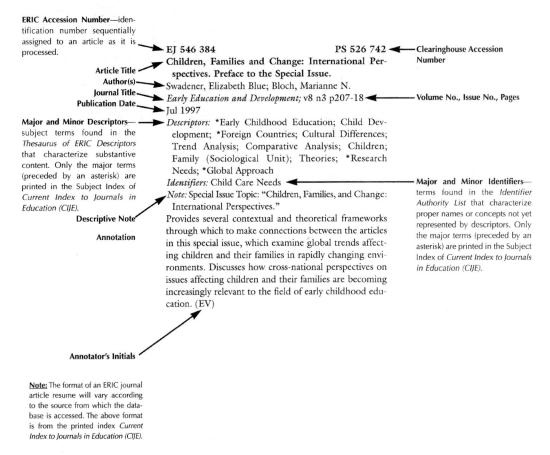

ERIC Accession Number—identification number sequentially assigned to an article as it is processed.

EJ 546 384   PS 526 742 ◄ **Clearinghouse Accession Number**

Children, Families and Change: International Perspectives. Preface to the Special Issue.
— **Article Title**

Author(s) ► Swadener, Elizabeth Blue; Bloch, Marianne N.

Journal Title ► *Early Education and Development;* v8 n3 p207-18 ◄ **Volume No., Issue No., Pages**

Publication Date ► Jul 1997

Major and Minor Descriptors—subject terms found in the *Thesaurus of ERIC Descriptors* that characterize substantive content. Only the major terms (preceded by an asterisk) are printed in the Subject Index of *Current Index to Journals in Education (CIJE).*

► *Descriptors:* *Early Childhood Education; Child Development; *Foreign Countries; Cultural Differences; Trend Analysis; Comparative Analysis; Children; Family (Sociological Unit); Theories; *Research Needs; *Global Approach

Identifiers: Child Care Needs ◄ **Major and Minor Identifiers**—terms found in the *Identifier Authority List* that characterize proper names or concepts not yet represented by descriptors. Only the major terms (preceded by an asterisk) are printed in the Subject Index of *Current Index to Journals in Education (CIJE).*

Descriptive Note *Note:* Special Issue Topic: "Children, Families, and Change: International Perspectives."

Annotation Provides several contextual and theoretical frameworks through which to make connections between the articles in this special issue, which examine global trends affecting children and their families in rapidly changing environments. Discusses how cross-national perspectives on issues affecting children and their families are becoming increasingly relevant to the field of early childhood education. (EV)

Annotator's Initials

Note: The format of an ERIC journal article resume will vary according to the source from which the database is accessed. The above format is from the printed index *Current Index to Journals in Education (CIJE).*

FIGURE 13.4   Sample ERIC journal article resume.

From *All About ERIC,* National Library of Education, Office of Educational Research and Improvement, U. S. Department of Education, 1999, p. 5.

educational researchers. Several general resources databases, including *Dissertation Abstracts International (DAI), EBSCOHost, JSTOR,* and *UnCover,* are useful for educational research. *DAI,* which may be searched electronically or manually in some libraries, provides access to abstracts of dissertations and selected theses from over 1,000 participating accredited higher education institutions.

EBSCOHost, JSTOR, and *UnCover* are available only by electronic means. The first two databases provide full text electronically for some articles in education. *UnCover* permits searches for journal citations and the tables of contents in some journals. Table 13.1 describes the content, coverage, and information available for these databases.

TABLE 13.1

Databases for Educational Research

Database	Content	Dates of Coverage	Information Available
Major Education Databases			
ERIC	Abstracts of educational studies and articles from professional educational journals and documents	1966–present	Citation, abstract
Education Abstracts Full Text	Full-length abstracts of articles from periodicals, books, and yearbooks	1983–present (electronic version)	Citation, abstract (1994–present), full text (1996–present)
Education Index	Information about books and articles, including author, title, and source	1929–present (paper); 1983–present (electronic version)	Citation
Major Social Sciences Databases			
PsycINFO	Comprehensive information about psychology plus relevant material from other disciplines, including education	1987–present	Citation, abstract
Social Science Citation Index	Electronic access to Web of Science databases; covers relevant items from leading scientific and technical journals	1982–present	Citation, abstract
Social Work Abstracts	Citations to journal articles on wide range of social work issues	1977–present	Citation, abstract
General Resources Databases			
Dissertation Abstracts International	Index to dissertations and selected theses in multiple subject areas including education; abstracts provided from 1980 to present	1961–present	Citation, abstract
EBSCOHost	Electronic access to full text for over 1,000 journals; abstracts and indexing for over 3,100 scholarly journals, including education	1990–present	Citation, abstract, full text
JSTOR	Electronic access to full-text articles in limited education journals	1980–present	Citation, abstract, full text
UnCover	Electronic access to journal citations and tables of contents in several fields, including education	1988–present	Citation, occasional summary from contents

Scope of the Search

The major scope question is whether the search will be exhaustive. Be advised that undertaking a complete search of the literature related to a problem area is a time-consuming task.

If the search is to be less than exhaustive, you must decide how to limit it. Will the recency of information determine what you review? If so, how will you decide the cutoff date? Will the availability of materials be the limiting factor? If yes, does "availability" include securing materials through interlibrary loan? These are a few of the ways to limit searches.

Electronic ERIC searches can be limited in many ways. In fact, most of the explanatory information items listed in the margins of Figures 13.3 and 13.4, including dates, descriptors, publication types, and others, can be used individually or in combination to limit searches.

If you work on a literature review as part of a graduate program, check with your adviser about the expectations for the scope of your search and the subsequent review. Reviews for research proposals may sometimes be less extensive than reviews in final research papers. In other cases, "proposals" comprise the beginning chapters of theses or dissertations and must contain complete reviews.

Search Strategies

Many libraries offer assistance with search strategies either in live sessions conducted by reference librarians or through electronic tutorials. In some instances, you may meet with reference librarians on an individual basis to discuss your search. Take advantage of this assistance unless you already know how to conduct searches. The time spent in these activities pays large dividends because well-planned searches yield more usable information more quickly than do searches conducted haphazardly.

Systematic database searches require the use of subject indexing terms, such as descriptors or keywords. All articles and documents included within the ERIC and *PsycINFO* data bases, for example, have assigned descriptors that enable potential users to locate their resumes. (Note the descriptor listings in Figures 13.3 and 13.4.)

The descriptors and their definitions are listed in the thesauri for these data bases. In many locations, the thesauri are available online, which makes their use relatively easy. Using appropriate descriptors in your search strategy means that you are likely to obtain more relevant information than you would without them.

For example, the counselor researcher who pursues study of acting-out behaviors might use the *Thesaurus of ERIC Descriptors* to find these subject descriptors: emotional disturbances, aggression, and adaptive behavior. If the counselor wants to find records indexed under all three of these concepts, she or he would use the "AND" operator. The computer will access all the

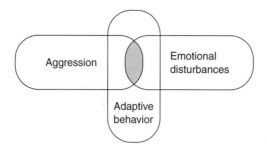

(a) Search showing use of the "AND" operator

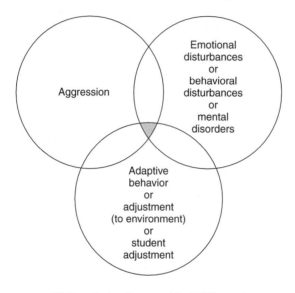

(b) Search showing use of the "OR" operator

FIGURE 13.5   Examples of "AND" and "OR" search strategy operators.

records contained in the intersection of the three concept sets (see Figure 13.5a).

If the counselor wants more information than this strategy locates, she or he can use the *Thesaurus* to locate additional relevant descriptors and add these into the search using the "OR" operator. Use of the "OR" operator tells the search program to locate documents and articles indexed with either descriptor (see figure 13.5b).

Keyword searches may be used to retrieve records. These searches normally "find" more items or records than do descriptor searches. However, keyword searches may locate records less pertinent to the topic.

Use of Search Results

Following the searches, you may have long lists of citations and abstracts for reports and articles related to your problem area. You may also have full texts of some reports and articles. What do you do with this information? How do you make sense of it?

You have your own unique ways of working with information that will be put to good use in this project. To expedite the processes, however, consider systematizing them:

1. Develop and use a consistent system for notes.

If you are expected to use a particular style manual for references in your review, write all references in this style when you first make them and insert the appropriate reference into every set of notes.

As you develop notes, also plan a simple method by which they can be retrieved, such as by topic, date, type of procedure (e.g., participants, instrumentation), or another method. If you develop hard copy notes, use only one side of large cards or paper. If your notes are made on the computer, develop a filing system that allows for ready access. These strategies allow you to sort information when you begin preparation of the review.

Abstract the important information from the literature and summarize it in your own words. This will curb any tendency to overuse direct quotations in the review. It's also faster. Even if your budget allows copies of the reference materials, it's worthwhile to make margin notes in your own words.

2. Budget your time.

Plan ahead how to use work time. For example, if you must work at a library, plan what you wish to accomplish before you go there. Complete your index searches separately from other tasks. If you plan to read materials in the library, allow some large chunks of time. Frustrations are likely to set in if you start a reading session only to realize that you must attend class or the library is closing.

Find out if the library offers as a service the location of reports, copying of reports, or both. This service probably has costs, but the time saved may outweigh the costs.

Read abstracts carefully and skim reports and articles before reading them in detail. Be aware of the consequences in terms of time if you read materials unrelated to your topic. Keep to your plan.

The desired outcome of using the search results should be an understanding of the knowledge base for your research problem. This study of the literature should make you aware not only of the major ideas, but also of the relationships among them.

✠ Preparation of an Initial Draft of the Literature Review

Your understanding of the knowledge base is expected to grow as you prepare the literature review because you will be studying the referenced material in detail. A good plan is to select a justification, then prepare the literature review as an argument that supports the justification.

Selection of the Justification

As part of your reflections about the literature, consider how your project will contribute to the knowledge base in the problem area. Recall the four justifications for projects discussed in Chapter 3. These are:

- There is little or no existing research in a particular problem area.
- Some research exists, but it is insufficient to be considered reliable as a solution to the research problem.
- There is a lot of research, but the findings are conflicting or contradictory. Researchers seek information that clarifies the findings for their particular setting.
- Two or more theories explain the same phenomenon, but each predicts different outcomes of a common action. Researchers conduct research to find out which theoretical orientation to follow.

Which of these justifications fits your project? If necessary, reread Chapter 3 for the meanings of these justifications. Remember, too, that your literature review must support the justification selected for your project.

Support of the Justification

Once you have selected a justification, consider how you will support it. Of course, the literature review provides a context for understanding the research problem, but it also supports whichever justification your project is expected to fulfill.

Well-prepared literature reviews are organized around major ideas that enable readers to understand the problem. Reread the paragraph summaries in Figure 3.1 from the literature review for Preservice and Inservice Secondary Teachers' Orientations toward Content Area Reading (A5). Notice that the review begins with general information about belief and practice relationships, then progressively moves toward discussion of literature closely related to the project.

Your review will differ in content and perhaps in length, but you should use the same basic plan. Begin with general information or a little history about the topic. Then move through a series of ideas that explain what is and isn't known about the problem. Some statements will comment on the strengths and weaknesses in existing research. Your review should use both explanation and critique statements (see Table 3.1).

Prepare an outline for your review. Use the themes that you want to emphasize as the major headings. These may resemble the paragraph summaries shown in Figure 3.1. Because a major reason for making this outline is to order the content, examine the flow of ideas before you decide that the task is complete. An outline may also help you to identify instances in which you should read additional research.

In the author's experiences, preparation of an outline of this type is difficult because the task requires management of several major ideas simultaneously. Depending on the complexity of the ideas, an outline may have to evolve over time—time that allows ideas to take shape, to be revised, and to be reshaped. In other words, for most individuals this is not a task to be completed within a few hours. The time and effort required to prepare an outline is well spent because actually writing the review is relatively easy once the main points and their sequence are established.

Working from the outline, prepare a complete initial draft of the literature review. Completion of this draft usually brings a sense of accomplishment and closure about the processes. You can add other references and edit the review in later drafts.

Development of the References List

Ordinarily, you are expected to list references for all works cited in the review in a special section called References or Bibliography. The guidelines for the formulation of this list are typically described in a style manual such as the *Publication Manual of the American Psychological Association* (1994) or *The*

E X E R C I S E   1 3 . 2

This exercise encourages you to word an initial research problem and prepare a draft of an initial literature review.

1. For at least one of the topics identified in Exercise 13.1, complete both of the following:
   • Apply the three selection criteria: your interest in the problem area, your ability to manage the problem should you decide to proceed with it, and the educational significance of investigating the problem.
   • Try to word the topic as a research problem. Use the brainstorming exercises suggested in this chapter section, as needed, to broaden or narrow the topic into a workable problem.

2. Circle the keywords in your initial problem statement. Use the *Thesaurus of ERIC Descriptors* to locate descriptors that reflect the meanings of the keywords.

3. Decide the scope of your search, then plan and execute a search within the relevant databases. Study the search results to become acquainted with the related literature.

4. Based on the results of the search, prepare an initial draft of the literature review through these stages:
   • Select one justification for your project that best fits the situation.
   • Prepare an outline for the literature review that supports this justification.
   • Prepare a complete initial draft of the literature review that fits the outline.
   • Develop a references list or bibliography.

Chicago Manual of Style (1993). Your graduate adviser or the funding agency for which you prepare a proposal usually specify a particular style manual.

⚔ Reconsideration and Revision of the Problem Statement

Soon after you complete the initial literature review, reflect again on your problem statement. Is this problem, as stated, viable or workable? Your answer must address two issues: the words selected to communicate your ideas and the ideas that underlie your words.

If your goal is explanation, have you communicated whether you seek an understanding of the meaning of a topic, variable, or phenomenon? Or are you attempting to understand or describe relationships among "parts" of the topic, variable, or phenomenon? Have you clarified which "parts" you want to understand or which relationships you are considering?

If your goal is prediction, does the literature establish that the variables of your study are related? Is this relationship strong enough that knowledge of one variable could reasonably be expected to predict knowledge of the other?

If your goal is control, does the literature establish that the variables of your study are related? Is there good reason to believe that a cause-and-effect relationship exists between the variables you've chosen to investigate?

Once you have answered these questions, think about the audience that will read your problem statement. In many cases, graduate committee members and funding agency reviewers expect to see research problems cast as purpose statements. These typically use declarative sentences to announce the main thrust of the problem, followed by questions that elaborate the details.

Clarify whether your study is a quantitative or qualitative project. For a quantitative project, each specific question should be answerable with "yes" or "no" upon completion of the study. In qualitative projects, specific questions are open-ended. Figure 13.6 contains examples of rudimentary purpose statements that will be elaborated on in Chapter 14.

Qualitative Project

The purpose of this project is to investigate factors that potentially affect student retention of content taught in school. Specifically, this project will explore answers to these questions:

1. What are optimal circucmstances under which students learn school curriculum content?
2. What seems to influence students' retention of content?

Quantitative Project

The purpose of this project is to investigate selected variables that may affect student retention of content taught in school. Specifically, this project will answer these questions:

1. Is student enthusiasm for school curriculum content related to retention of this content?
2. Is the type of presentation strategy for learning the content, whether teacher- or student-centered, related to retention?

FIGURE 13.6   Examples of rudimentary purpose statements for qualitative and quantitative research projects.

✖ Revision of the Literature Review and References List

Literature reviews typically undergo one or more content revisions, form revisions, or both before they can be considered as finished. Content revisions include additions, deletions, or both types of information and may use focus strategies, integration strategies, or both. Form revisions include general editing and wording changes along with language and mechanics usage corrections.

Content Revisions

During the first revision, it's a good idea to see if the draft contains adequate information about each major point in the outline and that the appropriate references are included. In the throes of composing the initial draft, it's easy to overlook a subheading or even a major heading. Serious content omissions should be remedied before proceeding with revisions. Be sure to revise the references list as you make changes in the review.

In subsequent revisions, use *focus strategies* to center the content on the topics. Eliminate information that does not serve a purpose because leaving it may detract attention from your key points. Also, add information that clarifies your points. Because you know the literature much better than do most of your readers, you must provide enough details to ensure understanding.

Integration strategies can also effect content changes because authors use these to bring information together. Rather than reporting studies separately, investigators often state their gist and refer to all the studies in one citation. Here are two examples from Wentzel (1997, p. 411):

> . . . several authors have suggested that feelings of belongingness and of being cared for can foster the adoption and internalization of goals and values of caregivers (Baumeister & Leary, 1995; Connell & Wellborn, 1991; Noddings, 1992).
>
> Academic effort represents an important index of academic motivation (Maehr, 1984), as well as a significant predictor of grades and test scores (Wentzel, Weinberger, Ford, & Feldman, 1990).

In the first example, three sources obtained similar findings about the effects of caregivers on students' goals and values, so all three sources are mentioned in the same citation. The second example displays research findings about relationships among four variables (i.e., academic effort, academic motivation, grades, test scores). The integration of these ideas into one sentence with two citations allows readers to quickly grasp the connections among the variables. See these examples in the introduction to A7.

A focused, integrated literature review provides readers with important information about your problem and the knowledge surrounding it. This type of review also makes clear why you want to investigate the particular problem.

Form Revisions

These revisions include the mechanics and organization of the review. Use of an outline to construct the review should help with organization. Literature reviews are usually considered as formal papers that require standard English and proper grammar. Of course, word-processing programs can help with these concerns.

Before you decide the review is complete, take time to read the paper aloud just as it's written. Pause wherever you placed punctuation. With careful listening, you may recognize needed wording changes to help the ideas flow freely.

Before you decide that the references list is complete, check again to see that all references cited in the review are included. Also, check the form for your entries in the references list against the style manual.

E X E R C I S E   1 3 . 3

In Exercise 13.2, you created an initial problem statement and literature review. Use the following suggestions to sharpen or focus these items.

1. Check to see that the purpose of your project is portrayed clearly in your problem statement. If necessary, phrase your problem statement as a purpose. Use Figure 13.6 as an example.

2. Check your initial literature review against the outline to be sure the review is complete. If necessary, add information to the literature review to ensure its completeness.

3. Apply focus and integration strategies. These eliminate unnecessary information and clarify your points.

4. Read your review for form, including mechanics and organization.

Summary

Several recursive subtasks involved in the creation of problem statements and literature reviews are the topics of this chapter. Recursion is important because problem statements and literature reviews, though separate, are closely related, complex tasks.

Experiences, educational literature, or some combination usually provide an initial research problem area. Scanning a published research review can help you learn the boundaries of the knowledge about the problem area.

As part of actually producing an initial problem statement, you should apply three criteria: your interest in the problem, your ability to manage it, and the educational significance of the problem. You may need to adjust the wording of your initial problem. Problems that are too broad or too narrow are difficult to pursue.

Completing one or more literature searches is necessary prior to preparing the review. Several databases, especially ERIC, provide access to large quantities of educational literature. You must decide if your search is to be exhaustive, and if it is not, how you will limit it. Once you obtain the literature, apply your preferred ways of studying it and relating it to your problem.

Through your study of the literature, you will select a justification for your study and outline the literature review to support this justification. Next, you should produce an initial draft of the review that makes use of the outline. As you mention references in the review, include them in a references list or bibliography in the required format.

Following this task, think again about the problem as you stated it, to be sure it communicates your goal of research. Make revisions as needed. When the problem is appropriately stated, revise the content and form of the literature review.

Questions for Discussion

1. Discuss the advantages and disadvantages of using a recursive sequence for the subtasks (see Figure 13.1 for one example) in the creation of problem statements and literature reviews.
2. Locate the index to the *Handbook of Research on. . .* (select your own topic, e.g., *Curriculum, Educational Administration*). Read the content in one section of interest to you. Discuss how this information might be helpful if your research problem were on this topic.
3. Sometimes graduate students undertake the study of research problems that are proposed by their advisers. Discuss potential benefits and drawbacks for these students.
4. Explain why the production of the literature review should precede planning the research project.

Creation of Proposals for Research Projects

❖ **Initiation of a Research Proposal**
❖ **Treatment Procedures in Experiments**
  Definition of Levels
  Assignments to Participants
  Personnel and Costs
❖ **Data Source Procedures**
  Participant Sources
  Selection Strategies
  Nonparticipant Sources
  Costs
❖ **Instrumentation, Data Collection, and Handling Procedures**
  Strategies for Numerical Data
  Strategies for Verbal Data
  Circumstances for Data Collection
  Personnel and Costs

❖ **Data Analysis Procedures**
  Strategies for Quantitative Analyses
  Strategies for Qualitative Analyses
  Personnel and Costs
❖ **Summary of the Method Section**
❖ **Time Line**
❖ **Budget**
❖ **Introduction to the Project**
  Introduction
  Purpose of the Study
  Educational Significance
  Definitions
  Summary
❖ **Title**
❖ **Completion of the Proposal**
  Review Board Approval

A **research proposal** contains a research problem, a literature review, and plans for the collection and analysis of data to solve the research problem. Most proposals have several sections, each serving an important purpose. As a foundation for the project, the **introduction to the project** delineates the research problem and provides information about the need for and the worth of the project. The *literature review* shows how the proposed project is expected to fit with and extend existing knowledge about the problem. The *method* section describes the procedures by which the researcher expects to collect and analyze data to solve the research problem. Finally, the *references,* or *bibliography,* document the sources of information included within the proposal.

This chapter is intended to help you integrate the problem statement, literature review, and references list that you created in Chapter 13 into a research proposal. You will also apply pertinent information from the chapters on quantitative and qualitative methods in parts III and IV to develop the method section of this proposal.

Goal

To enable you to:

- develop a proposal for a research project of your choice.

⚔ Initiation of a Research Proposal

Completion of a problem statement and Literature Review represents a significant step toward the creation of a research proposal. Your completion of these components satisfies the first two systematic processes in educational research: identify the problem and review known information in the problem area.

Through the preparation of the research problem, you have also selected the goal of your research project, which prescribes the general method for data collection and analysis. If your goal is explanation, you will embark on a qualitative, historical, or descriptive project, depending on your problem statement. If your goal is prediction, your project will use descriptive methods. If your goal is control, you will use experimental methods.

The third and fourth systematic processes are to collect data about the problem and to analyze and interpret data, respectively. A research proposal contains your plans for both systematic processes through the inclusion of data source, instrumentation, data collection, handling, and analysis procedures, plus treatment procedures for experiments. In all projects, these procedures must be related.

For example, data source procedures should be related to instrumentation procedures. Interviews can be used to collect data in projects with small numbers of participants, but a different collection strategy is required with large numbers of participants. Despite their interconnectedness, procedures are described in this chapter under separate headings for clarity. Figure 14.1 displays the relationships between research problems and procedures.

⚔ Treatment Procedures in Experiments

If the goal of your project is control, the treatment procedures will influence data source, instrumentation, and data collection and analysis procedures. Of course, if your goal is explanation or prediction, treatment procedures do not apply.

Definition of Levels

In the preparation of a proposal for an experiment, your initial task is to operationally define the treatment. That is, you will describe the actions that research personnel use with participants as they undergo treatment. The descriptions should provide details about how the circumstances in which participants learn, work, live, or play change as a result of this project. What do participants do differently from their regular routine? You must define treatment levels clearly for all intended comparison(s).

One of these options is typically the basis for the comparison of performances between:

1. before-and-after treatment for one group,
2. one group that receives treatment and another group that receives no treatment, or
3. two or more groups that receive different levels of treatment.

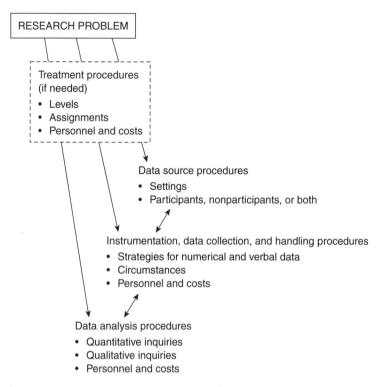

FIGURE 14.1   Relationships between research problems and procedures.

In comparisons 1 and 2, only one level of treatment is defined. However, comparison 3 requires definitions of two or more treatment levels.

For each treatment level, definitions should include answers to these questions: What exactly do the participants do? For what length of time in hours, weeks, or months do participants engage in the treatment? Which materials, supplies, or equipment do participants use as they engage in the treatment?

As examples, review two reports of experiments in Appendix A. In their Treatment subsection, Holmes and Keffer (1995) define one level of treatment in a comparison with no treatment (see A4). On the other hand, Gettinger (1993) defines three treatment levels in the Procedures subsection (see A1).

If you are conducting an experiment, you want to be sure that the manipulated variable(s) is(are) responsible for any changes in the responding variable(s). Therefore, consider the possible effects of extraneous variables on the projected test of cause-and-effect. You may decide to account for some extraneous variables by building them into the design.

As described in Chapter 6, an extraneous variable can be included in the design as an independent variable. For example, if you're concerned about the possible effects of age on the dependent variable, use a factorial design in which you assign age as an independent variable. Or you may hold age constant by using participants only of a certain age. Either action will minimize the possible effects that age might have on the dependent variable.

Assignments to Participants

How treatment levels are assigned to participants is an important contributor to the validity and reliability of data. Ideally, treatment levels are assigned randomly to *individuals* because this method provides unbiased groups, alike except for their treatment levels.

In the real world, however, schools, day-care centers, and other institutions may require that researchers assign treatments to *groups* rather than to individuals. Sometimes in school-based research, the groups are class sections. Random assignment of treatment to groups is preferred over nonrandom assignment.

Personnel and Costs

In some instances, you may be the only treatment administrator. In other instances, teachers or fellow graduate students may serve in this role. Regardless of your choice, include answers to the following questions in your treatment procedures: Who will administer treatment? What expertise must administrators have? Do the individuals selected as administrators require training?

Funds for payment of treatment administrators' time spent in training or for travel expenses may be required. In addition, expenses for supplies, materials, or equipment should be anticipated. What are the costs of specialized materials for the treatment levels? Estimates of these costs should be included in your budget.

E X E R C I S E   1 4 . 1

This exercise should help you to plan the treatment procedures of your research proposal. Answer these questions *only* if you are planning an *experiment* based on the problem or purpose statement you created in Chapter 13.

1. Define the treatment level(s) for each group within the comparison(s). Describe what participants will do and the materials, supplies, or equipment they will use. Describe the duration of treatment, including start and stop dates.

2. Describe the method by which treatment will be assigned to participants, whether individually or to groups.

3. Describe the personnel, in terms of their expertise, who will administer treatment. If you plan to offer training sessions for them, briefly describe the content and length of time required. Briefly describe any materials to be used in the training sessions.

4. Consider the costs associated with treatment procedures. List the items needed and their projected costs.

⋈ Data Source Procedures

Educational researchers typically use participants as their chief data sources, and use nonparticipant sources infrequently. However, the opposite situation usually applies to educational historians.

Participant Sources

Before you can collect data from participants or involve them in treatment, you must obtain their informed consent. If participants are minors, you must obtain consent from their parents or guardians. Informed consent means that individuals know the likely risks and potential consequences of being involved as participants. They also have the right to withdraw from the project at any time and to remain anonymous. Researchers must take appropriate precautions to protect the confidentiality of any data collected from participants (Ethical Standards of the American Educational Research Association, 1992). Additional discussion about participant consent is included in the final subsection on Review Board Approval.

In all quantitative inquiries, you should answer these questions: Are the participants likely to produce data across the range of variations within the variable(s)? Are there adequate numbers of participants available to provide data? If your project involves experimentation, you must determine if the variables of interest can be studied with the individuals expected to serve as participants. Is the treatment appropriate for them in terms of their ages, abilities, and interests?

For qualitative studies, your major concern should be the information richness of the projected research setting. In addition, decide if you will have access over a sufficiently long period to gather valid data. Will you have the type of access to participants that allows the use of appropriate data collection strategies?

Selection Strategies

The choice of selection strategies should be determined by how you plan to use the results. A random sampling selection strategy is necessary if you expect to generalize your results beyond the research setting that produced data. However, nonrandom-based sampling strategies are appropriate for research intended to answer questions for a specific situation.

Regardless of the choice of selection strategies, plan to describe fully the participant selection procedures. If you use a random sampling strategy, carefully describe the target population from which you will draw samples as well as the details of the selection strategy. These descriptions clarify the bases on which you expect to make generalizations.

If your choice is a purposive sampling strategy, explain why it is purposive. These reasons should be grounded in your descriptions of the information-richness of the setting and how your sample takes advantage of this richness.

For other nonrandom samples, describe the situations clearly. If you're claiming, for example, that the sample uses quotas, describe the bases for the quotas. Failure to discuss the bases for sampling may lead readers to believe that you have a convenience sample.

Nonparticipant Sources

Nonparticipant data sources include documents and artifacts housed in libraries, archives, government or school board offices, private businesses, and historical societies. Because these items may be scattered in a variety of locations, retrieving the documents, artifacts, or both is a major part of the procedures, but the use of electronic databases can assist with these procedures.

In some instances, documents at distant locations can be copied and sent to you. In other instances, however, you must go to wherever the documents and artifacts are located to study them. Both these operations can mean costs that become part of the budget.

Costs

Costs associated with data source procedures include travel to research settings or places where documents and artifacts are housed. Other potential costs include expenses related to obtaining permission from participants or their parents or guardians. For example, the costs of printing and distribution of permission forms should be part of your budget.

E X E R C I S E   14.2

This exercise should help you to plan the data source procedures of your research proposal. Answer these questions as they apply to the problem or purpose statement you created in Chapter 13. Take into account any treatment procedures you have planned for this project.

1. Complete this section if your project requires *participants* as data sources.
   a. Describe the research setting for your project in terms of the participants and their characteristics. If your project is a qualitative study, describe the degree of information-richness of the setting. If the project is a quantitative study, describe the numbers of participants your study requires. Discuss these matters with your committee, as needed.
   b. Explain what you expect to do with the results of your study. That is, do you plan to generalize the findings to a well-defined population? If yes, define this population and choose a random sampling strategy to select the groups for your comparison. Include accommodations for any variables that you wish to build into your design, either by holding them constant or by measuring them as pretests in experiments.

      If you do not plan to generalize the results, then describe the basis on which you will select samples for this project that allow you to answer your research questions for a specific situation.

   c. Consider the costs associated with data source procedures. List the items needed and their projected costs.
2. Complete this section if your project requires *nonparticipant* data sources.
   a. Identify the required documents, artifacts, or other nonparticipant data sources. Try using one or more electronic databases to locate these sources. Consult with reference librarians, as needed.
   b. Once you identify the possible locations of data sources, determine the feasibility of your being able to use them. Consult with reference librarians or other knowledgeable individuals. Communicate with individuals at the locations where the data sources are located, as needed.
   c. If you can obtain the data sources, plan the procedures by which you will access and study them. Stop work on the project if you find that the data sources are inaccessible.
   d. Consider the costs associated with data source procedures. List the items needed and their projected costs.

⚔ Instrumentation, Data Collection, and Handling Procedures

These procedures encompass your plans for the selection and administration of the strategies by which you will collect and handle data. Quantitative researchers typically collect mostly numerical data and anticipate reducing them to descriptive statistics. On the other hand, qualitative researchers collect mostly verbal data with intentions of reducing them to themes or hypotheses.

Strategies for Numerical Data

In *experiments,* you will measure each responding variable, and in *descriptive studies,* you will measure each variable. Whether you use existing strategies or devise your own, these collection devices must supply data at the appropriate level of measurement required to answer the research questions. Commonly used strategies include selected response tests, examinations, rating or ranking instruments, and closed-ended interviews. Moreover, the selected strategies must yield valid and reliable measures suited to your intended data analyses.

If instruments or strategies exist, indicators of their validity and reliability of measurement of data may also exist. In particular, commercially published instruments often have this information within their technical manuals. If you prepare your own instruments, you must determine the validity and reliability of measurement for data collected with these instruments.

Be especially aware that instruments should be sensitive to detect changes in variables. For example, if you plan to measure student achievement after 6 weeks of treatment, it's a good idea to use an achievement test specially prepared to measure the objectives within your project. Questions on a standardized achievement test, such as the *Stanford 9*, do not usually detect small changes because these tests measure achievement over a broad range.

Also, select strategies suited to the participants' developmental abilities. To illustrate, instruments that require reading ability will be ineffective unless participants can read at levels that allow them to answer the questions. It's especially important that participants be able to follow instructions for answering questions.

As part of planning, think about how the data will be handled following their collection. How will the instruments be scored or evaluated? Where will data be stored? Who will enter data into computer files? Who is in charge of these tasks? To ensure reliability of the data, these procedures must be uniform.

Strategies for Verbal Data

If your project uses qualitative methods, your plans should include collection of data about a specified phenomenon. You will typically choose one or more strategies that provide verbal data. Observations, open-ended interviews, constructed response instruments, document analyses, and artifact analyses are strategies commonly used in qualitative research. Because your project is unique, you will probably develop the strategy or strategies to fit your research question and the setting(s) for your project. For additional information about strategies, see Marshall and Rossman (1999), Chapter 4.

It's a good idea to try your strategies with individuals similar to those in your research setting, prior to the start of the project. If you plan open-ended interviews, for example, the collection of trial data may point out weaknesses in the questions that can be remedied prior to their use in the research setting.

The strategy or strategies you select must fit with your access to the setting. If your access is unrestricted, you will decide on your role. Do you plan to be a complete participant, a participant-as-observer, observer-as-participant, or a complete observer? Do you plan to change your adopted role during the course of data collection? Are other researchers working with you to collect data? If so, will their activities be compatible with yours and strengthen the reliability of the data?

The officials who grant your access to a research setting could potentially restrict your time on the campus or the type of contact you have with participants. You will be obliged to honor the arrangements that you make about access whenever you choose your role.

In advance of data collection, plan how you will handle raw data once the collection processes begin. Who will transcribe video- or audiotapes? Which information from observations will be put into field notes? Where will hard copies of these items be stored? How will data be entered into computer programs? How soon after the beginning of data collection will analysis begin? As these examples indicate, many details must be dealt with in data collection and handling and it's difficult to anticipate exactly how to account for them. Planning ahead will help.

Circumstances for Data Collection

The circumstances in which data are collected can influence their validity and reliability. Therefore, the conditions and schedule under which data are collected are important.

Classrooms are ideal as data collection sites for school-based research if participants associate pleasant or neutral feelings with them. If you use another location, select one where participants can feel comfortable. This is particularly important if you collect data through interviews.

The time of day at which data are collected can affect the quality of data. At the end of a school day, for example, participants may be fatigued so that data collected then are different from data collected earlier in the school day. Unseasonable weather and contemporary events (e.g., pep rallies) can also affect data collection. It's wise to arrange latitude in the time line to allow you to change dates for data collection if unforeseen circumstances warrant.

Also, in quantitative inquiries especially, anticipate how you will collect data from participants who are not available during regularly scheduled collections. Incomplete data require adjustments in analysis procedures and severe attrition can jeopardize the validity of the data.

Personnel and Costs

At a minimum level, all data collectors and handlers must be familiar with a standard set of instructions. Who will collect and handle data in your project? Will it be you alone or you and others (e.g., teachers, school administrators, or fellow graduate students)? Because it's your project, you must know the tasks involved and know how to do them. Other personnel may require training to be well-oriented to the procedures; you are the person who will plan and offer any required training sessions.

Costs for instrumentation, data collection, and handling must be considered. You will need to purchase any commercially published materials unless these are available through the school or organization where your project is located. Paper and pencil instruments that you devise also have printing costs. How many copies of instruments are required? For other strategies, consider whether special equipment, such as videotaping machines or computer equipment, is needed for the data collections. Possible costs also include travel either to the research setting(s) or to distant libraries or document locations. Funds required for any of these expenses should be included in the budget.

This exercise should help you to plan the instrumentation, data collection, and handling procedures of your research proposal. Apply these procedures to the problem or purpose statement you created in Chapter 13. Take into account all procedures you have planned for this project.

1. Complete this section if your project requires *numerical* data.
   a. Identify each variable(s) that must be measured and the level of measurement (e.g., interval) at which you plan to analyze data.
   b. Take into account the projected number of participants and identify an instrument *type* suitable for data collection for each variable. Consult Appendix B for suggestions.
   c. Identify at least one instrument or strategy for measuring each variable and explain your rationale for choosing it.

   Be sure the instrument or strategy meets your requirements for levels of measurement, validity of measurement, and reliability of measurement. Use one or more of these options to help with this identification:

   - Consider instruments mentioned in the literature that might be appropriate for measuring variable(s) in your project. If these are published instruments, read reviews in a reference such as *The Mental Measurements Yearbooks* (Buros, 1999) or consult the technical manual for the instrument to find this information.
   - If the instruments in the literature were researcher-developed, see if those instruments were published as part of a research report. Or contact the researchers to obtain additional information about the instruments. (If you decide to use them, you must secure permission from the developer.)
   - Develop your own instrument(s) to measure variables based on information from the literature. Plan a brief trial study to obtain data for evaluating the validity and reliability of measurement. For specific information, consult measurement and evaluation references, consultants, or both for assistance.

2. Complete this section if your project requires *verbal* data.
   a. Identify the phenomenon and name particular aspects of it on which you will collect data.
   b. Take into account the projected information-richness of the research setting and the professional access you have to the participants. Choose one or more strategies, at least by type, for data collection. Consult Appendix B for suggestions.
   c. Consider strategies mentioned in the literature that might be appropriate for data collection in your project. Develop your strategy and briefly try it in a trial situation. That is, if you plan to use interviews, prepare and try out interview questions. If you plan observations, try taking field notes.

3. Describe the circumstances in which data are to be collected. Identify where and on which dates data collection will take place, who will collect data, and what type of training the data collector(s) will have for these procedures.

4. Describe the procedures for handling data following their collection. Identify who will score the instruments or transcribe the tapes. Indicate whether data will be entered into computer files, and who will handle these tasks.

5. Consider costs associated with instrumentation, data collection, and handling procedures. List the items needed and their projected costs.

✘ Data Analysis Procedures

Plans for data analysis procedures are a vital part of your research proposal and are essential in a complete proposal. Data analysis procedures usually differ for quantitative and qualitative projects because of differences in the types of data.

Strategies for Quantitative Analyses

The research design and the measurement level of data suggest that you use either analyses of group data or analyses of associations among data. As Chapter 8 indicates, you will probably choose the former if your design is a survey, causal-comparative, or experimental project. You will calculate an appropriate measure of central tendency and variation based on the measurement level for each group. If data are interval or ratio, several options exist. If data are nominal or ordinal, however, options are limited.

If your design is for a correlation or prediction study, you are likely to calculate correlation coefficients, regression coefficients, or both. Again, the measurement level of data must be taken into account.

If your samples are random, you may plan to test one or more null hypotheses through the use of inferential statistical analyses. These analyses test for statistical significance at a probability level of your choice. Calculations for both the descriptive and inferential statistical procedures can be made with a computer program.

Within the data analysis procedures, include answers to the following questions: Which descriptive statistics will be calculated? Which hypotheses, if any, will be subjected to inferential statistical testing? Which inferential statistical tests and which levels of probability are projected for use?

Strategies for Qualitative Analyses

If your project is qualitative, anticipate how you will handle data analyses. Will you use manual coding or computer-assisted coding? If your choice is a computer program, which one? Will you use an existing set of codes or will you devise codes from the data? If you plan to use existing codes, how and where can they be located? Approximately how many levels of coding do you anticipate doing? How will you organize the analysis procedures to keep track of them?

Marshall and Rossman (1999) provide detailed information in Chapter 5 about recording, managing, and analyzing data. They also discuss planning time and resources for qualitative projects in Chapter 6.

Personnel and Costs

It's wise to plan for the personnel involved in anticipated data analyses. Who will handle the data analysis procedures? Will individuals other than you be involved? Do these individuals require training to handle these procedures? Are consultants needed?

If costs are associated with personnel or data analysis procedures, place estimates in the budget. For example, a data analysis consultant may provide basic advice without cost but may charge a fee for extended consultations. Include purchase of computer software or data processing services in the budget, if necessary.

✹ Summary of the Method Section

In a few paragraphs, summarize the procedures you describe in the method section. Your purpose is to help readers understand how the different sets of procedures work together to enable you to collect and analyze data to answer your research questions.

E X E R C I S E   1 4 . 4

This exercise should help you to plan the data analysis procedures of your research proposal. Apply these procedures to the problem or purpose statement you created in Chapter 13. Take into account all the procedures you have planned for this project.

1. Complete this section if your project requires analyses of *numerical* data.
   a. Identify which one of these analyses your research design and the measurement levels of your data suggest—an analysis of group data or an analysis of associations among data.
   b. Identify the appropriate descriptive statistics to be calculated using the collected data. Explain how you will use these statistics in the analysis from question 1a to answer your research questions for the project participants.
   c. Identify whether you plan to conduct inferential statistical analyses. If you do, describe your purpose and identify the inferential statistical test(s) that you anticipate using. Provide a rationale for your choice of test(s).
   d. Consider the costs associated with these data analysis procedures. List the items needed and their projected costs.

2. Complete this section if your project requires analyses of *verbal* data.
   a. Describe your approach to coding data. Indicate whether you will use manual or computer-assisted coding and if you will use existing codes. Tell approximately the number of levels of coding.
   b. Describe how you will organize the analysis procedures to keep track of them.
   c. Consider the costs associated with these data analysis procedures. List the items needed and their projected costs.

✹ Time Line

As you develop the treatment, data source, instrumentation, data collection, handling, and analysis procedures, you should devise a chronological sequence or time line by which to implement them. As minimum information, the time line should include projected dates for the initiation and completion of major project activities. Include leeway for changes, if possible.

Additional information such as names and locations of research set-tings, names of personnel and their major responsibilities, and specific hours of the day for particular activities may also be included. By projecting this time line for your research activities, you may avoid difficulties in the imple-mentation of the plan. Be sure to check with your committee chair about specific requirements for the time line.

✖ Budget

Most projects involve costs. Therefore, it's wise to plan a budget, regardless of its size. Budgets are usually planned around major headings such as (1) personnel; (2) equipment, supplies, and materials; and (3) travel. Item-ize the expenses for each set of procedures under one of these major head-ings and provide a total. If you are preparing a proposal to request funding, you will indicate the amount of funds needed to carry out the procedures.

To summarize information presented in previous sections, some proj-ects require personnel costs for those who administer treatment, collect and handle data, or perform data analyses. If personnel are required to partici-pate in training sessions, you may also have to pay for the time they spend in training. Consultants often provide their services without charge to graduate students, but extended consultant services can require payment.

Experiments may require the purchase of instructional or laboratory materials, supplies, or equipment. Data collection and handling may require funds for the purchase of instruments, printing, scoring, data entry, video-tapes, or other items.

Projects may require transportation costs for travel to research setting(s) by researchers, consultants, or both. Other costs include mailing and shipping charges of supplies or data.

✖ Introduction to the Project

The introduction to the project section usually contains five subsections: an unlabeled introduction, plus subsections labeled as purpose of the study, ed-ucational significance, definitions, and summary. This introduction to the study is different from introductions in published research studies. Note these differences in the following discussion.

Introduction

This initial two- or three-paragraph subsection sets the stage for the problem. In quantitative projects, mention the variables and the probable setting in which the problem is to be investigated. In qualitative projects, describe the phenomenon and the setting in which the problem is to be studied. Include other information, as needed, that points readers toward the purpose state-ment located in the next subsection. Remember, too, that an introduction may provide information about the organization of the section. Ordinarily you do not label the introduction or cite literature here.

Purpose of the Study

Use the rudimentary purpose statement that you created in Chapter 13 to begin this section. Briefly discuss and cite a few references that support the problem as being real (i.e., practical or theoretical) and in need of an answer. Describe one of the justifications for study discussed in Chapters 3 and 13. This justification is the one that you elaborated in the literature review.

Educational Significance

This subsection provides readers with an estimate of the worth of your study because here you must explain how educators are likely to benefit from answers to your research questions. For example, will the answers influence instruction, staff development, teacher education, instructional materials selection, or other issues? In order to estimate the educational significance of your study, examine the literature to see why answers to the problem are important to educators. Support from the literature makes a much stronger case for educational significance than does personal opinion alone.

Definitions

The definitions subsection briefly describes the phenomenon or the variables in operational terms. That is, the definitions provide meanings for phenomena or variables as you use them in your project. For a qualitative project, identify the phenomenon under investigation and briefly describe the strategies by which you plan to collect data. Also describe your role in data collection (e.g., participant-as-observer). This section should clarify how triangulation, if any, is used in this project.

For a quantitative project, identify each variable that you intend to measure and indicate the strategy or strategies used for its measurement. Briefly describe each level of treatment for the independent variables in experiments and use the definitions to clarify the cause-and-effect relationship that is tested.

Summary

To conclude the introduction to the project, summarize all the information in the section in a few paragraphs. This summary reminds readers of what they read and prepares them for the literature review, the major section that follows.

⚔ Title

At some point, you probably adopted a title for your research proposal. This was a working title that served to identify the variables or phenomenon of your project.

Now it is time to prepare a title for the completed proposal. As indicated in Chapter 3, this title should communicate an abbreviated form of your research problem. Either the phenomenon or variables and goal of research should be clear. In addition to these important attributes, provide information about the scope or range of interests within this project.

✎ Completion of the Proposal

At this point, you are ready to collate the proposal sections, add finishing touches, and submit the proposal for review(s). Proposal sections are usually arranged as follows:

> Title
> Introduction to the Project
>> Introduction (unlabeled)
>> Purpose of the Study
>> Educational Significance
>> Definitions
>> Summary
> Literature Review
> Method or Procedures
>> Treatment (if applicable)
>> Data Source
>> Instrumentation, Data Collection, and Handling
>> Data Analysis
>> Summary
> References

The literature review and references sections are those you prepared in Chapter 13. Preparation of the remaining sections is described in this chapter. The time line and budget may be included as proposal sections or appended to the proposal.

Once you have completed the proposal, take time to reread it in its entirety. Check to be sure that all sections and subsections are included. There should be a flow to the sections that allows readers to follow your line of reasoning. Check on the flow yourself. Ask a trusted colleague to read your proposal to check for flow and for completeness.

Your committee may also read your proposal and provide feedback about its content and organization. Work toward attaining the committee members' signatures on your proposal. Doing so ensures that they and you realize the expectations you are to meet for the project.

If you plan to use human participants, you will also need at least one independent review of your proposal. Work with your committee to prepare information for review board approval, which is described in the next subsection.

Review Board Approval

In almost all projects involving human participants, researchers must have their procedures approved by an institutional review board prior to the start of activities that involve participants. These boards have as their major purpose to ensure that every part of a research effort protects as strongly as possible the rights of individual participants (*Ethical Principles in the Conduct of Research with Human Participants,* 1982; Ethical Standards of the American Educational Research Association, 1992).

Figure 14.2 contains an excerpt from a university institutional review board application concerning work with participants, called human subjects. Note the specific questions concerned with their recruitment, how they will be informed about risks, how they can withdraw, and how their privacy is to be maintained.

If your research project is part of university requirements, discuss the review processes with your committee. This proposal will probably require approval by the university institutional review board if you plan to work with participants. If your research activities take place in schools or at other educational facilities, institutional review boards at those locations may also review your proposal. Or these boards may examine the approved statement from the university institutional review board.

E X E R C I S E   14.5

This exercise should help you to plan the remaining procedures of your research proposal. Apply these procedures to the problem or purpose statement you created in Chapter 13. Take into account all the procedures you have planned for this project.

1. Create a two- or three-paragraph summary of the method section that highlights and shows relationships among the important procedures.

2. Create a time line that displays the projected start and stop dates for major procedures. Include details that describe times of day, personnel, locations, and others. Consult with your committee about these details. Be sure that the dates selected allow the procedures to mesh. That is, data source selection must be complete prior to the start of data collection and treatment should conclude prior to the final data collection in quantitative studies.

   If you are planning a qualitative project, estimate the number of data collection, analysis, and interpretation cycles and their dates.

3. Create a budget for your proposal. Look through all the major sets of procedures for items needed and projected costs. Collate these items and costs into the following expense categories:
   • Personnel
   • Materials, supplies, and equipment
   • Travel

4. Create the introduction to the project section. Include an unlabeled introduction, a modified purpose of the study (from the one in Chapter 13), educational significance, definitions, and summary. See the section with this title for details.

5. Create a title for the project. Use the criteria for titles described in Chapter 3, Criteria for Evaluation.

6. Arrange the proposal sections as suggested in the Completion of the Proposal section. Read the proposal to check for completeness and for flow. Secure at least one additional reader to provide feedback about the proposal before submitting it to your committee.

1. **GENERAL PURPOSE OF THE RESEARCH:**

2. **DATA OBTAINED BY:**   Questionnaire ( )   Telephone ( )   Interview

Observation   ( )   Experiment ( )   Secondary Source

Other (explain)

3. **PROJECT DESCRIPTION**: The IRB must have sufficient information, nontechnical and detailed, about what will happen with/to subjects to evaluate/estimate the risks. Assurance from the investigator, no matter how strong, will not substitute for a description of the transactions between investigator and subject. If a questionnaire is used, attach a copy. (When visual or auditory stimuli, chemical substances, or other measures might affect the health of the subjects, a statement from a qualified person or other appropriate documentation will aid in evaluating the nature of any risk created. In questionable cases, the IRB will require such documentation.)
[Summary of Methodology]

4. **SUBJECT SELECTION:** Will subjects be less than 18 years of age?   Yes ( )   No ( )

How many subjects will participate? _____   Male ( ) Female ( ) Age _____to
_____

Will subjects be students at Arizona State University?   Yes ( )   No ( )

Source: _____

5. **How** will subjects be selected, enlisted or recruited?

6. **How** (in writing) will subjects be informed of procedures, intent of the study, and potential risks to them?

7. **How** (in writing) will subjects be informed they may withdraw at any time without prejudice?

8. **How** will subjects' privacy be maintained and confidentiality guaranteed?

FIGURE 14.2   Excerpt from *Application for the Conduct of Research Involving Human Subjects,* Arizona State University Institutional Review Board.

Summary

This chapter describes the tasks involved in designing the procedures to collect and analyze data for a research problem prepared previously. This problem specifies the general methods for these procedures through the identification of the goal of research.

If an experiment is planned, the definition of treatment levels and assignments of the levels to participants are two of the initial tasks. The decisions about treatment affect procedures in all the other components of the design.

Data source procedures should specify whether data are to be collected from participants or nonparticipant sources. In projects in which participants provide data, the procedures should describe how participants were selected, including any well-defined population they represent.

Instrumentation, data collection, and handling procedures describe the strategies by which data will be collected. These procedures should contain details about who collects data, the circumstances for collection, and how data are handled once they are collected. These procedures should be aligned closely with the procedures planned for analyses.

All the procedures sections should be organized into a proposal that contains an introductory section containing the project purpose, the literature review from the previous chapter, and the procedures. A time line and budget may be included as proposal sections or as appendices.

Addition of the references section for all the sources cited completes most proposals. Once complete, the proposal should be reviewed carefully to see that all information has been included. Most proposals will need approval of institutional review boards before researchers can begin any data collection.

Questions for Discussion

1. Explain how careful and systematic planning of research procedures contributes to the validity of data for analysis, and to the reliability of data for analysis.
2. Graduate students sometimes do not include data analysis procedures in research proposals because these procedures cannot be applied until the data are collected. Discuss the advantages and disadvantages of planning the analysis procedures as part of the proposal.
3. This chapter discusses the construction of the introduction to the project and the title as the final steps in the production of a research proposal. Describe the advantages and disadvantages of doing these tasks in this sequence.

Answers to Selected Exercises

Exercise 1.1

1. A5 Preservice and Inservice Secondary Teachers' Orientations Toward Content Area Reading has all the sections—introduction, method, results, discussion, and references. All are labeled, except the introduction.

Exercise 2.1

2a. Qualitative inquiry seems to be indicated because communication patterns suggests a phenomenon. Notice the open-endedness of the question. The data gathered to answer this question would likely be verbal descriptions.

2b. This question infers the goal of explanation or description of the phenomenon. The researcher is trying to grasp the nature of communication patterns.

5a. Quantitative inquiry is the likely choice because perceptual motor development and eye-hand coordination are known variables. The data gathered to answer this question would likely be numerical information about the degree to which eye-hand coordination is shown. Verbal descriptions could be collected, but these would be supplementary.

5b. The question calls for control as a goal. The researcher wants to manipulate the variable, perceptual motor development, to see if changes occur in eye-hand coordination.

Exercise 2.2

2. Use of a qualitative method is appropriate to answer this question. As indicated, the researcher wants to explore the phenomenon of communication patterns. Use of qualitative procedures would encourage gathering many types of information from parents of at-risk students, counselors, and others who work with at-risk students.

5. An experiment is required in this case. Probably two groups of first graders would be used to make comparison possible. One group would receive perceptual motor development, but the other would not. Another approach is to use only one group, evaluate their eye-hand coordination at the beginning, provide perceptual motor development training, and reevaluate eye-hand coordination. A third approach might be to use two groups of first graders and give each group different amounts of perceptual motor development training.

Exercise 3.1

1. The authors provide background information about the topic of their report through this explanatory statement.

Exercise 3.2

A3 A Phenomenological Study with Youth Gang Members: Results and Implications for School Counselors

1. Perceptions of gang membership, including how gangs function, is the phenomenon of interest in this research project; its underlying goal of research is explanation. This project uses qualitative methods for solution.

4. The primary justification stated in the report is to assist a newly hired high school counselor to increase her own knowledge of gangs. This justification is not connected directly to the literature review.

Exercise 4.1

2. The accessible population consists of students enrolled in high school foreign language classes. There's insufficient information to determine whether more than one high school or more than one teacher is involved. The sampling selection strategy is convenience because these students are those available to Mr. Charles. There's no mention of any actual sampling strategies.

Exercise 4.2

1. Based on the information given, Ms. Bordeaux probably used a purposeful sampling strategy. Through her observations, she observed a range of interactions among at-risk middle school students and teachers. After she determined the range, she asked for classrooms in which the interactions were different—one in which they were positive and one in which they were negative.

Exercise 4.3

A4 A Computerized Method to Teach Latin and Greek Root Words: Effect on Verbal SAT Scores

2a. The participants were planning to enter college by virtue of their enrollment in college preparatory-level English and would be likely to take the SAT. Therefore, they are ideal for this study. The original numbers of participants (see Table 1) are large enough to provide data about the full range of variations within these variables.

The participants were volunteers, which means the selection strategy was nonrandom. The participants do not necessarily represent any larger population. Therefore, their data are not necessarily like data that might be gathered from a larger group. Volunteers may have special qualities or reasons for participation that are not shared with nonvolunteers.

Exercise 5.1

1. Both flexibility-of-thinking and problem-solving capabilities in social studies must be measured. Both variables could be measured with either selected-response or constructed-response strategies such as tests, examinations, inventories, rating strategies, or ranking strategies. With large numbers of participants, researchers would likely use selected-response strategies rather than constructed-response strategies because the former would be more economical to administer and evaluate than the latter.

Both variables are constructs, therefore the measures would need construct validity of measurement. These constructs should be measured as the literature describes them.

Exercise 5.2

2. Nominal—Designations as males or females are simple classifications.
4. Ordinal—These are rankings; the rank of "excellent" may or may not be the same distance from "very good" as "very good" is from "good."
5. Ratio—Years of formal schooling could mean any number, including zero.

Exercise 5.3

2. To have verbal exchanges, Ms. Bordeaux would need to function as a participant-as-observer or as a complete participant. She would probably use informal conversations to check the accuracy of collected data.

Exercise 5.4

A5 Preservice and Inservice Secondary Teachers' Orientations Toward Content Area Reading

2a. The researchers need numerical data about teacher orientations to content area reading to answer their research questions. The "belief" instruments provide these data.

The researchers provide good evidence for the validity of data collected with their strategies. The researchers used knowledgeable university personnel who showed high levels of interrater reliability in agreements that the belief statements and lesson plans measured what they purported to measure.

Exercise 6.1

3. This is a true experiment, probably a posttest only control group design. There's no mention of a pretest, but there is a posttest. Participants are assigned to treatment levels (i.e., videotaped lectures, live lectures) by random assignment.

Exercise 7.1

2. This question suggests a causal comparative design. The researchers would gather data on students' abilities to suggest solutions to social problems and see if there is a pattern with measures of student intellectual developmental levels.

Other researchers might view this question as a correlation study and attempt to determine the magnitude and direction of a relationship between middle school students' intellectual developmental levels and their abilities to suggest solutions to social problems. Both variables can be measured and the data can be associated.
3. This question could be investigated through several designs. A meta-analysis of research studies on the topic of optimal age for formal schooling could provide status information. A survey study of experienced teachers who teach children at the beginning of formal schooling could also provide status information. A causal comparative study involving students who began formal schooling at different ages could also provide an answer.

Exercise 8.1

1b. About 68% of the students in Mr. B's class scored between 84 and 92 points. This is the interval of scores that includes one standard deviation above and one standard deviation below the mean.

1d. Juanita and Bill's earned scores of 86 each do not represent comparable performances. Juanita's score of 86, two points less than the class mean, is within one standard deviation below the mean. Bill's score of 86, 10 points above the mean, is approximately one-and-a-half standard deviations above the mean in his class. Bill's score is better than Juanita's.

Exercise 8.2

2a. An appropriate correlation coefficient for measuring the association between grade point average (interval measure) with gender (nominal measure) is either point biserial or biserial.

Exercise 8.3

A5 Preservice and Inservice Secondary Teachers' Orientations toward Content Area Reading

3. The descriptive results named in the Results section include frequencies and percentages of preservice and inservice teachers in each orientation on the two questions of the study (see Table 1). These statistics satisfy the project goal (explanation) and design (causal comparative).

     The researchers make a broad statement (i.e., "Preservice and inservice teachers . . . reading develops) about the meaning of the descriptive statistics in Table 1. The researchers did *not* answer the research questions for the participants with these descriptive statistics, although they could have done so.

Exercise 9.1

1a. N; This hypothesis states the no difference hypothesis about swim times for two groups that had different types of instruction.

Exercise 9.2

1a. The descriptive statistics tested are means for the two groups.

1b. These data are of ratio measure and a parametric test can be used, provided the numbers of participants in the two groups approaches 30 or more.

1c. A *t*-test could be used to see if there's a statistically significant difference between the means. Or a one-way analysis of variance could be used for the same purpose.

Exercise 9.3

1b. Data from the administrators showed a positive statistically significant correlation between emotional exhaustion and level of stress. The association among these data is so rare that it would happen by chance alone once in 1,000 times.

2b. The predictor variables of task-based stress, satisfaction, administrative coping, conflict-mediating stress, competitive approach, physical health, and administrative stress combined explain 47% of the variance within the criterion variable, emotional exhaustion.

Exercise 9.4

A4 A Computerized Method to Teach Latin and Greek Root Words: Effect on Verbal SAT

1. The researchers have these descriptive statistics available to use in inferential statistical tests: pre- and posttest means and standard deviations for the tested and untested groups and pre- and posttest means and standard deviations for the groups who had and did not have computer instruction. Pretesting/no pretesting and computer instruction/no computer instruction are the values of the independent variables in this project.

Exercise 11.1

1. This is probably a primary source with information provided by an eyewitness or a print copy of the address. Note that the date of 1834 fits with the time period of this study.

Exercise 12.1

1. Interpretation—Gmelch and Gates cite research from two different researchers as part of the explanation of their own findings.
3. Conclusion—This statement answers the researchers' question.

Exercise 12.2

A3 A Phenomenological Study with Youth Gang Members: Results and Implications for School Counselors

3. The conclusion of this project is the paragraph that begins, "Finally, we wrote. . ." These statements answer the research question, What is your experience of being a member of a gang? The conclusion seems warranted based on the information reported in the analyses of interviews.
4. The conclusion states a clear solution to the researchers' problem in terms of the project phenomena. These researchers are particularly careful to focus their conclusion on the particular gang members from whom they gathered data; they clearly limited the conclusion.
5. These researchers offered several recommendations in the form of implications for school counselors. For example, the researchers suggest that school counselors should foster a sense of identity and self-respect among the individual students with whom they work. Given the comments that participants shared with the researchers, this recommendation is appropriate. One of the chief reasons for becoming a gang member is to find a sense of belonging.

Appendix A
Research Reports

The reports included here are generally representative of those published in journals and are selected to be of interest to teachers, counselors, staff developers, and administrators. Some reports reflect the use of quantitative inquiry, but others use qualitative methods. Experimental, descriptive, qualitative, and historical methods are represented in these reports. Several subject areas and age or grade levels of participants are featured.

References to these reports are noted throughout the text in illustrations and in exercises. The reports include:

A1: Gettinger, M. (1993). Effects of error correction on third graders' spelling. *Journal of Educational Research, 87,* 39–45.

A2: Larson, B. E., & Parker, W. C. (1996). What is classroom discussion? A look at teachers' conceptions. *Journal of Curriculum and Supervision, 11,* 110–126.

A3: Omizo, M. M., Omizo, S. A., & Honda, M. R. (1997). A phenomenological study with youth gang members: Results and implications for school counselors. *Professional School Counseling, 1,* 39–42.

A4: Holmes, C. T., & Keffer, R. L. (1995). A computerized method to teach Latin and Greek root words: Effect on verbal SAT scores. *Journal of Educational Research, 89,* 47–50.

A5: Konopak, B. C., Readence, J. E., & Wilson, E. K. (1994). Preservice and inservice secondary teachers' orientations toward content area reading. *Journal of Educational Research, 87,* 220–227.

A6: Gmelch, W. H., & Gates, G. (1998). The impact of personal, professional and organizational characteristics on administrator burnout. *Journal of Educational Administration, 36,* 146–159.

A7: Wentzel, K. R. (1997). Student motivation in middle school: The role of perceived pedagogical caring. *Journal of Educational Psychology, 89,* 411–419.

A8: Tolley, K. (1996). Science for ladies, classics for gentlemen: A comparative analysis of scientific subjects in the curricula of boys' and girls' secondary schools in the United States, 1794–1850. *History of Education Quarterly, 36,* 129–153.

A9: Thomas, W. B., & Moran, K. J. (1992). Reconsidering the power of the superintendent in the Progressive Period. *American Educational Research Journal, 29,* 22–50.

A1

Effects of Error Correction on Third Graders' Spelling

Maribeth Gettinger
University of Wisconsin-Madison

ABSTRACT   An error-correction procedure was implemented as part of regular classroom spelling instruction for third-grade students. The procedure included two major components: (a) error imitation and correction and (b) repeated practice to mastery. A multigroup pretest-posttest design was used to compare the effectiveness of the corrected-test procedure with two control conditions—standard practice and practice with a reduced number of words. Significantly higher weekly spelling test scores and teacher ratings document the effectiveness of the experimental intervention over both control conditions. The present study provides evidence for the generalizability of error correction and practice procedures to regular classroom instruction.

A variety of theoretical positions and applied techniques for enhancing children's spelling performance have appeared in the literature in the last decade (Brown, 1990). Many recent developments in spelling instruction have evolved from merging traditional methods of teaching spelling (presenting a list of words on Monday and testing them on Friday) with new perspectives in information processing (Gerber & Hall, 1987). One instructional component that is common to most effective techniques is the provision of immediate, corrective feedback. The effectiveness of feedback stems, in part, from the enhancement of memory, attention, and discrimination necessary to learn spelling patterns. Several investigators have found error-correction strategies to be successful with normally achieving spellers (Foxx & Jones, 1978) as well as with both learning-disabled students (Ollendick, Matson, Esveldt-Dawson, & Shapiro, 1980) and children with mental retardation (Matson, Esveldt-Dawson, & Kazdin, 1982; Stewart & Singh, 1986).

A variation of the error-correction method was originally developed by Jobes (1975) and later used by Kauffman, Hallahan, Haas, Brame, and Boren (1978) to improve the spelling performance of a learning-disabled boy. This procedure incorporates contingent error imitation and correction, whereby children's pretest errors are rewritten by the teacher prior to modeling the correct spelling. Gettinger (1985) found that the addition of visual cues that highlight the error part(s) of misspelled words, paired with having students (rather than teachers) directing their own practice, further enhanced the overall effectiveness of the procedure. Gerber and his associates (Gerber, 1984a, 1984b, 1986; Nulman & Gerber, 1984) also demonstrated the efficacy of error imitation and modeling with disabled learners.

Specifically, Gerber (1984b, 1986) has shown that learning-disabled children can learn to spell a list of 10 words with 100% accuracy and to transfer learned phonetic

Journal of Educational Research, vol. 87, no. 1, pp. 39–45, October 1993. Reprinted with permission of the Helen Dwight Reid Educational Foundation. Published by Heldref publications, 1319 Eighteenth St., NW, Washington, DC 20036-1802. Copyright © 1993.

elements to a similar, rhyming list of words under two conditions: (a) They receive corrective feedback using the contingent imitation/modeling procedure of Kauffman et al. (1978). (b) They are given repeated opportunities to spell the entire word list correctly. The addition of a repeated-trials component is important for two reasons. First, low-achieving children characteristically take longer to master academic tasks than do their normally achieving peers (Gettinger, 1984b). Thus, the allocation of sufficient time to learn words maximizes the effectiveness of an error imitation and correction procedure with all children. Second, the provision of repeated dictation tests allows for a trial-by-trial analysis of qualitative changes in children's spelling attempts over time. This type of analysis yields more informative diagnostic data than can be obtained from simply knowing the number of words spelled correctly.

Whereas Kauffman et al. (1978) attributed the effectiveness of their corrected-test procedure to focused attention and forced discrimination between the error imitation and correct spelling, Gerber (1984b) offered an alternative cognitive problem-solving explanation. Gerber's analyses revealed that children's spelling attempts over trials reflected qualitatively better approximations of correct spelling. In other words, children demonstrated a gradual improvement in their understanding and application of orthographic rules rather than rote memorization of increasingly longer strings of letters. Thus, he posited that repeated exposure to both error imitations and correct spellings does more than focus children's attention; it also increases their efficiency in managing and applying orthographic knowledge. Gerber concluded that the use of a contingent imitation/ modeling procedure and repeated trials to criterion leads to qualitative improvements in spelling among disabled children.

Regardless of the theoretical explanation underlying the effectiveness of error-correction procedures, spelling problems may persist for many children because regular classroom instruction does not afford students sufficient time to master correct spellings, nor does it provide adequate corrective feedback. Findings from several investigations with poor spellers suggest that poor spelling ability may be attributed, in part, to instructional factors (Bryant, Drabin, & Gettinger, 1981; DeMaster, Crossland, & Hasselbring, 1986; Foster & Torgesen, 1983; Gettinger, 1984a; Gettinger, Bryant, & Fayne, 1982; Graham & Freeman, 1985). Researchers agree that allowing students to devise their own methods for studying spelling words is not as effective as providing a systematic error-correction and practice procedure.

Given that poor spelling may be caused by instructional factors, several researchers have examined the content of spelling curriculum or surveyed teachers to determine the nature of current instructional practices (Cronnell & Humes, 1980; Graham, 1983; Morris, Nelson, & Perney, 1986; Vallecorsa, Zigmond, & Henderson, 1985). Despite the fact that teachers are familiar with effective research-based techniques of their classrooms, the spelling procedures used in most classrooms are based primarily on commercially prepared materials. The presentation of 15 to 20 words each week and the use of a "pretest on Monday, posttest on Friday" instructional pattern characterize traditional teaching approaches. According to Vallecorsa et al. (1985), classroom teachers depend heavily on commercial materials and do not incorporate empirically valid techniques for teaching spelling, even when they are aware of those procedures.

Although there is general agreement that error-correction procedures may be effective for improving children's spelling performance, the literature is lacking in field-based studies in which corrected-test procedures are implemented and evaluated as part of classroom instruction. One reason that teachers may fail to use practices supported by research is that many procedures are typically conducted in a restricted format and rely on one-to-one or small-group instructional methods that may be difficult to implement in an actual classroom setting (Cronnell & Humes, 1980). Furthermore, data are seldom provided concerning children's performance during their regular classroom spelling assignments or on weekly spelling tests that typically include up to 20 words rather than 5 to 10 words.

In light of this apparent discrepancy between classroom practices and research-supported procedures, in the present study I addressed the extent to which a treatment procedure that has been shown to be effective with poor spellers in controlled investigations can be effectively implemented in regular education classrooms with all children. Collectively, the outcome data from the spelling intervention studies cited above show that children demonstrate improvement in spelling performance when (a) sufficient time is allocated for mastery, (b) feedback is provided that allows students to compare their errors with correct spellings, and (c) practice is student directed to minimize the supervisory time required of teachers. I examined the application of an intervention incorporating all three treatment components by third-grade students. The treatment was implemented as part of the spelling instruction in the class. Students' performance, evaluated on the basis of weekly spelling tests and teacher ratings, was compared with that of students who received traditional spelling instruction and practice. I predicted that students who received the error-correction intervention would evidence higher spelling accuracy than would students who received no additional modification beyond their standard spelling practice, or whose practice was optimized by dividing their words into smaller, daily chunks (Bryant et al., 1981; Gettinger et al., 1982).

Method

Participants

Students in three third-grade classes participated in this study. The classrooms included predominantly White (89%), middle-class children in a suburban school district. Because the purpose of this investigation was to evaluate the effectiveness of error correction as part of classroom instruction, all the children in each class were invited to participate. The sole criterion for participation was parental consent, which was obtained for all but 3 children from two different classes. There was a total of 65 children across the three classes who participated (31 boys and 34 girls). The students in the total sample had an average chronological age of 8 years, 2 months and a mean grade equivalent score from the Test of Written Spelling (Larson & Hammill, 1976) of 3rd grade, 1 month. Age and standardized spelling test performance were comparable across the three classrooms. Assignment of intact classrooms to experimental conditions was random.

Spelling Curriculum

All participating classes used the Lippencott Basic Spelling curriculum (Glim & Manchester, 1982). In this curriculum, there are 15 words for each weekly lesson that are grouped by visual similarity and commonality of orthographic rules (affixes, sound-letter correspondence, etc.). The series has 35 weekly lessons that include a review lesson every seventh week. As part of the regular spelling instruction, the participating teachers used a 5-day study plan with a pretest on Monday, 20-min independent study periods on Tuesday, Wednesday, and Thursday, and a final test on Friday. For purposes of this investigation, the six lessons that occurred between review lessons constituted one unit. One six-lesson unit was taught prior to the intervention, one unit during, and one unit subsequent to the intervention.

Procedure

Data were collected during three 6-week phases as part of the spelling instruction in each class. The first phase was a baseline or preintervention phase; the second phase was intervention; and the final phase was generalization or postintervention. Prior to baseline, classrooms were randomly assigned to one of three instructional conditions. These consisted of two comparison conditions, standard and reduced number, and an experimental condition. The three conditions varied in the nature of spelling practice that students received.

In the standard-condition classroom (Class A), 21 students (10 boys and 11 girls) received their regular spelling practice. On Monday, the students were given a pretest on the lesson's 15 words. Approximately 20 min were allocated on Tuesday, Wednesday, and Thursday for students to complete spelling workbook exercises, write sentences containing each word, or study words on their own or with another student. Weekly spelling tests were administered on Friday. The reduced-number condition in Class B (10 boys and 14 girls) was similar to the standard condition, except that the weekly 15-word lists were divided into three smaller sets of 5 words each. Students were instructed to select 5 different words for independent study on Tuesday through Thursday. To ensure the integrity of this condition, children made separate word cards for each 5-word set and studied only those words on a designated day. The rationale for including the reduced-number condition was to determine if the experimental condition would enhance spelling performance beyond simply minimizing the size of daily word units to study.

In the experimental-condition classroom (Class C), 20 students (11 boys and 9 girls) implemented an error-correction and practice procedure during their independent study time on Tuesday through Thursday. Working in pairs (2 students who sat next to each other), students tested each other on the day's 5-word set. Students then corrected their own tests in the following manner: for each incorrect word, the students first looked at how the word was spelled and then wrote the word in exact imitation of the misspelling adjacent to it. Next, they looked at the correct spelling and wrote it adjacent to the error imitation and repeated the word to themselves. After writing the error imitation and correct spelling, students circled in red and studied the part(s) of the word that were misspelled, in both the error imitation and the correct model. Following the error imitation and correction, students carried out three practice steps on their own: First, they looked at the word and repeated it; then they turned the card over and wrote the word, circling the error part; and, finally, they checked the spelling. After this practice, paired students retested each other. This sequence of testing, error imitation and correction, practice, and retesting continued until all words in the set were spelled correctly. Each retesting was scored as one learning trial. If students reached mastery before the end of the allocated time period, they were instructed to study the words or do workbook exercises on their own.

Measures

Three measures of spelling performance were collected for 18 weeks across the three experimental phases (i.e., baseline, intervention, generalization). Two measures of spelling accuracy—dictated lists and dictated stories—and a third measure reflecting teachers' evaluation of children's spelling were obtained for every child. A learning-rate measure and quality ratings were also obtained for experimental-group children during the intervention phase.

Spelling accuracy. Scores (number correct; possible range = 0 to 5) on weekly dictation spelling tests were used as the primary outcome measures of spelling performance. In keeping with the standard procedures in classrooms, students exchanged and graded each other's papers. I rescored all the tests; interscorer agreement between me and the students was consistently 100%. The median test-retest reliability coefficient, determined by correlating scores on weekly tests that were administered during baseline, was .92.

Spelling accuracy was also evaluated on the basis of the number of target words spelled correctly in a dictated story administered at the conclusion of each 6-week curriculum unit. Thirty words were selected at random from the total list of 90 words that were taught in a 6-week unit. Fifth-grade students in the same school used the 30 words to write a story during their creative writing lessons. A dictated-story spelling measure was used instead of student-generated writing samples to control for difficulty and complexity of vocabulary and syntax. Rather than my developing standard stories for dictation, I incorporated this activity into a creative writing lesson for older students. The stories were judged to be equivalent in difficulty by both third- and fifth-grade teachers.

Teacher ratings. Classroom teachers completed a global rating for students in their classrooms every 3 weeks (prior to, during, and subsequent to the intervention phase). The three teachers were instructed to rate children on weekly spelling test performance and general spelling accuracy for writing activities during the previous 3 weeks (e.g., essays and sentences). Ratings ranged from 1 (far below average) to 5 (far above average). Test-retest reliability, based on the correlation between the two ratings completed during baseline, was .83. The purpose of global ratings was to determine the social validity of treatment effectiveness data. Each teacher had at least 4 years of teaching experience and reported no difficulty in being able to complete the global ratings. There was a strong relationship between teachers' ratings and spelling accuracy on words presented in dictated lists ($r = .89$) and dictated stories ($r = .80$).

Trials-to-criterion and orthographic ratings. During the 6-week intervention phase, children in the experimental group tested themselves on each 5-word set until they reached a criterion of 100% accuracy. The number of learning trials (retests) required to reach criterion (TTC) was averaged across the 3 study days. TTC was an index of learning rate in the experimental condition; comparable learning-rate measures were not obtained for the standard or reduced-number conditions because they did not incorporate the repeated-practice component.

The quality of experimental children's weekly posttests during the intervention phase was evaluated independently by two raters who had been trained to an agreement level of 100% prior to the initiation of the study. The raters used a classification scheme, based on previous developmental scoring procedures (Gentry, 1978, 1981; Henderson & Beers, 1980), by which the quality of each spelling attempt on the posttest was rated on a 5-point scale. The rating categories were as follows: 1 = preliterate (strings of letters and nonletters without regard for letter-sound correspondence, e.g., ops for eagle); 2 = prephonetic (plausible representations of one or more, but not all, phonemes, e.g., ec for eagle); 3 = phonetic (representation of every phoneme as each sounds, e.g., egl for eagle); 4 = transitional (representation of all phonemes with some knowledge of English orthography, e.g., egul for eagle); and, 5 = correct. Each student received a qualitative score ranging from 15 to 75 for each test.

Treatment Integrity

During the intervention phase, the testing and practice papers of children in the experimental group were collected by the classroom teacher at the end of the daily study sessions. Thus, I was able to check the adherence of each child to the error imitation and correction, practice, and mastery testing procedures. An independent rater and I checked the papers at the end of each week to see that the appropriate procedures had been used. This check confirmed that the experimental treatment procedures were carried out appropriately by children in the experimental group during the intervention phase.

Results

The average number of words spelled correctly on weekly tests for each classroom is presented in Table 1. These figures reflect class averages for the three 6-week spelling curriculum units that were covered during the baseline, intervention, and generalization phases in each classroom. The three classrooms did not differ significantly in average weekly test performance on Unit 1. The mean accuracy across six tests was 69%, 72%, and 66% for Classes A, B, and C, respectively. An analysis of variance (ANOVA) on Unit 2 (i.e., during treatment implementation) and Unit 3 (i.e., posttreatment generalization accuracy scores did reveal a significant difference among classes, $F(2, 62) = 4.90$, $p < .05$, for Unit 2 and $F(2, 62) = 3.31$, $p < .05$, for Unit 3. Children in Class C, on average, obtained significantly higher weekly spelling test scores during the intervention and generalization phases than did children in the other two classes (see Table 1 for class averages).

Similar results were obtained for spelling accuracy scores based on dictated stories for Unit 2 words. Again, the classrooms showed comparable performance in spelling accuracy during baseline; average accuracy was 66%, 68%, and 63% for Classes A, B, and C, respectively. An ANOVA on Unit 2 words revealed a significant difference among classes, $F(2, 62) = 4.34$, $p < .05$, with students in Class C achieving higher accuracy (87%) than either Class A (69%) or Class B students (65%). Although higher accuracy was maintained by Class C students on Unit 3 words dictated in story format (82% accuracy versus 67% and 68%), this observed difference did not reach statistical significance, $F(2, 62) = 2.36$, ns.

Finally, mean teacher ratings (averaged across the two rating periods) were similar across the three classes during baseline (see Table 1). In the intervention phase, there was a significant difference among ratings, $F(2, 62) = 3.82$, $p < .05$. Parallel to the higher obtained weekly spelling test scores, students in Class C received overall higher ratings ($M = 4.3$) than did students in Class A ($M = 3.4$) or Class B ($M = 3.2$). Again, although higher teacher ratings were maintained in Class C during the generalization phase, the observed difference was not statistically significant, $F(2, 62) = 2.31$, ns.

Table 2 provides an analysis of the mean trials-to-criterion (TTC) scores (averaged across 3 days) and quality ratings for weekly tests during the intervention phase for experimental-group children. There was variation among children in the average number of learning trials needed to spell all words in a set correctly (highest range during Week 1 = 1.0 to 3.7). This indicates that, during Week 1, the slowest student took as much as three to four times the number of repeated learning trials to reach criterion as the fastest student.

An examination of the mean TTC scores indicates that the number of learning trials tended to decrease across weeks for all subjects. For example, the total average TTC for the first week of the intervention phase was 2.4, whereas the total average TTC for the last week of intervention was 1.6. That finding suggests that the error imitation and correction procedure and repeated practice may have improved children's acquisition rates as well as their spelling accuracy.

Also, there was limited variability in the quality of ratings across weeks (see Table 2). This was caused by (a) the high number of correct spellings on weekly tests that each received 5-point ratings and (b) the limited number of spellings that received ratings below 3 (phonetic). In general, children's spelling errors reflected performance at the phonetic or, more frequently, the transitional level. Nonetheless, the quality ratings in Table 2 show a gradual improvement across weeks.

TABLE 1

Average Spelling Accuracy on Dictated Lists and Stories and Teacher Ratings Across Conditions

Measure/unit	Class: Experimental condition			
	Class A (*n* = 21) standard	Class B (*n* = 24) reduced number	Class C (*n* = 20) experimental	*F*
Spelling accuracy: Weekly tests[a]				
Unit 1	10.3	10.8	9.9	0.27
(Baseline)	(3.6)	(4.3)	(3.9)	
	69%	72%	66%	
Unit 2	10.7	10.6	13.9	4.90*
(Intervention)	(3.3)	(3.8)	(4.2)	
	71%	71%	93%	
Unit 3	11.1	10.3	13.1	3.31*
(Generalization)	(3.3)	(3.6)	(3.8)	
	74%	69%	87%	
Spelling accuracy: Dictated stories[b]				
Unit 1	19.8	20.3	18.9	0.16
(Baseline)	(6.3)	(9.1)	(9.4)	
	66%	68%	63%	
Unit 2	20.6	19.5	26.2	4.34*
(Intervention)	(7.4)	(7.7)	(8.1)	
	69%	65%	87%	
Unit 3	20.1	20.5	24.8	2.36
(Generalization)	(6.8)	(7.0)	(7.3)	
	67%	68%	82%	
Teacher ratings[c]				
Unit 1	3.1	3.5	3.3	0.49
(Baseline)	(1.2)	(0.9)	(1.8)	
Unit 2	3.4	3.2	4.3	3.82*
(Intervention)	(1.1)	(1.4)	(1.5)	
Unit 3	3.2	3.1	3.9	2.31
(Generalization)	(1.4)	(1.1)	(1.3)	

Note. Numbers in parentheses are standard deviations. % equals percentages of correct spelling words.
[a]Mean number spelled correctly on weekly tests (possible range = 0 to 15), averaged across 6 weeks. [b]Mean number spelled correctly in context of dictated story (possible range = 0 to 30). [c]Mean ratings averaged over two periods (possible range = 0 to 5).
*$p < .05$.

TABLE 2

Average Trials-to-Criterion and Orthographic Quality Ratings for the Experimental Group Across Interventions

Measure	Week of intervention					
	1	2	3	4	5	6
TTC[a]						
Mean	2.4	2.6	2.1	1.7	1.8	1.6
Range	1.0 to 3.7	1.0 to 3.3	1.0 to 2.9	1.0 to 2.8	1.0 to 2.8	1.0 to 2.5
Quality rating[b]	67.9	71.3	70.1	73.4	72.9	73.8

[a]TTC averaged across 3 days of practice. [b]Possible range = 15 to 75.

Discussion

The results of this study show that an error imitation and correction procedure with repeated practice yielded higher weekly spelling test performance among third-grade students than either traditional spelling instruction or modified standard instruction in which the number of words to be learned (15 words) was broken down into smaller sets of 5 words for daily study. The significantly higher spelling test scores for experimental-group children were maintained 6 weeks following the intervention phase, suggesting that students continued to implement the error correction and practice procedures during generalization. Perhaps the most significant aspect of this study is that the intervention was implemented successfully as part of students' regular classroom instruction, thus demonstrating the validity and utility of laboratory techniques in classroom practices.

The error correction and practice procedure that I used in this investigation incorporated cognitive and behavioral factors that have been linked to spelling achievement. Research has shown that the ability to detect and correct spelling errors is related to spelling achievement. Children with spelling problems tend to require more salient cues and more practice to facilitate error detection and correction. Imitating errors, modeling correct spellings, and highlighting error parts appeared to provide necessary and immediate feedback to enhance children's error monitoring.

The positive effects of the experimental procedure may be attributed, in part, to two additional treatment components. First, the actual studying of spelling words was primarily a teacher-determined, student-controlled activity. Although the study procedure itself was teacher determined rather than student determined (i.e., students did not devise their own study strategies; the teacher instructed them on how to study words), students implemented and monitored the procedure with minimal teacher involvement. The differential effectiveness of study conditions that vary in terms of teacher versus student control has not been clearly established; however, research has consistently documented that student-controlled interventions can be at least as effective as teacher-controlled instruction (Gettinger, 1985; Graham & Freeman, 1985). Because student-controlled procedures may result in productive, organizational learning behaviors and minimize the supervisory time required of teachers, student-controlled study procedures in other academic areas may warrant continued use and further investigation.

Second, the experimental procedure incorporated some degree of cooperative learning by having children test each other in pairs. Van Oudehoven, van Berkum, and Swen-Koopmans (1987) have documented that studying in pairs produced better spelling than studying individually. In attributing benefits to these latter components (degree of teacher versus student control and working in pairs), one should note that neither was experimentally manipulated. That is, each component was inherent in the implementation of the experimental intervention; however, they were not necessarily excluded from either the standard or reduced-number conditions. For example, several children elected to work in pairs during the 20-min daily study periods in the comparison classrooms.

The trials-to-criterion (TTC) data obtained for the experimental group during intervention phase has the potential for providing both diagnostic and remedial information. First, it is apparent that students differed in the amount of time they needed to learn an assigned set of spelling words. The students required individually variable exposure time to the correction procedure before they were able to spell an entire set of words correctly. Cronnell and Humes (1980) observed that spelling textbooks frequently offer little opportunity for students to practice writing the words to be learned. Because the amount of time spent in learning is related to school achievement in general, programs that provide insufficient practice may not be effective with poor spellers. Consistent with research on mastery learning, students in this study required fewer trials to reach criterion on successive weekly word lists. Thus, initially slower rates of skill acquisition may be partially remediated by providing sufficient opportunities to compare and contrast misspellings with correct models and by establishing a criterion level of performance.

The limited variability of the orthographic quality ratings precluded a detailed analysis of qualitative changes in spelling attempts across weeks. Overall, the students in this investigation began at a fairly high developmental level (transitional) compared with younger or more delayed students in other studies in which improvements in spelling quality were evident after repeated exposure to the correction procedure (e.g., Nulman & Gerber, 1984). The observed increase in quality ratings was due primarily to an increase in the number of words spelled correctly, rather than to improvements in the quality of errors per se.

To summarize, although the provision of corrective feedback, whereby students compare and contrast their spelling attempts with correct models, has been studied in laboratory analogue research, few studies have extended their findings to the classroom. The present investigation offers direct evidence of the effectiveness of a research-based spelling intervention in regular classroom instruction. The superiority of the experimental intervention over more standard procedures raises some question about the appropriateness of the "pretest on Monday, posttest on Friday" procedure often used for teaching spelling (Cronnell & Humes, 1980). The control conditions essentially simulated this procedure, because students were instructed to study the words on their own between the pretest and posttest. The results indicate that students may benefit from having their Monday-to-Friday study time, including spontaneous writing, more structured to achieve maximum performance in spelling.

References

Brown, A. S. (1990). A review of recent research on spelling *Educational Psychology Review. 2*, 365–397.

Bryant, N. D., Drabin, I. R., & Gettinger, M. (1981). Effects of varying unit size on spelling achievement in learning disabled children. *Journal of Learning Disabilities. 14,* 200–203.

Cronnell, B., & Humes, A. (1980). Elementary spelling: What's really taught. *Elementary School Journal, 81,* 59–64.

DeMaster, V. K., Crossland, C. L., & Hasselbring, T. S. (1986). Consistency of learning disabled students' spelling performance. *Learning Disability Quarterly 9,* 89–96.

Foster, K., & Torgesen, J. K. (1983). The effects of directed study on the spelling performance on two subgroups of learning disabled students. *Learning Disability Quarterly, 6,* 252–257.

Foxx, R. M., & Jones, J. R. (1978). A remediation program for increasing the spelling achievement of elementary and junior high school students. *Behavior Modification, 2,* 211–230.

Gentry, J. R. (1978). Early spelling strategies. *Elementary School Journal, 79,* 88–92.

Gentry, J. R. (1981). Learning to spell developmentally. *The Reading Teacher, 34,* 378–381.

Gerber, M. M. (1984a). Orthographic problem-solving ability of learning disabled and normally achieving students. *Learning Disability Quarterly, 7,* 157–164.

Gerber, M. M. (1984b). Techniques to teach generalizable spelling skills. *Academic Therapy, 20,* 49–58.

Gerber, M. M. (1986). Generalization of spelling strategies by LD students as a result of contingent imitation/modeling and mastery criteria. *Journal of Learning Disabilities, 19,* 530–537.

Gerber, M. M., & Hall, R. J. (1987). Information processing approaches to studying spelling deficiencies. *Journal of Learning Disabilities, 20,* 34–42.

Gettinger, M. (1984a). Applying learning principles to remedial spelling instruction. *Academic Therapy, 20,* 41–48.

Gettinger, M. (1984b). Measuring time needed for learning to predict learning outcomes. *Exceptional Children, 51,* 244–248.

Gettinger, M. (1985). Effects of teacher-directed versus student-directed instruction and cues versus no cues for improving spelling performance. *Journal of Applied Behavior Analysis, 18,* 167–171.

Gettinger, M., Bryant, N. D., & Fayne, H. R. (1982). Designing spelling instruction for learning-disabled children: An emphasis on unit size, distributed practice, and training for transfer. *Journal of Special Education, 16,* 339–443.

Glim, T. E., & Manchester, F. S. (1982). *Lippincott basic spelling.* New York: Harper & Row.

Graham, S. (1983). Effective spelling instruction. *Elementary School Journal, 83,* 560–568.

Graham, S., & Freeman, S. (1985). Strategy training and teacher- vs. student-controlled study conditions: Effects on LD students' spelling performance. *Learning Disability Quarterly, 8,* 267–274.

Henderson, E. H., & Beers, J. W. (1980). *Developmental and cognitive aspects of learning to spell: A reflection of word knowledge.* Newark, DE: International Reading Association.

Jobes, N. K. (1975). *The acquisition and retention of spelling through imitation training and observational learning with and without feedback.* Unpublished doctoral dissertation, George Peabody College for Teachers, Nashville.

Kauffman, J. M., Hallahan, D. P., Haas, K., Brame, T., & Boren, R. (1978). Imitating children's errors to improve their spelling performance. *Journal of Learning Disabilities, 11,* 217–222.

Larsen, S., & Hammill, D. (1976). *Test of Written Spelling.* Austin, TX: Pro-Ed.

Matson, J. L., Esveldt-Dawson, K., & Kazdin, A. E. (1982). Treatment of spelling deficits in mentally retarded children. *Mental Retardation, 20,* 76–81.

Morris, D., Nelson, D., & Perney, J. (1986). Exploring the concept of "spelling instruction level" through the analysis of error types. *The Elementary School Journal, 87,* 181–200.

Nulman, J. A. H., & Gerber, M. M. (1984). Improving spelling performance by imitating a child's errors. *Journal of Learning Disabilities, 17,* 328–333.

Ollendick, T. H., Matson, J. L., Esveldt-Dawson, K., & Shapiro, E. S. (1980). Increasing spelling achievement: An analysis of treatment procedures utilizing an alternating treatments design. *Journal of Applied Behavior Analysis, 13,* 645–654.

Stewart, C., & Singh, N. (1986). Overcorrection of spelling deficits in moderately mentally retarded children. *Behavior Modification, 16,* 355–365.

Vallecorsa, A. L., Zigmond, N., & Henderson, L. A. (1985). Spelling instruction in special education classrooms: A survey of practices. *Exceptional Children, 52,* 19–24.

Van Oudehoven, J. P., van Berkum, G., & Swen-Koopmans, T. (1987). Effect of cooperation and shared feedback on spelling achievement. *Journal of Educational Psychology, 79,* 92–94.

Address correspondence to Maribeth Gettinger, Department of Educational Psychology, Educational Sciences Building, 1025 West Johnson Street, Madison, WI 53706.

A2

What Is Classroom Discussion? A Look at Teachers' Conceptions

Bruce E. Larson,
University of Washington

Walter C. Parker,
University of Washington

Discussion has enjoyed high status among forms of classroom interaction, but its status is effectively cancelled by its low frequency. Recitation persists[1] and is "seemingly invulnerable to repeated criticisms."[2]

---

[1]John I. Goodlad, *A Place Called School* (New York: McGraw-Hill, 1984); Susan S. Stodolsky, Teresa L. Ferguson, and Karen Wimpelberg, "The Recitation Persists, But What Does It Look Like?" *Journal of Curriculum Studies* 13, no. 2 (1981): 121–130; James Hoetker and William P. Ahlbrand Jr., "The Persistence of Recitation," *American Educational Research Journal* 6, no. 2 (1969): 145–167.

[2]Courtney Cazden, *Classroom Discourse* (Portsmouth, NH: Heinemann, 1988), p. 30.

Ironically, and adding insult to the instructional reformer's injury, junior and senior high school teachers and college teachers often call their recitations "discussions." When teachers lecture or seek answers to questions they pose, they often claim that this interaction could be called a discussion. For example, a semester-long study of middle school teachers revealed that the teacher talked for 87.8 percent of the class period during lessons that the teacher believed were discussions.[3]

The objective of the grounded theory study reported here was to build the first layer of an explanatory theory of teachers' conceptions of discussion. This foundation would contain detailed descriptions of a few teachers' notions of classroom discussion; from these, some initial "grounded hypotheses" could be constructed.[4] These statements in turn could be refined and elaborated in subsequent studies of teachers in various subject areas, grade levels, and cultural milieus. A grounded theory of this sort should be useful to researchers who are studying the persistence of recitation under the guise of discussion, often in lower-track settings, and to school administrators and practitioners who are committed to improving instruction.

Review of Related Literature

Classroom discussion serves several purposes. First, it is arguably the centerpiece of democratic education because it engages students in *the* essential practice of democratic living;[5] second, it nurtures critical thinking and moral reasoning;[6] third, it helps students understand the topic being discussed;[7] and fourth, it teaches the skills of discussion itself.[8] Discussion can accomplish all this because it is a unique form of classroom talk and a very special group dynamic: discussion requires students and teacher to talk back and forth at a high cognitive and affective level, both with one another and with the subject matter being discussed. "What they talk about," Dillon writes, "is an issue, some topic that is in question for them. Their talk consists of advancing and examining different proposals over the issue."[9]

[3]Nathan Swift and C. Thomas Gooding, "Interaction of Wait Time Feedback and Questioning Instruction on Middle School Science Teaching," *Journal of Research in Science Teaching* 20, no. 8 (1983): 721–730.

[4]Barney G. Glaser and Anselm L. Strauss, *The Discovery of Grounded Theory: Strategies for Qualitative Research* (New York: Aldine De Gruyter, 1967); Anselm L. Strauss and Juliet Corbin, *Basics of Qualitative Research: Grounded Theory, Procedures and Techniques* (Newbury Park, CA: Sage Publications, 1990).

[5]Shirley H. Engle and Anna Ochoa, *Education for Democratic Citizenship: Decision Making in the Social Studies* (New York: Teachers College Press, 1988); Donald W. Oliver and James P. Shaver, *Teaching Public Issues in the High School* (Logan, UT: Utah State University Press, 1966); Walter C. Parker, "The Possibilities of Discussion" (paper presented at the annual meeting of the College and University Faculty Assembly of the National Council for the Social Studies, Detroit, November 1992).

[6]Meredith D. Gall and Joyce P. Gall, "Outcomes of the Discussion Method," in *Teaching and Learning Through Discussion: The Theory Research and Practice of the Discussion Method,* ed. William W. Wilen (Springfield, IL: Charles C. Thomas, 1990), pp. 25–44; Fred M. Newmann, "The Curriculum of Thoughtful Classes," in *Higher Order Thinking in High School Social Studies: An Analysis of Classrooms, Teachers, Students, and Leadership,* ed. Fred M. Newmann (Madison: University of Wisconsin, National Center on Effective Secondary Schools, 1988), pp. 1–35; F. Clark Power, Ann Higgins, and Lawrence Kohlberg, *Lawrence Kohlberg's Approach to Moral Education* (New York: Columbia University Press, 1989).

[7]James T. Dillon, *Using Discussion in the Classroom* (Philadelphia: Open University Press, 1994); Suzanne Miller, *Creating Change: Towards a Dialogic Pedagogy,* Report Series 2.18 (Albany, NY: National Research Center on Literature Teaching and Learning) (ERIC Document Reproduction Service No. ED 349 582, 1992); Ronald G. Tharp and Ronald Gallimore, *Rousing Minds to Life: Teaching, Learning, and Schooling in Social Context* (Cambridge: Cambridge University Press, 1988).

[8]David Bridges, *Education, Democracy and Discussion* (Windsor, England: NFER, 1979); James T. Dillon, *Using Discussion in the Classroom* (Philadelphia: Open University Press, 1994); William W. Wilen, "Forms and Phases of Discussion," in *Teaching and Learning Through Discussion: The Theory, Research and Practice of the Discussion Method,* ed. William W. Wilen (Springfield IL: Charles C. Thomas, 1990) pp. 3–24.

[9]James T. Dillon, *Using Discussion in the Classroom* (Philadelphia: Open University Press, 1994), p. 7.

Democratic Citizenship

Democratic societies are dynamic and changing, for democracy is a way of life.[10] In this view, "democracy is not already accomplished, needing only protection, but a path that citizens in a pluralist society try to walk together. It is this commitment that unites them, not a culture, language, or religion."[11] Therefore, citizens should not merely elect those who will govern them, but participate in self-governance themselves. This is "strong" democracy.[12] The act of voting is only one of many important roles of a citizen. Also needed is a willingness and ability to interact with others on matters of common concern.

Discussion is the chief medium for this interaction. Competence in the skills of discussion is required if citizens are to engage in fruitful discussions. These skills include listening (with an ear to considering opposing opinions), encouraging participation, making and supporting claims, helping the group move through obstacles, and developing together a shared understanding of the problem.[13] Classroom discussions might be thought of as citizenship laboratories in which students of different race, ethnicity, gender, social class, and ability learn how to engage one another on matters of common concern.

Conceptions of Classroom Discussion

Conceptual models of discussion have been developed. These attempt to lay out the necessary and sufficient conditions for discussion,[14] characteristics of different types of discussions,[15] and the influence of teacher questions on classroom discussion.[16] According to such models, recitation is characterized by teacher-dominated classroom talk. It entails an interaction pattern between teacher and student similar to the following: the teacher initiates a statement or question; the student responds; the teacher provides feedback or evaluation. Discussion, on the other hand, is "an educative and group conversation between teacher and students about subject matter at the higher cognitive levels."[17] Bridges identified three defining conditions: (1) discussants put forward more than one point of view on a subject; (2) discussants are disposed to examine and be responsive to different points of view put forward; and

---

[10]John Dewey, "Democracy and Education," in *Democracy and Education: The Middle Works of John Dewey, 1899–1924,* vol. 9, ed. J. A. Boylston (Carbondale, IL: Southern Illinois University Press, 1985).

[11]Walter C. Parker, "Curriculum for Democracy," in *Democracy, Education and Schooling,* ed. Roger I. Soder, John I. Goodlad, and Kenneth A. Sirotnik (San Francisco: Jossey-Bass, in press).

[12]Benjamin Barber, *Strong Democracy* (Berkeley: University of California Press, 1984); Benjamin Barber, "Public Talk and Civic Action: Education for Participation in a Strong Democracy," *Social Education* 53, no. 6 (1989): 355–356, 370.

[13]David Mathews, *Politics for People* (Urbana: University of Illinois Press, 1994); Donald W. Oliver and Fred M. Newmann, *Taking a Stand: A Guide to Clear Discussion of Public Issues* (Middletown, CT: Xerox Corporation/American Education Publications, 1967).

[14]David Bridges, *Education, Democracy and Discussion* (Windsor, England: NFER, 1979); David Bridges, "Discussion and Questioning," *Questioning Exchange* 1 (1987): 34–37; Sophie Haroutunian-Gordon, *Turning the Soul: Teaching Through Conversation in the High School* (Chicago: The University of Chicago Press, 1991); Suzanne Miller, *Creating Change: Towards a Dialogic Pedagogy,* Report Series 2.18 (Albany, NY: National Research Center on Literature Teaching and Learning) (ERIC Document Reproduction Service No. ED 349 582, 1992).

[15]Donna E. Alvermann, David G. O'Brien, and Deborah R. Dillon, "What Teachers Do When They Say They Are Having Discussions of Content Area Reading Assignments: A Qualitative Analysis," *Reading Research Quarterly* 25, no. 4 (1990): 296–322; Meredith D. Gall and Joyce P. Gall, "Outcomes of the Discussion Method," in *Teaching and Learning Through Discussion: The Theory, Research and Practice of the Discussion Method,* ed. William W. Wilen (Springfield, IL: Charles C. Thomas, 1990), pp. 25–44; Thomas W. Roby, "Models of Discussion," in *Questioning and Discussion: A Multidisciplinary Study,* ed. James T. Dillon (Norwood, NJ: Ablex, 1988), pp. 163–191.

[16]James T. Dillon, *Using Discussion in the Classroom* (Philadelphia: Open University Press, 1994); Francis P. Hunkins, *Teaching Thinking Through Effective Questioning,* 2nd ed. (Boston: Christopher-Gorden, 1995); Thomas W. Roby. "Models of Discussion," in *Questioning and Discussion: A Multidisciplinary Study,* ed. James T. Dillon (Norwood, NJ: Ablex, 1988), pp. 163–191.

[17]William W. Wilen and Jane J. White, "Interaction and Discourse in Social Studies Classrooms," in *Handbook of Research on Social Studies Teaching and Learning,* ed. James P. Shaver (New York: Macmillan), p. 489.

(3) discussants have the intention of developing their knowledge and understanding and/or judging the matter discussed.[18]

Roby created a five-level model showing how teacher questioning influences classroom discussion.[19] The levels range from recitation-style questions (what Roby calls a "quiz show") to student-determined questions with no educational purpose or intended resolution (Roby's "bull session"). One step removed from the quiz show is the "problematical discussion," where the teacher uses questions that address a puzzling problem. Next is the "informational discussion" in which questions, whether from teacher or students, verify statements made in the discussion. Closest to the bull session is the "dialectical discussion." In this, questions encourage the exchange of multiple opinions and perspectives.

Before descriptions and recommendations regarding classroom discussion proceed much further, a study of what teachers think should be helpful. As it stands, discussion is defined by researchers without benefit of teachers' views. Accordingly, the conceptions of social studies teachers, for whom the recitation/discussion confusion is a very old problem, were examined.

The main research question was, What are teachers' conceptions of discussions in high school social studies classes? There were four related questions:

- According to teachers, what are the defining characteristics of classroom discussion?
- What purposes do teachers believe classroom discussions serve?
- Do teachers hold more than one conception of discussion?
- What seems to influence teachers' conceptions of discussion?

Method

Data Source

A purposive sample of three teachers was selected. To minimize variation in conceptions due to school setting, subject matter, and students, we chose teachers who all taught U.S. history in the same 26-year-old high school located in a middle-class suburb. The school's enrollment is 1,100 and growing. The three teachers were nominated by the building principal as teachers who were effective and thoughtful. Also, each teacher claimed to use discussion frequently.

One teacher, "Bill," is 40 years old and has been a social studies teacher for all his 18 years of teaching. He has an undergraduate and a master's degree in history, is actively involved in the National Council for the Social Studies, and presents workshops frequently at state social studies conferences. Bill teaches 11th grade U.S. history as well as a course entitled Current World Problems.

"Linda" is 44 years old and has been the social studies department chair for the past 8 years. She has been teaching for 22 years. She has an undergraduate degree in English, with a minor in social science, and a master's degree in secondary education. She has been teaching U.S. and world history, psychology, and sociology for the past 11 years. Before that she mainly taught American literature.

"Tom" is 46 years old and has been a teacher for 22 years. He has both an undergraduate and a master's degree in history. He has taught U.S. and world history for all of his teaching career. He is the only teacher at the school who teaches an Advanced Placement U.S. History course.

---

[18]David Bridges, *Education, Democracy and Discussion* (Windsor, England: NFER, 1979).

[19]Thomas W. Roby, "Models of Discussion," in *Questioning and Discussion: A Multidisciplinary Study*, ed. James T. Dillon (Norwood, NJ: Ablex, 1988), pp. 163–191.

Data

Data were of three kinds: responses to an interview schedule, responses during a think-aloud task, and observations of classroom teaching. In the interview, teachers described the mental image that came to mind when they heard the term "classroom discussion," distinguished between an ideal discussion and an imperfect one, gave examples of discussion, and listed educational rationales for discussion. The think-aloud exercise, which explored these teachers' notions of ideal discussions, followed a technique suggested by Anderson.[20] Five vignettes of classroom interaction, each a paragraph long, were composed. These drew on Roby's five-level model described earlier.[21] Each vignette describes a discussion in the classroom of one of five teachers (Jim, Kerry, Jack, Chris, and Brian). Jim's vignette describes a "quiz show," Kerry's a "problematical discussion," Jack's an "informational discussion," Chris's a "dialectical discussion," and Brian's a "bull session." The teachers ordered the vignettes from the one most like a discussion in their classroom to the one least like it, thinking aloud and sharing their reasoning all the while. Then, using their top-ranked vignette, the teachers sketched on a seating chart the interaction patterns they thought would obtain during such a discussion, again thinking aloud. A classroom observation of each teacher leading a discussion was the third source of data.

Analysis

These teachers' conceptions of discussion were induced through the use of a variation of the "constant-comparative"[22] or "iterative" technique.[23] This procedure involves alternating stages of data collection and analysis. Accordingly, during the interview phase, a list of conceptions was gradually constructed. Following the interview with Bill, an initial list was made. Then Linda was interviewed, and the list of conceptions drawn from the first interview was revised to include the new data. This revision entailed three steps: adding categories, refining (sharpening) categories, and elaborating (further illustrating) existing categories. These steps were repeated after the interview with Tom. In the think-aloud phase, the three teachers completed the ordering and drawing tasks, thinking aloud as they did so, and the list of conceptions developed in phase one was revised. In the classroom observation phase, the evolving list of conceptions was revised again as new data were juxtaposed with existing categories. In the end, a set of five reasonably well-illustrated categories was achieved.

The following section illustrates this procedure by showing how one of the conceptions emerged: "discussion as application of knowledge." Afterward, all five conceptions are presented.

Analysis Illustration

Analysis began with an examination of the interview responses of the first teacher, Bill. Two themes emerged quickly, both related to purposes of discussion: (1) discussion helps motivate students, and (2) discussion helps students link school topics to the nonschool world. These categories were named "motivation" and "knowledge generalization." Three responses were grouped under "motivation": discussions help

[20]John R. Anderson, *Cognitive Psychology and Its Implications* (San Francisco: W.H. Freeman and Company, 1980).

[21]Thomas W. Roby, "Models of Discussion," in *Questioning and Discussion: A Multidisciplinary Study,* ed. James T. Dillon (Norwood, NJ: Ablex, 1988), pp. 163–191.

[22]Barney G. Glaser and Anselm L. Strauss, *The Discovery of Grounded Theory: Strategies for Qualitative Research* (New York: Aldine De Gruyter, 1967); Anselm L. Strauss and Juliet Corbin, *Basics of Qualitative Research: Grounded Theory, Procedures and Techniques* (Newbury Park, CA: Sage Publications, 1990).

[23]Matthew B. Miles and A. Michael Huberman, *Qualitative Data Analysis: A Sourcebook of New Methods* (Beverly Hills, CA: Sage, 1994).

students gather and present information to classmates; discussions encourage students to take responsibility for their own learning; and discussions help teachers introduce an upcoming unit. Three other responses were categorized under "knowledge generalization": discussions give students opportunities to understand and explain current events; discussions encourage students to theorize about the relationship among two or more current events (e.g., citywide increases in unemployment and increases in robberies could be connected to economic despair); and discussions help students examine possible solutions to community problems.

Next, Linda's interview responses were compared with the categories developed from Bill's responses. Although Linda's responses did not cause a revision of the first category, "motivation," they did prompt a sharpening of the second category, "knowledge generalization." Three aspects of knowledge generalization were added to the picture: exploring consequences of historical events (e.g., In what ways does the Civil War have an impact on us now?); connecting school-learned information to societal issues (e.g., Can we take our knowledge about gun control and make a recommendation to the city council?); and group problem solving (e.g., using discussion in cooperative learning activities). Linda explained that discussion encouraged students to infer from particular details solutions to general issues (e.g., using specific details about the homeless in Seattle to address the general issue of society's responsibility to the homeless). She called this a "process of induction." This label suggested a different way of thinking about how discussions can help students generalize information. Each example previously coded under "knowledge generalization" was reexamined. Each alluded to this notion of moving from particular to general knowledge. Renaming the category "induction" seemed to capture this interpretation.

Two slightly different properties of "induction" emerged in Tom's responses: discussion encourages the application of textbook information to current situations, and discussion promotes comparisons between historical and contemporary events. Tom also explained that discussion encouraged in-depth treatment of information and challenged students to reexamine some of their preconceptions. However, the process was slow and required more class time than lecturing. Because the existing categories seemed not to capture these data well, a third category, called "learning-in-depth," was created to accommodate them.

The second phase of data collection and analysis, the think-aloud tasks, now began. Bill ordered the five vignettes as follows, from the one that is most like a discussion in his own classroom to the one least like it:

Most   Brian's "bull session"
        Chris's "dialectical discussion"
        Kerry's "problematical discussion"
        Jack's "informational discussion"
Least   Jim's "quiz show"

Bill thought Brian's discussion was most like his own, provided that Brian did three things: (1) encouraged learning through discussion, (2) encouraged students to change their minds, and (3) required preparation. According to Bill,

> the teacher needs to provide the students with some kind of a catalyst—a reading, a quote, a passage—and they're supposed to read it, consider it, and be super critical of it before they walk into this arena. If [Brian] wasn't doing this, this is not a form of discussion that I would buy into. It's just a discussion for the sake of discussion.

Bill believed discussions ideally would encourage students to understand different points of view. Such discussions would challenge students to explore the subject being discussed for perspectives other than their own. These ideas were coded under each category—"motivation," "learning-in-depth," and "induction." Clearly, the properties of these three categories were entangled. Bill commented that he "moved through" his material more slowly when he used discussion. After a discussion, however, he believed his students had a deeper understanding of the information (i.e., they were able to relate historical occurrences to contemporary events after a discussion). The "learning-in-depth" category appeared to be similar to induction. In-depth understanding helped discussions move from specific details to general application. Therefore, learning-in-depth was merged into induction, because the former provided illustrations for and added properties to the latter.

Think-aloud data from Linda contributed examples to the motivation category. Discussions motivated students, she believed, to collect and "induce" ideas from information they gathered. For example, when students knew they would be discussing how the North American Free Trade Agreement could be beneficial 20 years from now, they spent many hours researching this topic outside of class. Discussions also motivated students to examine information more thoughtfully. For example, Linda told of a discussion about inalienable human rights in which students wanted to examine the perspectives of Haitian immigrants in Florida. It became apparent in these statements that she believed discussions motivated students to form and use knowledge inductively. Motivation was not a category distinct from induction, perhaps; rather, it helped the discussions become more fully and genuinely inductive. What initially had been categorized as motivation now contributed properties to the growing category of induction. Now only one omnibus category remained.

Tom believed that discussion encouraged students to apply knowledge learned in class to situations and circumstances outside class. Originally this statement was categorized under induction. However, his idea that discussion prepared students to apply knowledge prompted a revision of that category label. Following a review of all of the previous examples under induction, it appeared that "application" described this conception more accurately. Moving from the particular to the general was only one way that discussion encouraged application. The ultimate purpose of discussion in the application category was not merely to move from particular to general, or to motivate students, or to learn about a topic in depth. The purpose driving this conception of discussion was to encourage a way of understanding information that encouraged usage in a variety of configurations and settings.

This brief sketch of category generation should help convey the constant-comparative procedure by which this one conception of discussion was constructed. Other conceptions evolved in similar fashion. In all, the interviews provided 11 categories. The list grew to 16 during analyses of the think-aloud task. Data gathered in classroom observations did not cause addition of new categories or alteration of existing categories. Just as "discussion as application" emerged in the integration of 4 categories (motivation, knowledge generalization, induction, and in-depth learning), the final list of 5 conceptions emerged from the comparison and integration of the 16. Comparing new data with emerging categories provided additional properties and examples that first expanded the number of categories and later caused us to collapse them into the conceptions given below.

Findings and Hypothesis

This section presents the five conceptions that eventually emerged. According to the canons of the grounded theory approach, they are *hypotheses* that are *grounded* in data and *tentative,* pending additional rounds of data gathering and analysis. As such, they provide an initial layer of understanding of teachers' conceptions of discussion.

Because they are hypotheses, this discussion uses the present tense and speaks generally of "teachers" rather than of "these three teachers."

Discussion as Recitation

Teacher-dominated classroom talk characterizes this conception of discussion. Teachers emphasize its utilitarian value: when they want to "cover" a large amount of information, assess students' understandings, or review for a test, this type of discussion is preferred. A comment by Linda is illustrative:

> This is not my choice of how discussion is to be used, but it does serve a definite educational purpose. If I were reviewing for a test, or after a chapter/unit had been covered, it is an effective way to make sure the students had read the textbook and understand the main points presented in the book. There are definite times for this use of discussion, and it is not a completely invalid method.

This conception of discussion follows a three-step interaction pattern between teacher and student: (1) teacher statement/question; (2) student response; (3) teacher feedback/evaluation.[24] When teachers want to control the subject being discussed and transmit particular information, they act to constrain interactions so they occur only between the teacher and a student, not one student and another. If teachers pose questions, decide who speaks, and evaluate student responses, interactions among students are unlikely. Recitation provides just this control.

In this kind of discussion, teachers are able to distribute information to students quickly and efficiently. When teachers are "in a hurry to cover information," they rely on lecture or recitation. In fact, when they are not lecturing, this type of discussion is the main way teachers attempt to transmit facts and ideas to students. Also, when teachers want specific answers to their questions, recitation is the type of discussion used. As Tom said, when a specific answer is desired, "not using recitation is like pulling teeth sometimes."

Discussion as Teacher-Directed Conversation

Another way teachers conceive of discussion is as a conversation that the teacher leads and controls. This involves more student-student interaction than in recitation—hence it has more the feel of a conversation—and the purposes are different: teachers want their students to understand multiple perspectives, or they want to encourage a deeper understanding of the topic being discussed. Still, the conversation is tethered to a teacher-selected question or topic.

During one class session, Tom directed students' conversation by continuously referring back to an opening question (i.e., "Why should we be responsible for the homeless?"). When asked why he held his students' comments so closely to this question, he responded:

> Well, if [the question] is not addressed, then the discussion will not serve the purpose of giving information to the students. The teacher needs to have the factual knowledge in mind in order to make sure the information being discussed is accurate and correct. It is nice to have opinions, but they have to lead to something. For example, if the discussion is on abortion, and

---

[24]This accords with the description of recitation reported by William W. Wilen and Jane J. White, "Interaction and Discourse in Social Studies Classrooms," in *Handbook of Research on Social Studies Teaching and Learning*, ed. James P. Shaver (New York: Macmillan, 1991), pp. 483–495.

all that is thrown out is a bunch of opinions about abortion, then the result doesn't necessarily lead to any end goal.

A common purpose of this kind of discussion is the development of multiple perspectives on the topic at hand. Teachers direct these discussions, but students' experiences and perspectives are elicited. Linda led such discussions by bringing up topics on which she knew her students' opinions would differ. Her goal for these discussions was not to reach a consensus or draw a conclusion but to "engage" students and draw out their ideas about the topic:

> Well, they are engaged with the topic . . . participating and bringing alternative ideas to the topic. Most of my topics hardly ever [permit] only one way to look at something.

Linda felt this use of discussion was necessary because the students, as budding citizens, needed practice understanding one another's viewpoints.

Bill had a different approach when using discussion to examine different perspectives. He set up "contrived" discussions set during certain historical periods. Bill used role playing to challenge students to understand how decisions were made and what people believed. For example, his students role-played discussions among congressmen in 1789. Students researched a role, then assumed that character and reenacted a congressional hearing. Some students represented people from the present as well and entered the discussion by bringing knowledge that was different or unknown in the 1700s. As this diverse group tried to converse on a specific topic, students addressed multiple points of view across multiple eras of history.

Discussion as Open-Ended Conversation

Not every discussion involves the teacher as monitor of the discussion and keeper of the topic. During open-ended discussions, teachers do not direct the conversation so much as join it. Teacher and students alike make comments and offer opinions. At times, open-ended discussions turn into debates and heated arguments. Bill maintained that open-ended discussions provide students with

> . . . tremendous freedom to explore ideas. [The teacher] is not telling them what avenue they have to follow. I mean they may start talking about document "Y" but may end up in what seems to an outsider a completely unrelated area. And I don't have any problem with that. I think it helps students understand that their world is interconnected; that mature, intellectual ideas are interconnected.

Open-ended discussions also provide students with the experience of interacting linguistically with one another. This matters a great deal to teachers. The classroom, they believe, can be a safe environment for tackling controversial issues in a diverse group. Students need this experience, teachers believe. "You're building confidence," Bill said.

> Most of these people don't have the confidence right now to stand up in front of the school board meeting or public library committee. . . . I really don't care where the students are in terms of opposing or supporting [a topic] when we're all done with this 20-minute discussion. . . . And, it's fun! I mean, dialogue—that kind of an exchange in a nonmalicious environment, in a nonthreatening environment—can be fun.

Linda's comments illustrate roughly the same point:

> I mean, they know a lot of things. But they haven't the experience. So sometimes we bounce it off each other for the experience. And, I really don't see my role as pedagogical. I mean, I really don't think I'm the one to say *these* are the values, and *these* are the facts and *these* are the rights, and *these* are the wrongs and you have to agree. I try to be fairly neutral, and I try to be non-confrontational. What I also try to present are the alternatives to the whole thing. . . . But it doesn't work unless they are engaged; it doesn't work unless they really want to be here; if they are willing to talk, you hope they have some ideas they are willing to share because it is good preparation. . . . While there is some value in letting students talk about issues that are pressing on their minds and want to talk about, this would be the most valuable if the discussion is tied to the course/content.

It is important to note that open-ended conversations center on a particular concept, piece of information, or question. While they may have an open end, they do not have an open beginning. When asked if discussions were open for any topic that the students wanted to talk about, teachers quickly express that the value of open-ended discussions is the freedom students have to talk about a subject or issue any *way* they want, not necessarily to talk about any *topic* they want. Moreover, this topic has to meet two criteria: it must fit into the curriculum and be a topic that students know about beforehand. Again, Bill illustrates:

> These young people can't walk in just cold, [with the teacher] saying, "OK, just talk." There's something that is predetermining the topic of discussion. If not, this is not a form of discussion that I would buy into. If it's just a discussion for the sake of discussion, it might be fine for a homeroom class. It would be a nice homeroom class activity, but not necessarily an academic activity.

Discussion as Posing Challenging Questions

Although teachers frequently combine questioning and discussion, the purpose of questioning under this conception is to challenge students' beliefs and ideas. Discussion as posing challenging questions differs from recitation because teachers are not seeking particular answers. It differs from teacher-directed conversations because teachers' questions are not intended necessarily to lead to a certain end. It differs from open-ended conversations because teachers direct the discussion with specific questions. The teachers in our sample called this the "Socratic method," and each claimed to use it.

Linda conceptualized it as "never give them any answers . . . The whole business of Socrates was to ask questions, and never give you any answers, but pose problems in questions, and not draw things to a close."

When Bill, using what he referred to as "Socratic dialogue," led a discussion by posing challenging questions, he commonly answered student questions with more questions. He often rephrased students' statements as questions. Later, Bill explained this use of discussion:

> I see myself coming in and engaging people in almost a Socratic dialogue . . . Throw questions, prompt. I do that an awful lot in that kind of setting. Large groups especially. I do a lot of role-playing . . . where I take on a persona, I take on a position that I know will spark a reaction from the audience. And I at times take that to the extreme. It's my opportunity in class to

be an actor, and basically to elicit dialogue and a reaction from them [with questions]. But not in a chaotic sense. Again, with some structure so that whether it's a reaction of an individual or a small group of people, other folks are in the background listening to that . . . and then having an equal opportunity to react. I see my role at times as helping them paraphrase one another's reactions [by asking repeated questions].

Under this conception, questions direct students' thinking about a topic, but answers are not the end goal. Rather, the goal is sharpening the process of thinking. Tom questioned students as "the devil's advocate." He tried to question anything that was said, hoping his students would "logic through the information and be more thoughtful about the ideas they formed."

Discussion as Application

Discussion is a way for students to bring into the here and now knowledge formed about the then and there. Additionally, it is a way for them to take into the world knowledge that was formed initially in the classroom. This conception involves, then, a present and proximate application of remote and, perhaps, historical knowledge as well as the generalization to nonschool settings of knowledge acquired in school. Linda stated that her

> main point for discussion is that . . . you can effectively use the inductive process . . . . How does what we learned about "there and then" relate today? How is it similar, how is it different, and what are some conclusions we can draw?

Bill emphasized that

> it is the *process* [of discussion] that I'm most intrigued with. I think the process of dialogue, of exchanging ideas, is fundamental to a democratic society. If they can do it in this artificial environment, then I think I'm guaranteed . . . that they will then continue those kinds of dialogues at their places of employment, at the dinner table at home, or in a public forum.

Finally, Tom offered the following observations:

> What I use discussions for are to make analogies and to make connections between the past and the present . . . discussion is used as a way to make kids think more than anything else . . . to make them think a little bit more, think about anything, instead of just regurgitate [information].

Summary

Thumbnail descriptions of the five conceptions are listed here. Brief illustrative statements from the participating teachers are included, and the phase of data gathering in which the statement was made is noted in parentheses.

Discussion as recitation. Teacher asks questions, students respond, and teacher evaluates responses. Information is distributed quickly and efficiently:

> If I were reviewing for a test . . . or wanted to make sure students had read the book and understand the main points presented, I will lead a discussion [that seeks specific answers to questions]. (Interview data)

Discussion as teacher-directed conversation. Teacher directs a conversation with students to help them understand a topic or "point." Students are encouraged to contribute any information they know, and teacher judges its relevance to the lesson's objective:

There are . . . discussions that I try to construct that definitely will get students from point A to point B. There is a light bulb that I want to ultimately turn on, whether it's a piece of knowledge, or a concept I want them to understand. (Interview data)

Discussion as open-ended conversation. Teacher and students freely share what they know about a predetermined topic. Teacher introduces the topic, then participates in the discussion, but does not direct it:

[This gives] tremendous freedom to explore ideas. [Students] may start talking about document Y but may end up, in what seems to an outsider, in a completely unrelated area. I think it helps students understand that intellectual ideas are interconnected. (Think-aloud data)

Discussion as posing challenging questions. Teacher poses questions to students but doesn't evaluate responses. Instead, additional questions are asked to challenge student assumptions and logic, and to develop thinking skills:

Ask questions, and never give any answers. [I] pose problems in questions, not drawing things to a close [in order to make students think]. (Think-aloud data)

Discussion as application. Teacher and students apply knowledge of the past to the present and apply knowledge acquired in class to other situations and circumstances. Students generalize particular facts and ideas to the larger world:

How does what we learned about "there and then" relate today? How is it similar, how is it different, and what are some conclusions we can draw? (Interview data)

Factors Influencing Conceptions and Uses of Discussion

This findings/hypotheses section concludes with a brief look at the fourth ancillary question: What seems to influence teachers' conceptions of discussion? Based on the data gathered, another hypothesis seems reasonable: Teachers select three aspects of the classroom milieu as pivotal determinants of how they conceptualize and use discussion: (1) maturity of students, (2) classroom personality, and (3) lesson objective.

Maturity of students. Teachers do not use discussion in the same way across their several classes. They discriminate, more likely conducting discussion in classes that have what they call more "mature" students—students they describe as some combination of older, more knowledgeable, less defensive, and more socially adept:

Sophomores [as opposed to seniors] . . . argue more than discuss. They are very determined. . . . There is a need to be right. They like that power and control. (Interview data)

Classroom personality. Interactions between teachers and students are influenced by characteristics unique to each classroom of students. Class size, gender, behaviors, cultural composition, and students' attitudes influence teachers' judgments as to the appropriateness of discussion:

Classrooms have personalities. . . . I can't [discuss] the same thing with one class that I can with the other. It's just the mix. (Think-aloud data)

Lesson objective. Teachers are more directive or controlling in discussions when they believe they need to "cover" or "get through" a body of information that students need in order to engage in an informed conversation. Teachers are less controlling when students already possess or can spend time gathering background information before the discussion begins:

> What has really made this dialogue, this discussion, as rich as it was is the painful research that we did. They went in and they may have looked at 200 articles between them, and then ultimately brought all of that back into this arena. (Classroom observation, aside to observer)

Conclusion

This study generated categories and hypotheses grounded in data gathered from teachers. It did not test conclusions already formed. It is important, nonetheless, to note points of convergence between the ideas developed here and ones in the related literature. These findings elaborate a conclusion drawn by McNeil—that instruction is beholden to teachers' desire to achieve and maintain classroom control.[25] McNeil found that "defensive teaching" reserves higher-status pedagogies for settings in which teachers feel more secure. This practice may sometimes be wise, but it also may be largely illusory—based perhaps on race and class prejudices about "these students."

A new construct emerging from the present study is that teachers have differentiated conceptions of discussion in relation to classroom control. True, teachers will classify recitation as discussion, as others have found, but this is not their only conception of discussion.[26] For example, teachers distinguish between recitation-style discussions and conversation-style discussions, and they theorize about which instructional settings and groups of students allow for different kinds of discussion.

This study has built only a first layer of an understanding of teachers' conceptions of discussion. Five conceptions were developed, along with three influences. Companion studies are needed, of course, in other subject areas and settings; and as a consequence, some conceptions and influences will be eliminated and others added. Gradually they can be pulled together into reasonably sound generalizations—a background against which teachers and supervisors can reflect and act upon classroom practices and teacher educators can provide more appropriate instruction on discussion itself. A next step in this research series is to concentrate attention on two urban high schools in which the U.S. history curriculum is differentiated ("honors," "basic," and "special education") and on 12th grade "senior problems" courses in which discussion is more likely to be treated as part of the curriculum, taught directly as a method of public discourse, rather than only implemented as an instructional method.

BRUCE E. LARSON is a high school teacher and doctoral candidate in education, 122 Miller, DQ-12, University of Washington, Seattle, WA 98195. Phone: 206-543-6636; fax: 206-543-8439. WALTER C. PARKER is Professor of Education, 122 Miller, DQ-12, University of Washington, Seattle, WA 98195.

[25]Linda McNeil, *Contradictions of Control: School Structure and School Knowledge* (New York: Routledge and Kegan Paul, 1986).

[26]See, for example, Donna E. Alvermann, David G. O'Brien, and Deborah R. Dillon, "What Teachers Do When They Say They Are Having Discussions of Content Area Reading Assignments: A Qualitative Analysis," *Reading Research Quarterly* 25, no. 4 (1990): 296–322.

A3

A Phenomenological Study with Youth Gang Members: Results and Implications for School Counselors

Michael M. Omizo
Sharon A. Omizo
Marianne R. Honda

The word *gang* usually invokes fear and trepidation among many law-abiding citizens. There is a new urgency and renewed interest in youth gangs due to the increasing diversity of gangs in the United States (Huff, 1990). While gangs have been associated with big cities such as Chicago or Los Angeles, other cities such as Honolulu are also affected by the impact of youth gangs. In fact, the Honolulu Police Department identified 45 gangs on the island of Oahu alone. Membership in these gangs is estimated at more than 1,000, with the majority of individuals ranging in age from 14 to 24 years (Rockhill et al., 1993).

The public's perception of gang activities includes images of drug trafficking, drug/substance abuse, violent and criminal acts, destruction of public and private property, and graffiti. Confrontations between gangs may occur, often claiming the lives of innocent victims. These highly visible and publicized activities of youth gangs have far-reaching effects on the general community (Compas, Hinden, & Gerhart, 1995).

According to Hagedorn (1990), gangs are growing in number and size throughout the nation. A problem related to this growth is in the increased range of illegal activities in which members are involved. Maxson and Klein (1990) reveal that violence is escalating, weaponry, becoming more sophisticated, and younger children joining gangs. Researchers (Maxson & Klein, 1990) have reported that people are now tending to stay in gangs longer, even after reaching adulthood.

Although many people associate negative connotations with youth gangs, they often serve a number of important psychological functions (Wang, 1994). A sense of belonging, self-identity, status, and emotional support are some positive consequences associated with gang membership (Clark, 1992; Rockhill et al., 1993; Virgil, 1988). Basic developmental needs are met and important values are instilled by membership in youth gangs. Gangs provide an opportunity to gain peer respect, group respect, and a sense of security (Chesney-Lind et al., 1995). Loyalty, responsibility, and conforming to group norms represent virtues that are valued by persons in youth gangs and the mainstream culture (Virgil, 1988).

The increase in the size and violence of youth gangs makes it imperative that teachers, counselors, administrators, and social service professionals recognize the variables which contribute to an adolescent's decision to join a gang. Effective preventative interventions that address these factors must be developed to deter youth from turning to gangs. These interventions should look at ways of channeling and redirecting the positive aspects of gangs into more constructive, socially acceptable outlets.

Omizo, M., Omizo, S., and Honda, M., "A Phenomenological Study with Youth Gang Members: Results and Implications for School Counselors." *Professional School Counseling*, vol. 1, no. 1, October 1997, pp. 39–42. Reprinted by permission.

In addition to prevention. understanding the dynamics of gangs and the role they play in the lives of their members is essential to deal responsibly and effectively with gang-affiliated youth. By the secondary school years, some individuals will already belong to a gang. It is important that existing programs are evaluated and adapted to meet the needs of the individual, family, and community. In doing so, problems associated with gang membership, such as alienation, dropping out of school and illegal activities, can be minimized.

As a newly hired counselor in a high school which includes gang members, one of the researchers wanted more information on how to help this population. She contacted a faculty member from a local university, who was her former advisor, to do some research to help her, as well as other school counselors. The researchers decided to conduct a qualitative study using a phenomenological approach to get a better understanding of the experiences of being a gang member.

The purpose of this article is to share eight male adolescents' perceptions of their gang membership using a phenomenological research model. The basic research question was "What is your experience of being a member of a gang?" Implications for future interventions by school counselors are then articulated.

Method

The participants included eight male gang members from one high school. The members ranged in age from 13 to 17 and were Southeast Asian or Samoan. They all attended an urban high school on Oahu, Hawaii. The boys were selected from 2 programs which provide extra-curricular support services for gang members.

Procedure

The phenomenoloical research model explores personal experiences as perceived by the participants, who are referred to as co-researchers (Husserl, 1962; Keen, 1975). Giorgi (1970) reported that the phenomenological model provides a deeper and more comprehensive understanding of human behavior as compared to other models of research. Researchers who conduct this type of research need to immerse themselves in the material to better understand and appreciate the experience of the co-researchers (van Manen, 1984).

According to Kornfeld (1988), conducting phenomenological research has two phases. The first phase begins with epoche. The researchers record on paper their biases, stereotypes, and assumptions as completely as possible, discuss these, and then tear up the paper to get rid of these thoughts symbolically. The process allows an openness to examining the phenomenon being studied.

The second phase involves recording, clustering, and synthesizing categories to discover themes. The interview statements of each co-researcher are analyzed for texture and structure. Texture is the characteristic of the phenomenon as it appears in everyday life. Feelings, thoughts, images, and events are included as texture. Structure is the part of the phenomenon that does not vary. Structure evokes and precipitates feelings and thoughts. Structures are often covered up by textures. Researchers need to be patient and wait for meanings to emerge and not impose their ideas, values, and biased interpretations. The goal for the researcher is to evaluate the co-researchers' experiences by integrating the textual and structural descriptions. This process needs to be completed for each co-researcher and for all the co-researchers combined.

Researchers

The three researchers have counseling backgrounds and have had experience with phenomenological research. Each researcher interviewed two or three co-researchers. The researchers developed questions to be used within a semi-structured format. The researchers were not looking for specific responses. They were interested in gaining a deeper understanding of gang membership. The following are examples of questions which were used:

> What are some of the reasons that made you join a gang?
> What are advantages of being a gang member?
> What are some disadvantages of being a gang member?
> How has being in a gang affected school?
> How has being in a gang affected your home situation?
> How has being a gang member affected you socially?

We used counseling skills to establish a relationship, interview, probe, clarify, summarize, integrate, and gather information.

We began the study with process of epoche. We wrote down our biases and predictions relative to the researchers' questions. The following were included: Being part of a gang has many disadvantages; gang members are involved with illegal activities; members of gangs do not do well in school; at-risk youth are often involved with gangs; and gang members use drugs and carry weapons. These biases were discussed and, in an effort to disperse them, the papers they were written on were torn up.

Following participant permission, each co-researcher was interviewed for approximately one hour by one of the researchers. The interviews were tape recorded and later transcribed verbatim. The interviewing began with general questions to establish rapport. As the dialogue became smooth, genuine, and comfortable, the co-researchers were told the purpose of the study.

Analyses of the Interviews

To analyze the information, all the interviews were listened to first to get a general idea of the information provided. Following the method used, by Moustaka (1987), Kornfeld (1988) and Omizo and Omizo (1990), the data were analyzed for each co-researcher and then for the entire group.

We first listed every expression related to the research question. The following are examples:

> "The gang members are always there for me."
> "Sometimes the initiation of new members scare me."
> "I've made good friends."
> "We fight for our rights."
> "Our gang does not want any kind of trouble."

The expressions were reduced to recurring experiences to identify general categories that related to the research questions. The three categories that the authors came up with were: (a) sense of belonging, (b) self-esteem, and (c) protection. Statements reflecting the categories are as follows:

Sense of Belonging

> "I like being around guys that I can count on."
> "We help each other out all the time."
> "I don't have anyone at home to help me out - the gang is there to do things with."

Self-Esteem

"I feel important when I'm with the gang."
"We are on top at school and around the neighborhood."
"It feels good to have others want to be with you."

Protection

"The gang won't let anything bad happen to any member."
"I feel safer being with the gang."
"No one will try to do anything to me."

Next, the expressions were delimited to eliminate expressions that did not lead to understanding the individual's experiences of gang membership. Expressions such as "We like to eat pizza" and "My brother works for Burger King" were not included.

The authors proceeded to identify themes. All expressions found previously that were implicit or explicit representations of a common experience were labeled. The themes included emotions, images, and other sensory experiences. The themes were: sense of belonging; self-esteem; and social/recreational. Themes and sample expressions included the following areas:

Sense of Belonging

"It feels great to have friends all the time."
"Since my family is hardly around, I spend most of my time with the gang."
"Being in a gang makes the time go by quickly."

Self-esteem

"The gang makes everybody feel good."
"I feel good that I can help others."
"I like being bad (positive connotation)."

Social/Recreational

"We always do stuff together."
"The gang gives me something to do."
"We play basketball til late at night, sometimes."

A textual description of the feelings and thoughts of the co-researchers was developed. The gang members felt that being a member of the gang made them feel like an important part of a group. They liked being depended upon and being able to depend on others. Gang membership made them feel important and respected by others. In addition, being part of the gang made the co-researchers feel safer.

A structural description of the precipitating conditions that produce the thoughts, images, feelings, and events followed. Structure includes the specific events and situations relative to gang membership. These include being involved with social and recreational activities, feeling safer and protected in threatening situations, and having a substitute family.

Finally, we wrote a summary description reflecting the textural-structural content. It seems that being a member of a gang had many positive aspects. The co-researchers like being part of a gang and depending on each other. They also felt better about themselves because of helping others and knowing that others are there for them. Gang membership also provides them with things to do such as going to parties and playing sports. A few negative aspects were mentioned such as parents' disapproval of them being in gangs, sometimes doing things that they did not feel were quite right, and not being able to be with friends who were not in their gangs.

Implications for School Counselors

The prevalence of gangs in contemporary society reflects a breakdown of communities, schools, and homes (Maxson & Klein, 1990). School counselors should address the immediate needs that gangs fulfill, such as belongingness, identity, and protection. They should also deal with the long-term effects of gang membership; for example the inability to cope with the demands of adult roles due to poor social skills or lack of marketable job skills. The complex nature of gangs requires prevention and treatment on multiple levels. School counselors can play a pivotal role in the provision of such services.

Individual Counseling

When working with individuals, school counselors should foster a sense of identity and self-respect. This may be achieved through the recognition of personal achievement, strengths, and abilities. With some students, the counselor may have to start with positively acknowledging very basic behavior such as tutoring the student in homework assignments or even being in school.

Another objective of individual counseling for a gang member may be to establish and encourage a connection with legitimate groups such as sports teams, school clubs, or community organizations. Membership in these socially approved groups may meet the adolescents' need for belongingness, as well as influence the development of prosocial identity.

The counselor could also address issues such as drug abuse, dealing with peer pressure, and developmental issues. The counselor would also be a positive adult role model.

Group Counseling

Direct client services provided by the school counselor should also include a group counseling component. A group setting may be especially effective with gang members as it provides the structure and opportunity to interact with peers in a nongang setting. Groups could address issues which are relevant to this population. Interacting with others in a cohesive group environment could improve adolescents' social and interpersonal skills, enabling them to acquire important behaviors for effective and satisfying relationships.

Working with Families

Sometimes, gangs serve as surrogate families. Families of gang youth are typically socially disorganized, poor, and from ethnic minorities. School counselors could help families improve communication skills, parenting skills, anger management, coping skills, and problem-solving skills.

An important responsibility for counselors is educating parents about gangs and gang activities. Parents may not know what to look for as signs of gang involvement, the seriousness of the problem, or what to do if they do suspect gang affiliation. When dealing with a parent, the counselor should communicate concern, openness, and support. If the parent is a recent immigrant or has limited English ability, an interpreter should be obtained.

The counselor can also serve the function of a resource person with an awareness of various community agencies and resources to which families of gangs or delinquent youth can be referred. The counselor may link the family up with services for legal advice, financial assistance, or family counseling. In this capacity, counselor knowledge of both the family situation and outside resources is critical.

School Intervention

An indirect, but important, service that school counselors can provide is that of consultant for the school staff. In this role, counselors may conduct in-service, training sessions for teachers and administrators on gang awareness. By increasing awareness of gangs and signs of gang activity, the counselor is equipping the staff to recognize problems so that early intervention is possible. It is important to share with staff the needs gangs feel and to brainstorm and integrate proactive measures.

Counselors might also conduct in-service training on proactive classroom management, cooperative learning, or interactive teaching techniques. Schools must provide meaningful experience for students, and realize that the standard requirements for graduation and curriculum do not fit every student. Providing options to traditional school programs and exploring alternative teaching methods may help reduce alienation and increase school involvement (Mulvey, Arthur, & Reppucci, 1993).

School counselors should be advocates for opportunities and services which meet the diverse needs of the student population. By offering early intervention programs such as conflict resolution, peer counseling, drug prevention, anti-violence curriculum, athletic and other after-school activities, schools can help steer youth away from gangs.

Concerned counselors and teachers can work together with parents of at-risk gang youth to discourage gang participation. With this team approach, students may be exposed to new ways of relating to others, a changing view of themselves, and to a higher commitment to school. Developing a partnership between school and home creates a win-win situation. The individual, school, and society profit when an individual diverts from delinquent, antisocial behavior, and acquires the skills to lead a productive life. By training school staff and working with parents to address the problem, students have a wider base of support and can receive guidance from a variety of sources.

Community Organizations and Interventions

Counselors must venture beyond the cultures of the school boundaries in order to make a significant and lasting impact on the gang problem. A proactive approach is essential, and school counselors can take various measures to aggressively address issues that encourage youth involvement with gangs. Perhaps the most efficient way to accomplish this is to promote community involvement combating street gangs. By educating the community and increasing awareness about gangs, school counselors can equip communities with accurate information to deal effectively with the problem.

An additional role that counselors must fill is that of community resource person. School counselors can educate the public on the direct and indirect effects that gangs have not only on its members and their families, but also on society as a whole. The perception of gangs as a narrow problem affecting certain individuals must be broadened to address the detrimental effects they have on neighborhoods and entire communities. By encouraging community ownership of the problem, we can begin to direct attention to social disorganization which provides the context within which gangs thrive.

By increasing community involvement, gang crime can be reduced or prevented. School counselors can help organize anti-gang events such as graffiti clean-ups, extracurricular social activities, and neighborhood watch programs. Furthermore, school counselors should strive to nurture a coherent community in which youth can play a constructive and meaningful role, providing an alternative to criminal gangs as a source of social status and self-esteem.

Summary

This article has presented the results of phenomenological study on gang member-ships and its implications for school counselors. The results support previous research on the reasons for adolescents joining gangs and the benefits of being a gang mem-ber (Chesney-Lind et al., 1995; Clark, 1992; Virgil, 1988). Although the results may also be applied to other gangs, the reader is cautioned to not overgeneralize these re-sults to gangs comprised of other ethnic group members.

Counselors play a crucial role in making available a variety of services to youth gang members. These services include providing individual counseling and group counseling, working with families, serving as consultant to the staff of the school, and advocating for at-risk students. In addition, counselors should attempt to involve the community in providing services for this population.

References

Chesney-Lind, M., Lesien, M. B., Allen, J., Brown, M., Rockhill, A., Market, N., Liu, R., & Joe, K. (1995). *Crime, delinquency, and gangs in Hawaii.* Honolulu, HI: Center for Youth Research, University of Hawaii at Manoa.

Clark, C. (1992). Deviant adolescent subcultures: Assessment strategies and clinical interventions. *Adolescence 27,* 289–93.

Compas, B. E., Hinden, B. R., & Gerhart, C. A. (1995). Adolescent development: Pathways and processes of risk and resilience. *Annual Review of Psychology, 46,* 265–93.

Giorgi, A. (1970). *Psychology as a human science.* New York: Harper & Row.

Hagedorn, J. M. (1990). Gang research in the nineties. In C.R. Huff (Ed.). *Gangs in America* (pp. 240–257). Newbury Park, CA: Sage.

Huff, C. R. (1990). *Gangs in America.* Newbury Park, CA: Sage.

Husserl, E. (1962). *Ideas.* [W.R. Boyce Gibson (trans.)]. New York: Macmillian.

Keen, E. (1975). *A primer in phenomenological psychology.* Lanham, MD: University Press.

Kornfeld, A. S. (1988). Sixth grade girl's experience of stress: A phenomenological study. Unpublished doctoral dissertation, Union for Experimenting Colleges and Universities, Cincinnati, OH.

Maxson, C. L., & Klein, M. W. (1990). Defining and measuring gang violence. In C. R. Huff (Ed.), *Gangs in America.* (pp. 71–100). Newbury Park, CA: Sage.

Moustaka, C. (1987). *Rhythms, rituals, and relationships.* Detroit, MI: Harlo Press.

Mulvey, E. P., Arthur, M. M. W., & Reppucci, N. D. (1993). The prevention and treatment of juvenile delinquency: A review of the research. *Clinical Psychology Review, 13,* 133–167.

Omizo, M. M. & Omizo, S. A. (1990). Children and stress: Using a phenomenological approach. *Elementary School Guidance and Counseling, 25*(1), 30–36.

Rockhill, A., Chesney-Lind, A. J., Batalon, N., Garvin, E., Joe, K., & Spina, M. (1993). *Surveying Hawaii's youth: Neighborhoods, delinquency and gangs.* University of Hawaii, Social Science Research Institute.

van Manen, M. (1984). Practicing phenomenological writing. *Phenomenological Pedagogy, 2,* 36–68.

Virgil, J. D. (1988). Group processes and street identity: Adolescent Chicano gang members. *Ethos, 16,* 421–445.

Wang, A. Y. (1994). Pride and prejudice in high school gang members. *Adolescence, 29,* 279–291.

Michael M. Omizo, Ph.D., is professor and chairperson, University of Hawaii at Manoa; Sharon A. Omizo, M.Ed., R.D., is consultant dietitian, Leabi Hospital Hawaii; and Marianne R. Honda, M.Ed., is school counselor, Kaimuki High School, Hawaii.

A4

A Computerized Method to Teach Latin and Greek Root Words: Effect on Verbal SAT Scores

C. Thomas Holmes
Ronald L. Keffer

ABSTRACT   The effectiveness of using a computer program over a 6-week period to teach high school students to use Latin and Greek root words for deciphering English terms, to increase their scores on the verbal portion of the Scholastic Aptitude Test (SAT), was studied.

When Latin was taught in a way that emphasized the derivation of English words, knowledge of English vocabulary was increased (Berelson & Steiner, 1964). Between 60% and 80% of English words are derived from Latin (Masciantonio, 1985). The exact percentage of English words that come from Latin may vary in the experience of different people. The number of words of Latin origin used daily by a physician may be high, whereas a mechanic may use many fewer. Greek also produces English derivatives. Booth (1980) suggested that 75% of English words can be attributed to "Latin/Greek" derivations. It is a reasonable notion, then, that a knowledge of the key root words from these parent languages will improve vocabulary and, consequently, scores on tests such as the Scholastic Aptitude Test (SAT).

If English vocabulary were derived from Latin terms on a one-to-one basis, that is, if students had to learn one Latin term for each English term they decoded, it would not be an efficient strategy to approach English vocabulary through Latin. In fact, one Latin term can provide sufficient information to enable one to decode many English terms. Masciantonio (1977) emphasized that the student "who knows the meaning of the Latin word *aqua* (water) finds such English words as aquarium, aqueduct, aquatic, aquamarine, Aquarius, and aqueous easier to understand" (p. 376).

Luyster (1980) examined the frequency and percentage of words containing Latin prefixes and roots in a basic elementary reading vocabulary, the Harris-Jacobson Core List. She found that the frequency of Latin-derived terms increased as grade level increased. By the sixth grade, 65% of the words listed contained a Latin

Journal of Educational Research, vol. 89, no. 1, pp. 47–50, September/October 1995. Reprinted with permission of the Helen Dwight Reid Educational Foundation. Published by Heldref Publications, 1319 Eighteenth St., NW, Washington DC 20036-1802. Copyright © 1995.

root or prefix that appeared in the core list 10 or more times. Teaching a relatively small number of Latin roots and prefixes, consequently, may enable a student to decipher and use a relatively large number of English words.

In reviewing studies of year-long programs of Latin study designed to maximize its overall effect upon student performance in language arts, Masciantonio (1977) concluded that these programs were effective. LaFleur (1981) found that on the 1980 test "the SAT verbal average for those students taking the Latin Achievement Tests was 144 points higher than the national average for all students" (p. 254). Students taking the German and Russian Achievement Tests were outscored significantly by the Latin students. LaFleur's conclusion was that the higher scores of the Latin students probably should not be attributed to the fact that Latin may attract superior students, because students of German and Russian also are likely to be superior students. LaFleur (1982) also reported that the same results were present the following year when students taking the Latin Achievement Test scored higher on the verbal section of the SAT than did students taking the achievement test in all other foreign languages.

Although there has been some disagreement among researchers as to what the effects of the study of Latin are upon vocabulary skills, the more recent studies indicate that Latin has a positive effect on vocabulary and other English language skills (LaFleur, 1985). Of interest to us in the present study is the question of whether a program of study of Latin terms that is short term can have a significant positive effect upon SAT verbal scores.

Coaching for the SAT

Two studies by the Federal Trade Commission (1978, 1979) investigated the question of whether short-term coaching can have a positive effect on SAT scores. Although they dealt with only two commercial coaching schools, they found that coaching at one of the schools raised mean total SAT scores by 40 points, and by 50 points in the other school.

Hulsart (1983) reviewed several studies designed to answer questions about whether short-term preparation can effect positive changes in SAT scores. No general conclusion can be reached. The 10 studies vary in their conclusions. Hulsart's conclusion was confirmed and expanded upon by Becker (1990). Her analysis of over 50 studies of the effectiveness of coaching for the SAT indicated that many uncertainties remained, although the more rigorous published studies found an average gain of only 9 points on the verbal portion of the SAT. The studies in her analysis varied widely in results; many were flawed because they lacked comparison groups or did not take advantage of random assignment.

Method

A Solomon four-group design was used in this study. Subjects were assigned randomly to each of the four groups (see Table 1). Group 1 took a pretest, participated in the use of the computer program designed to teach Latin and Greek root words and how to use them to decode English words, and took a posttest. Group 2 took the pretest and the posttest. Group 3 participated in using the computer program and took the posttest. Group 4 took the posttest.

Participants

Volunteers for the study were solicited from all the college-preparatory-level English classes at one high school in northeast Georgia; 115 subjects were recruited. The high

TABLE 1

Descriptive Data for the Four Groups

	Group			
	1	**2**	**3**	**4**
Original number	28	30	29	28
Final number	15	19	19	17
Used the program	Yes	No	Yes	No
Mean computer hours	7.9	NA	8	NA
Number of Latin students	3	1	5	3
Previous SAT experience	8	6	5	7
Male/female	5/10	7/12	10/9	1/16
Mean age	15.7	15.5	15.6	15.6
Pretested	Yes	Yes	No	No

school population had a mixed sociocultural background. Approximately 15% were Black, and 16% received free or reduced-price lunches. The participants in this study were, however, not representative of the school population as a whole; none received free or reduced-price lunches, and only 4 of the 115 volunteers were Black.

The county is rural, and about 12,000 of its 22,000 population live in the county seat. Of the students who graduated from the school in 1990, 59% enrolled in a college, 14% enrolled in vocational training, 7% enlisted in the military, and 20% found full-time employment. The 108 seniors who took the SAT the previous year scored a verbal mean of 399 and a mathematics mean of 438. These scores fall well below the national average.

Using a table of random numbers, we assigned participants randomly to the four groups. A pretest, the verbal portion of a retired SAT, was administered to the participants in Groups 1 and 2. The following week, participants in Groups 1 and 3 began to use the computer program designed to drill them in Latin and Greek root words and in the use of these roots to decipher English terms. These sessions continued for 6 weeks.

Treatment

The computer program that we used in this study was based on the Apple Hypercard system. The Latin terms used in the program were chosen by consulting the *Dictionnaire Frequentiel et Index Inverse de la Langue Latine* [Dictionary of frequency and word forms from Latin] (Le Laboratoire d'Analyse Statistique des Langues Anciennes de l'Universite de Liege, 1981). This source listed Latin terms according to the frequency with which they appeared in certain ancient Latin works of prose and poetry. Working on the assumption that those terms that appeared most frequently in Latin also would be most prolific in producing English terms, we constructed a list of the 150 most frequently used nouns, verbs, and adjectives.

Each of the 150 terms chosen for frequency was tested by consulting the following sources: *Latin-English Derivative Dictionary* (Schaeffer, 1960), *14 Basic Roots and the Key to 100,000 English Words* (McNamara, 1983), *English from the Roots Up: Help for*

Reading, Writing, Spelling, and SAT Scores, Volume 1 (Lundquist, 1989), *The Latin Elements in English Words* (Lee, 1959), *Greek and Latin in English Today* (Krill, 1990); "A Basic Latin Vocabulary Along Etymological Lines" (Else, 1952), *Latin Words of Common English* (Johnson, 1931, *Latin and Greek in Current Use* (Burriss & Casson, 1949), and *The Contribution of Latin to English* (Brown, 1942). Those terms that did not produce at least five English derivatives were purged from the list; we retained 90 Latin roots.

We derived the Greek roots used in this study by consulting *English Words from Latin and Greek Elements* (Ayers, 1986), *Greek and Latin in English Today* (Krill, 1990), *English from the Roots Up: Help for Reading, Writing, Spelling, and SAT Scores* (Lundquist, 1989), and the *Greek-English Derivative Dictionary* (Schaeffer, 1963). We chose the Greek roots that appeared most frequently in these sources and that were prolific in producing English derivatives. Eleven Greek roots were included, making a total of 101 Latin and Greek roots in the program. Approximately 800 English derivatives were included.

Participants receiving the treatment were allowed two 45-min periods each week to use the computer program. One time slot was available in the morning before school and three were available after school. Time was limited because of the limited access to computers.

The first active screen the student encountered contained a scrolling list of all 101 Latin and Greek terms. Above the list was a definition of one of the terms. If the student correctly matched the definition to one of the terms, the computer responded that the answer was correct and allowed the student to go on to the next card, which contained the same scrolling list, but a new definition. If the answer was incorrect, the student was asked to try again. The student could not advance in any way except by matching terms and definitions correctly.

When a student was unable to find correct answers, he or she could choose a button at the bottom of the first screen. That button was marked with a large question mark. When chosen, the first card in the Help Stack, which contained a scrolling list of the root terms in a simplified form, appeared. When the student chose one of the terms in the list, a new card appeared with the root term at the top, the English definition below it, and a scrolling list of the English derivatives below that.

The students were told initially that they had two objectives in using the computer program. The first objective was to be able to go through the first stack of cards without error, demonstrating that they had learned the meanings of the root terms. Because this was the prime objective, the student had to choose the correct meanings in the first stack from the beginning each time he or she started the program. Even if one had reached card 72 previously, one had to give the correct responses to the first 72 cards at the outset of the new session in order to reach card 73.

Learning English derivatives was the second objective. Students were instructed that because improving SAT scores was their goal, learning to recognize the root words in English words had to be accomplished once the meanings of the roots were mastered. No correct strategy for deciphering English terms was offered, but students were instructed to develop their own strategies while learning the root terms and derivatives.

At the end of the 6-week treatment period, the posttest was administered. It consisted of a retired SAT verbal portion, but a different one from the pretest. We derived the scores for both the pretest and posttest by using the formula supplied by the College Entrance Examination Board (1988). The range of possible scores was 200 to 800.

TABLE 2

Two-Way Analysis of Variance for Posttest Means

Variable	SS	df	MS	F	p
Treated/untreated	1,539.57	1	1,539.57	3.69	.03
Pretested/unpretested	547.29	1	547.29	1.31	.26
Interaction	86.63	1	86.63	.21	.65
Within	27,516.86	66	416.92		
Total	29,690.35	69			

TABLE 3

Posttest Means and Standard Deviations

Group	Treated	Untreated	Total
Pretested			
M	384.67	354.74	369.70
SD	68.75	80.79	
Unpretested			
M	417.37	368.82	393.10
SD	100.82	83.06	
Total	401.02	361.78	

Findings

Random assignment to groups should have ensured that the groups were equivalent. To test that proposition, we conducted an analysis of variance (ANOVA) with the pretest means for the two groups that had been pretested. This showed no significant difference between the groups, $F(1, 32) = .85$, $p = .36$. We conducted a second ANOVA for all four groups on accumulative grade average. No significant difference was found among the four groups of students. $F(3, 66) = 1.06$, $p = .37$. Because no initial achievement differences were observed after random assignment to the groups, we relied on a two-way ANOVA to test the null hypotheses.

We calculated the two-way ANOVA using the posttest score means for the four groups as measures of treatment effect and pretesting effect. We also tested for possible interaction between pretesting and treatment.

No significant interaction, $F(1, 66) = .65$, $p = .21$, and no main effect for pretesting, $F(1, 66) = 1.31$, $p = .26$, were observed. There was, however, a significant main effect from the treatment, $F(1, 66) = 3.69$, $p < .03$. The mean score for participants who received the treatment, the computer program that taught the use of Latin and Greek root words in deciphering English terms, was approximately 40 points higher than the mean of the control groups (see Tables 2 and 3).

Discussion

The population standard deviation for the SAT was reported as 100 (Becker, 1990), so the 40-point average difference between treated and untreated groups represents about .4 standard deviation. This difference occurred after only an 8-hr average study time over a 6-week period.

Consideration of the findings of this study in view of the research discussed in the introduction led to certain conclusions. Though research in computer coaching for the SAT and in coaching for the SAT in general provided no definitive indication that there was one approach to the problem of low SAT scores that could satisfy the needs of schools and school administrators, the research did indicate that some methods had led to significant rises in SAT scores. Clearly, the designs of a number of these studies were flawed, and the studies were inappropriate to answer the questions posed through them. The nature of the coaching provided was not described in some studies. Researchers who investigated the effects of the teaching of Latin upon English verbal skills uniformly found a positive effect and disagreed only on the magnitude of the effect.

Research indicates that short-term solutions to the problem of low SAT scores should be viewed with skepticism. Meta-analyses of coaching effects also indicate that questions of external validity threaten the usefulness of most studies of this question. One factor that is difficult to accurately measure is the motivational level of the participants in any study. Determination and eager application may enhance the effects of even a mediocre coaching program. With these caveats in mind, we suggest that in some instances rapid improvement in SAT verbal scores, of an order of magnitude approaching .4 standard deviation, may be achieved. Because of its relative strength with regard to both internal and external validity, the Soloman four-group design of this study lends credence to these conclusions. Nonetheless, the subjects were volunteers recruited at one northeast Georgia high school, and generalizability may be limited.

A knowledge of Latin and Greek root words has improved the English skills of students through a broad range of grade levels. Students of our times are highly motivated to become involved in any activity that has the flavor of a "video game." The combination of these two factors may be one approach that can work to improve verbal skills for many students.

References

Ayer, D. M (1986). *English words from Latin and Greek elements* (2nd ed). Tucson: University of Arizona Press.

Becker, B. J. (1990). Coaching for the scholastic aptitude test: Further synthesis and appraisal. *Review of Educational Research, 60.* 373–417.

Berelson, B., & Steiner, G. A. (1964). *Human behavior: An inventory of scientific findings.* New York: Harcourt, Brace, & World.

Booth, F. M. (1980). A high school administrator's defense of Latin. *The Classical Outlook, 57*(4), 84–85.

Brown, C. B. (1942). *The contribution of Latin to English.* Nashville: Vanderbilt University Press.

Burriss, E. E., & Casson, L. (1949). *Latin and Greek in current use* (2nd ed.), Englewood Cliffs, NJ: Prentice Hall.

College Entrance Examination Board. (1988). *10 SATs plus advice from the college board on how to prepare for them.* New York: College Entrance Examination Board.

Else, G. F. (1952). A basic Latin vocabulary along etymological lines. *The Classical Weekly, 45*(15), 241–255.

Federal Trade Commission. (1978). *The effects of coaching on standardized admission examinations: Staff memorandum of the Boston Regional Office of the Federal Trade Commission.* Washington, DC: Federal Trade Commission, Bureau of Consumer Protection.

Federal Trade Commission. (1979). *The effects of coaching on standardized admission examinations: Revised statistical analyses of data gathered by Boston Regional Office of Federal Trade Commission.* Washington, DC: Federal Trade Commission, Bureau of Consumer Protection.

Hulsart, R. (1983). *Source book on preparation for college admissions tests: ACT-PSAT-SAT.* Denver: Colorado Department of Education.

Johnson, E. L. (1931). *Latin words of common English.* New York: D.C. Heath.

Krill, R. M. (1990). *Greek and Latin in English today.* Wauconda, IL: Bolchazy-Carducci Publishers.

LaFleur, R. A. (1981). Latin students score high on SAT and achievement tests. *The Classical Journal, 76*(3), 254.

LaFleur, R. A. (1982). 1981 SAT and Latin achievement test results and enrollment data. *The Classical Outlook, 77*(4), 343.

LaFleur, R. A. (1985). 1984: Latin in the United States twenty years after the fall. *Foreign Language Annals, 18*(4), 341–346.

Le Laboratoire d'Analyse Statistique des Langues Anciennes de l'Universite de Liege. (1981). *Dictionnaire frequentiel et index inverse de la langue Latine* (Dictionary of frequency and word forms from Latin). Liege, Belgium: Author.

Lee, L. (1959). *The Latin elements of English words.* Englewood Cliffs, NJ: Exposition Press.

Lundquist, J. (1989). *English from the roots up: Help for reading, writing, spelling, and SAT scores* (Volume 1). Bellevue, WA: Literacy Unlimited.

Luyster, E. M. (1980). *The frequency and percentage of words containing Latin prefixes and roots in the Harris-Jacobson Core List.* Master's Thesis, Kean College. Kean, NJ.

Masciantonio, R. (1977). Tangible benefits of the study of Latin: A review of research. *Foreign Language Annals, 10*(4), 375–382.

Masciantonio, R. (1985). Say it in Latin. *Principal, 64*(4), 12–14.

McNamara, R. S. (1983). *14 basic roots and the key to 100,000 English words.* Oxford, OH: American Classical League.

Schaeffer, R. F. (1960). *Latin-English derivative dictionary.* Oxford, OH: American Classical League.

Schaeffer, R. F. (1963). *Greek-English derivative dictionary.* Oxford, OH: American Classical League.

Address correspondence, including requests for the list of roots and derivatives, to C. Thomas Holmes. G-10 Aderhold Hall, The University of Georgia, Athens, GA 30602.

A5

Preservice and Inservice Secondary Teachers' Orientations Toward Content Area Reading

Bonnie C. Konopak
Louisiana State University

John E. Readence
University of Nevada at Las Vegas

Elizabeth K. Wilson
University of Alabama

ABSTRACT This study examined preservice and inservice secondary teachers' orientations toward content area reading and instruction. Instruments included two sets of belief statements and three sets of lesson plans; for comparison, each instrument incorporated three explanations of the reading process. Based on their selection of statements and plans, preservice teachers favored an interactive model of reading but a reader-based instructional approach, whereas inservice teachers held reader-based beliefs in both areas. In addition, both groups selected primarily reader-based vocabulary and comprehension lessons but varied in their choices of decoding lessons. Further, only teachers holding reader-based beliefs consistently chose corresponding vocabulary and comprehension plans.

During the past 15 years, research on teacher effectiveness has shifted its focus from just observing behaviors in the classroom to examining the relationship between the way teachers think and what they practice (Clark & Peterson, 1986; Shavelson & Stern, 1981; Shulman, 1986). The underlying assumption is that teachers' thoughts about different components of the instructional process can influence their classroom plans and actions (Armour-Thomas, 1989). As one in a series of investigations on the belief-practice relationship, we attempted to determine the theoretical orientations of preservice and inservice secondary teachers regarding content area reading and instruction. By focusing on these two groups, we examined how academic and professional experience might influence teachers' thoughts and decisions as a basis for future research on classroom practices.

Research on teaching was once dominated by a unidirectional, process-product approach that focused on classroom behaviors and achievement; current research has developed a broad, recursive approach involving teachers' beliefs, decision making, and interactions with students (see Clark & Peterson, 1986, for a review). In particular, teachers' beliefs regarding teaching and learning are considered critical components supporting the planning and implementation stages of instruction. By examining these beliefs, researchers can address their influence on, and how they are influenced by, classroom events.

In reading education, the extent to which teachers' thoughts influence instructional decision making and behavior has been debated. One position suggests that

Journal of Educational Research, vol. 87, no. 4, pp. 220–227, March/April 1994. Reprinted with permission of the Helen Dwight Reid Educational Foundation, Published by Heldief Publication 1319 Eighteenth St., NW, Washington DC, 20036-1802. Copyright © 1994.

teachers do possess theoretical beliefs toward reading and that their plans and subsequent actions are filtered through these understandings. As Harste and Burke (1977) stated "Despite atheoretical statements, teachers are theoretical in their instructional approach to reading" (p. 32). Subsequent research (Richardson, Anders, Tidwell, & Lloyd, 1991; Rupley & Logan, 1984; Stern & Shavelson, 1983) supported this premise, indicating that methods and materials are selected or ignored based on teachers' beliefs about reading and learning processes. As an illustration, Richardson et al. found that upper elementary teachers' beliefs, as assessed in ethnographic interviews, were consistent with their reading comprehension instruction; for example, teachers who believed reading involved learning a set of skills regularly used basal texts and focused on different word-attack approaches.

However, other investigators (Duffy & Ball, 1986; Lampert, 1985) emphasized factors external to the teacher, which can be even more influential. Here, the focus was on the sociocultural and environmental realities of the classroom that can constrain the implementation of belief-supported instruction. As Duffy and Anderson (1982) noted, although teachers can state theoretical aspects related to reading and instruction, their practice is actually governed by complex, contextual variables. For example, Hoffman and Kugle (1982) found that teachers' verbal feedback to students during reading instruction was not consistent with their beliefs about the reading process and concluded that decisions made regarding instruction were generally situational.

To further examine this issue, Kinzer (1988) compared the beliefs and instructional choices of preservice and inservice elementary teachers regarding the reading process. He hoped to discern how experience affected these teachers' beliefs, as well as the consistency between their beliefs and choices of instruction. For comparison, he used two written instruments (Kinzer & Carrick, 1986): (a) two sets of belief statements on how reading takes place (theoretical model) and how reading develops (instructional approach) and (b) three sets of lesson plans on syllabication, vocabulary, and comprehension (specific application). Each set was constructed to incorporate three divergent explanations of the reading process: *text based* (Gough, 1985); *reader based* (Goodman, 1985), and *interactive* (Rumelhart, 1985). According to Leu and Kinzer (1987), these three explanations represent different points on a continuum of explanations; text-based and reader-based plans are situated near the ends, and interactive plans are situated "somewhere in the middle" (p. 39) and related to both. (Note that although Kinzer used different labels for explanations in different instruments, for the purposes of this study, we used one set of labels across instruments.)

The explanations for how reading takes place differed by source of meaning and role of the reader. That is, (a) text-based plans assumed that meaning resides in the text for the reader to attain, (b) reader-based explanations assumed that meaning resides in the reader who encounters the text, and (c) interactive plans assumed that meaning resides in the text and in the reader who uses both written and experiential information to make meaning. The explanations for how reading develops differed by the nature and delivery of instruction. That is, (a) text-based plans assumed that instruction focuses on mastery of separate, sequential skills; (b) reader-based explanations assumed that instruction holistically involves all language processes; and (c) interactive plans assumed that instruction is differentially delivered depending on different stages of development. Aspects of both how reading takes place and develops were represented for the three sets of lesson plans. That is, text-based plans focused on a teacher-directed, discrete skills lesson; reader-based plans emphasized a student-centered, whole language lesson; and interactive plans emphasized a teacher-directed lesson based on individual student differences.

Based on his subjects' choices of statements and lessons, Kinzer (1988) found that the two groups were similar in their beliefs about the reading process, but to different degrees. That is, preservice teachers primarily chose reader-based explanations, whereas the inservice teachers were more equally distributed between reader-based and interactive explanations. In addition, in examining the correspondence between the teachers' beliefs and lesson choices, Kinzer found that teachers in both groups who held reader-based beliefs were generally consistent in choosing corresponding lesson plans, although preservice teachers were more consistent than inservice teachers across all instruments. He concluded that, similar to Duffy and Anderson's (1982) findings, the practicing teachers' responses and inconsistencies may have been influenced somewhat by their actual experiences in the classroom, whereas the preservice teachers' views may have been more unified because of their lack of experience.

In the present study we attempted to determine the beliefs and decisions of preservice and inservice secondary teachers regarding content area reading and instruction. By addressing this population, we hoped not only to extend Kinzer's (1988) findings but also to develop a basis for future research on the relationship between theoretical beliefs and actual practice. The major questions addressed were: (a) Do preservice and inservice teachers hold different theoretical orientations concerning reading and instruction in the content areas? and (b) Are preservice and inservice teachers consistent in their theoretical orientations concerning the reading process and instructional decision making?

Method

Subjects

Subjects for this study were 58 preservice and 46 inservice secondary teachers enrolled in education courses at a large southeastern university. Approximately 65% of the preservice teachers were women and 35% were men; 25% were juniors, 55% seniors, and 20% postbaccalaureate students. These subjects were enrolled in two sections of a required undergraduate content reading methods course that were taught by the same instructor. Approximately 70% of the inservice teachers were women; they were enrolled in eight graduate-level secondary education courses that were taught by different instructors. Based on identical course questionnaires, preservice teachers indicated no prior field or teaching experience, whereas inservice teachers indicated 1 through 15 years of teaching experience. In addition, the two groups indicated the same eight subject area specialties: English, fine arts, foreign language, mathematics, physical education, science, social studies, and vocational education.

Materials

Kinzer's (1988) instruments were adapted to reflect a content area emphasis appropriate for use with secondary teachers. The two sets of belief statements on how reading takes place and how it develops each contained 15 statements, 5 text based, 5 reader based, and 5 interactive. All were modified through minor wording changes. For example, an original statement on how reading takes place read: "There is usually only one acceptable answer to a question from a story," whereas the revised statement read: "There is usually only one acceptable answer to a question from a text." In addition, an original statement on how reading develops read: "Children should receive many opportunities to read materials unrelated to specific school learning tasks," whereas the revised statement read: "Students should receive many opportunities to read materials other than the textbook in the content areas (e.g. newspapers, literature, magazines, etc." (See Appendix A for the two complete sets of belief statements.)

The three sets of lesson plans on decoding, vocabulary, and instruction were written according to the format of the original plans, outlining student and teacher behaviors as well as instructional activities. Each set contained a text-based, a reader-based, and an interactive plan. Briefly, text-based plans stressed that (a) the text is the primary source of information, (b) the students learn through drill and practice of individual skills, and (c) the teacher stipulates the correctness of student responses. Reader-based plans emphasized that (a) the students bring meaning to the text, (b) the students use their prior knowledge to anticipate and confirm their understanding; and (c) the teacher models and guides the lessons. Interactive plans stressed that (a) the students use both text information and personal knowledge to develop meaning, (b) the students use a variety of reading strategies that are appropriate for them, and (c) the teacher directs the lessons but allows for individual student differences. (See Appendix B for the complete lesson set on vocabulary instruction.)

Validity. To establish content validity, we asked two professors and two doctoral students in reading education to classify the belief statements and lessons according to the different explanations and to offer suggestions for revisions. Among the raters and researchers, there was .91 agreement on the classification of statements and .96 agreement on the classification of lesson plans. Based on suggestions, we revised six belief statements: Three statements were rewritten to distinguish between reader-based and interactive explanations, and three statements were rewritten to reflect differences between text-based and interactive explanations. In addition, on the decoding instructional lesson set, wording changes were made to more clearly distinguish reader-based and interactive lessons.

Reliability. To establish reliability, we conducted a test-retest procedure that examined the consistency of teachers' theoretical orientations across two versions of the instruments. The participants included 125 preservice and inservice content teachers representing 10 subject areas. All were enrolled in summer school education courses; preservice teachers in undergraduate classes and inservice teachers in graduate classes. Based on course questionnaires, preservice teachers had no prior classroom experience, whereas inservice teachers had 2 through 20 years' teaching experience.

All the teachers were randomly assigned one version of the instruments during the first week of class and the alternate version, with statements and lessons reordered, during the second week of class. The procedure for administration and scoring was identical to that used in the study (see the Procedure section). Consistency of theoretical orientations across versions was determined by percentage of agreement for each teacher group. Across instruments, consistency was .86 for all teachers, .84 for preservice teachers, and .89 for inservice teachers.

Procedure

The procedure for data collection was the same for both preservice and inservice teachers. Two researchers administered the instruments in the subjects' university classrooms. Subjects first were given the 15 belief statements on how content reading takes place and were asked to circle 5 statements that best represented their beliefs in that area. Next, they performed the identical task concerning their beliefs about how reading develops in the content areas. Finally, they were asked to choose one lesson each for decoding, vocabulary, and comprehension instruction that they ideally would use with an average content class. The instrumentation for preservice teachers was administered at the beginning of the first class of the semester; the instrumentation for inservice teachers was administered at the beginning of class within the first 2 weeks of the same semester. All the subjects completed the instruments within 30 min.

Scoring. Following Kinzer's (1988) procedure, we scored each set of instruments to classify subjects' beliefs and lesson choices as representative of a particular explanation of reading. For the two sets of belief statements, teachers choosing a majority of statements that reflected one explanation (i.e., text based, reader based, interactive) were classified as that explanation. In addition, teachers choosing a distribution of statements that reflected more than one explanation were classified as interactive; as noted earlier, this explanation related to both text-based and reader-based views and reflects components of each (Leu & Kinzer, 1987). (See Appendix C for the frequency of statements chosen.) For the three sets of lesson plans, teachers choosing a particular lesson (e.g., text based) in each instructional area were classified as that explanation.

Results

Group Differences on Theoretical Orientations

For Research Question 1, we conducted chi-square statistics to examine differences between preservice and inservice teachers on their theoretical orientations, using 2 × 3 (Teacher Groups × Explanations) contingency tables for the two sets of belief statements and the three sets of lesson plans. When global significant differences were found, we conducted post hoc chi-square analyses (Marascuilo, 1966) to determine the source of the significance.

Beliefs about the reading process. Preservice and inservice teachers varied in their orientations concerning how reading takes place but were similar in their orientations about how reading develops (see Table 1). On how reading takes place, a statistically significant difference was found between groups; our findings on post hoc tests indicated that preservice teachers chose more interactive explanations, whereas inservice teachers selected more reader-based explanations. We found no statistically significant difference on how reading develops; both groups primarily chose a reader-based instructional approach.

Lesson plan choices. A statistically significant difference between groups was found only for the comprehension lesson plan set; inservice teachers selected more reader-based plans than did preservice teachers (see Table 2). For decoding lessons, both preservice and inservice teachers were distributed across the three explanations, whereas for vocabulary lessons, the two groups were primarily reader based.

Match Between Reading Beliefs and Lesson Choices

For research Question 2, we conducted separate chi-square analyses to examine the match between each teacher group's beliefs about reading and its instructional choices. Analyses included 1 × 2 (Belief × Lesson Match/Not Match) contingency tables for each possible belief and lesson combination.

Preservice teachers. Table 3 provides the frequency of belief-lesson match for preservice teachers. We found statistically significant results for how reading takes place for reader-based explanations and vocabulary and comprehension lessons. That is, those teachers favoring a reader-based model of reading chose more reader-based vocabulary and comprehension lessons. For how reading develops, we found similar results; only teachers holding reader-based beliefs selected more corresponding vocabulary and comprehension plans. No statistical significance was found for other belief-lesson combinations.

Inservice teachers. We found similar results on belief-lesson matches for inservice teachers (see Table 4). For both how reading takes place and how reading develops, those teachers choosing a reader-based model of reading selected significantly more corresponding reader-based vocabulary and comprehension lessons. Again, other belief-lesson combinations were not statistically significant.

TABLE 1

Frequencies and Chi-Square Values of Belief Statement Orientations for Preservice and Inservice Teachers

Teachers	Text based		Reader based		Interactive		χ^2
	n	%	n	%	n	%	
How reading takes place							
Preservice	1	2	16	28†	41	70†	8.20*
Inservice	0	0	26	57	20	43	
How reading develops							
Preservice	4	7	32	55	22	38	4.00
Inservice	2	4	34	74	10	22	

Note. Preservice n = 58; inservice n = 46.
*p < .05.
†Post hoc significant at p < .05.

TABLE 2

Frequencies and Chi-Square Values of Lesson-Plan Orientations for Preservice and Inservice Teachers

Variable	Text based		Reader based		Interactive		χ^2
	n	%	n	%	n	%	
Decoding							
Preservice	28	48	12	21	18	31	2.92
Inservice	16	35	16	35	14	30	
Vocabulary							
Preservice	17	29	30	52	11	19	5.49
Inservice	5	11	27	59	14	30	
Comprehension							
Preservice	5	09	38	66†	15	25	8.59*
Inservice	0	00	41	89	5	11	

Note. Preservice n = 58; inservice n = 46.
*p < .05.
†Post hoc significant at p < .05.

TABLE 3

Frequencies of Belief-Lesson Match and Chi-Square Values for Preservice Teachers

	Text based (out of 1 possible match)	Reader based (out of 16 possible matches)	Interactive (out of 41 possible matches)
How reading takes place			
Decoding	0	4	12
Vocabulary	1	11*	10
Comprehension	0	13**	12

	Text based (out of 4 possible matches)	Reader based (out of 32 possible matches)	Interactive (out of 22 possible matches)
How reading develops			
Decoding	2	6	5
Vocabulary	1	19***	4
Comprehension	1	23****	7

Note. Preservice $n = 58$.

*$\chi^2 = 8.59$, $p < .01$; **$\chi^2 = 15.91$, $p < .001$; ***$\chi^2 = 9.41$, $p < .01$; ****$\chi^2 = 20.84$, $p < .001$.

TABLE 4

Frequencies of Belief-Lesson Match and Chi-Square Values for Inservice Teachers

	Text based (out of 0 possible matches)	Reader based (out of 26 possible matches)	Interactive (out of 20 possible matches)
How reading takes place			
Decoding	—	10	7
Vocabulary	—	16*	7
Comprehension	—	24**	3

	Text based (out of 2 possible matches)	Reader based (out of 34 possible matches)	Interactive (out of 10 possible matches)
How reading develops			
Decoding	2	14	1
Vocabulary	1	23***	4
Comprehension	0	30****	1

Note. Inservice $n = 46$.

*$\chi^2 = 8.92$, $p < .01$; **$\chi^2 = 39.83$. $p < .0001$; ***$\chi^2 = 17.54$. $p < .001$: ****$\chi^2 = 45.35$, $p < .0001$.

Discussion

The purpose of the present investigation was to examine preservice and inservice secondary teachers' theoretical orientations regarding reading and instruction in the content areas. The findings are limited by the hypothetical nature of the written tasks; teachers were not studied in real instructional situations where decisions might be made differently. In addition, we examined only three broad theoretical orientations that we predetermined; discrete beliefs as reflected by individual statement selections were not analyzed. Further, these subjects were studied only in relation to their degree of teaching experience; possible differences among the eight content areas represented were not examined. Given these limitations, the results indicate that the groups varied somewhat in their orientations across instruments but were similar in their consistency between beliefs and lesson choices.

The first research question on the theoretical orientations of preservice and inservice teachers indicated differences between groups, as well as within groups, across instruments. On the belief statements, preservice teachers favored an interactive explanation of how reading takes place, whereas inservice teachers selected a reader-based explanation; however, both groups primarily chose a reader-based explanation of how reading develops. Such results indicate preservice teachers' lack of unity in their orientations toward a reading model and an instructional approach, whereas inservice teachers showed more consistency. It may be that these inservice teachers had developed unified explanations of the reading process based on their background in education course work and their teaching experiences, whereas the preservice teacher had not yet had these opportunities.

However, preservice and inservice teachers were more similar in their lesson choices. For decoding lessons, both groups were distributed across the three explanations, varying somewhat in their proportions of text-based, reader-based, and interactive orientations. These responses may have been caused by a lack of emphasis on decoding as a skill in secondary education course work, as well as actual teaching, so that these groups relied more on traditional or mixed approaches. For vocabulary and comprehension instruction, both groups primarily favored reader-based lessons, corresponding with these teachers' beliefs about an instructional approach or how reading develops. In particular, inservice teachers were overwhelmingly reader based on comprehension, suggesting a strong academic and teaching emphasis in this instructional area.

The second research question on the consistency between teachers' beliefs about the reading process and their instructional choices showed statistically significant results only for reader-based orientations and corresponding vocabulary and comprehension lessons. For inservice teachers, these results were not unexpected given the high percentage of responses for these orientations (see Tables 1 and 2). For preservice teachers, the results were somewhat surprising; although their orientation on how reading develops was primarily reader based, their orientation on how reading takes place was interactive. Again, it may be that preservice teachers had not yet developed unified explanations of how reading takes place and actual instruction. Further, an interactive explanation may lie on a continuum between text-based and reader-based explanations and thus is somewhat related to both (Leu & Kinzer, 1987). Consequently, while teachers may favor interactive beliefs, they may choose a more pure form of instruction.

When comparing these results with Kinzer's (1988) findings, one notes similarities and differences between elementary and secondary teachers. In both studies, preservice and inservice teachers generally held reader-based and interactive orientations across belief statements and lesson choices; a text-based emphasis was found only for secondary teachers on the decoding lessons. In addition, the relationship between belief statements and lesson plans was also similar; teachers in both studies were consistent only when holding reader-based orientations.

However, a major difference between the studies concerned the teachers' relative emphases on reader-based and interactive orientations. Preservice elementary teachers were more consistently reader based than their secondary counterparts, perhaps because of course and field experience differences in elementary and secondary education curricula. In addition, inservice elementary teachers held fewer reader-based orientations and were less consistent across instruments than were inservice secondary teachers. It may be that classroom conditions for elementary reading (e.g., use of basal texts, school/district required skill objectives) are prohibitive to belief-supported instruction (e.g., a whole-language approach). In contrast, inservice secondary teachers may have fewer external constraints that restrict the implementation of their instructional choices.

Overall, these results provide some support for research that suggests that teachers' theoretical orientations about the reading process are reflected in their instructional decision making (Stern & Shavelson, 1983). Given the limitations of the present research, in future studies we will examine the beliefs and choices of secondary teachers in relation to their actual practice, that is, a comparison among what they believe, what lessons they choose, and what they do in real classrooms. In addition, teachers' selection of individual belief statements, in addition to their broad theoretical orientations, will be examined in light of their observed plans and activities. Further, these studies will focus on separate content areas in order to investigate possible differences according to subject discipline. By studying these components we hope to better describe the complexities of the teaching and learning experience.

Appendix A

Beliefs Regarding How One Reads*

1. Before students can comprehend a text, they must be able to recognize all the words and/or symbols in a textbook page.
2. Students' background knowledge and experience play a major role in their comprehension of a text.
3. Students who are weak at word-recognition skills usually cannot compensate for this weakness with other components of the reading process.
4. Before students read a text, it is often useful for them to discuss experiences involving the topic being studied.
5. There is usually only one acceptable answer to a question from a text.
6. Teachers should normally provide instruction aimed at developing all components of the reading process.
7. If students are weak in one component important to the comprehension process, it is still possible for them to read and comprehend a text.
8. The meaning of a text is usually a joint product of reader knowledge and text information.
9. Teachers should normally expect and encourage students to have different interpretations of a text.
10. If readers do not comprehend a text in the way an author intended, we usually say they have misunderstood the text.
11. Teachers should normally discuss with students what they know about a topic before they begin reading a text.

*Text-based statements: 1, 3, 5, 10, 12; reader-based statements: 2, 4, 9, 11, 15; interactive statements: 6, 7, 8, 13, 14.

12. When students summarize a text, they should usually restate what the text says.
13. Expectations about a text topic are often as important as accurate recognition of words during the reading process.
14. Readers use a variety of strategies as they read a text—from sounding out unfamiliar words to guessing familiar words in rich context.
15. The best readers of a text are those who have learned to predict upcoming text.

Beliefs Regarding How Reading Develops*

1. It is important for content teachers to provide clear, precise presentations during skill instruction.
2. Students should receive many opportunities to read materials other than the textbook in the content areas (e.g., newspapers, literature, magazines).
3. In deciding how to teach a text topic, teachers should consider the varying abilities of the students.
4. Reading, writing, speaking, and listening are closely related learning processes.
5. Students learn content best when the material is broken down into specific skills to be taught by teachers.
6. Students should be tested frequently to determine if they have mastered what was taught.
7. Some students learn best by reading widely and often; others learn best through direct instruction.
8. Teachers should model how to learn from text material so that students gradually acquire their own independent reading strategies.
9. Opportunities should be created in the content areas to encourage students to read.
10. Not all poor readers benefit from more direct and structured learning experiences.
11. Teachers should have a list of reading skills appropriate for their content area and make certain that students learn these skills.
12. Much of what is learned in the content areas can be attributed to what is taught by the teacher.
13. It is important to consider students' differing reading abilities when selecting and using text materials.
14. Students can acquire a great deal of knowledge about learning to learn through adult models.
15. Teachers should generally spend more time working with less proficient readers than with more proficient readers.

Appendix B

Vocabulary Lesson Plans*

The teacher identifies several terms which may be unfamiliar to the students as they read the text. The teacher decides to utilize the following procedure:

---

*Text-based statements: 1, 5, 6, 11, 12; reader-based statements: 2, 4, 8, 9, 14; interactive statements: 3, 7, 10, 13, 15.

*Lesson 1: interactive; Lesson 2: reader based; Lesson 3: text based.

Lesson 1

1. The teacher explains that the students may be unfamiliar with some of the words they encounter in the upcoming reading selection. The teacher writes the words on the board and recites them to the students. The students are asked to provide definitions for the words.
2. The teacher has prepared a transparency with the words used in sentences. Using the context of the sentence, the students attempt to provide definitions for the words. The teacher provides the correct definitions for any not provided by the students and asks them to use each word in a sentence.
3. Before the students begin the reading assignment, the teacher provides a brief overview of the material. With this information, the students are asked to predict the usage of the new vocabulary word in the text.
4. After reading the text selection, the students write the vocabulary words and definitions in their own words in their notebooks.
5. The students are asked to write a passage using the terms. The teacher provides the topics according to the students' abilities.
6. The following day, the students take a quiz that involves matching some definitions with the words. The students use the other words by writing their own sentences.

Lesson 2

1. Before the students read the text, the teacher explains that the student may be unfamiliar with some of the words they will encounter in the upcoming reading selection.
2. The teacher writes these words on the board and asks the students to use the words in sentences. If some of the words are unfamiliar to the students, the teacher uses those words in sentences and asks the students to define them by using the context of the sentences.
3. Then the teacher asks the students to describe situations where they may have encountered or read about the terms. The teacher asks other students how these situations may be familiar to them. Then the students are asked to apply the definitions to other possible situations.
4. Following the discussion, the teacher provides different materials which contain the words used in a variety of ways. The class works in groups, analyzing the material and engaging in discussion about the meaning of the terms.
5. After reading the text selection, the students are asked to discuss their interpretations of the reading and the vocabulary words.
6. The following day, for a quiz grade, the students are asked to convey the meaning of the words in any type of writing passage.

Lesson 3

1. The teacher writes the vocabulary words on the board and reads the words aloud. The students are asked to recite the words and provide definitions. The teacher writes the correct student definitions and any that were not provided by the students on the board.
2. Then the teacher shows the students a transparency with the terms used in sentences. The students are asked to read each sentence aloud and recite the meanings of the new terms.

3. The teacher has prepared another transparency with sentences and missing words. The students are asked to fill in the blanks with the appropriate vocabulary words.

4. After this exercise, the students are asked to read the text selection. On a transparency, the teacher has written the sentences from the text containing the vocabulary words, leaving a blank where the term belongs. The class is asked to fill in the blanks and provide definitions of the terms.

5. Students are instructed to write the terms and the teacher's definitions in their notebooks.

6. The following day, the students are given a multiple-choice quiz—the vocabulary word is provided as well as three possible choices. For each question answered incorrectly, the students are required to write each term and its definition five times.

Appendix C

Frequencies of Statement Selection for How Reading Takes Place and How Reading Develops: Preservice and Inservice Teachers

Belief statement	Pre	In	Total	Belief statement	Pre	In	Total
How reading takes place				How reading develops			
1	18	6	24	1	21	10	31
2	43	38	81	2	47	40	87
3	8	0	8	3	27	31	58
4	29	29	58	4	37	35	72
5	0	0	0	5	8	4	12
6	41	23	64	6	11	7	18
7	25	20	45	7	10	7	17
8	31	23	54	8	12	20	32
9	31	20	51	9	43	31	74
10	1	2	3	10	5	6	11
11	19	25	44	11	11	4	15
12	5	3	8	12	8	2	10
13	13	12	25	13	25	21	46
14	24	28	52	14	13	10	23
15	2	1	3	15	12	2	14
Total	290	230	520	Total	290	230	520

References

Armour-Thomas, E. (1989). The application of teacher cognition in the classroom: A new teaching competency. *Journal of Research and Development in Education, 22,* 29–37.

Clark, C. M., & Peterson, P. L. (1986). Teachers' thought processes. In M. C. Wittrock (Ed.), *Handbook of research on teaching* (pp. 255–296). New York: Macmillan.

Duffy, G., & Anderson L. (1982). *Final report: Conceptions of reading progress* (Research series No. 11). East Lansing, MI: Institute for Research on Teaching, Michigan State University.

Duffy, G., & Ball, D. (1986). Instructional decision-making and reading teacher effectiveness. In J. Hoffman (Ed.), *Effective teaching of reading: Research and practice* (pp. 163–180). Newark, DE: International Reading Association.

Goodman, , K. S. (1985). Unity in reading. In H. Singer & R. Ruddell (Eds.), *Theoretical models and processes of reading* (3rd ed., pp. 813–840). Newark, DE: International Reading Association.

Gough, P. (1985). One second of reading. In H. Singer & R. Ruddell (Eds.), *Theoretical models and processes of reading* (3rd ed., pp. 661–686). Newark, DE: International Reading Association.

Harste, J. C., & Burke, C. L. (1977). A new hypothesis for reading teacher research: Both the teaching and learning of reading are theoretically based. In P. D. Pearson (Ed.), *Reading: Theory, research, and practice* (pp. 32–40). Clemson, SC: National Reading Conference.

Hoffman, J. V., & Kugle, C. L. (1982). A study of theoretical orientation to reading and its relationship to teacher verbal feedback during reading instruction. *Journal of Classroom Interaction, 18,* 2–7.

Kinzer, C. K. (1988). Instructional frameworks and instructional choices: Comparisons between preservice and inservice teachers. *Journal of Reading Behavior, 20,* 357–377.

Kinzer, C. K., & Carrick, D. A. (1986). Teacher beliefs as instructional influences. In J. Niles & R. Lalik (Eds.), *Solving problems in literacy: Learners, teachers & researchers* (pp. 127–134). New York: National Reading Conference.

Lampert, M. (1985). How do teachers manage to teach? Perspectives on problems in practice. *Harvard Educational Review, 55,* 178–184.

Leu, D. J., & Kinzer, C. K. (1987). *Effective reading instruction in the elementary grades.* Columbus, OH: Merrill.

Marascuilo, L. A. (1966). Large-sample multiple comparisons. *Psychological Bulletin, 65,* 280–290.

Richardson, V., Anders P., Tidwell, D., & Lloyd, C. (1991). The relationship between teachers' beliefs and practices in reading comprehension instruction. *American Educational Research Journal, 28,* 559–586.

Rumelhart, D. E. (1985). Toward an interactive model of reading. In H. Singer & R. Ruddell (Eds.), *Theoretical models and processes of reading* (3rd ed., pp. 722–750). Newark, DE: International Reading Association.

Rupley, W. H., & Logan, J. W. (1984). *Elementary teachers' beliefs about reading and knowledge of reading content.* (ERIC Document Reproduction No. ED 258 162)

Shavelson, R. J., & Stern, P. (1981). Research on teachers' pedagogical thoughts, judgments, decisions, and behavior. *Review of Educational Research, 51,* 455–498.

Shulman, L. S. (1986). Those who understand: Knowledge growth in teaching. *Educational Researcher, 15,* 4–14.

Stern, P., & Shavelson, R. (1983). Reading teachers' judgment, plans, and decision-making. *The Reading Teacher, 37,* 280–286.

Address correspondence to Bonnie C. Konopak, Office of the Dean, Louisiana State University, 221 Peabody Hall, Baton Rouge, LA 70803-4707.

A6

The Impact of Personal, Professional and Organizational Characteristics on Administrator Burnout

Walter H. Gmelch and Gordon Gates
Washington State University, Pullman, Washington, USA

Owing to difficult and challenging times, the position of school administrator appears less appealing to other educators. High school principalships have attracted fewer aspirants in recent years and are viewed by many as burnout positions. In response, popular writers and academic researchers have added volumes to the literature in the past decades on school administrator stress and burnout. Since 1980, over 90 studies have explored the causes, responses, and consequences of administrator stress and burnout. These research studies have examined several levels or stages of stress from its nature (Chicon and Koff, 1980), types and sources (Feitler and Tokar, 1981; Gmelch and Swent, 1984), responses (Gmelch, 1988; Swent, 1983), and consequences (Bloch, 1978; Friesen and Sarros, 1989) to administrators' coping effectiveness (Hiebert and Mendaglio, 1988). Most of these data-based studies have investigated the sources of burnout while fewer have explored the associations between burnout and stress, coping, job performance, and satisfaction and such mediating variables as support systems, role conflict, personality, gender, and age. Much yet remains unknown about the associations, relationships, and influences of stress and burnout with these other personal, professional, and organizational characteristics.

There is a growing body of evidence which links the effects of burnout on job satisfaction, performance, and health (Blix *et al.*, 1994; Gmelch *et al.*, 1984; Keller, 1975) as well as the intervening impact of support systems (Sarros and Sarros, 1992), personality (Friedman and Rosenman, 1974), role conflict and ambiguity (Gmelch and Torelli, 1994; Kottkamp and Mansfield, 1985; Schwab and Iwanicki, 1982), and personal characteristics such as age and gender (Blix *et al.*, 1994; Dey, 1994). Thus, the purpose of this study is to broaden the investigation carried out in previous research. Specifically, the study possesses the following three objectives: to identify the most salient personal, professional, and organizational characteristics contributing to administrator burnout; to determine those correlational relationships that are most salient; and to assess the role of social support's impact on job satisfaction, burnout, and performance.

Data from the present study of school administrators were used previously to establish the correlational link between stress and burnout (Torelli and Gmelch, 1993), coping and stress (Gmelch and Chan, 1995), and the influence of role ambiguity and conflict on stress and burnout (Gmelch and Torelli, 1994). This study does not replicate the analyses of these earlier works, rather it is an extension. The analysis of the present study attempts to determine the most relevant personal, professional, and organizational variables that have been uncovered through previous research as sources of administrator stress and burnout. Further, the present study includes the social support response items which have been unexamined in previous analyses of the

Journal of Educational Administration, vol. 36, no. 2, 1998, pp. 146–159. Copyright © MCB University Press, Bradford, UK. Reprinted by permission.

data. Such an understanding should increase present knowledge to present facets of administration which need closer attention, modification of practice, and organizational restructuring to reduce the stress and burnout experienced by administrators.

Theoretical Framework

Occupational Stress and Burnout

A number of models have emerged since the 1970s which identify several components of stress. The conceptual cornerstone of the present study is formed from components of these earlier works, especially that of McGrath (1976).

First, McGrath's model hypothesized that there are six dimensions of stress. However, most subsequent measures of job-related stress identify fewer dimensions than McGrath's six (e.g. Indik *et al.*, 1964). A study by Gmelch and Swent (1984) sought to overcome these discrepancies in stress measures and developed the Administrative Stress Index. Through factor analysis, four sources of stress were identified which approximate McGrath's six hypothesized dimensions:

1. role-based stress, perceived from administrator's role-set interactions and beliefs or attitudes about his or her role in the schools;
2. task-based stress, arising from the performance of day-to-day administrative activities, from telephone and staff interruptions, meetings, writing memos, and reports, to participating in school activities outside of the normal working hours;
3. boundary-spanning stress, emanating from external conditions, such as negotiations and gaining public support for school budgets; and
4. conflict-mediating stress, arising from the administrator handling conflicts within the school such as trying to resolve differences between and among personnel, resolving parent and school conflicts, and handling student discipline problems.

Second, McGrath explained stress as a four-stage, closed-loop process beginning with situations in the environment (A), which are then perceived by the individual (B), to which the individual selects the response (C), resulting in consequences for both the individual and the situation (D), which closes the loop. Each of the four stages is connected by the linking process of cognitive appraisal, decision, performance and outcome. The four stages postulated by McGrath also have served as sound building blocks for the development of later stress models. Each subsequent model appears to have been personalized with appropriate feedback loops, mediating variables, and process variables embellishing the relationship among the four basic stages in a manner that meets the research and application needs of each job/role being investigated.

One example of these later stress models is the Administrator Stress Cycle (Gmelch, 1982). Basically, the first of the four stages of this model is initiated when an administrator experiences one or more of the sources of stress. Stage two consists of the perception or interpretation of the stressors by the individual. Administrators who perceive demands as harmful or demanding will experience stress within their lives and approach their work with intensity. The classic study of the effect of Type A behaviour and health by Friedman and Rosenman (1974) highlights the impact of perception on stress.

The third stage of the cycle presents choices to the individual. In this stage the administrator responds to the stressor, if it is perceived to be harmful, threatening, and/or demanding. Individuals use coping strategies when they believe they can counteract the stressor. A coping strategy is effective to the degree that it assists the individual in a positive manner.

The fourth stage of the stress cycle, consequences, takes into account the long range effects of stress. The negative consequences of stress can include headaches, ulcers, illnesses, or other physical disabilities. Maslach and Jackson (1981) separated the consequences of stress into three dimensions of burnout: emotional exhaustion, depersonalization, and feelings of low personal accomplishment. Emotional exhaustion identifies that aspect of burnout which is associated with low levels of energy and the feeling of being drained. Depersonalization is the dimension of burnout which is connected to feelings of lost identity and meaningfulness. And finally, low personal accomplishment is that aspect of burnout where individuals feel dissatisfied with their accomplishments and/or believe that their actions no longer make a difference.

Study Design

Subject Sample

In the spring of 1991, 1,000 subjects were stratified and randomly selected from each of the following four categories in public school administration: 250 elementary principals, 250 junior high/middle school principals, 250 high school principals, and 250 superintendents. Each administrator was mailed an Administrator Work Inventory (AWI). A total of 740 were returned for a 74 per cent response rate. However, due to missing data, 656 surveys were used for data analysis. Responses by administrative position were consistent across all levels (169 elementary school principals, 149 junior high/middle school principals, 177 high school principals, and 161 superintendents).

Measurements

The AWI is comprised of six instruments, plus a seventh section on general information. The following instruments in the inventory will each be explained: the Administrator Stress Index (Gmelch and Swent, 1984), the Maslach Burnout Inventory (Maslach and Jackson, 1981, 1986), the Administrative Role Questionnaire (Rizzo et al., 1970), the Sayles Type A Personality (Caplan et al., 1980), the Support Climate instrument (Caplan et al., 1980), and the Bem Sex-Role Inventory (Bem, 1975, 1981).

Administrator Stress Index (ASI). The ASI, developed and validated by Gmelch and Swent (1984) contains over 30 items. Respondents are asked to indicate perceptions of various situations as sources of concern. Using a five-point Likert-type scale of rarely or never bothers me to frequently bothers me, respondents indicate their level of stress. Furthermore, for each item, respondents are asked to indicate on a five-point Likert-type scale their perceived coping ability from not at all effective to very effective. This method for quantifying emotional reaction has been used successfully both clinically (Hiebert and Fox, 1981) and in survey instruments (Gmelch et al., 1984; Hiebert and Mendaglio, 1988). From a factor analysis by Koch et al. (1982) and by Gmelch and Torelli (1994), four stress factors and four coping factors have been identified. The four stress factors and accompanying coping factors are the following: task-based, role-based, conflict-mediating, and boundary-spanning.

Maslach Burnout Inventory (MBI). The MBI is recognized and used extensively throughout research on burnout and the helping professions (Cordes and Dougherty, 1993). It contains 22-seven point Likert-type scale questions and has been tested, validated, and normed for educators. Three dimensions of burnout are assessed: emotional exhaustion, depersonalization, and personal accomplishment. Personal accomplishment is reversed scored such that reduced personal accomplishment is related to burnout.

Administrative Role Questionnaire. This 14-item instrument was developed by Rizzo et al. (1970) to determine the level of perceived role ambiguity (reverse scored) and role conflict. A psychometric evaluation of this instrument across six samples concluded that its use is justified (Schuler *et al.* 1977; Tracy and Johnson, 1981). Also, a few studies using multiple methods have found agreement between the questionnaire and interview data on role conflict and ambiguity (e.g. Caplan et. al., 1980).

Social Support Questionnaire. This component of the survey was adapted from Caplan's study of job demands and worker health at the University of Michigan (Caplan, et. al., 1980). Thoits (1982) argues that social support must include elements of both sources and types of support, not merely the amount of support individuals feel they receive. This section of the survey is composed of nine questions allowing respondents to indicate on a five-point Likert-type scale the degree to which they receive support from their immediate supervisor, colleagues, family and friends, as well as the type of help received in solving work related problems, heavy workload, and constructive feedback on performance.

Type A Personality. The Type A Personality component of the survey is comprised of ten questions. Developed by Sayles (in Caplan, et. al., 1980) from Friedman and Rosenman's Type A behaviour research (1974), the Sayles Type A Personality instrument attempts to identify the degree to which individuals possess Type A behaviour traits. Again this component of the AWI is composed of Likert-type scale questions.

While research studies assess Type A Personality (Schaubroeck *et al.*, 1994) as a unidimensional construct, factor analysis of the 10-item Sayles Type A Behaviour questionnaire revealed two factors: work competition and challenge (see Table I). The first factor, explaining 28.6 percent of the total variance, is composed of items which reflect the respondents' competitiveness. The second factor, explaining

TABLE I

Factor Analysis of Administrative Style

Variables	Factors	
	Competition	Challenge
It seems as if I need 30 hours a day to finish all the things I'm faced with	0.787	
In general, I approach my work more seriously than most people I know	0.778	
I guess there are some people who can be nonchalant or easy going about their work, but I'm not one of them	0.758	
Sometimes I feel like I shouldn't be working so hard, but something drives me on	0.662	
In comparison to most people I know, I'm very involved in my work	0.510	
I thrive on challenging situations. The more challenges I have, the better		0.796
I've often been asked to be an officer of some group or groups		0.628
I hate giving up before I'm absolutely sure that I'm licked		0.480
My achievements are considered to be significantly higher than those of most people I know		0.163
Percentage of total variance explained after rotation	28.64	18.65

18.6 per cent of the total variance, is composed of items which reflect the degree to which respondents thrive on situational challenges.

Bem Sex-Role Inventory (BSRI). Developed by Sandra Bem (1981), the BSRI attempts to assess individuals tendency towards four sex-role trait categories: undifferentiated, masculine, feminine, and androgenous. An androgenous individual is one who possesses both high masculine and feminine sex-role traits, while the undifferentiated scores low in both. A masculine individual scores high in the masculine sex-role traits and low in the feminine traits, while a person identified as feminine scores the reverse. The Bem inventory measures 30 personality characteristics of respondents on a seven-point Likert-type scale of never or almost never true to always or almost always true.

General information. A total of 14 questions comprised the demographic section of the AWI to assess variables in the personal area (age, gender, physical health, hours of exercise) and professional area (position, years in administration, years in current position, hours of overtime worked, administrative performance, and job satisfaction). With respect to job satisfaction, physical health, and current performance, administrators were asked to assess each dimension on a five-point Likert-type scale. The organizational domain assessed grade level of school, number of students in school, and number of students in the school district.

Dependent and Independent Variables

The dependent variables for this study were the three subscales of the MBI: emotional exhaustion, depersonalization, and personal accomplishment. The independent variables included age, years as administrator, satisfaction with current position, current performance as an administrator, physical health, role conflict, role ambiguity, overall level of stress felt as an administrator, and total level of coping with stress. Other independent variables were the social support questions, the four stress factors (task-based, role-based, conflict-mediating, and boundary-spanning), the four coping factors (task-based, role-based, conflict-mediating, and boundary-spanning), and the Type A personality factors (competitive and challenge). The independent discrete variables of gender, level of position (elementary, middle/junior, high school, and superintendent), and sex-role classification (undifferentiated, masculine, feminine, and androgenous) were dummy coded into dichotomous variables for analysis (Tabachnick and Fidell, 1983).

Data Analysis

Percentage distributions were generated for the demographic information. Further, Persons-Product Moment correlations were computed for analysis of relationships between the dependent and independent variables. Interactive stepwise multiple regression analysis ($p = 0.05$) using Systat 5.1 occurred to develop models for predicting emotional exhaustion, depersonalization, and personal accomplishment. These models provide the best estimate using the fewest independent variables for understanding the associations between these independent and dependent variables. Through this process theoretical tenets may be compared to that which is found in practice. However, one problem with this process is that the models may be tailored to this data set.

Results

Demographics

The average subject was 47 years of age and had 14 years of administrative experience. Of the administrators, 23 per cent were female and 77 percent were male. Most administrators had been in their present position for six years and worked an average of 54 hours a week. For those who wanted to work overtime, seven hours a week was normal. The majority of respondents stated that they would choose administration again if they were given the choice. Administrators surveyed, on average, worked in school districts with a student population of around 8,500. Furthermore, the average size school for principals was around 550 students. Generally, the administrators attributed 65 per cent of their total stress in their lives to their work, while feeling that they coped with stress effectively. Finally, these administrators felt that they were performing their jobs well and were very satisfied with administration.

Correlation Analysis

Pearson-product moment correlations provide insights into the strength and direction of the relationships between variables. All coefficients $r = 0.08$) reported below are significant at $p = 0.05$ level, while coefficients ($r = 0.13$) are significant at the $p = 0.001$ level. The strongest correlations, and significant at $p = 0.001$, are found between the burnout dimension of emotional exhaustion and level of stress ($r = 0.57$), task-based stress ($r = 0.51$), and conflict-mediating stress ($r = 0.41$). Strong negative correlations exist between stress and coping ($r = -0.54$), that is, the more effective an administrator's coping ability the less stress he or she reported experiencing.

The strongest negative correlations exist between job satisfaction and the burnout dimension of emotional exhaustion ($r = -0.47$), and less convincing correlations were found for the other dimensions of burnout (depersonalization $r = -0.18$, and personal accomplishment $r = 0.26$). Each of these correlations, between the three dimensions of burnout and job satisfaction, infer that those with higher levels of job satisfaction experience less burnout. Also strong inverse associations were found to exist between job satisfaction and role-based stress ($r = -0.38$), task-based stress ($r = -0.33$), and the overall level of stress ($r = -0.36$). Conversely, positive correlations were found between job satisfaction and overall coping effectiveness ($r = 0.26$), as well as for role-based coping ($r = 0.37$) and tasked-based coping ($r = 0.36$).

Strong associations have already been reported from this data set between emotional exhaustion and the four stress factors (Torelli and Gmelch, 1993), and the four coping factors (Gmelch and Chan, 1995). Given the fact that the other burnout dimensions (depersonalization and personal accomplishment) are highly intercorrelated ($r = 0.76$), it appears that emotional exhaustion is most sensitive to the impact of stress and the other independent variables.

The two Type A Personality factors, work competition and challenge, appear to have an opposite relationship on the variables assessed in this study. The competitive Type A approach has a slight, but negative association with physical health ($r = -0.10$) whereas challenge has a slightly positive relationship with health ($r = 0.11$). The same pattern held true with regard to each of the stress factors (e.g. competition was positively correlated with the stress factors and challenge was negatively correlated with the four stress factors). The associations between competition and emotional exhaustion ($r = 0.30$), challenge and emotional exhaustion ($r = -0.10$), and challenge and personal accomplishment ($r = 0.18$) support the perspective that administrators who have adopted a competitive approach tend to report experiencing greater levels of stress than those who view the sources of stress as challenging.

The most significant correlation with administrative performance was job satisfaction ($r = 0.36$). Performance was also positively associated with the Type A Personality factor of challenge ($r = 0.24$), but not with competition ($r = 0.01$). Those variables that were found to be negatively correlated with administrative performance above the ($r = 0.20$) level were conflict-mediating stress, task-based stress, overall level of stress, and emotional exhaustion. Conversely, the stress coping factors were found to be positively correlated with administrator performance. Overall, it is interesting to note that administrative performance was more associated with effective coping (boundary-spanning $r = 0.22$, role-based $r = 0.22$, conflict-mediating $r = 0.24$, and task-based $r = 0.16$) than by the stress factors.

Finally, while the support-stress paradigm was verified for faculty by Neumann and Finaly-Neumann (1991), the exploration into administrative stress has yet to be investigated. In this study, the role of social support's impact on job satisfaction, burnout, and performance was assessed. Preliminary analysis revealed that the three sources of assistance (supervisor, colleagues, and family) were highly correlated across the type of help received. Therefore, for simplification the nine items were combined to three sources of assistance. Of these three sources (supervisor, colleagues, and family), support from one's supervisor has the strongest correlation with job satisfaction ($r = 0.29$) and support of family is correlated the strongest with administrators' perception of their performance as administrators ($r = 0.23$). Support of colleagues was moderately associated with satisfaction ($r = 0.18$) and performance ($r = 0.14$). A weaker correlation was found between the burnout dimensions and social support of family and friends than from support of supervisor or support of colleagues. A moderate level of association was found between personal accomplishment and the three sources of support (supervisor, colleagues, and family and friends). Overall, however, support of supervisor seemed to be the social support factor that is most consistently correlated at a level of significance. Support of supervisor is correlated with emotional exhaustion ($r = -0.12$), depersonalization ($r = -0.12$), and personal accomplishment ($r = 0.18$), remembering that personal accomplishment is reversed from the other two dimensions.

Multiple Regression Analysis

Stepwise multiple regression analysis was used to determine which variables were significant at the $p = 0.05$ level for predicting burnout on each of the three dimensions. This process removes from a model variance due to the correlation between the independent variables. Thus, the models show the unique contribution of each independent variable to the predictive models for each dependent variable. As shown in Table II, seven variables explaining 47 per cent of the variance were statistically significant in predicting emotional exhaustion for educational administrators.

The independent variables explain less of the variance for depersonalization and personal accomplishment than for emotional exhaustion. The regression analysis shows that emotional exhaustion is most easily explained by the variables assessed in this study. Time pressures (task-based stress), competition (Type A behaviour), administrative stress, and conflict impact administrator's feelings of emotional exhaustion, resulting in job dissatisfaction. Both effective coping and good health are positive resisters to emotional exhaustion. While emotional exhaustion appears linked with the time and conflict pressures of the position, both the other dimensions of

TABLE II

Multiple regression analysis

Variable	Significance	R^2(explained variance)
Emotional exhaustion		
Task-based stress	0.00	0.25
Satisfaction	0.00	0.10
Administrative coping	0.00	0.04
Conflict-mediating stress	0.00	0.02
Competitive approach	0.00	0.02
Physical health	0.00	0.02
Administrative stress	0.00	0.02
Total R^2		0.47
Depersonalization		
Ambiguity	0.00	0.06
Conflict-based stress	0.00	0.02
Total R^2		0.08
Personal accomplishment		
Ambiguity	0.00	0.11
Boundary-spanning coping	0.00	0.02
Satisfaction	0.00	0.02
Family support	0.00	0.01
Total R^2		0.16

burnout (depersonalization and feeling of low personal accomplishment) are most influenced by role ambiguity.

Discussion

Multidimensionality of Burnout

It has been argued by others that unless burnout is tested as a multidimentional construct, little progress will be made in determining its linkages to other variables (Byrne, 1992; Maslach and Jackson, 1986). This assertion was confirmed by the correlation analysis and supported by that literature reconfirming the intercorrelated paths leading from personal, professional, and organizational characteristics to the three dimensions of burnout and the consequences of health and performance.

Intercorrelated paths. Furthermore, just as emotional exhaustion and personal accomplishment are clearly linked to job performance, job performance is strongly related to positive health, effective coping, job challenge, stress, role conflict, and ambiguity, and job satisfaction. An administrator's health is impacted by a number of personal and professional variables such as, on the positive side, exercise, coping, job

TABLE III

Administrator burnout dimensions: influences, remediation and buffers

Dimensions	Influences	Remediation	Buffers
Emotional exhausion	Task stress Conflict stress Competition Administrative stress	Time management Negotiation/mediation skills Self-awareness Stress management	Satisfaction Administrative coping Physical health
Depersonalization	Ambiguity Conflict stress	Role clarification Negotiation/mediation skills	No buffers correlated
Personal accomplishment	Ambiguity	Role clarification	Boundary coping Satisfaction Family support

satisfaction, and administrative performance, and negatively by role conflict and ambiguity, stress, and emotional exhaustion.

Influences on Administrative Burnout

In general, emotional exhaustion stands as the central construct since it is most responsive to the variables of job intensity (time, stress, competition, and conflict) and negatively associated with job satisfaction and effective coping. Depersonalization and reduced personal accomplishment are highly intercorrelated ($r = 0.76$), reflecting their joint association with the variable of job ambiguity. Since these constructs of burnout reflect differential influences from personal, professional, and organizational variables, they will be discussed separately, using Table III as a guideline, in terms of:

1. identification of negative influences;
2. suggestions for remediation of the influences; and
3. variables acting as burnout mediators.

Emotional exhaustion. Clearly emotional exhaustion stands as the central construct of administrator burnout with seven variables explaining 47 per cent of the variance. On the downside, the four variables that accentuate emotional exhaustion reflect the intensity of administration:

1. the task-based stress characterized by interruptions, participating in activities outside school hours, too heavy a workload, meetings, and writing reports, memos, and other communications;
2. the conflict-mediating stress riddled with trying to resolve differences with and between students, parents, teachers, and superiors;
3. the competitive nature of Type A behaviour—trying to finish things up, taking work more seriously than others, and a hard-driving work ethic; and
4. the overall level of stress administrators feel.

Administrator preparation programmes and on-the-job training should emphasize basic administrative survival skills such as effective time management, principled negotiation and mediation training, and programmes to develop self-awareness and understanding of the emotional intensity of administration. As one colleague stated: "The reason some administrators burn out so quickly is that they burn so brightly."

While the influence of intensity represents the hot spots contributing to emotional exhaustion, administrators also appear to have burnout buffers such as good physical health, effective coping techniques, and most significantly, being satisfied with their jobs.

Depersonalization and personal accomplishment. Job ambiguity provided the most significant influence on both depersonalization and personal accomplishment dimensions of burnout. If administrators experience unclear job conditions—not knowing exactly what is expected of them, how much authority they have, unclear goals, and what has to be done—how then can they feel fulfilled and accomplished? These unclear job underpinnings need to be addressed. Better dialogue and understanding should occur to clarify job requirements and expectations. The stress administrators experience from constantly encountering other people on a conflict basis also contributes to depersonalization.

In addition, boundary-spanning requirements of the job such as complying with rules and regulations, negotiating contracts, and gaining public approval for programmes also adds to administrators feeling of low personal accomplishment. On the positive side, administrators who experienced feelings of low personal accomplishment found a burnout buffer from the support they received from their families.

Social Support as a Mediating Variable

Although social support is investigated in most studies as a single construct, recent research suggested that it should be viewed both by source and type (Sarros and Sarros, 1992). Further, Beehr *et al.* (1976) inferred from his analysis that social support may be the cure for stress-related disorder. The AWI asked nine questions to assess the three types of support in terms of help with work-related problems, workload, and performance feedback as well as three sources—supervisors, colleagues, and family and friends. Owing to the intercorrelations, the nine items were combined by the three sources of assistance. As expected, most of the significant correlations were with supervisory support, especially beneficial with regard to role conflict and ambiguity as well as role-based stress and overall stress. Supervisory support also correlated positively with role-based coping and job satisfaction.

As the social support research has been refined and expanded by the Sarros and Sarros' (1992) study and this study, it is becoming more apparent that support is both ambiguous and inconclusive as a resource for burnout prevention and stress reduction. Also, these findings suggest that social support is a multifaceted resource that works better in some situations depending on the source of the stress.

Clearly, support from one's supervisor has a greater impact than the other sources investigated in this study. For instance, administrators' support from their supervisors appears to be critical to help reduce the feelings of role conflict and ambiguity as well as role-based stress. While this study did not confirm strong correlations between support and burnout, others have testified that support from a supervisor can help alleviate educator burnout (Jackson *et al.*, 1986; Sarros and Sarros, 1992). However, further research is still recommended.

Conclusion

Administrators in Need of a Clock and Compass

While other studies have investigated two or three variables as they relate to burnout, the uniqueness of this study is the use of multiple independent variables assessed and related to burnout. This study used regression analysis to sift out the less influential variables and accentuate those with the most salient influence on burnout. Only the burnout dimension of emotional exhaustion was explained by a significant per cent of variance, most of which related to task-based stress. Little variance for depersonalization and personal accomplishment was explained by the plethora of independent variables; however, role ambiguity revealed the greatest variance in both cases.

Therefore, different strategies must be taken for separate dimensions of burnout in order to pave a more manageable road currently travelled by educational administrators. The time-pressure and intensity with which administrators travel their road must be modified in order to moderate the emotional exhaustion experience along the way. Also, it is not just the pace of the travel, but the ambiguous direction which leads administrators to a place often characterized by feelings of depersonalization and lack of personal accomplishment. To properly navigate the road of administration and reduce the influence of burnout, administrators must be equipped with both a better clock and compass for the journey ahead.

References

Beehr, T.A., Walsh, J.T. and Taber, T.D. (1976), "Relationship of stress to individually and organizationally valued states: higher order needs as a moderator," *Journal of Applied Psychology,* Vol. 61, pp. 41–7.

Bem, S.L. (1975), "Sex role adaptability: one consequence of psychological androgyny," *Journal of Psychology and Social Psychology,* Vol. 31, pp. 634–13.

Bem, S.L. (1981), *Bem Sex Role Inventory—Professional Manual,* Consulting Psychologist Press, Inc., Palo Alto, CA.

Blix, A.G., Cruise, R.J., Mitchell, B.J. and Blix, G.G. (1994), "Occupational stress among university teachers," *Educational Research,* Vol. 36 No. 2, pp. 157–69.

Bloch, A.M. (1978), "Combat neurosis in inner city schools," *American Journal of Psychiatry,* Vol. 135 No. 10, pp. 1189–92.

Byrne, B.M. (1992) *Investigating Causal Links to Burnout for Elementary, Intermediate, and Secondary Teachers,* American Educational Research Conference, San Francisco, CA.

Caplan, R.D., Cobb, S., French, J.R.P., Van Harrison, R. and Pinneau, S.R. (1980), *Job Demands and Worker Health: Main Effects and Occupational Differences.* US Government Printing Office, Washington, DC.

Chicon, D.J. and Koff, R.H. (1980), "Stress and teaching," *NASSP Bulletin,* Vol. 64, pp. 91–104.

Cooper, C.L. and Marshall, J. (1976), "Occupational sources of stress: a review of the literature relating to coronary heat disease and mental ill health," *Journal of Occupational Psychology,* Vol. 49, pp. 11–29.

Cordes, C.L. and Dougherty, T.W. 1993), "A review and an integration of research on job burnout," *Academy of Management Review.* Vol. 18 No. 6, pp. 621–56.

Dey, E.L. (1994), "Dimensions of faculty stress: a recent survey," *Review of Higher Education,* Vol. 17, pp. 305–22.

Feitler, F.C. and Tokar, E.B. (1981), "Teacher stress: sources, symptoms, and job satisfaction," paper presented at American Educational Research Association, Los Angeles, CA.

Friedman, M. and Rosenman, R.H. (1974), *Type A Behavior and Your Heart,* New York, NY.

Friesen, D. and Sarros, J.C. (1989), "Sources of burnout among educators," *Journal of Organizational Behavior,* Vol. 10, pp. 179–89.

French, R.P. and Caplan, R.D. (1972), "Organizational stress and individual strain," in Marrow, A.J. (Ed.), *The Failure of Success,* AMACOM, New York, NY.

Gmelch, W.H. (1982), *Beyond Stress to Effective Management,* Wiley & Sons, New York, N.Y.

Gmelch, W.H. (1988), "Research perspectives on administrative stress: causes, reactions, responses, and consequences," *Journal of Educational Administration,* Vol. 26 No. 2, pp. 134–40.

Gmelch, W.H. and Chan, W. (1995), "Administrator stress and coping factors: a transactional analysis," *Journal of Personnel Evaluation in Education,* Vol. 9, pp. 275–86.

Gmelch, W.H., Lovrich, N.D. and Wilke, P.K. (1984), "Stress in academe: a national perspective," *Research in Higher Education,* Vol. 20 No. 4, pp. 477–90.

Gmelch, W.H. and Swent, B. (1984), "Management team stressors and their impact on administrators' health," *The Journal of Educational Administration,* Vol. 22 No. 2, pp. 192–205.

Gmelch, W.H. and Torelli, J.A. (1994), "The association of role conflict and ambiguity with administrator stress and burnout," *Journal of School Leadership,* Vol. 4, pp. 341–56.

Hiebert, B. and Fox, E.G. (1981), "The reactive effects of self-monitoring anxiety," *Journal of Canadian Psychology,* Vol. 28, pp. 187–93.

Hiebert, B. and Mendaglio, S. (1988), "A transactional look at school principal stress," *Research Report,* University of Calgary.

House, J.S. (1982), *Work Stress and Social Support,* Addison-Wesley, Philippines.

Indik, B., Seashore, S.E. and Slesinger, J. (1964), "Demographic correlates of psychological strain," *Journal of Abnormal and Social Psychology,* Vol. 69, pp. 26–38.

Jackson, J.E., Schwab, R.L. and Schuler, R.S. (1986), "Toward an understanding of the burnout phenomenon," *Journal of Applied Psychology,* Vol. 71 No. 4, pp. 630–40.

Kahn, R.L., Wolfe, D.M., Quinn, R.P. and Snoek, J.D. (1964), *Organizational Stress: Studies in Role Conflict and Ambiguity,* John Wiley & Sons, New York, N.Y.

Keller, R.T. (1975), "Role conflict and ambiguity: correlates with job satisfaction and values," *Personnel Psychology,* Vol. 25, pp. 57–64.

Koch, J.L., Tung R., Gmelch, W. and Swent, B. (1982), "Job stress among school administrators: factorial dimensions and differential effects," *Journal of Applied Psychology,* Vol. 67 No. 4, pp. 493–9.

Kottkamp, R.B. and Mansfield, J.R. (1985), "Role conflict, role ambiguity, powerlessness and burnout among high school supervisors," *Journal of Research and Development in Education,* Vol. 18 No. 4, pp. 29–38.

McGrath, J.E. (1976), *Handbook of Industrial and Organizational Psychology,* Rand-McNally College, Chicago, IL, pp. 1351–95.

Maslach, C. and Jackson, S.E. (1981), "The measurement of experienced burnout," *Journal of Occupational Behavior,* Vol. 2, pp. 99–113.

Maslach, C. and Jackson, S.E. (1986), *Maslach Burnout Inventory—Manual,* Consulting Psychologist Press, Inc., Palo Alto, CA.

Neumann, Y. and Finaly-Neumann, E. (1991), "Determinants and correlates of faculty burnout in US research universities," *Journal of Educational Administration,* Vol. 29 No. 3, pp. 80–92.

Rizzo, J.R., House, R.J. and Lirtzman, S.I. (1970), "Role conflict and ambiguity in complex organizations," *Administrative Science Quarterly,* Vol. 15, pp. 150–63.

Sarros, J.C. (1988), "Administrator burn out: findings and future directions," *Journal of Educational Administration,* Vol. 26 No. 2, pp. 184–96.

Sarros, J.C. and Sarros, A.M. (1992), "Social support and teacher burnout," *Journal of Educational Administration,* Vol. 30 No. 1, pp. 55–69.

Schuler, R.S., Aldag, R.J. and Brief, A.P. (1977), "Role conflict and ambiguity: a scale analysis," *Organizational Behavior and Human Performance,* Vol. 20, pp. 119–28.

Schaubroeck, J., Ganster, D.C. and Kemmerer, B.E. (1994), "Job complexity, Type A behavior, and cardiovascular disorder: a prospective study," *Academy of Management Journal,* Vol. 37 No. 2, pp. 426–39.

Schwab, R.L. and Iwanicki, E.F. (1982), "Perceived role conflict, role ambiguity and teacher burnout," *Educational Administration Quarterly,* Vol. 18 No. 1, pp. 60–74.

Swent, B. (1983), "How administrators cope with stress," *Theory Into Practice,* Vol. 22 No. 1, pp. 70–4.

Tabachnick, B.G. and Fidell, L.S. (1983), *Using Multivariate Statistics,* Harper & Row, New York, NY.

Thoits, P.A. (1982), "Conceptual, methodological and theoretical problems in studying social support as a buffer against life stress," *Journal of Health and Social Behavior,* Vol. 23, pp. 145–9.

Torelli, J.A. and Gmelch, W.H. (1993), "Occupational stress and burnout in educational administration," *People and Education,* Vol. 1 No. 4, pp. 363–81.

Tracy, L. and Johnson, T.W. (1981), "What do the role conflict and role ambiguity scales measures?," *Journal of Applied Psychology,* Vol. 66 No. 4, pp. 464–9.

Whitaker, K.S. (1992), "Principal burnout and personality type: do relationships exist?," *Record in Educational Administration,* Vol. 13 No. 1, pp. 87–95.

A7

Student Motivation in Middle School: The Role of Perceived Pedagogical Caring

Kathryn R. Wentzel
University of Maryland College Park

This study examined adolescents' perceptions of pedagogical caring in relation to their motivation to achieve positive social and academic outcomes in middle school. A longitudinal sample of 248 students was followed from 6th to 8th grade. Perceived caring from teachers predicted motivational outcomes, even when students' current levels of psychological distress and beliefs about personal control, as well as previous (6th grade) motivation and

Wentzel, K., "Student Motivation in Middle School: The Role of Perceived Pedagogical Caring." *Journal of Educational Psychology,* vol. 89, no. 3, 1997, pp. 411–419. Copyright © 1997 the American Psychological Association. Reprinted with permission.

performance, were taken into account. Eighth-grade students characterize supportive and caring teachers along dimensions suggested by N. Noddings (1992) and models of effective parenting (D. Baumrind, 1971). Teachers who care were described as demonstrating democratic interaction styles, developing expectations for student behavior in light of individual differences, modeling a "caring" attitude toward their own work, and providing constructive feedback. The implications for understanding links between teacher behavior and student achievement are discussed.

Why are some children eager to engage in classroom activities whereas others devalue and disengage from the learning process? Researchers of achievement motivation often attribute these distinct motivational orientations to intrapersonal cognitive processes (e.g., Bandura, 1986; Dweck & Leggett, 1988; Weiner, 1992; Wigfield & Eccles, 1992). Others have attributed a powerful role to teaching and instruction (e.g., Ames & Ames, 1984; Rosenholtz & Wilson, 1980; Slavin, 1987).

Of interest for the present research is that recent studies have linked interpersonal relationships between teachers and students to motivational outcomes (e.g., Birch & Ladd, 1996; Pianta, 1992; Wentzel & Asher, 1995). Explanations for why these noninstructional aspects of classroom life are related to student effort and engagement have not been well developed. However, several authors have suggested that feelings of belongingness and of being cared for can foster the adoption and internalization of goals and values of caregivers (Baumeister & Leary, 1995; Connell & Wellborn, 1991; Noddings, 1992). With respect to schooling, this explanation translates into the notion that students will be motivated to engage in classroom activities if they believe that teachers care about them.

According to Noddings (1992), the academic objectives of schools cannot be met unless teachers provide students with a caring and supportive classroom environment (see also Noblit, 1993). However, even the most basic questions concerning the influence of caring on student motivation have not been addressed empirically. For instance, to what extent do caring and supportive teachers motivate student behavior when other student characteristics are taken into account? If "caring" teachers do make a difference, then what makes a teacher an effective "caregiver" in the eyes of students?

The present study provides an initial attempt to address these questions by identifying characteristics of pedagogical caring in middle school and examining the relation of perceptions of caring teachers to young adolescents' motivation to achieve academic and social outcomes. Studies of teacher characteristics and teacher-student relationships have not been frequent with young adolescents in middle school. However, transitions from elementary to middle school often result in heightened levels of mistrust between teachers and students, student perceptions that teachers no longer care about them, and a decrease in opportunities for students to establish meaningful relationships with teachers (Eccles, 1993; Harter, 1996. Therefore, perceptions of caring from teachers might be a critical factor that motivates middle school students to engage in the social and academic activities of the classroom.

Two specific questions concerning teacher caring and student motivation were addressed: (a) To what extent do adolescents' perceptions of caring teachers predict efforts to achieve positive social and academic outcomes at school? and (b) How do middle school students characterize a caring, supportive teacher? With respect to the first question, perceptions of caring teachers were examined in relation to 8th graders' academic effort and pursuit of prosocial and social responsibility goals. These social and academic aspects of motivation are important in that the pursuit of goals to behave in prosocial and socially responsible ways has been related consistently and positively to academic motivation and performance as well as to social competence (Wentzel, 1991, 1993). Academic effort represents an important index of academic motivation (Maehr, 1984), as well as a significant predictor of grades and test scores (Wentzel, Weinberger, Ford, & Feldman, 1990).

In this study, students' perceptions rather than observers' or teachers' reports of caring were the focus of interest. Previous research has documented that correlations between adolescents' subjective reports of caregiving and observers' or parents' reports are typically weak or nonsignificant (Feldman, Wentzel, & Gehring, 1989). It is particularly important to note, however, that adolescents' perceptions of caregivers' behavior tend to be more powerful predictors of independent assessments of social and emotional outcomes than reports from other informants (Feldman et al., 1989). In light of these findings, students' subjective interpretations of teachers' behavior were the focus of interest in this study.

Teachers as Providers of Care and Support

Teachers are rarely mentioned by adolescents as having a significant or important influence in their lives (Galbo, 1984; Reid, Landesman, Treder, & Jaccard, 1989). Adolescents often rate teachers as providing aid and advice (Lempers & Clark-Lempers, 1992; Reid et al., 1989) but only as secondary sources relative to parents and peers (Furman & Buhrmester, 1992). In contrast, studies of social support provide evidence that perceptions of supportive teachers are related to student outcomes in important ways. Specifically, perceived support from teachers is a significant predictor of young adolescents' motivation and academic achievement (Felner, Aber, Primavera, & Cauce, 1985; Goodenow, 1993; Wentzel & Asher, 1995). Wentzel (1996) suggests that when perceived support from parents, peers, and teachers is considered jointly, perceived support from teachers has the most direct link to students' interest in school.

Although suggestive, these studies of perceived support from teachers are limited in their ability to shed light on relations between students' perceptions of caring teachers and classroom motivation. For instance, perceptions that teachers are supportive and caring might simply be a proxy for psychological well-being. Indeed, research on adults and older adolescents suggests that perceived social support is related to positive aspects of adjustment because it serves to alleviate or at least lessen the negative effects of stress (Cohen & Wills, 1985). It is possible, therefore, that students who perceive teachers to be supportive are motivated to do well simply because they experience less distress and negative affect when presented with academic and social challenges at school.

Other psychological variables also might explain links between perceived support from teachers and students' effort and engagement in the classroom. For example, as conceptualized by Connell and his colleagues (Connell, 1985; Skinner & Connell, 1986), perceived control is a belief about why events occur, with unknown reasons, internal, personal attributes, and powerful others being the primary sources of control. Of particular relevance for the present research is that internal control beliefs have been related positively to perceived social support (Lakey & Cassady, 1990). Research on college students also indicates that beliefs about control are related to how well students learn, regardless of the quality of instruction (Perry & Tuna, 1988). It is reasonable to expect, therefore, that students' beliefs that teachers are caring and supportive reflect, in part, their beliefs about personal control at school.

Finally, it is not clear whether students' perceptions of their teachers will be related to their classroom motivation when past levels of motivation and performance are taken into account. Is classroom motivation a fairly stable, internal student characteristic by the time young adolescents finish middle school, or can motivation change in response to feelings of being supported and cared for by teachers? The present study addressed this issue by using a longitudinal design, whereby relations between perceived caring from teachers and motivation in eighth grade were studied while controlling for previous levels of motivation and actual performance in sixth grade. To account for the possibility that perceptions of caring teachers are a proxy for other student characteristics, I also assessed students' psychological distress and control beliefs. Perceptions of caring teachers also might reflect actual classroom practices. Therefore, perceived caring in eighth grade was examined as a function of classroom teacher while controlling for previous perceptions of caring teachers.

Characteristics of Pedagogical Caring

A final issue that was addressed by the present study concerns what it means to be a teacher who "cares": What is it that students believe teachers do to communicate an ethic of care in their classrooms? Noddings (1992) suggested that caring teachers (a) model caring behavior to their students, (b) engage students in dialogues that lead to mutual understanding and perspective taking, and (c) expect as well as encourage students to do the best they can given their abilities. In the family socialization literature, models of effective caregivers also underscore the importance of modeling (Bandura, 1986), as well as democratic communication styles and expectations to live up to one's unique potential (Baumrind, 1971). In addition, socialization models stress consistent rule setting and structure, and expressions of warmth and approval as components of effective parenting (Baumrind, 1971, 1991; Grusec & Goodnow, 1994).

From the perspective of students, however, little is known about what constitutes effective caregiving in the classroom. When students complain, "Teachers don't care about me," are they voicing a need for a personal friend or, as the parenting literature might suggest, a need for more structure and guidance or perhaps more warmth and approval? To gain insight into this dimension of pedagogical caring in middle school, I asked students to generate characteristics of caring as well as uncaring teachers. Student responses were analyzed with respect to the five dimensions of effective caregiving as suggested by Noddings (1992) and the family socialization literature: modeling, democratic communication styles, expectations for behavior, rule setting, and nurturance.

Method

Participants

Eighth-grade students ($N = 375$) from a sixth- through eighth-grade suburban middle school in a mid-Atlantic state participated in the study. A subset ($n = 248$) of these students were followed for 3 years, with initial data collection occurring at the end of their sixth-grade year. The longitudinal sample was composed of 125 boys and 123 girls; 92% were White, 2% Black, 2% Hispanic, 3% Asian American, and 1% other ethnic status. All students participated unless they were absent on the day the questionnaires were administered or parent permission was denied.

Procedure

All measures were administered by Kathryn Wentzel during regular class sessions. In sixth grade, students attending classes of all academic subjects were surveyed

(17 classroom teachers); in eighth grade, students were surveyed during English class (3 classroom teachers). Students were told that all of their answers would be confidential and that they did not have to answer any of the questions if they did not want to. At both Time 1 (sixth grade) and Time 2 (eighth grade), teachers remained in their classrooms while students filled out the questionnaires. Data were collected from students in late spring. Achievement data were obtained from student files at the end of the sixth-grade academic year.

Measures

Background information. Students were asked to fill out a general information sheet at the beginning of the session, indicating their sex and ethnicity (White, African American, Hispanic, Asian, and other). Because the sample was predominantly White, race was not included as a variable in analyses.

Perceived caring from teachers. The present study used a measure of social support that focused specifically on the notion of caring (cf. Cauce, Felner, & Primavera, 1982). Perceived caring from teachers was measured in sixth and eighth grade by the Teacher Social and Academic Support subscales of the Classroom Life Measure (Johnson, Johnson, Buckman, & Richards, 1985). A sample item of the 4-item Teacher Social Support subscale is "My teacher really cares about me" (1 = *never*, 5 = *always*). The 4-item Teacher Academic Support subscale asks about perceived support for learning, such as "My teacher cares about how much I learn." Students were instructed to respond to the items with respect to their teachers in general, rather than with specific teachers in mind.

Social and academic caring scores were related significantly and positively (*r*s = .67 and .73, *p* < .001, in sixth and eighth grade, respectively) and therefore averaged to form composite scores. Cronbach alphas were .89 and .91, and means and standard deviations were 4.25 and .75 and 3.70 and .91, for perceived caring in sixth and eighth grade, respectively.

Psychological distress. Distress was measured with the Weinberger Adjustment Inventory—Short Form (Weinberger, Feldman, Ford, & Chastain, 1987). This scale contains 12 items that tap anxiety (e.g., "I worry too much about things that aren't important"), depression (e.g., "I often feel sad or unhappy"), low self-esteem (e.g., "I'm not sure of myself"), and low well-being (e.g., "I'm the kind of person who has a lot of fun"; reverse scored). Responses are made on 5-point scales, 1 = *false* and 5 = *true*, and then averaged to yield a distress score. Weinberger et al. reported that the items have an internal consistency of .87 and a 1-week test-retest reliability of .83. The mean and standard deviation for the present sample were 3.34 and 1.07, respectively.

Control beliefs. Self-reports were obtained using the cognitive subscales of Connell's (1985) Multidimensional Measure of Children's Perceptions of Control. The subscales assess three aspects of perceived control: (a) Unknown (e.g., "When I get a good grade in school I usually don't know why I did so well," 4 items); (b) Powerful Others (e.g., "When I do well in school, it's because the teacher likes me," 4 items); and (c) Internal (e.g., "If I want to do well in school, it's up to me to do it," 4 items). Responses are made on 4-point scales (1 = *not at all true* and 4 = *always true*).

Internal consistency (Cronbach's alpha) in the present sample was .67, .71, and .74 for the Unknown, Powerful Others, and Internal subscales, respectively. For Unknown control, $M = 1.85$ and $SD = .59$; for Powerful Others control, $M = 1.88$ and $SD = .59$; for Internal control, $M = 3.32$ and $SD = .65$.

Pursuit of social goals. Pursuit of social goals was assessed when students were in sixth as well as eighth grade. Prosocial goal pursuit was measured with a 3-item prosocial goal scale (Wentzel, 1994) that asks about efforts to share and help peers with academic problems. A sample item is "How often do you try to share what you've learned with your classmates?" At Time 1 (6th grade), M = 3.55 and SD = .75, Cronbach's α = .73; at Time 2 (8th grade), M = 3.16 and SD = .87, Cronbach's α = .78.

Social responsibility goal pursuit was assessed with a 3-item scale that asks how often students try to follow classroom rules. A sample item is "How often do you try to do what your teacher asks you to do?" At Time 1, M = 3.87 and SD = .81, Cronbach's α = .79; at Time 2, M = 3.64 and SD = .87, Cronbach's α = .81.

Academic effort. Academic effort also was assessed when students were in sixth and eighth grade. For each academic subject (English, mathematics, social studies, science), students were asked "How often do you really try in each of these classes?" and "How often do you really pay attention during each of these classes?" Responses were made on 5-point scales (0 = *never* to 4 = *always*). For each question, responses were averaged across the four subject areas. The correlations between the "try" and "pay attention" scores were .46 and .69, p < .001, for sixth and eighth grade, respectively. Consequently, composite academic effort scores were computed by averaging the two scores (M = 3.20; SD = .56 for 6th grade, and M = 3.02; SD = .65 for 8th grade).

Irresponsible and prosocial behavior. In sixth grade, irresponsible behavior was assessed using a peer nomination procedure (see Wentzel, 1991). Students were asked to indicate from lists of classmates who "breaks the rules, does things you're not supposed to." Because middle-school students do not stay with one group or in one classroom all day, and therefore come into contact with a large number of peers, it was necessary to create a list of names that did not require students to rate all of the children with whom they share classes. Sixth-grade students were organized into six instructional teams and attended classes consisting only of team members. Therefore, students were given lists of 25 names of same-sex classmates randomly selected from their team. Students were instructed to cross out the names of classmates they did not know. The random selection procedure resulted in each student rating a unique set of names and in each student receiving an average of 25 ratings. As such, randomly assigned and distinct sets of informants assessed classroom behavior. Students were asked to circle the names of the classmates on each list who fit the behavioral description: students could circle as many or as few names as they wanted.

For each student, an irresponsible behavior nomination score was calculated: The percentage of nominations each child received was computed by dividing the number of nominations each child received by the total number of times the child's name appeared on the nomination list and was not crossed out as someone unknown to the nominator. Then, to correct for nonnormal distributions, arc sin transformations were computed. Finally, scores were standardized within team.

To assess prosocial behavior, I asked students to nominate students in their class on the following characteristics: "Who cooperates and shares?" and "Who helps other kids when they have a problem?" Scores were computed in the same way as irresponsible behavior scores. The two prosocial behavior scores were significantly related (r = .47, p< .001) and therefore averaged to form a composite score.

Academic achievement. End-of-year cumulative grade point average (GPA), based on averaged English, science, social studies, and mathematics final grades, was used as the index of achievement. Grades were obtained from student files at the end of their sixth-grade academic year and coded such that a failing grade equals 0 and an "A" = 4.00 (M = 2.50; SD = .89).

Characteristics of caring teachers. On a sheet of paper titled, "Who Cares?", students were asked "How do you know when a teacher cares about you? List three things that teachers do to show that they care about you." Underneath, students were asked "How do you know when a teacher does not care about you? List three things that teachers do to show that they don't care about you."

Results

Does Perceived Caring From Teachers Predict Students' Pursuit of Social Goals and Academic Effort?

Correlations. Zero-order correlations are shown in Table 1. Perceived caring from teachers was related significantly and positively to students' pursuit of prosocial and social responsibility goals and to students' academic effort. Perceived caring also was related significantly and positively to internal control beliefs and negatively to powerful other and unknown control beliefs, and to students' reports of distress. Finally, sixth-grade prosocial goal pursuit and prosocial behavior were related significantly to eighth-grade prosocial goal pursuit; sixth-grade social responsibility goal pursuit and irresponsible behavior were related significantly to eighth-grade social responsibility goal pursuit; and sixth-grade academic effort and GPA were related significantly to eighth-grade academic effort.

Gender differences. Mean differences as a function of gender also were examined with a series of one-way analyses of variance (ANOVAs). Significant differences were found for perceived caring from teachers, $F(1,374) = 4.13$, $p< .05$; distress, $F(1,374) = 3.72$, $p< .05$; pursuit of prosocial goals, $F(1,374) = 10.95$, $p< .001$; pursuit of social responsibility goals, $F(1,374) = 4.14$, $p< .05$; and GPA, $F(1,374) = 44.62$, with girls having significantly higher scores than boys. Boys were significantly more likely to report higher levels of control by powerful others than were girls, $F(1,374) = 4.97$, $p < .05$. Significant gender differences in unknown and internal control beliefs, and academic effort were not found: Given these findings, subsequent analyses controlled for the potentially confounding influence of gender.

Regression analyses. A series of hierarchical regression analyses were conducted to examine relations between perceptions of teacher caring and motivation outcomes, when controlling for student characteristics, previous motivation, and previous academic and behavioral competence. For each model, Time 1 variables were entered first, students' gender, distress, and control beliefs were entered second, and the perceived caring variable was entered last.

As shown in Table 2, perceived caring accounted for a significant increment to R^2 in each model when added at the last step—$\Delta R^2 = .07$, $F(1, 166) = 8.82$, $p < .001$ for prosocial goal pursuit; $\Delta R^2 = .09$, $F(1, 166) = 15.19$, $p < .001$ for responsibility goal pursuit; and $\Delta R^2 = .07$, $F(1, 166) = 14.79$, $p < .01$ for academic effort). In other words, change in students' motivation from sixth to eighth grade could be explained in part by students' perceptions of their eighth-grade teachers, even after past behavior, students' gender, psychological distress, and control beliefs were taken into account.

Standardized beta weights for each variable at the last step of each model also are shown in Table 2. Perceptions of caring from teachers were a significant, independent predictor of each motivation outcome when all other variables were taken into account.

Classroom Effects

The focus of this research was on students' perceptions of teacher caring. It is possible, however, that classroom teacher effects might explain students' perceptions. To

TABLE 1

Intercorrelations Among Variables

Variable	1	2	3	4	5	6	7	8	9	10	11	12	13
1. T2 Prosocial goal pursuit	—												
2. T2 Responsibility goal pursuit	.50***	—											
3. T2 Academic effort	.46***	.67***	—										
4. T2 Perceived teacher caring	.39***	.45***	.36***	—									
5. T2 Distress	.04	-.10*	-.13**	-.23***	—								
6. T2 Internal control	.21***	.25***	.26***	.27***	.01	—							
7. T2 Powerful others control	-.13**	-.35***	-.32***	-.25***	.22***	-.18***	—						
8. T2 Unknown control	-.10*	-.34***	-.25***	-.22***	.26***	-.04	.46***	—					
9. T1 Prosocial behavior	.18***	.07	.09	.14**	.01	.02	-.08	-.08	—				
10. T1 Prosocial goal pursuit	.32***	.19***	.16**	.20**	-.04	-.07	-.05	-.13*	.16***	—			
11. T1 Irresponsible behavior	-.08	-.10*	-.03	-.12*	-.13*	.01	.05	.08	-.23***	-.12**	—		
12. T1 Prosocial goal pursuit	.18***	.30***	.34***	.20**	.02*	-.11*	-.12*	-.20***	.18***	.34***	-.38***	—	
13. T1 Academic effort	.17***	.21***	.33***	.13**	-.07	-.11*	-.22***	-.19***	.19***	.35***	-.31***	.59***	—
14. T1 Grade point average	.17***	.15***	.18***	.18***	-.04	.04	-.16**	-.22***	.44***	.13**	-.48***	.23***	.36***

Note. T1 = Time 1 (sixth grade); T2 = Time 2 (eighth grade).

*$p < .05$. **$p < .01$. ***$p < .001$.

TABLE 2

Predictors of Social Goal Pursuit and Academic Effort: Multiple Regressions

Predictor	Prosocial Goal Pursuit		Responsibility Goal Pursuit		Academic Effort	
	β	ΔR²	β	ΔR²	β	ΔR²
Step 1		.13***		.07***		.14***
T1 Motivation	.26***		.19**		.19**	
T1 Behavior	.02		.13*		.09	
Step 2		.09***		.26***		.19***
Sex	.14*		.09		−.01	
Internal control	.09		.16*		.17**	
Powerful others control	−.06		−.14*		−.20**	
Unknown control	−.02		−.23***		−.05	
Distress	.04		.10		.04	
Step 3		.07***		.09***		.07***
Teacher caring	.31***		.34***		.31***	
Total		.29***		.42***		.40***

Note. Standardized beta weights at the last step are shown. Time 1 (T1; sixth grade) motivation variables were prosocial goal pursuit, social responsibility goal pursuit, and academic effort. Time 1 behavior variables were prosocial behavior, irresponsible behavior, and grade point average.

*p < .05. **p < .01. ***p < .001.

examine this possibility, I analyzed eighth graders' perceptions of teacher caring as a function of classroom teacher while controlling for perceptions of teacher caring in sixth grade. Results of an analysis of covariance (ANCOVA) indicated that teacher effects were nonsignificant, $F(2, 110) = 1.94$. Therefore, changes in perceived teacher caring from sixth to eighth grade could not be attributed to attending classes with one of the three eighth-grade English teachers.

What Makes a Teacher an Effective Caregiver?

The larger group of 375 eighth graders provided information concerning characteristics of caring teachers. Responses to the "Who Cares?" questionnaire were coded initially into six categories: modeling, democratic interactions, expectations for behavior, nurturance, rule setting, and other. On the basis of the frequency and content of responses, within-category distinctions were made. For caring and uncaring characteristics, expectations for behavior was subdivided into expectations for the student as a person and as a learner, and democratic interactions was subdivided into communication style and equitable treatment and respect. Full descriptions and examples of responses representing each category are shown in Table 3. Inter-rater agreement was 97% for caring categories and 95% for the uncaring categories; agreement was based on 8% of responses.

The percentage of responses for each category also are shown in Table 3. The largest percentage of responses characterizing caring and uncaring teachers pertained to expectations for behavior (43% for caring teachers and 28% for uncaring teachers) and democratic interactions (20% for caring teachers and 43% for uncaring

TABLE 3

Students' Responses: Teachers Who "Care" and "Do Not Care"

Description of Categories and Examples	% of Responses: Teachers Who Care	% of Responses: Teachers Who Do Not Care
Modeling		
Focus is on indications that the teacher cares about teaching.	23	7
Caring examples: makes a special effort, teaches in a special way, makes class interesting		
Not caring examples: doesn't care about your grades, teaches a boring class, gets off task, teaches while students aren't paying attention		
Democratic interactions		
Communication style: Focus is on the act of communication itself.		
Responses reflect that lines of communication are open and reciprocal rather than the content of communication.	16	31
Caring examples: talks to you, pays attention, asks questions, listens		
Not caring examples: screams, yells, ignores, interrupts		
Equitable treatment and respect: Focus is on honest and fair treatment, as well as keeping promises.	4	1
Caring examples: trusts me, tells you the truth		
Not caring examples: embarrasses, insults, picks		
Expectations based on individuality		
Student as a person: Focus is on a recognition of student's individuality, and concern with the student's nonacademic functioning.	13	4
Caring examples: asks what's wrong, talks to me about my problems, acts as a friend		
Not caring examples: forgets name, doesn't ask why I'm sad, does nothing when I do something wrong		
Student as a learner: Focus is on a recognition of the student as having unique academic skills, problems, and contributions to make to the class.	30	24
Caring examples: asks if I need help, takes time to make sure I understand, calls on me		
Not caring examples: doesn't explain things or answer questions, doesn't try to help you		
Nurturance		
Focus is on teacher's informal and formal evaluations of student work.	10	12
Caring examples: checks work, tells you when you do a good job, praises me		
Not caring examples: sends to office, gives bad grades, doesn't correct work		
Other: Vague answers ("nice to me, helps me"), all references to personal attributes, or responses that do not fit into the other categories.	5	11

Note. N = 375. Percentage for each of the caring and not caring response sets was based on a total of 1,125 responses (three characteristics for each category were obtained from each student).

teachers). Students did not mention rule setting and consistent enforcement of rules as characteristics of caring or uncaring teachers.

Discussion

This research was designed to answer two questions: (a) To what extent do adolescents' perceptions of caring from teachers predict efforts to achieve positive social and academic outcomes at school? and (b) How do middle-school students characterize a caring, supportive teacher? Results suggest that perceptions of caring teachers are related to students' academic efforts and to their pursuit of prosocial and social responsibility goals. These relations were robust when students' previous motivation and performance, and current control beliefs and distress were taken into account. When asked to describe teachers who care, students generated responses that correspond closely to dimensions of effective parenting. Teachers who care were described as demonstrating democratic interaction styles, developing expectations for student behavior in light of individual differences, modeling a "caring" attitude toward their own work, and providing constructive feedback.

Significant relations between perceived caring from teachers and students' efforts to achieve academic as well as social outcomes raise important issues concerning the role of social factors in explaining students' motivation to achieve. For the most part, current theories of motivation focus on variables that describe the psychological functioning of a student, such as goal orientations (e.g., Dweck & Leggett, 1988), beliefs about ability (e.g., Bandura, 1986), and beliefs about control (Weiner, 1992). In a related vein, student motivation also has been attributed to relatively objective aspects of teaching and instruction. For instance, researchers have documented significant relations between classroom reward structures (Ames & Ames, 1984), classroom organization (e.g., Rosenholtz & Wilson, 1980; Slavin, 1987), and the curriculum (e.g., Renninger, Hidi, & Krapp, 1992) on the one hand, and student motivation and academic work on the other.

The results of the present study, however, suggest that models of motivation based on psychological or instructional variables be extended to include students' perceptions of relationships with others, especially perceptions that teachers care about them. Although this work has begun (e.g., Birch & Ladd, 1996; Connell & Wellborn, 1991; Harter, 1996; Pianta, 1992), the processes that underlie significant relations between perceptions of caring teachers and students' motivation are not well understood. Until experimental interventions provide evidence of cause-effect relations, the present findings must be interpreted with caution. However, changes in students' motivation from sixth to eighth grade were explained, in part, by eighth graders' perceptions of their teachers. Therefore, the results of the present study provide strong evidence in support of the notion that students are more likely to engage in classroom activities if they feel supported and valued.

What makes students feel valued? Students' descriptions of teachers who care and do not care provide some insight. Recall that students described caring teachers as providers of very specific types of support: students' responses could be coded reliably along dimensions of modeling, expectations based on individual differences, democratic interactions, and nurturance.

Although speculative, the potentially positive impact of each of these teacher characteristics on student motivation could be explained in light of the literature on intrapersonal aspects of motivation. For instance, communicating expectations that students' behavior will reflect their best intentions and abilities should teach students to attribute their behavior to internal, controllable causes (a desirable attributional style; see Weiner, 1992). Providing opportunities for autonomous decision making and democratic interaction styles should foster the development of positive beliefs about personal autonomy and competence (see Ryan & Powelson, 1991). Finally, nurturance and approval should promote the development of positive feelings of self-worth (see Covington, 1992). These linkages between teacher behavior and student outcomes require systematic investigation. However, identification of noninstructional teacher characteristics that correspond to the development of students' motivational belief systems could provide valuable information for the improvement of classroom practice and the development of positive motivational orientations toward school.

The descriptive data also provide initial evidence that models of effective caregiving in the home can be generalized to the study of effective caregiving at school. In particular, they suggest that socialization processes known to result in the internalization of parental goals and values might also motivate students to pursue goals that are valued by adults at school (see also Eccles, 1993; McCaslin & Good, 1992). More focused investigations concerning the continuity of caregiving across home and school contexts is clearly needed in this regard. For instance, lack of common understanding among parents, teachers, and students concerning what it means to care might explain why some students become alienated and disengaged from the educational process.

The results of this study are intriguing in that much of the previous research linking the perceived availability of supportive adults to positive academic outcomes in middle school has been conducted with minority, inner-city, or low-achieving students (e.g., Cauce, Felner, & Primavera, 1982; Felner et al., 1985; Phelan, Davidson, & Cao, 1991). Therefore, this study adds to this work by suggesting that perceptions of supportive and caring relationships with teachers are important regardless of students' race or family background. However, Steinberg, Dornbusch, and Brown (1992) report that adolescents' perceptions of parenting dimensions similar to those highlighted in the present study predict positive school-related outcomes for White, middle-class children but not for Hispanic and African American adolescents. Therefore, the generalizability of the findings concerning characteristics of caring teachers to minority populations needs to be examined in future research.

Finally, might other processes explain these findings? One possibility is that students' perceptions of caring reflect general levels of social competence and the ability to form positive relationships with others. A recent study by Wentzel and Asher (1995), however, indicates that students without friends but who are well liked by teachers are highly motivated to achieve academically. Therefore, if positive interpersonal skills can explain the present findings, those skills that promote and sustain adult-child relationships rather than peer relationships are probably most relevant (see Montemayor et al., 1994).

Future research might profit by focusing on identifying additional student characteristics that predispose students to perceive teachers as caring or uncaring. The literature on peer relationships suggests that children who are socially rejected tend to believe that others are out to harm them when, in fact, they are not (Dodge & Feldman, 1990). Over time, these children develop relationships with their peers marked by mistrust and hostility. Similar research has not been conducted on student-teacher relationships. However, it is possible that students who believe that teachers do not like them or care about them might also be perceiving and interpreting these adult relationships in ways that are biased and unfounded. If true, then efforts to promote perceptions that teachers care are likely to be most successful if students are the primary target of intervention.

A limitation of this study is that students were not asked to respond with specific teachers in mind but rather about general perceptions that teachers care about them. Ethnographic research has documented the unique characteristics of caring classroom teachers and has highlighted the necessity of individualized attention to student needs in demonstrations of care (Noblit, 1993). Given this work, future studies also would benefit from assessments that focus on students' perceptions of specific teachers or on differences in student perceptions across multiple classrooms. The influence of teachers' beliefs about caring on their classroom practice and on subsequent student behavior also deserves careful attention.

In their review of the literature on teacher behavior and student achievement, Brophy and Good (1986) observed that "despite the importance of the topic, there has been remarkably little systematic research linking teacher behavior to student achievement" (p. 329). In their conclusions, they suggested that social and motivational outcomes need to be included in research on the role of teachers in students' lives. The results of the present study provide clear support for continued work in this area, especially with respect to ways in which students come to understand and appreciate what teachers do.

References

Ames, C., & Ames, R. (1984). Systems of student and teacher motivation: Toward a qualitative definition. *Journal of Educational Psychology, 76,* 478–487.

Bandura, A. (1986). *Social foundations of thought and action: A social cognitive theory.* Englewood Cliffs, NJ: Prentice Hall.

Baumeister, R. F., & Leary, M. R. (1995). The need to belong: Desire for interpersonal attachments as a fundamental human motivation. *Psychological Bulletin, 117,* 497–529.

Baumrind, D. (1971). Current patterns of parental authority. *Developmental Psychology Monograph, 4,* (1. Pt. 2).

Baumrind, D. (l991). Effective parenting during the early adolescent transition. In P. A. Cowan & M. Hetherington (Eds.), *Family transitions* (pp. 111–164). Hillsdale, NJ: Erlbaum.

Birch, S. H., & Ladd, G. W. (1996). Interpersonal relationships in the school environment and children's early school adjustment: The role of teachers and peers. In J. Juvonen & K. Wentzel (Eds.), *Social motivation: Understanding children's school adjustment.* New York: Cambridge University Press.

Brophy, J. E., & Good, T. L. (1986). Teacher behavior and student achievement. In M. Wittrock (Ed.). *Handbook of research on teaching* (pp. 328–375). New York: Macmillan.

Cauce, A. M., Felner, R. D., & Primavera, J. (1982). Social support in high-risk adolescents: Structural components and adaptive impact. *American Journal of Community Psychology, 10,* 417–428.

Cohen, S., & Wills, T. A. (1985). Stress, social support, and the buffering hypothesis. *Psychological Bulletin, 98,* 310–357.

Connell, J. P. (1985). A new multidimensional measure of children's perceptions of control. *Child Development, 56,* 1018–1041.

Connell. J. P., & Wellborn, J. G. (1991). Competence, autonomy, and relatedness: A motivational analysis of self-system processes. In M. R. Gunnar & L. A. Sroufe (Eds.), *Self processes and development: The Minnesota Symposia on Child Development* (Vol. 23, pp. 43–78). Hillsdale, NJ: Erlbaum.

Covington, M. V. (1992). *Making the grade: A self-worth perspective on motivation and school reform.* New York: Cambridge University Press.

Dodge, K. A., & Feldman, E. (1990). Issues in social cognition and sociometric status. In S. R. Asher & J. D. Coie (Eds.), *Peer rejection in childhood* (pp. 119–155). New York: Cambridge.

Dweck, C. S., & Leggett, E. L. (1988). A social-cognitive approach to motivation and personality. *Psychological Review, 95,* 256–272.

Eccles, J. (1993). School and family effects on the ontogeny of children's interests, self-perceptions, and activity choices. In J. Jacobs (Ed.), Nebraska Symposium on Motivation; Vol. 40. *Developmental perspectives on motivation* (pp. 145–208). Lincoln: University of Nebraska Press.

Feldman, S. S., Wentzel, K. R., & Gehring, T. M. (1989). A comparison of the views of mothers, fathers, and pre-adolescents about family cohesion and power. *Journal of Family Psychology, 3,* 39–60.

Felner, R. D., Aber, M. S., Primavera, J., & Cauce, A. M. (1985). Adaptation and vulnerability in high-risk adolescents: An examination of environmental mediators. *American Journal of Community Psychology, 13,* 365–379.

Furman, W., & Buhrmester, D. (1992). Age and sex differences in perceptions of networks of personal relationships. *Child Development, 63,* 103–115.

Galbo, J. J. (1984). Adolescents' perceptions of significant adults: A review of the literature. *Adolescence, 19,* 951–970.

Goodenow, C. (1993). Classroom belonging among early adolescent students: Relationships to motivation and achievement. *Journal of Early Adolescence, 13,* 21–43.

Grusee, J. E., & Goodnow, J. J. (1994). Impact of parental discipline methods on the child's internalization of values: A reconceptualization of current points of view. *Developmental Psychology, 30,* 4–19.

Harter, S. (1996). Teacher and classmate influences on scholastic motivation, self-esteem, and level of voice in adolescents. In J. Juvonen & K. Wentzel (Eds.). *Social motivation: Understanding Children's school adjustment* (pg. 11–12). New York: Cambridge.

Johnson, D. W., Johnson, R. T., Buckman, L. A., & Richards, P. S. (1985). The effect of prolonged implementation of cooperative learning on social support within the classroom. *The Journal of Psychology, 119,* 405–411.

Lakey, B., & Cassady, P. B. (1990). Cognitive processes in perceived social support. *Journal of Personality and Social Psychology, 59,* 337–343.

Lempers, J. D., & Clark-Lempers, D. S. (1992). Young, middle, and late adolescents' comparisons of the functional importance of five significant relationships. *Journal of Youth and Adolescence 21,* 53–96.

Maehr, M. L. (1984). Meaning and motivation: Toward a theory of personal investment. In R. E. Ames & C. Ames (Eds.). *Research on motivation in education* (pp. 115–144). New York: Academic Press.

McCaslin, M., & Good, T. L. (1992). Compliant cognition: The misalliance of management and instructional goals in current school reform, *Educational Researcher, 21,* 4–17.

Montemayor, R., Adams, G. R., & Gullotta, T. P. (1994). *Personal relationships in adolescence.* Thousand Oaks, CA:Sage.

Noblit, G. W. (1993). Power and caring. *American Educational Research Journal, 30,* 23–38.

Noddings, N. (1992). *The challenge to care in schools: An alternative approach to education.* New York: Teachers College Press.

Perry, R. P., & Tuna, K. (1988). Perceived control, Type A/B behavior, and quality of instruction. *Journal of Educational Psychology, 80,* 102–110.

Phelan, P., Davidson, A. L., & Cao. H. T. (1991). Students' multiple worlds: Negotiating the boundaries of family, peer, and school cultures. *Anthropology and Education Quarterly, 22,* 224–250.

Pianta, R. C. (1992). *Beyond the parent: The role of other adults in children's lives. New directions in child development: Vol. 57.* San Francisco: Jossey-Bass.

Reid, M., Landesman, S., Treder, R., & Jaccard, J. (1989). "My family and friends": Six- to twelve-year-old children's perceptions of social support, *Child Development, 60,* 896–910.

Renninger, K. A., Hidi, S., & Krapp, A. (1992). *The role of interest in learning and development.* Hillsdale, NJ: Erlbaum.

Rosenholtz, S. J., & Wilson, B. (1980). The effect of classroom structure on shared perceptions of ability. *American Educational Research Journal, 17,* 75–82.

Ryan, R. M., & Powelson, C. L. (1991). Autonomy and relatedness as fundamental to motivation and education. *Journal of Learning Disabilities, 19,* 500–503.

Skinner, E., & Connell, J. P. (1986). Control understanding: Suggestions for a developmental framework. In M. M. Baltes & P. B. Baltes (Eds.). *The psychology of control and aging.* Hillsdale, NJ: Erlbaum.

Slavin, R. E. (1987). Developmental and motivational perspectives on cooperative learning: A reconciliation. *Child Development, 58,* 1161–1167.

Steinberg, L., Dornbusch, S. M., & Brown, B. B. (1992). Ethnic differences in adolescent achievement: An ecological perspective. *American Psychologist, 47,* 723–729.

Weinberger, D. A., Feldman, S. S., Ford, M. E., & Chastain, R. L. (1987). *Construct validation of the Weinberger Adjustment Inventory.* Unpublished manuscript, Stanford University.

Weiner, B. (1992). *Human motivation: Metaphors, theories, and research.* Newbury Park, CA: Sage.

Wentzel, K. R. (1991). Relations between social competence and academic achievement in early adolescence. *Child Development, 62,* 1066–1078.

Wentzel, K. R. (1993). Social and academic goals at school: Motivation and achievement in early adolescence. *Journal of Early Adolescence, 13,* 4–20.

Wentzel, K. R. (1994). Relations of social goal pursuit to social acceptance, classroom behavior, and perceived social support. *Journal of Educational Psychology, 86,* 173–182.

Wentzel, K. R. (1996, March). *Social support and adjustment in middle school: The role of parents, teachers, and peers.* Paper presented at the biennial meeting of the Society for Research on Adolescence, Boston.

Wentzel, K. R., & Asher, S. R. (1995). Academic lives of neglected, rejected, popular, and controversial children. *Child Development, 66,* 754–763.

Wentzel, K. R., Weinberger, D. A., Ford, M. E., & Feldman, S. S. (1990). Academic achievement in preadolescence: The role of motivational, affective, and self-regulatory processes. *Journal of Applied Developmental Psychology, 11,* 179–193.

Wigfield, A., & Eccles, J. S. (1992). The development of achievement task values: A theoretical analysis. *Developmental Review, 12,* 265–310.

Received June 5, 1996
Revision received October 30, 1996
Accepted October 30, 1996

Correspondence concerning this article should be addressed to Kathryn R. Wentzel, Department of Human Development, Benjamin Building, University of Maryland, College Park, Maryland 20742. Electronic mail may be sent via Internet to kw52@umail.umd.edu.

A8

Science for Ladies, Classics for Gentlemen: A Comparative Analysis of Scientific Subjects in the Curricula of Boys' and Girls' Secondary Schools in the United States, 1794–1850

Kim Tolley

In 1864, the British government established the Taunton Commission to conduct an inquiry into the education of middle-class boys. Concerned about the status of the arts and sciences in the schools, the Commission directed its appointed inspectors to pay particular attention to scientific subjects. Almost as an afterthought, the Commission decided to investigate the conditions in girls' schools as well. From 1864 to 1868, inspectors traveled throughout Great Britain, observing classes, interviewing headmasters and headmistresses, and examining students in private, proprietary, and endowed schools. To their surprise, members of the Taunton Commission discovered that while the sciences maintained at best a marginal toehold in boys' schools, they were quite popular in girls' schools. While a boy's education centered around Latin and Greek, a girl's education included ample doses of botany, chemistry, natural philosophy, natural history, and physiology.[1]

Did comparable conditions exist in the United States? Based on data compiled from newspaper advertisements, published accounts of school examinations, and state superintendents' reports, this study demonstrates that similar conditions indeed existed in America during the first half of the nineteenth century. The data support the thesis that by 1840, the subjects of natural philosophy, chemistry, and astronomy had become more prevalent in American schools for middle- and upper-class girls than in comparable institutions for boys.[2]

The inclusion of scientific subjects in the courses of study of American female seminaries and academies in the early nineteenth century has been noted by historians of women's education. When Thomas Woody published his classic history of women's education in 1929, he included an appendix listing the subjects offered in 162 female seminaries between 1742 and 1871. Natural philosophy, astronomy, chemistry, and botany were among the ten subjects most frequently listed by the seminaries in Woody's sample. More recent studies have described in some detail the many opportunities afforded girls to study scientific subjects in their academies and seminaries. Until

---

[1] *Schools Inquiry Commission: General Reports of the Assistant Commissioners, Southern Counties*, VII (1867–68), [3966-VI] XXVIII, mf. 74.275–81, 71, 206–7; Patricia Phillips, *The Scientific Lady: A Social History of Women's Scientific Interests, 1520–1918* (London, 1990), 236. According to Phillips, the commission defined members of the middle classes as those occupying houses assessed at an annual value of twenty pounds or more. There were estimated to be between 974,000 children between the ages of five and twenty in this social class in approximately ten thousand educational institutions, most of which catered to boys.

[2] The term *middle class* is used loosely here to denote those members of society able to afford the tuition rates of private secondary schools during the early nineteenth century.

---

now, however, there has been insufficient data upon which to base a comparison of the relative emphasis placed on the sciences in boys' and girls' schools.[3]

It has been a long-standing paradigm in histories of science education to date the rapid infusion of the sciences into the secondary school curriculum from the publication dates of such writers as Thomas Huxley and Herbert Spencer in the 1850s and 1860s.[4] This study suggests that this paradigm has misled us in fundamental ways. While the writings of such men as Huxley and Spencer were undoubtedly pivotal in efforts to increase the science curriculum, first at the college, and then at the secondary level, this increase represented a marked change for only half of the American student population. While the decades after the 1860s saw an increase in the sciences in male colleges, boys' academies, and coeducational secondary schools, the data revealed here indicate that the sciences had already long formed a visible part of the schooling of American girls.

* * * * *

During the last decades of the eighteenth century, American reformers developed several rationales for the education of females, often basing their arguments on women's social roles as mothers, wives, and teachers. The education of women was crucial to the welfare of the state because the primary duties of motherhood included "the education for time and eternity of the next generation of immortal beings." As a wife, a woman "must be able to comprehend [her husband's] plans; she must sympathize in his feelings, or else she cannot be his helpmate." The demand for teachers created a need that could be admirably filled by educated females, because "Women [were] the very best teachers in the primary education of children," being "less expensive teachers than men."[5]

What was to be the proper course of study for girls? Because the mind of a woman, like that of a man, needed discipline, some educators argued that girls should be instructed in the "solid" branches of science rather than in the merely "ornamental" branches of drawing, painting, and needlework. Although classical studies had traditionally played the role of training the mind, many educators argued that science could serve the same function by training students to observe critically and think logically.[6]

Advocates of science touted its social and physical benefits. According to the well-known female educator Almira Hart Lincoln Phelps, scientific study would result "in enlarging [women's] sphere of thought, rendering them more interesting as companions to men of science, and better capable of instructing the young." Concerned

[3]See Thomas Woody, *A History of Women's Education in the United States* (New York, 1980; 1929), 1: 563–65. Although Woody did not specify the institutions represented in his collection of school catalogs, a perusal of his bibliography reveals catalogs from twenty states. See Deborah Jean Warner, "Science Education for Women in Antebellum America," *Isis 69* (Mar. 1978): 58–67; Christie Farnham, *The Education of the Southern Belle; Higher Education and Student Socialization in the Antebellum South* (New York, 1994). Farnham argues that the science courses offered in southern women's colleges compared favorably with those offered in men's colleges. Her conclusion must be interpreted with caution, however, since it appears to be based on a small sample of primary sources and does not include an analytical comparison of the actual textbooks used in these institutions.

[4]This view is promoted most recently by George E. DeBoer in *A History of Ideas in Science Education; Implications for Practice* (New York, 1991).

[5]The first quotation is from John Pierce Brace, nephew and successor to Sarah Pierce as head of Litchfield Female Seminary, and appears in Harriet Webster Marr, *The Old New England Academies founded before 1826* (New York, 1959), 105–6. The second quotation is from C. G. Memminger, "Address at the Opening of the Female High and Normal School in Charleston, South Carolina, 1859," in *A Documentary History of Education in the South before 1860*, ed. Edgar W. Knight (Chapel Hill, N.C., 1950), 5: 273. The last quotation is a statement by Joseph Emerson quoted in Marr *Old New England Academies*, 106.

[6]James Mulhern, *A History of Secondary Education in Pennsylvania* (Philadelphia, 1933), 394; Lorraine Smith Pangle and Thomas L. Pangle, *The Learning of Liberty: The Educational Ideas of the American Founders* (Lawrence, Ks., 1993), 102–3; Elizabeth Keeney, *The Botanizers: Amateur Scientists in Nineteenth-Century America* (Chapel Hill, N.C., 1992), 58ff. According to Keeney, Amos Eaton and Almira Hart Lincoln Phelps, sister of Emma Willard, were highly influential in promoting this view of the sciences among educators. For an example of similar views in a southern state, see "A Syllabus of a Course of Vacation Reading is Provided for the Students at South Carolina Female Collegiate Institute, 1836," in *A Documentary History of Education in the South*, ed. Knight, 5:412–13.

about the physical strength of young American girls, educators and doctors alike recommended botany, a subject many contemporaries viewed as particularly suited to females because "its pursuits leading to exercise in the open are conducive to health and cheerfulness."[7]

The rhetoric of natural theology, which portrayed the study of the natural world as spiritually and morally uplifting, made highly desirable the inclusion of the sciences into the curriculum. Natural theology, which gained popularity at the beginning of the eighteenth century in Great Britain, was founded on the premise that God could be known by consulting either Scripture or nature itself, both of which led to the same truths. Central to natural theology was the argument of design, in which the mechanism, instrumentality, or design in nature attested to the existence of an intelligent and benevolent Creator. "The analysis of science and revealed religion," proclaimed John Ludlow in his 1834 address at the opening of Albany Female Academy, "will ultimately terminate in the same point. . . . the invisible God." As did many members of the British and American scientific communities during this period, textbook authors frequently invoked natural theology as they extolled the benefits of studying the sciences. In a statement fairly representative of the period, the popular textbook author J. L. Comstock assured his readers that chemistry was a suitable vehicle for moral instruction, because "this subject teaches, that nothing has been formed by the fortuitous concurrence of atoms, but that even the 'stocks and stones' bear the impress of creative agency and design."[8]

While such influential Americans as Thomas Jefferson felt that the subjects of study most useful for American boys included both the classics and the sciences, relatively few reformers claimed that girls should study the classics. Traditionally, a classical education had been the prerogative of middle-class males, and it remained so until several decades into the nineteenth century.[9] Many educators looked to find rigor in a program for girls, not to the classics at first, but to the sciences.

During the eighteenth century, local grammar schools provided advanced education for boys, usually offering instruction in Latin and Greek. As the century progressed, the growth of scattered villages, the division of towns into school districts, and the growth of district schools accompanied a gradual decline in the number of grammar schools. To fill the void, advanced instruction was provided by increasing numbers of private schools and incorporated academies.[10]

Although science had been rarely included in the curricula of the colonial grammar or Latin grammar schools, a number of early academy charters included natural philosophy among the subjects to be offered, reflecting the newer views on education. The standard studies in boys' academies generally included the traditional

[7]Almira Hart Lincoln Phelps, *Lectures to Young Ladies* (Boston, 1833), 218. Almira Hart Lincoln Phelps quoted in Keeney, *The Botanizers*, 73–74.

[8]Peter J. Bowler, *Evolution: The History of an Idea* (Berkeley, 1989; 1984), 53; Thomas L. Hankins, *Science and the Enlightenment* (Cambridge Eng., 1985), 115; John Ludlow, *Address Delivered at the Opening of the New Female Academy in Albany, May 12, 1834* (Albany, N.Y., 1834), 7; J. L. Comstock, *Elements of Chemistry . . .* (New York, 1839), preface.

[9]See "Jefferson to J. Bannister Jr., October 15, 1785," in *A Documentary History of Education in the South*, ed. Knight, 2: 4–5. While Jefferson did not advocate a classical education for girls, such prominent educators as Catharine Beecher and Mary Lyon thought that girls should study the classics. For a general overview of women's education in the early nineteenth century, see Joan N. Burstyn and Thalia M. Mulvihill, "The History of Women's Education: North America," in *The International Encyclopedia of Education*, ed. Torsten Husén and T. Neville Postlethwaite (Oxford, Eng., 1994), 2: 6761–65. Woody, *A History of Women's Education*, 1: 413, 563–65. Woody noted that Latin was offered in the more prestigious female seminaries after 1810. His sample of 162 school catalogs reveals that more than 50 percent of the schools listed Latin between 1810 and 1870, and approximately 25 percent listed Greek grammar. However, Woody's sample should be interpreted with caution, since only the larger and wealthier schools would have published catalogs during this period.

[10]Theodore R. Sizer, ed., *The Age of the Academies* (New York, 1964); Ellwood Patterson Cubberley, *Public Education in the United States: A Study and Interpretation of American Educational History* (Boston, 1934), 29–31; Clifton Johnson, *Old-Time Schools and School-books* (New York, 1917), 147.

subjects of English, Latin, Greek, declamation, writing, and arithmetic, and some portion of the newer subjects of French, geography, logic, geometry, and natural philosophy or astronomy. A similar curriculum appeared in a variety of private institutions serving boys, known by such names as "Mr. Lyon's School for Boys," "John G. Nelson's School," or "Norristown Boarding School."[11]

From an early date, some boys' schools opened their doors to girls, educating females in a separate department. For example, Robert Leeth's school placed an advertisement in the *New York Gazette-Weekly Post Boy* in 1751, offering instruction to both sexes in "two handsome Rooms, with Fire-places, the one for Boys and the other for Girls." Near the end of the eighteenth century, a few teachers opened schools exclusively for girls, supporting their efforts financially with funds raised by selling shares. For instance, Sarah Pierce opened her school for girls in the dining room of her home in Litchfield, Connecticut, in 1791. Two pupils from her school, Catharine and Mary Beecher, opened the Hartford Female Seminary in 1823. Their school was incorporated in 1827, the same year as the parent school at Litchfield.[12]

Troy Female Seminary, which opened in 1821 under the leadership of Emma Willard, became an important center for the diffusion of new educational ideas in the early nineteenth century. The curriculum at Troy included mathematics, science, modern languages, history, philosophy, geography, and literature. Gifted speakers and prolific writers—such as Catharine Beecher; Emma Willard and her sister Elmira Hart Phelps; Zilpah Grant, head of Ipswich Female Seminary; and Mary Lyon, head of Mount Holyoke Seminary—were highly influential in disseminating the new views of female education. Many of their graduates became teachers in distant states, bringing these ideas to different parts of the country.[13]

Newspaper advertisements published in both northern and southern states during the 1820s reveal a growing number of schools claiming to provide a relatively advanced form of education for girls. Such institutions described themselves variously as female academies or seminaries, day schools, boarding schools, or ladies' select schools. Some enrolled students from the ages of eight to sixteen or eighteen; others admitted pupils at age twelve; still others, perhaps needing the extra tuition to stay afloat, admitted any prospective students that applied, even those younger than eight.[14] Because of the diverse nature of the schools serving females, for the purposes of this study, precollege institutions providing instruction Beyond learning to read and write are referred to simply as "secondary schools."

Newly founded girls' secondary schools advertised their courses of study in local newspapers in order to attract students. During the period from 1800 to 1845, such advertisements often provided a complete list of the subjects offered in a given school, sometimes accompanied with the titles of the textbooks used in various courses. Catharine and Mary Beecher's 1824 advertisement is representative in its degree of detail (see Plate 1). Although advertisements are unreliable as a means of evaluating either the content or method of the actual instruction delivered in educational institutions, as marketing tools, these sources illuminate the degree to which educational institutions differentiated their curricula according to the gender of their desired clientele.

[11]Sizer, *The Age of the Academies;* Johnson, *Old-Time Schools and School-books,* 147; Marr, *Old New England Academies,* 203; *Columbian Centinel,* 26 Dec. 1827; *Richmond Enquirer,* 24 Nov. 1835, 5 Aug. 1836.

[12]*New York Gazette-Weekly Post Boy* quoted in Thomas Woody, *A History of Women's Education in the United States,* 1: 225; Marr, *Old New England Academies,* 3.

[13]For a discussion on the influence of these female educators, see Anne Firor Scott, The Ever Widening Circle: The Diffusion of Feminist Values from the Troy Female Seminary, 1822–1872" in *History of Education Quarterly* 19 (Spring 1979): 3–25; Warner, Science Education for Women in Antebellum America," 58–67.

[14]Marr, *Old New England Academies.*

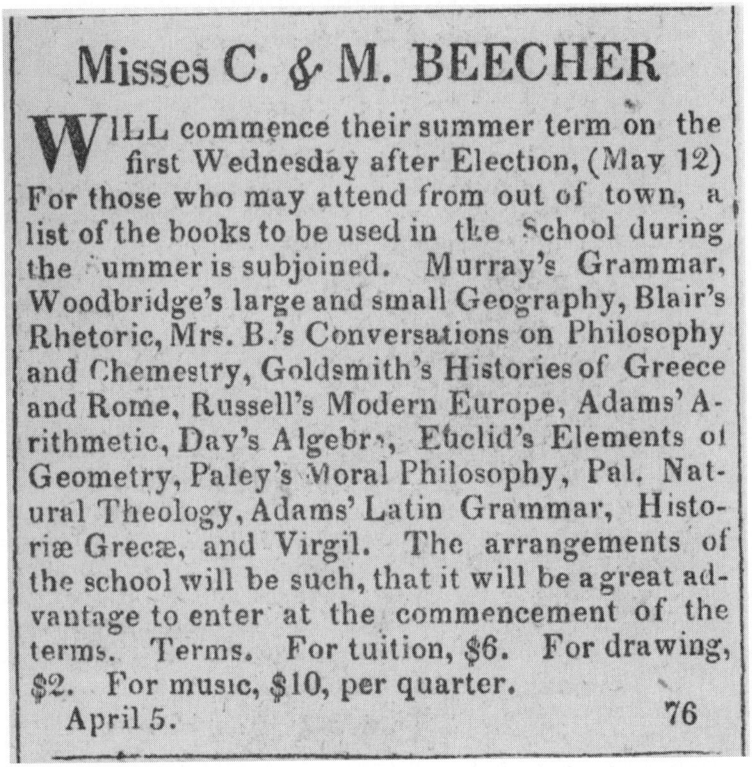

Misses C. & M. BEECHER

WILL commence their summer term on the first Wednesday after Election, (May 12) For those who may attend from out of town, a list of the books to be used in the School during the Summer is subjoined. Murray's Grammar, Woodbridge's large and small Geography, Blair's Rhetoric, Mrs. B.'s Conversations on Philosophy and Chemestry, Goldsmith's Histories of Greece and Rome, Russell's Modern Europe, Adams' Arithmetic, Day's Algebra, Euclid's Elements of Geometry, Paley's Moral Philosophy, Pal. Natural Theology, Adams' Latin Grammar, Historiæ Grecæ, and Virgil. The arrangements of the school will be such, that it will be a great advantage to enter at the commencement of the terms. Terms. For tuition, $6. For drawing, $2. For music, $10, per quarter.

April 5. 76

PLATE 1. An 1824 newspaper advertisement for Catharine and Mary Beecher's school in Connecticut. Courtesy of the Department of Special Collections, Stanford University Libraries.

During the first half of the nineteenth century, the curricula of girls' schools expanded enormously. Between 1800 and 1820, most female institutions offered reading, writing, grammar, geography, arithmetic, and plain needlework on a regular basis; for additional fees, students could study a foreign language (usually French) and an assortment of such ornamental subjects as drawing, painting, Dresden, or lacework as electives. But increasing criticism of the emphasis on ornamentals in girls' education, and a rising belief that girls were indeed endowed by nature with minds to be trained by discipline, led many schools to include such presumably solid subjects as natural philosophy, astronomy, chemistry, and (more rarely) botany during the 1820s and 1830s.[15]

In order to remain competitive in attracting students, schools advertised when they added new subjects to their courses of study, or when they added new teachers, textbooks, or scientific apparatus to their programs. A fairly typical example of the

[15]Emma Willard and her sister Almira Lincoln Hart Phelps actively promoted the ideas that a woman's education should include solid subjects. See Mulhern, *A History of Secondary Education in Pennsylvania,* 394; Woody, *A History of Women's Education in the United States,* 1: 108ff.

TABLE 1

Expansion of the Curriculum of Shocco Female Academy, North Carolina, 1818–30

1818	1823	1826	1830
Reading	Reading	Reading	Reading
Writing	Writing	Writing	Writing
Arithmetic	Arithmetic	Arithmetic	Arithmetic
Grammar	Grammar	Grammar	Grammar
Geography	Geography	Geography	Geography
Needlework	Needlework	Needlework	Needlework
Drawing	Drawing	Drawing	Drawing
Painting	Painting	Painting	Painting
	Spelling	Spelling	Spelling
	Astronomy	Astronomy	Astronomy
	Nat'l Phil	Nat'l Phil	Nat'l Phil
		Chemistry	Chemistry
		Botany	Botany
		History	History
		Music	Music
			Mythology
			Lacework

Source: Data compiled from newspaper advertisements included in *North Carolina Schools and Academies 1790–1840: A Documentary History* (Raleigh, N.C., 1915), ed. Charles L. Coon, 604–12.

curriculum expansion in girls' schools can be seen in the growing number of subjects advertised by North Carolina Shocco Female Academy from 1818 to 1830 (see Table 1).[16]

The tuition rates in newspaper advertisements indicate that the sciences never attained the core status of such basic subjects as reading, writing, or arithmetic. Nevertheless, girls' schools included scientific subjects, more often than the so-called ornamental subjects, in the basic course of studies, referred to as the English course. For instance, in a sample of thirty-one girls' schools in North Carolina, 42 percent included the sciences under the basic tuition, while 58 percent charged extra. In contrast, the so-called ornamental subjects, comprising music, painting, drawing, embroidery, and so on were almost always offered on a supplemental basis and were sometimes taught by adjunct faculty.[17] The additional tuition charged for the ornamental subjects was often as

[16]The samples of newspaper advertisements used in this study were selected on the basis of the specificity of their content. In many cases, it was not possible to tell from the advertisement whether the school served males or females, or both. Nor, in all cases, was the entire course of study provided. Some advertisers claimed to offer "the usual branches of education" in their schools, and such advertisements were too vague to be included in the samples. The samples included here are drawn from advertisements that clearly specified the gender served in the school and provided a detailed course of study.

[17]It is a fairly common misconception among historians of education that the so-called ornamental subjects were a staple in the schooling of early nineteenth-century American girls. This interpretation of the place of ornamentals in female education has been preserved for decades in Thomas Woody's 1929 study of female education, in which Woody claimed that "the [female] seminary continued to offer the friperies of filigree, painting, music, and drawing in far greater profusion" from the time of Emma Willard and Catharine Beecher. See Woody, *A History of Women's Education in the United States*, 1: 415.

much, or even greater than the tuition for the entire English course, which often in-cluded the sciences. In 1831, a girl seeking to study the subjects of drawing, painting, and music in the Wake Forest Female School had to pay twice the tuition of the English course:

> The course of instruction will be that usually pursued, viz; Reading, Writing, Arithmetic, History, Natural Philosophy and Astronomy, Composition, Plain Needle Work and Embroidery, Drawing and Painting, and Music on the Piano.
>
> The prices of Tuition for the Session of five months, will be; for the ordinary branches of an English Education $10—Needle Work and Embroidery $5—Drawing and Painting $5—Music on the Piano $15, payable always in advance.[18]

Although some of the most prominent female seminaries included such traditionally male subjects as Latin and Greek in their courses of study, only a minority of schools followed this pattern until later in the century, choosing instead to offer students an educational program deemed more suitable for females. During the second and third decades of the nineteenth century, an increasing percentage of institutions advertised a curriculum that included such subjects as astronomy, natural philosophy, chemistry, and, to a lesser extent, natural history. So prevalent was the addition of science to a girl's course of studies in North Carolina in 1826, that the female department of Tarborough Academy described its program as being "as extensive as at other Female Seminaries, including Chemistry, Astronomy, Natural Philosophy, Rhetoric and History." The Academy's advertisement added that "such as desire it, may be taught plain and ornamental Needle Work, Painting on Paper and Velvet, and Music." Similarly, the 1830 prospectus of Connecticut's New Haven Female Seminary claimed that its course of study embraced "all the scientific and ornamental branches necessary to complete the female education."[19]

Visitors from abroad were struck by the presence of scientific subjects in the schooling of American girls. The Englishwoman Frances Trollope, who lived in the United States for several years during the late 1820s, recounted her experience at the annual public exhibition of a Cincinnati girls' school, where she "perceived, with some surprise, that the higher branches of science were among the studies of the pretty creatures I saw assembled there." In 1850, the Swedish writer Fredrika Bremer concluded that American girls advanced as far in their scientific studies as did American boys: "opportunity is afforded [girls] to advance as far as the young men in study and the sciences, which have hitherto been considered as too difficult for them, are as easy for them to acquire as that superficial knowledge and accomplishment to which hitherto their education has been restricted."[20]

[18]*Raleigh Register,* 7 July 1831, quoted in *North Carolina Schools and Academies, 1790–1840: A Documentary History,* ed. Charles L. Coon (Raleigh, N.C., 1915), 533.

[19]Historian Christie Farnham argues that Latin appears more frequently in southern girls' schools than in northern institutions. See Farnham, *The Education of the Southern Belle,* 28–32. However, the sources examined for this study do not support Farnham's thesis. Newspaper advertisements published in North Carolina and Virginia reveal that relatively few girls' schools in these two southern states offered Latin. During the decade from 1810 to 1830, only seven (19 percent) of a sample of thirty-six North Carolina girls' schools included Latin in their advertised courses of study. Similarly, only four (13 percent) of a sample of thirty-one Virginia girls' schools mentioned Latin in advertisements published from 1835 to 1838. In contrast, ten (42 percent) out of a sample of twenty-four girls' schools in Connecticut, Massachusetts, New York, and Maryland advertised Latin from 1820 to 1842. See discussion in Kim Tolley, "The Science Education of American Girls, 1784–1932" (Ed.D. diss., University of California at Berkeley, 1996), ch. 8. Tarborough advertisement quoted in *North Carolina Schools and Academies,* ed. Coon, 79; New Haven prospectus quoted in Vera M. Butler, *Education as Revealed by New England Newspapers prior to 1850* (Ph.D. diss., Temple University, 1935), 188.

[20]Frances Milton Trollope, *Domestic Manners of the Americans* (New York, 1949; 1832), 82; Adolph B. Benson, ed., *America of the Fifties: Letters of Fredrika Bremer* (New York, 1924; 1853), 285.

In fact, relatively few American girls had either the leisure or financial means to study the sciences. Some of the textbooks published during the antebellum period reveal the assumptions of contemporaries about the social status of females who engaged in scientific investigation. For example, Richard G. Parker's *Juvenile Philosophy*, a popular elementary text, conveys scientific principles through the medium of a mother's conversation with her daughter. The elite status of this pair is implied in their surroundings and apparatus. One illustration depicts the two of them in a well-appointed drawing room, using a gold coin to perform a science experiment (see Plate 2).[21]

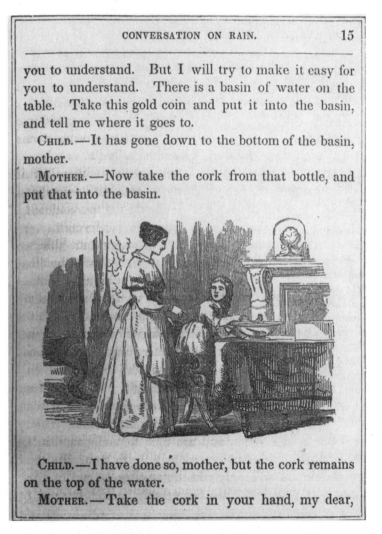

you to understand.   But I will try to make it easy for you to understand.   There is a basin of water on the table.   Take this gold coin and put it into the basin, and tell me where it goes to.

CHILD.—It has gone down to the bottom of the basin, mother.

MOTHER.—Now take the cork from that bottle, and put that into the basin.

CHILD.—I have done so, mother, but the cork remains on the top of the water.

MOTHER.—Take the cork in your hand, my dear,

CONVERSATION ON RAIN.   15

PLATE 2.   Courtesy of Cubberley Education Library, Stanford University Libraries.

[21]Richard Green Parker, *Juvenile Philosophy: or, Philosophy in Familiar Conversations Designed to Teach Young Children to Think* (New York, 1857; 1850), 15.

While the study of the sciences was largely the prerogative of the middle and upper classes, it was not restricted to the children of Anglo-Saxon, Protestant families. Indications of the movement to bring science into girls' courses of study can be found in some Catholic schools and in several academies serving Native Americans.

Although Catholicism was a minority religion of relatively new immigrants, some of the academies run by various orders of the Catholic church adapted to the newer American views of female education by offering scientific subjects to middle-class girls. For example, in 1842 the Maryland Carmelite Sister's Academy advertised natural philosophy, botany, and astronomy in its course of study, along with such other subjects as sacred history. In frontier St. Louis, the Society of the Sacred Heart reserved scientific subjects for the daughters of well-to-do families. In the Society's free school catering to indigent girls, students studied reading, writing, spelling, arithmetic, and religion. Advanced studies, offered in the 1830s for a small fee, included grammar, geography, and sewing. In contrast, girls in the Society's prestigious academy studied natural philosophy, astronomy, chemistry, and geography along with the other usual branches of a presumably solid education.[22]

The daughters of elites in the Cherokee Nation also received some instruction in scientific subjects. Since 1839, wealthier mixed-blood Cherokees had sent their daughters to the Fayetteville Female Academy in Arkansas, where they were instructed in geography and ancient history, logic, natural philosophy, literature, astronomy, and other subjects conducive to elevating the "female character in the Nation." Established in Tahlequah in 1843, another option for young Cherokee females was the Cherokee Female Seminary, where pupils studied a curriculum that included the natural sciences.[23]

In 1847, the Cherokee National Council enacted a law requiring the teachers of the Female Seminary to teach "all the branches of literature and science commonly taught in the academies of the United States." As a source of faculty for the Seminary, Cherokees looked to Mary Lyon's Mount Holyoke Female Seminary. According to the historian Devon A. Mihesuah, between 1839 and 1856, twenty-four Mount Holyoke alumnae taught among North American tribes. Modeled on the curriculum at Mount Holyoke Female Seminary, the course of study at Cherokee Female Seminary was distinguished from that in the Nation's common schools by its emphasis on literature and the sciences. In 1852, students in Cherokee common schools studied a basic course of reading, spelling, geography, and arithmetic. During the same period, the daughters of wealthier Cherokee families were instructed in such additional subjects as botany, natural philosophy, and astronomy.[24]

Facing educational restrictions more severe than those of any other ethnic group in the United States, African Americans had few opportunities to study the sciences. Before the Civil War, several states passed legislation outlawing the teaching of slaves.

[22]*Baltimore Sun,* 12 Aug. 1842; Nikola Baumgarten, "Education and Democracy in Frontier St. Louis: The Society of the Sacred Heart," *History of Education Quarterly* 34 (Summer 1994): 171–92. Baumgarten attributes the inclusion of scientific subjects in the Catholic curriculum to the influence of such female educators as Emma Willard and Catharine Beecher.

[23]Devon A. Mihesuah, *Cultivating the Rosebuds: The Education of Women at the Cherokee Female Seminary, 1851–1909* (Urbana, Ill., 1993), 21. According to the author, there were two Cherokee female seminaries. The earlier institution, established in 1843, was short lived. The second Cherokee Female Seminary, which is the subject of Mihesuah's book, was established in 1851.

[24]Ibid., 27.

In cases where common schools were established for their benefit, the quality of instruction provided to free African Americans was often both rudimentary and poor.[25]

In spite of enormous obstacles, however, free African Americans occasionally gained access to schooling generally reserved for elites. Such an individual was Charlotte Forten, who came of a middle-class free Philadelphia family. In the 1850s, she attended school with white students in Salem, Massachusetts. Her journal entries reveal that while a student at Higginson Grammar School, she studied geography, geology, natural philosophy, and entomology.[26]

What sort of science did girls encounter in their schoolbooks? An analysis of 54 astronomy, chemistry, and natural philosophy texts commonly used in male and female institutions reveals that boys and girls studied the same content: descriptive and physical astronomy, mechanics, pneumatics, hydrostatics, properties of matter, and so on. Before 1830, the science texts appearing in girls' schools generally included less mathematics than those in boys' schools; however, the introduction of algebra and geometry into their curricula during the 1830s and 1840s allowed some girls to undertake a mathematical study of the physical sciences at mid-century. For example, Alonzo Gray, an instructor in Brooklyn Female Academy, included algebraic formulae in his natural philosophy text, published in 1850 "for the use of pupils under the immediate instruction of the author" (see Plate 3). By the 1860s, the most difficult texts appearing in girls' schools were comparable in their mathematical complexity to those used in boys' schools, with the exception of military academies.[27]

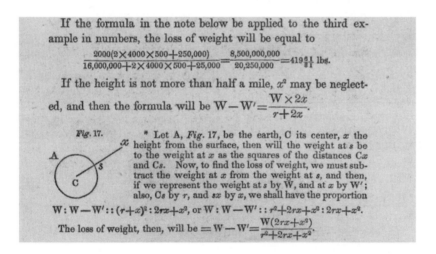

PLATE 3.   A representation of Newton's Law of Gravity, in Alonzo Gray's *Elements of Natural Philosophy* (1850). Courtesy of Cubberley Education Library, Stanford University Libraries.

---

[25]See Knight, ed., *A Documentary History of Education in the South*, 5: 459–515. For instance, in their 1845 report, the examining committee of the Boston schools noted that conditions were deplorable in the Smith school, an institution catering to the children of free African Americans. See "Boston Grammar and Writing Schools," in *Common School Journal 7* (Oct. 1845): 299–300; Caroline Alfred to Lucretia Crocker, 21 Feb. 1874, Caroline Alfred Letters, Freedman's Aid Society Papers, Massachusetts Historical Society. Conditions in the South after the Civil War were no better. Caroline Alfred, a teacher of free African Americans in Georgia, complained despairingly that "in the public colored school in this city great pains are taken that the pupils shall only learn to *read*."

[26]Brenda Stevenson, ed., *The Journals of Charlotte Forten Grimké* (New York, 1988), 1–31, 82, 63, 89, 105, 107–8, 122. The quotation is from her entry of 28 May 1854.

[27]Alonzo Gray, *Elements of Natural Philosophy* (New York, 1850), iii; Kim Tolley, "The Science Education of American Girls," ch. 3.

A variety of contemporary sources indicate that while the sciences maintained a relatively marginal presence in boys' academies before 1840, they were highly visible in girls' schools. Newspaper advertisements published in both northern and southern states reveal that a larger percentage of female institutions advertised scientific subjects than did male institutions during the same period. As shown in Tables 2–4, natural philosophy, astronomy, and chemistry comprised the most commonly advertised sciences in both male and female institutions. Botany appeared in a majority of girls' schools only after 1840.

TABLE 2

Percentage of North Carolina and Virginia Secondary Schools Advertising Various Sciences, 1800–1840

	Natural Philosophy	Astronomy	Chemistry	Botany	Mineralogy	Natural History
Girls' Schools (n=78)	74%	47%	54%	35%	5%	13%
Boys' Schools (n=86)	47%	22%	21%	2%	3%	1%

Source: Data compiled from newspaper advertisements for 61 Virginia schools published in the *Richmond Enquirer* (Virginia, 1835–38), and 103 schools included in *North Carolina Schools and Academies,* ed. Coon.

TABLE 3

Percentage of Secondary Schools in Selected Northern States Advertising Various Sciences, 1820–1842

	Natural Philosophy	Astronomy	Chemistry	Botany	Mineralogy	Natural History
Girls' Schools (n=24)	63%	50%	58%	25%	0%	4%
Boys' Schools (n=15)	53%	33%	53%	27%	20%	0%

Source: Data compiled from newspaper advertisements for 39 schools published in the *American Mercury* (Connecticut, 1820–29 [incomplete]); *Columbian Centinel* (Massachusetts, 1827–31); *Baltimore Sun* (Maryland, 1841–42); *New York Evening Post* (1 Aug. 1835–31 May 1836); *The Globe* (Washington, D.C., 1831); *Daily National Intelligencer* (Washington, D.C., 1825).

TABLE 4

Percentage of Pennsylvania Secondary Schools Offering Various Sciences, 1830–1889

	Natural Philosophy	Astronomy	Chemistry	Botany	Mineralogy	Natural History
Girls' Schools (n=90)	88%	67%	72%	77%	33%	—
Boys' & Coed Schools (n=116)	54%	47%	56%	33%	28%	—

Source: Data compiled from tables in James Mulhern, *A History of Secondary Education in Pennsylvania* (Philadelphia, 1933) 328–29, 428–29.

In comparing the results for northern and southern states, there appears to be little regional variation in the percentage of girls' schools advertising scientific subjects; the higher figures reported for Pennsylvania are attributable to the later time period (1830–89) represented by the schools in Mulhern's sample. However, although evidence is sketchy, the newspapers examined for this study indicate that a larger percentage of boys' schools in northern states advertised the sciences than did their southern counterparts, a trend that may have developed in response to the growing industrialization of the North.

While a girl's education commonly included doses of scientific subjects, a boy's education more often centered around Latin and Greek, particularly in the South. For example, in Virginia and North Carolina, Latin was the most frequently advertised subject in boys' academies and private schools from 1790 to 1840; 91 percent of boys' schools advertised Latin, and 85 percent advertised Greek. In contrast, only 18 percent of girls' schools advertised Latin, and a very meager 5 percent advertised Greek. In the North, only a slightly larger percentage of boys' schools than girls' schools advertised Latin, although female institutions usually offered the subject on an elective basis only.[28]

Another way to compare the curricula offered to the two sexes is to examine the courses of study in schools with both male and female departments. Of the 103 schools represented in the North Carolina sample, seven placed advertisements describing curricula for the male and female departments of the same institution.[29] Six of the seven institutions advertised a different science curriculum for their male and female departments. The curriculum of Vine Hill Academy exemplifies variations in the subjects available to middle-class males and females; the classics, higher mathematics, navigation, and surveying were offered to males, whereas natural philosophy, astronomy, chemistry, botany, and several other subjects were offered to females (see Table 5).

In New York's Genesee Wesleyan Seminary, which offered the same number of scientific subjects to both sexes in separate departments, girls predominated in the science courses. Despite the fact that males comprised 62 percent of the student body in 1834, enrollment data reveal that a significantly larger percentage of females than males studied the sciences (see Table 6). According to historian Nancy Beadie, "males, by contrast, dominated in Latin, algebra, Greek, Hebrew, bookkeeping, trigonometry, various branches of applied geometry (for surveying) and navigation."[30]

School examinations provide another source of information about the relative importance of scientific subjects in the curriculum. Newspapers occasionally published accounts of the examinations of the larger and more prestigious local academies and seminaries, often including the names of examinees and the subjects on which they were examined. While institutions may have included scientific subjects in their advertised courses of study in order to appeal to a broad market of parents and guardians, the published reports of examinations indicate to a far greater degree the subjects that students actually studied.

Because the success or failure of its students reflected on the quality of instruction at each institution, it is unlikely that subjects taught incidentally were included in

[28]This conclusion is based on an analysis of the newspaper advertisements mentioned in the above tables. Out of a sample of twenty-four girls' schools in New England states from 1820 to 1842, 42 percent advertised Latin, usually on an elective basis, in contrast to 47 percent of a sample of fifteen boys' schools.

[29]New Bern Academy in Craven County, Fayetteville Academy in Cumberland County, Tarborough Academy in Edgecome County, Greensborough Academy in Guilford County, Vine Hill Academy in Halifax County, Salisbury Academy in Rowan County, and Raleigh Academy in Wake County.

[30]Nancy Beadie, "Emma Willard's Idea Put to the Test: The Consequences of State Support of Female Education in New York, 1819–67," *History of Education Quarterly* 33 (Winter 1993): 543–62, 560n.

TABLE 5

Comparison of the Male and Female Courses of Study Advertised by Vine Hill Academy, North Carolina, 1837

Male Department	Female Department
Spelling	Spelling
Reading	Reading
Writing	Writing
Grammar	Grammar
Geography	Geography
History	History
Arithmetic	Arithmetic
Rhetoric	Rhetoric
Logic	Logic
French	French
Latin	_____
Greek	_____
Algebra	_____
Geometry	_____
Navigation	_____
Surveying	_____
_____	Natural Philosophy
_____	Chemistry
_____	Astronomy
_____	Botany
_____	Moral & Intellectual Philosophy
_____	Natural Theology
_____	Elements of Criticism
_____	Drawing & Painting

Source: Data compiled from the *Raleigh Star* (17 May 1837), in *North Carolina Schools,* ed. Coon, 176–77.

examinations. Public examinations were high-stakes performances, conducted orally, often in the presence of a large audience of relatives, ministers, trustees, and visiting preceptors from other schools. In an era when few forms of public entertainment were available, the examinations in some cases assumed the form of a spectacle. When Mary Lyon was teaching at Ipswich Female Seminary with Zilpah Grant, "public examination carryalls from Andover rolled over to Ipswich to help swell the audience." The examinations sometimes lasted for several days, no doubt creating an atmosphere of terror and excitement for students.[31]

[31]Mary Lyon quoted in Marr, *Old New England Academies,* 247. Depending on the school's charter, examinations might be held at the end of each term or more frequently. At Salisbury Academy in North Carolina, both private and public examinations were held. Each year was divided into two sessions, each session consisting of two quarters. At the end of each quarter, a committee of the Trustees was appointed to conduct the quarterly examination. The committee took the last two days of the quarter to examine the classes privately on their various studies. Twice a year, a public examination took place, and the Trustees' report of the public examination was published in the papers. See *Western Carolinian,* 19 Sep. 1820, in *North Carolina Schools and Academies,* ed. Coon, 360.

TABLE 6

Number and Percentage of Each Sex Enrolled in Science Courses at Genesee Wesleyan Seminary, New York, 1834

	Total Enrollment	Natural Philos.	Astronomy	Chemistry	Botany
Girls	144	85 (58%)	7 (5%)	33 (23%)	11 (8%)
Boys	232	64 (28%)	0 (0%)	20 (9%)	0 (0%)

Source: Nancy Beadie, "Emma Willard's Idea Put to the Test: The Consequences of State Support of Female Education in New York, 1819–67," *History of Education Quarterly* 33 (Winter 1993): 559–60n.

In their academies, boys were almost always examined on the classics and on such core subjects as geography, arithmetic, and grammar. For example, at North Carolina's Raleigh Academy in 1807, while the rest of his classmates endured questions on such topics as Horace, Virgil, Caesar, Selectae Veterii, Erasmus, Aesop's Fables, the Greek Testament, and Latin Grammar, Thomas Gales was the sole student examined on natural philosophy and astronomy, evidencing "by his ready and unembarrassed answers, his perfect acquaintance with them." It was not uncommon for a boys' academy to include natural philosophy or astronomy in its advertised course of study but to exclude these subjects from its examinations.[32]

Published accounts of examinations in North Carolina reveal that a greater percentage of girls' schools included scientific subjects in their exams than did boys' schools of the same period. Although the majority of girls were examined on such core subjects as geography, reading, spelling, and grammar, and on such ornamentals as fancy needlework and painting, it was not uncommon also to find classes of girls examined in natural philosophy, astronomy, or chemistry. Female students generally impressed their audience with their knowledge of various scientific subjects. For instance, in 1826, the examiners of Charlotte Female Academy noted with admiration that "the abstruse principles of Natural Philosophy and Astronomy were fully comprehended and understood by those who are yet but children."[33]

In New England, the examinations given in the common schools of Boston, Massachusetts, under the leadership of Horace Mann reveal a similar situation. The Boston common schools of this period offered free instruction to the children of Boston's citizens. Each school was really two schools in one, a writing school and a grammar school. The master of the writing school taught the subjects of writing, arithmetic, algebra, geometry, and bookkeeping, and the master of the grammar school taught the subjects of grammar, reading, geography, history, and sometimes natural philosophy and astronomy.[34]

[32]*Raleigh Minerva,* 4 June 1807, in *North Carolina Schools and Academies,* ed. Coon, 399. For example, this was a common practice of the Classical School in Charlottesville, Virginia, from 1835 to 1836. See the issue of the *Richmond Enquirer* for 10 Nov. 1835, which advertises its course of study, and the issue for 29 Dec. 1835, which reports its examinations.

[33]Of the schools that published reports of examinations, seven (78 percent) of nine girls' schools included scientific subjects, as compared to two (14 percent) of fourteen boys' schools. Data compiled from newspaper advertisements in Coon, ed., *North Carolina Schools and Academies. Catawba Journal,* 5 Dec. 1826, in *North Carolina Schools and Academies,* ed. Coon, 235–36; see also *Raleigh Star,* 10 Jan. 1812, in ibid., 601. The examiners' report discusses the students' extensive knowledge of astronomy in Mordecai's Female Academy in Warrenton, North Carolina.

[34]"Boston Grammar and Writing Schools," in *Common School Journal* 7 (15 Oct. 1845): 311–17. Lengthy extracts from the report of the Boston School Committee were published in numbers 19–23 of the *Journal* in 1845; Otis W. Caldwell and Stuart A. Courtis, *Then and Now in Education, 1845–1923: A Message of Encouragement from the Past to the Present* (Yonkers-on-Hudson, N.Y., 1925), 11, 14.

The School Committee of the City of Boston appointed a subcommittee in 1845 to examine the highest, or first class in each of the nineteen grammar schools in Boston. Five schools catered exclusively to girls, five to boys, and the remaining nine were coeducational. The students in the first classes were about to graduate, being on average fourteen years old. Among the tests created for this purpose were those in natural philosophy and astronomy. The same examinations were administered to each of the schools in the city, and the tabulated results published in detail, question by question and school by school.[35]

Thirteen of the nineteen common schools in Boston reportedly offered natural philosophy as an elective, and four offered astronomy on the same basis. Because taking the examinations in these subjects was optional, schools that did not provide instruction in astronomy or natural philosophy declined to submit scholars for questioning.[36]

All five of the girls' schools produced scholars for the natural philosophy examination, and two of these schools, Franklin and Johnson, produced scholars for the astronomy examination as well. In contrast, only two boys' schools produced scholars for the natural philosophy examination, and no boys' school consented to be examined on astronomy (see Table 7).

[35]Caldwell and Courtis, *Then and Now in Education*, 22–226. It is possible to identify the girls' and boys' schools from extracts of the Boston School Committee Report. Copies of the original tests are reproduced both in Caldwell and Courtis's text and in *Common School Journal* 7 (1 Dec. 1845): 361–63.

[36]Caldwell and Courtis, *Then and Now in Education*, 168–69; 342–43. Apparently neither astronomy or natural philosophy was offered in the Smith school, an institution catering solely to African American children; Smith declined to produce scholars for examination on either subject.

TABLE 7

Students in Boston Common Schools Examined in Natural Philosophy and Astronomy, 1845

Girls' Schools	Enrollment	Number Examined in Nat. Philos.	Number Examined in Astronomy
Bowdoin	508	45	0
Wells	307	27	0
Franklin	418	14	19
Hancock	509	20	0
Johnson	547	44	50
Total	2289	150	69

Boys' Schools	Enrollment	Number Examined in Nat. Philos.	Number Examined in Astronomy
Brimmer	513	35	0
Eliot	456	0	0
Adams	418	0	0
Mayhew	368	19	0
New South	136	0	0
Total	1891	54	0

Source: Data compiled from Otis W. Caldwell and Stuart A. Courtis, *Then and Now in Education, 1845–1923: A Message of Encouragement from the Past to the Present* (Yonkers-on-Hudson, N.Y., 1925), 342, 344.

Because students from both the top-ranked girls' and boys' schools took the examination in natural philosophy, it is possible to compare the relative performance of boys and girls. According to the examining committee, Bowdoin was the top-ranked girls' school, and Brimmer was the top-ranked boys' school. Although the scores overall were rather disappointing to the citizens of Boston, the girls' scores were much higher than those of the boys. The girls from Bowdoin correctly answered 36 percent of the questions on the natural philosophy examination, whereas the boys from Brimmer correctly answered only 19 percent.[37]

The evidence provided by newspaper advertisements, tuition rates, and reports of school examinations reveals a distinctly greater emphasis on scientific subjects in schools for middle-class girls than in similar institutions for boys. At first offered to the children of elites in academies and seminaries, the sciences began to appear more frequently in common schools in the late 1830s. A sampling of the school returns in Massachusetts reveals a substantial increase in the percentage of towns reporting the use of science textbooks in the common schools during a brief four-year period beginning in 1837.[38]

In order to understand why the sciences were more prevalent in girls' schools than in boys' schools before 1840, it is important to consider the social and cultural context influencing these institutions in the early nineteenth century. One explanation for the dominance of the traditional classical curriculum in boys' academies lies in the entrance requirements of local colleges. In 1810, the University of Pennsylvania required candidates to translate Caesar's *Commentaries* and Virgil, to translate English exercises into Latin, and to translate the Gospels from Greek. Thirty years later, admission requirements of male colleges generally covered parts of Caesar, Virgil, Cicero, the *Anabasis,* and the *Iliad.* For college-bound students, the years of study necessary to achieve mastery in the classics must have left little time for other subjects. Nathaniel True, a student at Maine's North Yarmouth Academy during the 1820s, recalled his classical studies as being all-consuming: "I sat up one night a week during the term without retiring and studied every night until midnight. I averaged more than eighteen hours a day in getting my two Latin lessons each day for recitation."[39]

A second reason for the durability of the classical curriculum was the social prestige of classical study in American nineteenth-century culture. Although the great majority of academy students may not have gone on to college, the attainment of classical knowledge conferred a gentlemanly polish on boys who eventually planned to

[37]Ibid., 182, 229. Ironically, although the examiners ranked Brimmer as the highest quality boys' school, its scholars were consistently outranked by other schools on the examinations in all subjects. The examiners, perhaps unable to see beyond the social status of Brimmer's students, nevertheless held unfailingly to a belief in the intelligence of the school's scholars: "The boys of the first class have . . . a general intelligence, which was perfectly obvious to the committee, but of which no record can appear in our tables" (ibid., 184). Caldwell and Courtis, *Then and Now in Education,* 342–44. In fact, the girls' schools Bowdoin and Wells ranked within the top three schools on each of the remaining examinations as well, a phenonomon that must be interpreted with caution. Generally, girls stayed in school longer than boys. In Boston, boys were required to leave school at the end of the term after their fourteenth birthday, while girls could remain until the end of the term after their sixteenth birthday. The average age of the girls examined at Bowdoin was fourteen years and eight months, while the average age of the boys at Brimmer was thirteen years. However, age alone did not account for all the differences in scores. On the history examination, for example, boys from Adams school, whose average age was only twelve years and eleven months, outscored the girls from Wells, whose average age was thirteen years and three months (Caldwell and Courtis, *Then and Now in Education,* 14, 330). See also "Boston Grammar and Writing Schools," in *Common School Journal* 7 (Oct. 1845): 292, 296–97.

[38]Data compiled from a random sampling of thirty towns each in *First Abstract of the Massachusetts School Returns for 1837* (Boston, 1838), and *Abstract of the Massachusetts School Returns, 1840–41* (Boston, 1841). In 1837, 17 percent of towns reported using natural philosophy textbooks in their common schools, 10 percent reported chemistry and 7 percent astronomy textbooks. In 1841, 73 percent reported using natural philosophy textbooks, 20 percent reported chemistry, 23 percent astronomy, and 3 percent natural history textbooks.

[39]Mulhern, *A History of Secondary Education in Pennsylvania,* 223–24; Woody: *A History of Women's Education in the United States.* 2: 163ff. True qouted in Ruth Arline Wray, *The History of Secondary Education in Cumberland and Sagadahoc Counties in Maine* (Orono, Me., 1940), 47.

manage their fathers' plantations or pursue a career in business. In their interviews with British middle-class parents in the 1860s, inspectors for the Taunton Commission discovered that parents simply did not wish to experiment with the education of their sons. Instead, parents expressed the belief that "to learn the classics was a definite mark of an upper class and clearly separated the education of their sons from that of a merely commercial school."[40] Americans were undoubtedly equally anxious to maintain or elevate the social status of their children.

The schoolmasters in boys' academies constitute a third factor in the resistance of these institutions to offer scientific instruction. Having been trained in the classics themselves, many instructors were probably reluctant to add new subjects to the curriculum. Often, those who defended Latin as the ideal educational instrument for mental training had vested interests in maintaining the status quo, being either schoolmasters or professors of Latin in college classics departments.[41]

A fourth influence on the curricula in male academies was the existing job market. Because there were relatively few profitable career opportunities for young men as physicists, astronomers, geologists, or botanists in the early nineteenth century, there was little incentive to promote these subjects in the academies on the basis of their vocational value. By the third decade of the century, the era of the great surveys was just beginning. In 1830, a writer noted that the science of geology was virtually unknown in the smaller communities of the United States: "A geologist in a retired town, engaged in his examination of rocks, is often surrounded by a collection of individuals, eying him with contempt; pity, or suspicion." Even forty years later, the appearance of a scientist in a small town was a novelty.[42] Although entrance to the medical profession required scientific study, those aspiring to become doctors traditionally studied the sciences in college after a rigorous classical training at the academy. A similar path, in which classical training preceded scientific study, lay ahead of those seeking to become professional scientists.

In fact, what might be termed vocational subjects were relatively scarce in academies before 1840. For example, while some forms of employment required knowledge of navigation, mensuration, or surveying, fewer than a third of academies in Pennsylvania and North Carolina provided instruction in these subjects before 1840. This state of affairs can be explained by the existence of competing institutions. Such institutions as mechanics' institutes and other evening schools offered vocational training to young men needing to work during the day. The following advertisement for an evening school in North Carolina is fairly representative: "The subscriber will open an Evening School . . . [where] will be taught Reading, Writing,

[40]As late as 1864, the state superintendent of Pennsylvania reported that "It is not probable that more than one-eighth of the students in the academies and seminaries pass on through a college course." Quoted in Rev. J. Fraser, *Report on the Common School System of the United States and of the Provinces of Upper and Lower Canada* (1867) [3857] XXVI.293 mf 73.216–20, 106. Taunton Commission report quoted in Phillips, *The Scientific Lady*, 239–40.

[41]For example, see William Hooper, "Imperfections of Our Primary Schools, 1833" in *North Carolina Schools*, ed. Coon, 729–50. Hooper was professor of ancient language in the University of North Carolina. In a speech designed to alert North Carolinians to the dangers posed by the new trends in education, Hooper announced that students entering Andover Academy "cannot decline their Greek nouns and verbs with any tolerable accuracy" (ibid., 734).

[42]Ralph S. Bates, *Scientific Societies in the United States* (Cambridge, Mass., 1965; 1945), 33; A. Hunter Dupree, *Science in the Federal Government: A History of Policies and Activities to 1940* (New York, 1964), 383–86; "Geological Studies," *American Annals of Education* 1 (Oct./Nov. 1830): 141; "Lucy Millington," unpublished manuscript by Liberty Hyde Bailey, file 1, box 8, Liberty Hyde Bailey Papers, Carl Kroch Library, Cornell University. Bailey, who grew up in South Haven, Michigan, wrote that he had seen only one botanist, a visiting lecturer in the town lyceum, before meeting Lucy Millington in 1876.

English Grammar, Geography, Arithmetic, Trigonometry, Mensuration of Surfaces and Solids, Navigation and Surveying."[43]

We can infer that many upper- and middle-class American parents considered the study of the sciences an unnecessary frill in the education of their sons. Marketing their programs to this audience through local newspapers, southern male academies advertised the classics far more frequently than the sciences. And whereas a greater percentage of institutions in some northern states advertised scientific subjects, in practice, classical study probably predominated in most northern institutions as well. It is likely that parents disdained the sciences because such subjects were not needed to gain entrance to college, had little value in imparting the gentlemanly polish of liberal culture, and afforded relatively few career opportunities. When he visited America in the 1850s, Swedish commentator Per Siljestrom noted with surprise that Americans appeared to hold the natural sciences in relatively low esteem.[44]

Although parents may not have considered the sciences quite good enough for their sons, they viewed them as acceptable for their daughters. The most important factor in the rise of scientific subjects in girls' schools is the novelty of the institutions themselves. Unlike boys' academies, which were preceded by the Latin grammar schools, there was no precedent for the curriculum in female seminaries. As a result, educational reformers seeking to bring the sciences into secondary schools were far more likely to succeed in girls' schools.

College entrance requirements, so influential in the male academies, held little sway over educational institutions for girls. Because colleges were generally not open to women before 1850, girls' schools were free of the burden of preparing students for entrance requirements in the classics. In addition, the study of the classics was traditionally the prerogative of males. In 1803, one writer who supported the education of girls nevertheless cautioned against allowing them to study the classics, advising parents to "Let your girls go in hand with your boys, as far as reading, writing, and accounts; there draw a line, for girls have nothing to do with Latin and Greek."[45]

The influence of trends from Europe undoubtedly played a part in the development of women's scientific interests in the United States. The eighteenth century witnessed an increase in the production of popular science in both Great Britain and France, and the numbers of science books written for a female audience gradually increased. These publications were primarily elementary textbooks for women and children, in which concepts of natural philosophy, chemistry, or natural history were conveyed through the medium of female characters, a format that effectively emphasized the appropriateness of women's scientific interests. Since the seventeenth century, there had been a steady flow of ideas from Great Britain and Europe to North America, and the same sources of transmission increased in the eighteenth century. Newspapers, books, pamphlets, and periodicals reprinted European and British articles and stories. In addition, personal contact by travel and correspondence guaranteed an exchange of ideas between countries. Soon, Americans published their own popular science books

---

[43]Data compiled from Mulhern, *A History of Secondary Education in Pennsylvania,* 328: Mulhern's sample of forty-seven academies (1750 to 1829) reveals that 9 percent offered mensuration, 19 percent surveying, and 13 percent navigation; data compiled from *North Carolina Schools and Academies,* ed. Coon: the advertisements of 56 academies from the period 1794 to 1840 reveal that 9 percent offered mensuration, 29 percent surveying, and 13 percent navigation. See *Columbian Centinal* (Boston, Mass., 6 Oct. 1827); *Raleigh Register* (30 Sep. 1828), in *North Carolina Schools and Academies.* ed. Coon, 494; Mulhern, *A History of Secondary Education in Pennsylvania,* 472; "A Night School," in *Raleigh Register,* 30 Sep. 1828, in *North Carolina Schools and Academies,* ed. Coon, 494.

[44]Per Siljestrom, *The Educational Institutions of the United States, Their Character and Organization.* (London, 1853), 393.

[45]Mulhern, *A History of Secondary Education in Pennsylvania,* 323; Woody, *A History of Women's Education in the United States* 2: 163; quoted in Mulhern, *A History of Secondary Education in Pennsylvania,* 391.

for women, and their texts quickly appeared on bookstore shelves next to European imports.[46]

The almost complete lack of public opposition to the study of science in girls' schools can be attributed to the tacit acceptance of this movement among many American scientists. For America's fledgling scientific community, there were benefits to be gained by encouraging females to study the sciences. First, as popularizers of science, women helped to create a supportive public. In an era when few public funds were available for scientific enterprises, the popularization of science ensured a public receptive to the necessary financing of experiments, surveys, and expeditions. Second, as consumers of popular science, women's numbers swelled the audiences at Lyceum lectures, helping to pay the salaries of male scientists who traveled the lecture circuit. Also, such scientists as Benjamin Silliman, Denison Olmsted, Asa Gray, and others wrote science textbooks and developed scientific apparatus for the use of academies and seminaries, and the royalties from the sales of these materials in girls' schools must have produced handsome profits. Third, as collectors of mineral and botanical specimens, women amateurs served as unpaid assistants aiding the research efforts of professional male scientists in herbaria, museums, and colleges.

The social and cultural influences briefly outlined here helped to create an educational climate in which scientific subjects easily gained entry into the curriculum of educational institutions for middle- and upper-class girls. While science was initially included in the courses of study of academies and seminaries, by the mid-nineteenth century its presence was also beginning to be felt in common schools.

The central conclusion of this study is that increasingly toward the middle decades of the nineteenth century, a young woman's education included the study of the sciences. The reported courses of study of early girls' schools, seminaries, and academies evidences a greater emphasis on scientific subjects than the curricula of similar, contemporary institutions for boys.

Historians of science have frequently noted the rapid entry of women into scientific fields in the United States in the latter half of the nineteenth century. Heretofore, explanations of this phenomenon have centered either on the extracurricular scientific literature increasingly aimed at a female audience during the late eighteenth and early nineteenth centuries, or on the opening of colleges and universities to women during the latter decades of the nineteenth century.[47] This study presents a consistent body of evidence to support the conclusion that a scientific curriculum was widely implemented in schools for American girls from the first decades of the nineteenth century. The science education of American girls in the antebellum period thus constitutes a likely and hitherto overlooked factor in the rise of science as a female interest after the Civil War.

[46]The exchange of ideas between America and Europe is discussed in Bernard Bailyn, "Political Experience and Enlightenment Ideas in Eighteenth-Century America," in *An American Enlightenment: Selected Articles on Colonial Intellectual History*, ed. Peter Charles Hoffer (New York, 1988), 134–46. For an overview of women's participation in natural history and their authorship of popular science books for women, see Marcia Bonta, *Women in the Field: America's Pioneering Women Naturalists* (College Station, 1991); Vera Norwood, *Made from This Earth: American Women and Nature* (Chapel Hill, N.C., 1993).

[47]See Margaret W. Rossiter, *Women Scientists in America: Struggles and Strategies to 1940* (Baltimore, Md., 1982), 1–28; Lynn Barber, *The Heyday of Natural History, 1820–1870* (Garden City, N.Y., 1980); Keener, *The Botanizers*.

Kim Tolley is a doctoral candidate at the University of California at Berkeley. She is also a lecturer in the School of Education at Saint Mary's College of California. She would like to thank Geraldine Jonçich Clifford, Roger Hahn, Larry Lowery, J. David Miller, Barbara Beatty, and an anonymous reviewer for their thoughtful comments and suggestions. This essay was awarded the Henry Barnard Prize for 1995.

A9

Reconsidering the Power of the Superintendent in the Progressive Period

William B. Thomas and Kevin J. Moran
University of Pittsburgh

Raymond E. Callahan's *Education and the Cult of Efficiency* advanced the widely accepted notion about superintendents being extremely vulnerable to myriad pressures and criticisms of various special interest groups. To test this vulnerability thesis, we followed the career path of a single school executive in three cities between 1914–1922. As an active and long-time influential member of the Department of Superintendence of the National Education Association, Ernest Clark Hartwell typified a stalwart, modern-day, career-bound superintendent who consistently controlled school affairs during his administration. More than merely surviving as a school executive, he built an educational empire by aligning himself with managerial elites and fellow career-bound superintendents. In our study of this first-generation progressive, we show how he won the right to dominate the affairs of schools, systematically applied a business ethos to his work, adopted antilabor practices to dash militant teachers' hopes for democratic control, and enlarged a state-sanctioned school bureaucracy to shield himself from public criticism in different institutional settings.

Raymond E. Callahan's noted work *Education and the Cult of Efficiency* advanced the widely accepted notion that "very much of what happened in American education since 1900 can be explained on the basis of the extreme vulnerability of our schoolmen to public criticism and pressure."[1] Callahan assumed that the precariousness of the office of the superintendent stemmed from the myriad pressures and criticisms of various special interest groups. He argued that "the professional survival of school superintendents depended on their ability to appease their most powerful and vocal critics. . . . Public opinion became a most powerful force as newspapers and popular journals featuring sensationalism and exposure reached an increasingly larger audience."[2] Callahan supported his contentions with an editorial from the *American School Board Journal* on the professional insecurity of school administrators. It too noted that "the tenure of the school superintendent is an uncertain one and that his position is attended with vexatious conditions."[3] Undoubtedly, some early 20th-century school executives were caught between Scylla and Charybdis, as are many contemporary superintendents, in their efforts to attend to a multitude of duties while appeasing many diverse groups. In Buffalo, New York, to cite a historical example, the superintendent complained that "the idea of a superintendent of schools being nominated in a party convention and going through a political campaign was

[1] Raymond E. Callahan, *Education and the Cult of Efficiency: A Study of the Social Forces That Have Shaped the Administration of the Public Schools* (Chicago: University of Chicago Press, 1962), viii.

[2] Ibid., 52–53.

[3] Ibid., 53.

Thomas, William and Moran, Kevin. "Reconsidering the Power of the Superintendent in the Progressive Period." *American Educational Research Journal,* vol. 29(1), pp. 22–50.

naturally abhorrent to superintendents elected by more or less cultured boards of education."[4]

Of late, the debate over Callahan's vulnerability thesis, which explains the behaviors of superintendents in the battle over school affairs, has resurfaced.[5] Proponents of his vulnerability thesis maintain that superintendents have reacted to conflicts and pressures as vulnerable employees rather than acting as powerful leaders or philosopher kings. Other scholars reject this vulnerability thesis on several grounds. Their counterarguments suggest that superintendents were far from being weak and vulnerable.[6] Cuban, for example, questions the persuasiveness of the single-cause explanation embodied in the vulnerability thesis. To explain the behavior of superintendents, he favors interpretations that consider the effects of economic, political, and demographic pressures upon the superintendent's office and also the impact of national trends, the business ideology of the period, and other progressive ideas. Each of these factors, he contends, might have influenced the development of different conceptions of administrative leadership styles and behaviors.[7] In further contrast to the vulnerability thesis, case studies show that the office of the superintendent was one of great power and that "the incumbents demonstrated repeatedly their invulnerability to business pressures whenever matters of educational policy were at stake."[8] Still other scholars who have examined the relationship between the superintendent and the school board conclude that, although boards have legitimacy and formal authority and are influential in policy-making, superintendents are normally more powerful due to their abilities to control board access to information, to set agendas at board meetings, and to use their professional expertise on educational matters.[9] Superintendents' knowledge, their professional stature, time in office, and staff assistance all seem to reinforce this power base that defenders of the vulnerability thesis downplay.

Indeed, past and present relationships between superintendents and school boards are dynamic and quite complex. In some instances, the longevity of superintendents has hinged on the power structure of the community, on the characteristics and composition of the school board,[10] or on the administrative style of the superintendent. Whether the board is appointed or elected, is polarized over volatile issues, is supportive of the superintendents' policies, or is dominated by members representing special interest groups may help to explain the rapid superintendent turnover that, for example, has occurred recently in 28 of the 45 districts comprising the Council of the Great City Schools.[11]

These determinants of superintendents' tenure notwithstanding, we contend that there may be a relationship between the vulnerability of school executives and their career aspirations. Carlson and House distinguish the career goals of superintendents to

[4]Henry P. Emerson, *Annual Report of the Superintendent of Education of the City of Buffalo, 1914–1915* (Buffalo, N.Y.: James D. Warren's Sons Co., 1915), 17.

[5]William E. Eaton, ed., *Shaping the Superintendency: A Reexamination of Callahan and the Cult of Efficiency* (New York: Teachers College Press, 1990).

[6]Barbara Berman, "Business Efficiency, American Schooling, and the Public School Superintendency: A Reconsideration of the Callahan Thesis." *History of Education Quarterly* 23 (Fall 1983): 297–321.

[7]Larry Cuban, *Urban School Chiefs Under Fire* (Chicago: University of Chicago Press, 1976),111–139.

[8]Timothy L. Smith, "Education and the Cult of Efficiency: A Study of the Social Forces That Have Shaped the Administration of the Public Schools (A Review)," *History of Education Quarterly* 4 (March 1961), 76–77.

[9]John Thomas Thompson, *Policymaking in American Public Education: A Framework for Analysis* (Englewood Cliffs, N.J.: Prentice-Hall, 1976) 48–49; L. Harmon Zeigler and M. Kent Jennings, *Governing American Schools: Political Interaction in Local School Districts* (North Scituate, Miss.: Duxbury, 1974); and James Koerner, *Who Controls American Education?* (Boston: Beacon, 1968).

[10]Donald McCarty and Charles Ramsey, *The School Managers: Power and Conflict in American Public Education* (Westport, Conn.: Greenwood, 1978).

[11]Ann Bradley, "Rapid Turnover in Urban Superintendencies Prompts Calls for Reforms in Governance," *Education Week* 10 (December 1990): 1, 34–35.

show how place-bound and career-bound school managers differ and how their differences may affect their job performance. Place-bound superintendents rely upon the loyalty of the local power structure and diverse community members. These superintendents plan to remain in their posts until retirement. They, therefore, perceive good public relations as a large part of their responsibilities and tend to take few risks that might alienate their community supporters. In contrast, career-bound superintendents remain detached from the local power structure and spend less time establishing a local constituency in the community. Instead, they build a referent group comprising a network of other career-bound school executives (like themselves), researchers and university professors, and state and national policymakers. As greater risk-takers, they view each new placement as a stepping stone to increased responsibilities and professional power.[12]

These differing assessments of the relative power and vulnerability of superintendents have opened the door for students of administrative theory and practice to explore the policies and actions of individual career-bound superintendents. To test historically the vulnerability thesis, we followed the career path of a single school executive from Sault Ste. Marie, Michigan, to St. Paul, Minnesota, and from there to Buffalo, New York, between 1915–1922. As the president (and long time influential member) of the Department of Superintendence of the National Education Association (1918) and the president of the New York Council of Superintendents (1922), Ernest Clark Hartwell typified a stalwart, modern-day, career-bound superintendent who consistently controlled school affairs in these three cities. During these years, he encountered many political issues and uncertainties that continue to plague today's superintendents. There were pressures from taxpayers and the business community, demanding greater returns for fewer tax dollars; assimilationists, who viewed schools as an institution for Americanizing or socializing less favored immigrant groups in urban centers; politicans or elected school board members, whose demands reflected the special interest of their respective constituents; parents groups, who looked to schools as ladders of mobility for their children; and militant teachers, seeking higher salaries, professional status, and decentralized control over educational decision making. Additionally, there were groups opposing in some way each of these pressure groups and their political agendas.

More than merely surviving as a school executive, Hartwell built an educational empire by aligning himself with managerial elites and fellow career-bound superintendents. As a mark of his early success, from 1916–1919, he secured public appropriations for school buildings amounting to $11,500,000. Given his reputation as an efficiency-minded school manager, when conflicts arose over teacher professionalism, merit pay, teacher loyalty, and teacher unionization, he proved invulnerable to mounting political pressures. As a member of a powerful network of superintendents in an era of reform, he gained total control over schools and their personnel and prevailed, as did his counterparts in New York, Pittsburgh, Detroit, and Cleveland. Unlike the urban superintendent whose average longevity on the job today is three years or less, Hartwell systematically applied a business ethos to his work: successfully adopted antilabor practices to subvert militant teachers' organizing activities; and enlarged a state-sanctioned school bureaucracy to shield himself from public criticism. With a centralized system of control, the legislature, courts, and media at his disposal, he was impervious to criticism. When groups of militant teachers attempted to gain concessions from him, he charged teachers with "inefficiency" and then fired their

---

[12]R.O. Carlson, *School Superintendents: Careers and Performance* (Columbus, Ohio Charles E. Merrill, 1972); Ernest House, *The Politics of Educational Innovation* (Berkeley, Calif.: McCutchan, 1974). See also Joel Spring, *American Education: An Introduction to Social and Political Aspects* (New York: Longman, 1991): 170–172.

outspoken leaders, thereby hastening teacher unionization. Hartwell, therefore, does not fit the picture of Callahan's "vulnerable" superintendent. This study of the superintendencies of a first-generation progressive shows how one powerful career-bound superintendent dominated the affairs of schools in a period of reform. Once having gained control, he then imposed a managerial style upon teachers and citizen groups who had hoped for democratic control and were strongly opposed to authoritarian administrative designs.

Ascending the Career Ladder Through Confrontation

In the late 19th century, school board members, commissioners of education, and superintendents in many large cities were elected public officials. To reform the potentially corrupting tendencies of this arrangement and the effects of ward politics upon school affairs, heads of local governments were authorized to appoint these school executives. In the search for apolitical school leadership, city officials drew from a business and professional community, whose members performed without pay what they believed to be a civic duty. Appointed boards of education and commissioners were concerned with reforms that emphasized stability and standardization that resulted in efficiency and control over outcomes of local schools. Given the vast responsibilities of operating large, modern, educational complexes, these board members and commissioners in turn appointed energetic superintendents as their chief advisers. The appointments of these aspiring career superintendents coincided with the superintendents' unrelenting campaign to gain firm control over the public schools. They sought power commensurate with the responsibilities of their offices. At the same time, elementary school teachers pressed for more democratization of their workplace. Their concerns included control over curriculum matters, textbook adoptions, and recruitment of and supervision over their group. We look first at the conflict between superintendent and teachers in St. Paul, Minnesota.

In St. Paul, the mayor had been authorized to appoint a commissioner of education. At that time, an appointive commissioner, as opposed to an elected one, offered city leaders some hope that public education might free itself from the outside interferences that had plagued so many other urban communities. St. Paul was characterized as "the Boston of the Middle West;" it was not only the state capital, distinguished for its important commerce, but it was "Republican in the sense of culture and conservatism" and it was the home of the merchant and professional classes.[13] It was also notable in that the duties for which the school boards were responsible in other cities were vested in the hands of a single commissioner of education.

Under this arrangement before the turn of the century, members of the male-dominated St. Paul Teachers' Association enjoyed relative control over some educational matters. The association had been the organization representing the city teachers' concerns to the local government, while advising the commissioner of education on related issues. Some teachers, however, had become discontented with the association's leadership, especially when it supported new school policies that forbade individual teachers from appearing before school authorities to negotiate with them about individual grievances. In 1898, therefore, these dissident teachers imported from Chicago the concept of a grade school teachers' federation to address the special interests of teachers and principals who worked in elementary schools. Their

[13] Missing footnote

group achieved some success in their struggle to participate in educational decision making. For example, the Grade Teachers' Federation won the right for their president to serve a five-year term on the Board of School Inspectors.

When St. Paul revised its charter in 1914, it confirmed teachers' explicit, though limited, role in the administration of schools. Teachers maintained responsibility for a number of affairs affecting their classrooms, including recommending textbook adoptions, designing courses of study, and proposing teaching methods. As further marks of their professionalism, the Grade Teachers' Federation invited lecturers to their meetings, sponsored university extension courses to upgrade their teaching skills, and underwrote the expenses of coworkers to attend educational workshops.[14] Finally, the Superintendent of Schools was required by the city's charter to meet monthly with the teacher-elected Board of Teachers to receive their advice on educational matters.

In 1916, School Commissioner Albert Wunderlich recruited the 33-year-old Ernest C. Hartwell from his superintendent's post in Sault Ste. Marie, Michigan. Born in Albion, Michigan, on May 14, 1883, Hartwell had earned his A.B. (1905) and A.M. (1910) degrees from Albion College and the University of Michigan, respectively, and received a Master of Pedagogy degree from New York State Normal College (1915). Later, New York State College and Albion College would confer Doctor of Pedagogy degrees upon him in 1915 and 1929. When Hartwell came to St. Paul, he typified David Tyack's characterization of the modern-day superintendent—married, Republican, male, Protestant, native-born into a favored ethnic group, and from a rural area or small midwestern town.[15] Typical of superintendents of his day, Hartwell began his career as superintendent of a smaller school district (Petoskey, Michigan, 1910–1915). He then progressed to a larger community (Sault Ste. Marie, Michigan, 1915–1916), where he created the first separate junior high school in Michigan's Upper Peninsula and laid the cornerstone for the community's new high school. While in Sault Ste. Marie, he adopted a business model of operation that emphasized efficiency and standardization. He pledged to a relatively homogeneous community that his efficiency plans would assure greater returns for their tax investments in education. At that time, Hartwell promised that standardized, scientifically managed schools could assure every eighth-grade graduate the skills necessary to read intelligently, write legibly, compute accurately, spell correctly, and speak grammatically.[16] When he left Michigan for St. Paul, however, his policies calling for efficiency and standardization had undercut the professional prerogatives that teachers in that city had fought for and won.

The first act that antagonized the St. Paul Grade Teachers' Federation was Hartwell's meeting with school principals to put an end to what he called teachers' "soldiering (loafing) on the job."[17] Accompanied by Commissioner Wunderlich, Hartwell visited a school to try to confirm his suspicions of teacher dawdling. Finding no evidence to substantiate his contentions, he insisted on formulating policies to increase supervision over teachers. To this end, he standardized penmanship instruction by adopting the exclusive use of the Palmer method. Teachers objected to this

---

[14]*Minutes of the Grade Teachers' Federation,* October 7, 1915–October 30, 1916, St. Paul Federation of Teachers Collection (hereafter Teachers' Collection), Box 1, Series 1, Walter P. Reuther Archives of Labor and Urban Affairs (hereafter WPRA), Wayne State University, Detroit, Mich.

[15]David B. Tyack, "Pilgrim's Progress: Toward a Social History of the School Superintendency, 1860–1960," *History of Education Quarterly* 16 (Fall 1976): 257–300; and David B. Tyack and Elisabeth Hansot, *Managers of Virtue: Public School Leadership in America, 1820–1980* (New York: Basic Books, 1982).

[16]"Development of Good Citizens through Organization Based on Business Principles Is First Aim of the Sault School System." *The Evening News* (Sault Ste. Marie), 20 December 1915, 1.

[17]"Two Stormy Years," p. 1, Teachers' Collection, Box 1, Series 1 (WPRA).

new policy, claiming that this standardization created hardships on low-income parents. It required them to purchase Palmer buttons, paper, manuals, pens, and diplomas for their children.[18] From the superintendent's perspective, standardization served as a mechanism to monitor instruction in the classroom closely and to screen applicants more efficiently for teaching positions. Hartwell required the recertification in the Palmer method of currently employed teachers, and threatened to fire those who did not meet the Palmer standard.[19] To monitor instruction, he hired, over more teacher protests, supervisors of penmanship, art, and music. He required teachers to submit weekly drills to their new superiors as evidence of teacher adherence to his mandates. At this time, superintendents across the nation justified adding a supervisory tier to school departments on the grounds that many teachers were inadequately trained to teach special subjects.

Members of the Grade Teachers' Federation reacted to this intrusion upon their professional sphere by engaging in activities to frustrate the work of the supervisors. Teachers voiced their strong disapproval in verse published in their organization's journal:

> Once upon a midnight dreary, while I pondered weak and weary,
> Over many a curious letter, Palmer drills just by the score;
> While I nodded, nearly napping, suddenly I heard a tapping,
> As of someone gently rapping, rapping at my study door—
> "Supervisor!" then I muttered, "Just another little bore,
> First just one and then some more. . . ."[20]

Teacher objections to the requirement of the Palmer concept and pedagogy did not impress the new superintendent. In fact, he took steps to stifle the Federation by mounting a public campaign against it, circumventing the powers of the Board of Teachers' advisory group and then appointing his own textbook committee to recommend book adoptions. The Federation accused Hartwell of duplicity, charging that his textbook committee adopted only textbooks from companies responsible for his recruitment to St. Paul.[21]

The Federation teachers viewed Hartwell's assault upon their domain as an attempt to relegate women to non-administrative matters, while subordinating them further in the educational hierarchy. They complained that for the most part, the early education of the nation's youth was placed in the hands of women; yet, the decisions of what to teach and how to teach young people continued to rest in the hands of men.[22] In her presidential speech to the Grade Teachers' Federation, Flora Smalley told the teachers:

> The struggle for democracy in the schools is nation-wide; the struggle is not ended yet and will not be until the happy day when the teacher has the right to make the course of study which she uses, to choose the textbooks with which she works, and to elect to office the people under whom and with whom she administers the school.[23]

[18]"Palmer Penmanship," *St. Paul Herald*, 19 August 1918, Teachers' Collection, Scrapbook, vol. 4 (WTRA).

[19]Ibid., 19 August.

[20]"A Ghost Story," *The Bulletin of the St. Paul Grade Teachers' Federation* 6 (February 1918); 2. Teachers' Collection, Box 1, Series 1 (WPRA)

[21]"Two stormy Years," op. cit., p. 2.

[22]"Woman's Century," *The Bulletin of the St. Paul Grade Teachers' Federation* 6 (February 1918): 4–6 (WPRA).

[23]Flora Smalley, "The President's Report," (1918), Teacher's Collection, Box 1, Series 1 (WPRA).

Smalley's address mustered the teachers to action against the superintendent. Prior to the 1920 ratification of the 19th amendment to the U.S. Constitution, women in Minnesota had been enfranchised, albeit only in educational matters. St. Paul's city charter, however, denied them this right. This disfranchisement exacerbated all the more the teachers' sense of deprivation and galvanized them into action. They therefore called for solidarity, which was in their view the mechanism through which males had controlled the world.[24]

Perhaps no administrative policy rankled the city's teachers more than did Hartwell's plan to implement a merit pay system. In 1908, the Federation had successfully averted a merit plan through an expose of the corrupt alliances between the then superintendent and the American Book Company. In the interest of the book company, merit pay had become a weapon to force teacher-run textbook adoption committees to recommend only those books published by companies favorable to the superintendent.[25] Teacher apprehensions resurfaced in 1917, when the Federation demanded higher salaries to keep pace with the cost of living.[26] Hartwell agreed in a statement to the press that teachers could not live on the present $500.00 starting salary. Not only was this amount insufficient to pay for insurance, recreation, professional development, and savings, he claimed, but St. Paul was at a disadvantage in the recruitment of good teachers since it could not compete with salaries offered in other cities.[27] Hartwell's commitment to salary increases, however, was conditional. He and the commissioner of education insisted that all increases must be linked to merit. The superintendent believed that a merit system was the best way to weed out teachers whom he deemed to be "inefficient." He proposed to draw upon a $25,000 fund that the city council had appropriated. In addition to using recommendations from principals and assistant superintendents for merit pay, Hartwell would rely upon those from the music, art, and penmanship supervisors he had appointed and whom some teachers and principals had ignored. The maximum salary for grade school teachers would be increased from $1,000 to $1,200.[28] Wunderlich endosed the merit plan, contending that the bonuses would ensure efficient and superior teaching. He also spoke out against teachers who were frustrating the plan's implementation, declaring: "Much duress and intimidation has [sic] been exercised by certain teacher-politicians to frighten teachers from expressing themselves on this matter. . . . I believe in running the schools in the interest of the children and not to the advantage of teacher-politicans."[29]

Already assigned by reason of gender to lower paying jobs, members of the Federation rejected the merit system for a host of reasons. They argued that the plan would set up an autocratic supervisory system in what should be the most democratic institution in the country—the schools. The plan would also create further subservience on the part of teachers. Federation teachers viewed merit pay as a weapon against certain teachers and a "cloak for disciplinary measures." They argued further that the supervisors would not have sufficient time to visit 600 classrooms in 200 days

[24]"The Women-Group," *The Bulletin of the St. Paul Grade Teachers' Federation* 6 (February 1918); 11–13 (WPRA).

[25]To prohibit further textbook profiteering, in 1911 the Minnesota state lawmakers legislated against these alliances between school personnel and book companies (*General Laws of Minnesota for 1911,* Chapter 43, Sec. 1–11, p. 61); Mayor Daniel W. Lawler, "An Open Letter to the People of St. Paul." 11 April, 1910, and "Getting from Under," *St. Paul Herald,* 6 July 1918, Teachers' Collection, Box 1, Series 1 (WPRA).

[26]Letter from the Salary Committee of the Grade Teachers' Federation to E.C. Hartwell, 2 August 1917, Teachers' Collection, Scrapbook, vol. 2 (WPRA).

[27]"Teacher Can't Live on St. Paul Salary," *St. Paul Daily News,* 19 October 1917, Teachers' Collection, Scrapbook, vol. 1 (WPRA).

[28]"$25,000 Bonus Plan Laid Out by Wunderlich," *St. Paul Pioneer Press,* 14 October 1917, Ibid.

of school.[30] Responding to the teachers' objections, Hartwell dismissed them simply as the typical argument against merit and denounced as costly the Federation's proposal for across-the-board salary increases. He then took his case to the business community. He addressed one civic group, stating that teacher salaries were low, but that St. Paul lacked an incentive for superior service:

> "There are teachers in St. Paul who have never taught a successful day in their lives, but who have been on the payroll for 25 years. . . . You would not run your business that way, yet you would not discharge all who do not come up to high standards—certainly you would not reward them."[31]

As the Superintendent's position became more uncompromising, the sparring between him and the Federation intensified. The group questioned the purpose of the merit plan, asking:

> Is it for the benefit of favorite teachers or for the benefit of the schools? There is nothing in the plan outlined by the commissioner which guarantees that it shall be effective for the end for which it is ostensibly designed— the strengthening of the teaching corps.[32]

As if the relationship between Hartwell and the teachers had not been strained enough, Commissioner Wunderlich issued a public declaration against the teachers, charging:

> The issue which has loomed large in St. Paul school affairs is the question of whether the school is to be run in a business-like way by the officials whom the people select and in the interest of the children, or whether it is to be dominated by a small group sometimes characterized by the people interested in good schools as "the educational I. W. W.s". . . . Sinister influences from outside the faculty and from outside the city have united to promote dissension in our teaching staff. . . . The time has come to put a stop to all of this.[33]

The battle over merit pay for teachers rose to such a fevered pitch that it polarized the city. On the one hand, there were those who supported the administration's position on the issues of merit. Columbia University professor George D. Strayer, who had only recently completed a survey of the St. Paul school district for a fee of $20,000,[34] supported the administration's claim that merit pay rewarded superior teaching. He contended that "to oppose a plan by which the competent are to be rewarded would be nothing short of a confession of incompetence."[35] He went on to charge: "Any teacher who would take a stand against a system based on her own individual worth is a coward who is conscious of her inability to earn an increase, and is

[29] "Bonus System for Teachers Adopted by Wunderlich," *St. Paul Dispatch,* 8 October 1917, Ibid. At this time, merit pay was not an isolated concern. For example, Superintendent Frank Spaulding grappled with this issue and spoke in similar terms when he described his efforts to implement merit pay plans during his various superintendencies. See Frank E. Spaulding, *School Superintendency in Action in Five Cities* (Rindge, N.H.: Richard R. Smith Publisher, 1955), 331.

[30] "Teachers Oppose Merit Pay Plan." *St. Paul Daily News,* 18 October 1917, Teachers', Collection, Scrapbook, vol. 1 (WPRA).

[31] "Raise Teachers' Pay on Merit Plan, Hartwell Advises," *St. Paul Pioneer Press,* 20 October 1917, Ibid.

[32] "The So-Called Merit System," Pamphlet, Teachers' Collection, Box 1, Series 1, 25 October 1917 (WPRA).

[33] "Grade Teachers' Federation under Wunderlich Ban," *St. Paul Daily News,* 28 October 1917, Teachers' Collection, Scrapbook, vol. 1 (WPRA).

[34] "Organized Labor Opposes Wunderlich's Merit Plan," *Minnesota Union Advocate,* 23 November 1917, Teachers' Collection, Scrapbook, vol. 2 (WPRA).

[35] "Give Best Pay in Good Teachers," *St. Paul Daily News,* 29 October 1917, Teachers' Collection, Scrapbook, vol. 1 (WPRA).

trying to cover the fact by loud protest." Strayer then recommended that teachers opposing the merit system be fired.[36]

Others who sided with the administration included some grade school principals. They did so on the basis of their belief in "law and authority."[37] Some teachers, loyal to the administration, condemned their coworkers' protest against merit pay as insubordination, and spoke in glowing terms of Hartwell's accomplishments in making the teachers work harder while lowering class sizes. Citizen groups also entered the fracas. Twenty-two civic clubs representing 3,000 mothers voted 18–4 in favor of the merit plan. Speaking before the Citizen Committee for Better Schools, Hartwell denied that the merit plan divided teachers into superior and inferior groups. However, he did not deny that it caused disharmony, but, as he quipped, "St. Paul was never signally conspicuous for harmony in its school system."[38]

On the other hand, opponents of the plan cited John Dewey's position that merit plans befog the issues and mislead the public, while creating fear and dissension among teachers.[39] The Housewives League and the Trades and Labor Assembly likewise opposed the concept. Organized labor equated the merit plan to the "speed-up" system being applied in some non-union factories.[40]

Because of public discord over the issue, the superintendent and the teachers compromised on a plan to raise only those teachers' salaries that were at the lower end of the scale until more funds were available. Commissioner Wunderlich eventually agreed to the compromise.[41] In effect, the teachers had "won the battle over merit pay but lost the war over control of educational affairs to the developing administrative hierarchies and their rating systems."[42]

Throughout this controversy, Hartwell raised the issue of teacher loyalty to his administration. He revived the old St. Paul Teachers' Association as a strictly "professional" organization. Claiming to be apolitical, this teacher organization aligned with the conservative National Education Association and was devoted to the administration. One effect of reviving this group was to isolate the more militant members of the Federation. Hartwell claimed that the newly resurrected organization would "promote better harmony in the future" and "curtail inherited strife."[43] He used this occasion to castigate the Federation publicly:

> "Teachers' organizations are a powerful influence, either for good or for harm in any school system. Most cities with organizations have a close and sympathetic cooperation between teachers and the superintendent. . . . Much of the bitterness and hostility of former years remains in our midst today. Hail to an organization in St. Paul that will work with the administration for harmonious and efficient operation of our schools."[44]

[36]"Strayer Lauds Merit System for Teachers," *St. Paul Dispatch*, 29 October 1917, Ibid.

[37]"Principals Favor Better Pay Plan," *St. Paul Daily News*, 30 October 1917, Ibid.

[38]"Citizens to Delay Merit Plan Move," *St. Paul Pioneer Press*, 6 October 1917, Ibid.

[39]"Labor to Oppose Wunderlich Plan," *St. Paul Pioneer Press*, 30 October 1917, Ibid.

[40]"Organized Labor Opposes Wunderlich's Merit Plan," op. cit.

[41]"The President's Report to the Grade Teachers' Federation," 1918, Teachers' Collection, Box 1, Series 1 (WPRA), "Teachers' Bonus Plan Abandoned," *St. Paul Daily News*, 8 January 1918; "Way Found to Pay Teacher Bonuses," *St. Paul Daily News*, 31 January 1918, Teachers' Collection, Scrapbook, vol. 2 (WPRA).

[42]Wayne Urban, *Why Teachers Organized* (Detroit: Wayne State University Press, 1982), 158.

[43]"Hartwell Praises Teacher Union," *St. Paul Dispatch*, 14 November 1917, Teachers' Collection, Scrapbook, vol. 2 (WPRA).

[44]"Hartwell Praises New Teacher Body," *St. Paul Dispatch,* 1 December 1917, Ibid.

[45]"Loyalty," *"The Bulletin of the St. Paul Grade Teachers' Federation* 5 (June 1917): 6 (WPRA).

Federation members viewed the formation of Hartwell's organization as a "company union," designed to undermine teachers' attempts to democratize their workplace. They worried that it was a device to draw the line between teachers who differed on merit policy, and those whom he had co-opted to his side. The Federation was reluctant to pledge blind allegiance, arguing that teachers had a right as trained educators to an independent opinion on a matter of school policy without the question of loyalty being involved. They had made known their position on loyalty in June of that year when they wrote: "Loyalty to the state should be part of our being; . . . loyalty to the individual is another matter. That must come from slow growth. Its ground work must be truth. It is the outcome of mutual trust on the part of the recipient as well as the giver."[45]

Instead of promoting harmony within the teaching force, the new teacher organization pitted teacher against teacher and principal against principal. Hostilities over issues of supervision, penmanship, merit, and teacher loyalty came to a dramatic climax in June, 1918. The commissioner followed Hartwell's recommendations to fire 14 grade school principals and teachers whom the superintendent has asked to resign but who had refused to do so. Some of these principals and teachers had been officers of the Grade Teachers' Federation. Evoking a 1911 law regulating teacher behavior, he ousted the educators on charges of "inefficiency" and an attitude of indifference toward the penmanship supervisor.[46] He then transferred 150 teachers to other schools where they would be disciplined by principals more loyal to his administration. In response to this assault upon the teaching force, on June 18, 1918, the Grade Teachers' Federation affiliated with the American Federation of Teachers (Local #28) and its umbrella organization, the American Federation of Labor. On this occasion, the Vice President of the National Women's Trade Union League told 125 grade school teachers: "A clinging vine isn't the fashionable kind of woman these war days. Too many women are working, and there is no chivalry in industry; therefore women must organize to protect themselves as well as they can."[47]

News of Hartwell's ironfisted administration had attracted the attention of the newly appointed school board in Buffalo, New York. This group was headed by the general manager of the Standard Oil Company and comprised four men and one woman drawn exclusively from a small group of business and professional leaders. Making a career move, Hartwell resigned his post in St. Paul and accepted a six-year contract in Buffalo for $7,000 (a $2,000 salary increase that St. Paul could not match). The *St. Paul Pioneer Press* and the *Dispatch,* owned by the brother of an executive officer in the pro-administration teacher association, placed most of the blame for Hartwell's departure on the militant teachers' rebellion against authority and discipline.[48] The St. Paul Association, a group of business and professional men, likewise lamented his departure and pledged its support to the commissioner of education in bringing about loyalty in the schools.[49]

Although Wunderlich had supported Hartwell's decisions in the teachers' dismissals, he later reconsidered amid a growing public outcry. In one instance, 140 citizens petitioned him to reinstate one of the ousted principals.[50] Numerous letters supporting the dismissed educators also appeared in the Independent and the

[46]At this time, when "efficiency" was applied to the teaching corps, it meant obedience to the duty constituted authorities. Laws relating to the terms under which teachers could be fired are found in *General Laws of Minnesota for 1911,* Chapter 96, Section 1–3, pp. 114–115. Letters of dismissal are on file in the Teachers' Collection, Box 1, Series 1 (WPRA).

[47]"125 Teachers Form Labor Union Here," *St. Paul Dispatch,* 20 June 1918, Teachers' Collection, Scrapbook, vol. 3 (WPRA).

[48]"School Situation in St. Paul for Frank Consideration," *St. Paul Dispatch,* 9 July 1918, Ibid.

[49]"S.P.A. Action to End Strife in Schools Being Planned," *St. Paul Dispatch,* 10 July 1918, Ibid.

[50]"Wunderlich Ignores Plea for Teachers," *St. Paul Pioneer Press,* 21 June 1918, Ibid.

Democratic local newspapers. In addition, many of the educators sought legal advice in their struggle against the administration. One attorney for the teachers argued that the dismissals were based on school politics and not on legitimate grounds: "The idea was that the Superintendent should crack the whip and that the teachers, like a lot of trained animals, should immediately jump through the hoop no matter where they landed or what they would run against."[51] Following Hartwell's departure, the commissioner relented. At a meeting of the commissioner, Hartwell's successor (S.O. Hartwell, no relation), and two supervisors, Mayor L. C. Hodgson received assurances that all teachers and principals, except two, would be reinstated. In the case of the exceptions, the committee agreed that age would likely hamper their ability to perform the required duties of their office.[52]

Strife Awaits Hartwell in Buffalo

Much like St. Paul, Buffalo had a history of partisan conflict over school affairs. Under a decentralized system of control, teachers had been able to influence the educational decision-making process. Individual school employees might approach the city council or school officials for redress of grievances, including matters pertaining to salary increases, leaves of absence, appointments, and promotions.[53] Typically, when the school board received a committee of teachers who presented recommendations for salary increases, the chair requested the delegation to make further recommendations on matters pertaining to curriculum reforms, including subjects that, in their judgment, should be dropped and "any other economies that in their judgment might be profitably practiced by the Board."[54]

School Superintendent Henry P. Emerson regarded as "evil and abhorrent" Buffalo's democratic localism, with its potential for political patronage. He opposed this system that vested in the hands of a popularly elected superintendent absolute powers of appointment: "The temptation to make appointments with reference to gaining political strength was greater than most men could resist." He regarded "inefficient teachers, the appointment of political favorites in the school department,. . . and the generally poor standards and low tone in the schools" as consequences of their being used for political purposes.[55] In addition to these concerns plaguing the school department, the issue of depressed salaries had emerged in 1910. When teachers demanded pay raises, school managers in Buffalo, like those in St. Paul, responded with a merit plan. At that time, the Teachers' Educational League (TEL), an organization of women elementary school teachers, challenged the merit idea. In their negotiations with city officials over salaries, the teachers garnered the support of the United Trades and Labor Council, affiliated with the American Federation of Labor.[56] In its support of the teachers, labor claimed that a merit system "places in the hands of the superintendent the power to promote his favorites and to punish those who may not meet his favor."[57] Teacher organizer Margaret Haley came to Buffalo to caution teachers against merit pay. She characterized it as a secret means to crush their organization,

[51]"Kyle Demands Council Probe of School System," *St. Paul Dispatch,* 17 July 1918, Ibid.

[52]Letter from Mayor L.C. Hodgson to Flora Smalley, President of the Grade Teachers' Federation, 27 August 1918, Teachers' Collection, Box 1, Series 1 (WPRA).

[53]"Teachers Make Spirited Statement in Refutation of Emerson's Arguments," *Buffalo Daily Courier,* 7 September 1910, 7.

[54]*Buffalo School Board Minutes* (22 May 1916): 74, Buffalo School Board Office, City Hall, Buffalo, N.Y. (hereafter Buffalo School Board Office).

[55]Henry P. Emerson, op cit., pp. 15–17.

[56]"School Teachers Have Now Become Labor Unionists," *Buffalo Daily Courier,* 11 June 1910, 7.

[57]"Teachers See Favoritism Plan in Merit System," *Buffalo Daily Courier,* 5 September 1910.

which had been agitating for salary increases, tenure, and professional status. She demanded: ". . . strike [it] down as a viper."[58]

The city of Buffalo was not exactly like St. Paul. It had a more diverse economy than did St. Paul, and it was the nation's third largest steel-producing center. Buffalo provided immeasurable employment opportunities in manufacturing for the diverse, uneducated, and unskilled immigrant populations flooding the city. Conservative English and German Protestant Republicans dominated most of Buffalo's institutions; however, the citizens were largely Democratic working-class Catholics, with a high concentration of Polish, Italian, and Irish residents.

Prior to Hartwell's arrival in Buffalo, a school bureaucracy was already in place with a school board, a board of examiners, a superintendent, and department directors and supervisors. In 1916, the state commissioner of education had announced new ordinances that placed the authority over teaching in the hands of the superintendent and financial affairs under the control of the school board.[59] Hartwell's predecessor had created a Bureau of Efficiency and Research that enlarged the school bureaucracy to include "an efficiency department for increasing the efficiency of the teaching service."[60] To raise the level of school efficiency in Buffalo, Hartwell acted as he had done in his former posts. He devised and implemented an educational blueprint, replete with efficiency rhetoric. His plans for Buffalo involved a 12-point model based on business principles promising to make the city's "educational plants pay dividends worthy of its investments."[61] To Hartwell, an efficiently operated school system was analogous to a large business corporation in which the people were the stockholders and the pupils were the products.[62] He held that if administrators applied business principles to progressive educational ideas, schools would then become efficient, stable organizations, more profitable to the students and the community. His ideas translated into a departmentalized educational bureaucracy with a team of associate superintendents, supervisors, and clerks. Under the direct supervision of his office, they were to administer all affairs pertaining to school personnel and account for all school supplies and facilities, minimizing waste in time and resources. The new superintendent implemented the classic example of what Callahan described as the cult of efficiency.

In cities across the nation, scientific management had become the linchpin of superintendents' administrative reforms. Typically, to promote their management schemes, superintendents made wide use of the media in the same manner in which muckrakers had attacked public schools in their popular journals. As these school managers accomplished their goals, they then wrote glowing, self-serving bulletins and annual reports to school boards and to the public, hailing the outcomes of their scientific managerial styles.[63] Like other superintendents and professors of educational administration at this time, Hartwell was aware that winning "enlightened, intelligent, and sympathetic public sentiment" was key to the success of his programs. He called for the depoliticization of schools through the application of the scientific

[58]"Thousands Hear Margaret Haley Inspire Teachers in Fight for Their Rights," *Buffalo Daily Courier*, 14 October 1910, 6.

[59]"Dr. Emerson Given Charge of Teaching," *Buffalo Evening News*, 27 January 1916, 15.

[60]*Buffalo School Board Minutes* (23 October 1916): 207, Buffalo School Board Office.

[61]Development of Good Citizens," op cit.

[62]E.C. Hartwell, "Financing the Public Schools," *Addresses and Proceedings of the 56th Annual Meeting of the NEA* 56 (1918): 605–607; E.C. Hartwell, "A Final Word," *The School Magazine* 1 (June 1919): 3–5.

[63]As an example of how another powerful superintendent made effective use of the media, Frank Spaulding attributed his successful 25 years of service (1895–1920) in five cities to his leadership style and his ability to win popular approval through the press. He recounted that by assuming full responsibility for the management of school programs and the efficient administration of the teaching staff, every one of his thousands of recommendations to the board had passed with few or no objections. Spaulding, op. cit., pp. 580–585; 690.

[64]E.C. Hartwell, "A New School Slogan," *The School Magazine* 1 (October 1918): 5.

method to educational decision making: "No community must expect efficient expenditure of money or a high quality of instruction until it is ready to eliminate absolutely from the management of its school petty politics, intrigue, and favoritism."[64] During his first months in office, he rallied school personnel and declared that every individual connected with the school system must become "a missionary in the cause of efficient schools."[65] Hartwell presented his plans for reforming the schools in the local newspapers and school bulletins.[66] To win public confidence in his "Buffalo Plan," he also gave speeches to civic groups. He prescribed the uniform use of standardized textbooks and mental and achievement testing,[67] daily attendance accounting, and an annual survey showing school continuation among recent elementary school graduates. He then required principals to publish these school outcomes in their commencement programs. He believed that surveys and annual reports from principals to his office, following a standardized format, allowed him to measure and to compare school outcomes in a scientific manner. He could then hold his principals and teachers accountable for attaining educational goals formulated by his administrative staff. Hartwell also instituted major reforms in teacher recruitment, training, supervision, and promotions. One program involved experienced teachers supervising teacher trainees. Following a top-down model, middle managers outlined courses of study for elementary schools and devised self-administered assessment scales "to assist the elementary school teacher in analyzing her efficiency."[68]

Another facet of his reforms in Buffalo was entailed in an $8.125 million proposal for 12 experimental, intermediate schools,[69] an idea that attracted national attention at NEA conferences[70] and won the support of the school board. Between 1918 and 1930, he built 27 elementary schools. He also created an Opportunity School for pupils with special educational needs, continuation schools for boys and girls who worked and attended school part-time, and an Adjustment School for boys posing disciplinary problems.[71] Hartwell viewed his educational program as a response to expanding school enrollment and a means to fit youth to their future roles as productive and "good citizens." To these ends, he expanded the vocational schools and occupational training in domestic science and manual arts.

Buffalo had a large and diverse population whose demands heavily taxed school resources. Responding to local and national imperatives to socialize the children of recent immigrants as expediently as possible, Hartwell noted:

> We are trying to assimilate into our democracy millions of foreigners, recruited from the slums of European cities, because as one large employer recently expressed it: "They had weak heads and strong backs." To combat these influences and to assist in producing an American citizenry with ideals

---

[65]Ibid., p. 4–5.

[66]Ernest C. Hartwell, "The Buffalo Plan," *The School Magazine* 1 (April 1919): 11–23.

[67]William B. Thomas, "Mental Testing and Tracking for the Social Adjustment of an Urban Underclass, 1920–1930," *Journal of Education* 168 (1986): 9–30.

[68]"Self-analysis for the Principal," *The School Magazine* 2 (November 1919): 3–4.

[69]"Intermediate Schools," *Buffalo School Board Minutes*, 11 December 1918, pp. 1105–1113, Buffalo School Board Office. See also Mary E. Finn, "'Democratic Reform,' Progressivism, and the Junior High Controversy in Buffalo (1918–1923)," *Urban Education* 18 (1984): 477–489.

[70]William B. Ittner, "The Intermediate School," *Addresses and Proceedings of the 57th Annual Meeting of the NEA,* vol. 57 (Chicago: University of Chicago Press, 1919), 328–331.

[71]William B. Thomas, "Schooling as a Political Instrument of Social Control: School Response to Black Migrant Youth in Buffalo, New York, 1917–1940," *Teachers College Record* 86 (Summer 1985): 579–592.

[72]E.C. Hartwell, Miscellaneous Speeches, Folder 2, Hartwell Collection, Buffalo and Eric County Historical Society, Buffalo, N.Y.

of respect for law, property, the rights of others, honesty, and decency, there is just one tax-supported institution—the public school.[72]

Accordingly, the superintendent imposed character training programs, which, in those schools where foreign pupils were concentrated, stressed traits such as obedience to and respect for authority, self-control, and patriotism.[73] In contrast to his earlier promises for universal literacy in the small-town midwest, Hartwell had significantly revised his educational plans to emphasize character training. He told a group of citizens in Buffalo that the test to be applied to teaching was whether children "had learned the lessons of character essential to sound citizenship" and that "the purpose of the public school has been to develop social usefulness and civic righteousness."[74] With all of these and other accomplishments in the first three years of the Hartwell superintendency in Buffalo, his admirers characterized his progress as "remarkable efficiency without extravagance of expenditure, work accomplished with a minimum of funds."[75]

In addition to administering schools in this second largest city in New York State, Hartwell was an active and powerful member of NEA. In 1918, he was chosen president of its Department of Superintendence. Upton Sinclair, in his muckraking exposé of the schools, characterized the department as "the great clearinghouse, where the bosses exchange experiences and perfect the technique of holding down the salaries of the teachers, breaking up their organizations, eliminating the rebels from the system, and making fast the hold of the gang."[76] Superintendents and professors of educational administration acting through the department comprised an "old boy" network. During their annual conferences, they exchanged ideas relevant to the solution of school problems and then returned to their respective communities to implement the innovations. One of their reforms, in particular, would mitigate the political vulnerability of their group's members by elevating the superintendent's post from that of "vote-chasing politician" to one of managerial professional.[77]

Hartwell echoed the anti-politics sentiments of his fellow superintendents in his 1920 address to the Department of Superintendence, when he endorsed attempts to remove the superintendency from the direct control of the NEA. He advocated an administrative organization removed from partisan politics, devoted to the problems of administrative policy, and composed exclusively of and led by career superintendents. Hartwell took the opportunity to assail the notion of a superintendent without power

---

[73]Buffalo Department of Education, *Character Training* (June 20, 1924); William B. Thomas, "A Quantitative Study of Differentiated School Knowledge Transmission in Buffalo, 1918–1931," *Journal of Negro Education* 57 (1988): 66–80; and William B. Thomas and Kevin J. Moran, "Social Stratification of School Knowledge in Character Training Programs of South Buffalo, New York, 1918–1932," *Journal of Education* 170 (1988): 77–94.

[74]E.C. Hartwell, Miscellaneous speeches and addresses, Folder No. 1, Dr. E.C. Hartwell Collection, Buffalo and Eric County Historical Society, Buffalo, N.Y. The superintendent's penchant for character building was not far afield from the prescription outlined by University of Illinois Professor of Education William C. Bagley, who wrote: "The pressing need, especially in the elementary school, is for strong teachers who can rigidly 'hew to the line' in all initial stages of habit building. Even scholarship could be sacrificed, if necessary, in attaining this end." In William C. Bagley, *Classroom Management: Its Principles and Technique* (New York: Macmillian, 1907), 18.

[75]"What Others Think of Progress in the Buffalo Schools," *The School Magazine* 3 (March 1921): 177.

[76]Upton Sinclair, *The Goslings: A Study of the American Schools* (Pasadena, Calif.: AMS Press, 1924), 227.

[77]In 1915 Ellwood P. Cubberly, a leading professor of education at Stanford University, predicted the emergence of a class of administrative professionals. At that time, he posited: "The recent attempts to survey and measure school systems and to determine the efficiency of instruction along scientific lines had alike served to develop a scientific method for attacking administrative problems . . .; all of these developments point unmistakably in the direction of the evolution of a profession of school administrators as distinct from the work of teaching on the one hand and politics on the other." Ellwood P. Cubberly, "Organization of Public Education," *Journal of Proceedings and Addresses of the 53rd Annual Meeting of NEA* 15–17 (August 1915), 93; also see Tyack and Hansot, op cit., pp. 121–128.

[78]Ernest C. Hartwell, "The Greatest Need in Public Education Today—Wise and Responsible Leadership," Speech presented to the Department of Superintendence of the NEA (4–10 July 1920), E.C. Hartwell Collection, File #M77-6, Buffalo and Eric County Historical Society, Buffalo, N.Y.

as being a contradiction analogous to a superintendent without responsibility. In his address, he also repudiated attacks on his own superintendency by his teachers in Buffalo. He stated that teachers had characterized him and fellow superintendents as "creatures of the capitalistic class . . . servile tools of the powers that prey." At the same time, he ridiculed the idea of teacher councils, groups of teachers whose function was to advise the school administration, which had been effectively implemented in Chicago under its female superintendent Ella Flagg Young: "I am unwilling to concede that there is not anything new in the idea of the teacher participating in the administration of schools . . . but, advice is one thing and responsibility is another." He added:

> I could wish nothing worse for the misguided dupe of all this shallow talk about "administrative despotism" than to have him or her obliged to teach for a year in a school where every teacher should be a "self-directing agent" and where no decision on any matter might be made until the local soviet could be assembled. . . . Teachers fare best under strong leadership. . . . In private business or public service, the power of decision is of necessity entrusted to administrative authority. . . . Order without law is impossible and law without executive authority is ineffective.[78]

Hartwell and superintendents like him were gaining some measure of the public trust necessary to attain the much sought after professionalization of their group. State education agencies, local and state legislatures, schools of education, and the courts supported these chief educational advisers to school boards and elevated them to the level of "expert."[79] Superintendents, who had advocated expanding school bureaucracies, came to enjoy publicly sanctioned autonomy in their control over large educational complexes. In effect, the office of the superintendent rose from "the status of a walking delegate of the school committee, . . . from a job which was passed around among retired ministers, briefless lawyers, and patientless doctors to a profession which required as much ability as was necessary for the management of a great business or industrial enterprise."[80] No longer "the shuttlecocks of politics," superintendents monopolized important decision-making powers. Their new powers were legitimized by a body of knowledge linked to the science of management and by public esteem for their graduate degrees in educational administration.

Ellwood Cubberly, a staunch advocate of professional status for school superintendents, praised this movement which would change "school administration from guesswork to scientific accuracy." He believed that application of the new science of education would have a far-reaching effect upon educational decision making, substituting for a system of favoritism one of objective measures of outcomes. A key aspect of the new school administration would be to secure the superintendent from

[79]In his address to the University Convocation of the State of New York, Hartwell lauded decisions to grant legal authority to school executives. Meanwhile, 1919 state laws codified school board powers to set educational costs, which the city council was then required to fund. State courts recognized this enlarging power that removed school executives "from political influence," while the state commissioner opposed any legislation to reverse this trend. He claimed that such attempts to do so would "practically nullify the control of school authorities over city schools [and] politicize the teaching service." See "Board of Education Has Exclusive Power over Teachers' Salaries," *Buffalo Express*, 18 November 1920; Frank B. Gilbert, "To Boards of Education and Superintendents of Schools of Cities," *The School Magazine* 3 (March 1921): 180. See also Magall Sarfatti Larson, *The Rise of the Professional: A Sociological Analysis* (Los Angeles: University of California Press, 1977), 186.

[80]Edwin C. Broome, "Strengthening the Superintendency," *Addresses and Proceedings of the NEA*, vol. 58 (Chicago; University of Chicago, 1920), 506.

[81]Ellwood P. Cubberly, *Public School Administration* (Cambridge, Mass.: Riverside Press, 1916), 325–329.

[82]Tyack and Hansot, op cit., p. 187.

removal at the hands of his political enemies.[81] The efficiency movement changed school supervision from the level of an occupation to that of a profession. Many superintendents were now planners and thinkers who designed programs for burgeoning urban school systems and then evaluated the outcomes as a guide for their subsequent decision making. A state-sanctioned, multi-level school structure shielded them from public interference in the management of school affairs. This status shift allowed superintendents to preempt a long-standing practice of teachers' negotiating with local and state politicians for decisions favorable to their group. Consequently, school personnel in Buffalo were no longer permitted to approach the city council or the board directly to redress grievances or to make salary adjustments. All requests were now to be routed through the chain of command.

Superintendents' continued press for a status befitting their position in the educational hierarchy exacerbated conflicts between their group and elementary school teachers, who sought professional autonomy from their administrative control. Tyack and Hansot contend that superintendents responded to these challenges of teachers for professional status by "giving them symbolic gains, . . . [while] promoting an ideology of professionalism that blurred actual lines of cleavage between . . . the administrators and teachers."[82] How, then, did Hartwell undercut the freedoms that teachers in Buffalo had previously enjoyed?

Vanquishing His Adversaries

Prior to Hartwell's arrival in Buffalo, the founder of the TEL, Mary A. O'Connor, had won the faith of nearly all of the grade school teachers and a number of citizen and labor groups. Her leadership in helping to obtain sabbaticals and salary increases prompted 97% of the teachers to petition the board to appoint her to an assistant superintendent's post, in the hope that she would succeed retiring Superintendent Emerson.[83] Emerson and the board, however, rejected the nomination and recruited Hartwell from St. Paul instead. Shortly after Hartwell's arrival, he immediately courted teacher militants to win their loyalty. Hartwell elevated O'Connor to principal on October 29, 1918. He assigned her to a small, dilapidated elementary school located in the Polish school district. Her appointment served two purposes. On the one hand, Hartwell appeased the elementary school teachers who had favored her appointment to an administrative post. On the other hand, her appointment might mitigate the teachers' loyalty to her by including her on his administrative team.[84] The appointment made O'Connor vulnerable to the discretionary powers of the superintendent, since newly ratified tenure laws protected teachers and not principals.

Initial courtesies between Hartwell and the TEL were short-lived.[85] Relations became abrasive following a series of confrontations over pay raises and TEL's right to lobby in the state legislature.[86] To discredit the teacher organization, Hartwell authorized school department heads and administrative supporters to mount a campaign against members of TEL. They did so in a manner similar to that in which pro-administration groups in St. Paul had acted. First, an elementary school principal united all of Buffalo's teaching and administrative associations into a confederation,

[83]*Buffalo School Board Minutes* (6 May 1918): 911; (13 May 1918): 926; (20 May 18): Buffalo 938; (27 May 1918): 944; (12 August 1918); 1031; Bufallo School Board Office.

[84]O'Connor would later testify under oath that Hartwell had offered her a $500.00 salary increase if she would use her influence with the grade school teachers in his interest. "Right to End of Teacher's Trial, Board Excludes All Evidence of Justification," *Buffalo Daily Courier,* 14 December 1920, 7.

[85]Teachers Honor Supt. Hartwell at Annual Feast," *Buffalo Daily Courier,* 15 December 1918, 75.

[86]William B. Thomas and Kevin J. Moran, "Women Teacher Militance in the Workplace, 1910–1922," *Paedagogica Historica* 27 (1991): 35–53.

comprised of six local educational organizations. However, the newly formed Buffalo Federation of Educational Associations excluded the TEL from its membership. The expressed aim of this organization was "to be loyal to the highest ideals of education and to those who are striving to bring about these ideals."[87] Second, leaders of the new federation printed, delivered by taxi to all schools throughout the city, and then distributed to every teacher in the school district a pamphlet criticizing TEL and its leader. Third, administrators attempted to intimidate members of the League. One principal met with the teachers of his school and demanded they resign from TEL or be forced out of their jobs. His action resulted in the resignation of four teachers from TEL.[88] A TEL member reported that on another occasion, Hartwell shook his finger at her and pounded his fist on his desk, threatening "I'm after you and I'll be after you as long as I am in Buffalo . . . . Get out of that organization."[89]

Responding to these attacks, TEL members drafted a resolution and sent it to the school board. They accused Hartwell of complicity in an attempt to undermine their organization. Taking their case to the public, TEL submitted its resolution to the press and also alleged financial improprieties on the part of Hartwell. These charges prompted the city's finance commissioner to authorize an embarrassing schoolwide audit, which later exonerated the superintendent. TEL then published a manifesto criticizing school supervisors as incompetent. In it, they characterized administrative supporters as "spineless trucklers" and attacked Hartwell's pet vocational education program as a "fad . . . creating a sordid sort of materialism."[90] Members of TEL had personal ties to labor, as many of the founding officers were of working-class origins.[91] Sympathetic with the plight of working-class children, who would most likely be tracked into dead-end vocational programs, Mary O'Connor cautioned: "With the growing power of the laboring classes, a thing for which in itself we rejoice, . . . the infantile vocationalism is more likely to condemn the boy or girl to narrow industrial and economic slavery."[92] Centralization of school affairs was anathema to O'Connor and her supporters. She was motivated in large measure by her concerns that more centralization over schools in New York State would remove teachers further from the center of decision making and assign them to what she characterized as positions of "day laborers." As teacher-superintendent relations lapsed into acrimony, O'Connor became resolute in her desire to win status for her group. She described the moral goal of TEL as one designed "to emancipate the teachers from the petty despotism of bosses and time servers, to inspirit them, to stiffen their backbone so they can stand upright and speak out their minds unafraid."[93] From her perspective, teacher advancement necessitated first and foremost the decentralization of managerial control over teachers.

The *American School Board Journal* portrayed Hartwell as "fearless and straightforward in dealing with school board members and teachers."[94] Indeed, its description was well-founded. As teachers in St. Paul had discovered, Hartwell had little patience with what he described as "unfit, incompetent" teachers who disobeyed his authority. He told the members of the Department of Superintendence, "They must be elimi-

---

[87]*Buffalo Foundation Directory*, p. 43. Buffalo and Erie County Historical Society, Buffalo, N.Y.

[88]Teachers' League Tenders Ovation to Miss O'Connor," *Buffalo Daily Courier*, 27 March 1920, 13.

[89]*Buffalo School Board Minutes* (11 October 1920): 1703–1704, Buffalo School Board Office.

[90]Teacher Educational League: Its History and Its Aims, June 1920," in *Buffalo School Board Minutes* (11 October 1920): 1694, Ibid.

[91]See William B. Thomas and Kevin J. Moran, "Centralization and Ethnic Coalition Formation in Buffalo, New York, 1918–1922," *Journal of Social History* 23 (1989): 139–140.

[92]Teachers' Educational League," op cit., p. 1694.

[93]Ibid., p. 1689.

[94]Mr. Hartwell Comes to Buffalo." *American School Board Journal* 57 (1918): 45.

nated." In his counterpoint to TEL's manifesto criticizing his administration, he charged that low salaries were due to the large numbers of "untrained, incompetent, and unfit" teachers. He observed how infinitely easier it was to get into the teaching profession than into a good labor union of plumbers, cigar makers, painters, or bricklayers. Yet, as he noted, teacher organizations were fighting for higher salaries and pressing for automatic increases and life tenure, with no recognition of merit or safeguarding the profession on its own account.[95]

In 1920, Hartwell carried out his threat to eliminate certain teachers when he presented two recommendations at a school board meeting. The first was that "no permanent contract as principal be given to Miss Mary A. O'Connor and that her probationary contract as principal be discontinued forthwith." He charged that she was an unsatisfactory principal and that she did not cooperate harmoniously with the other members of the department. The board unanimously accepted Hartwell's recommendation. The superintendent next called for the immediate suspensions of the remaining seven officers of TEL. Responding to charges of "inefficiency" similar to those that Hartwell had levied against the St. Paul teachers, the board unanimously approved the removal of the other seven TEL officers, pending a hearing.[96] The superintendent then dispatched a messenger to O'Connor's school, delivering notice of her immediate dismissal. Since one school board member was also business manager of the *Buffalo Commercial*, it was no coincidence that a reporter from the paper appeared at O'Connor's school to record her immediate reactions at the time she received notification of her dismissal. The following day, Hartwell appointed a less experienced principal to replace O'Connor at a salary $300.00 greater than that paid to her.[97]

News that the board had dismissed the popular O'Connor and suspended the teachers generated an immediate and profound sensation. Many teachers expressed indignation over the capricious act by the superintendent.[98] As a measure of support for their colleagues, some teachers threatened to strike, an action that O'Connor and the other TEL officers discouraged, since they believed the children would then suffer. Ethnic communities of Poles, Italians, and Irish rallied immediately behind the teachers. They condemned emphatically administrative actions as "undemocratic" and then demanded O'Connor's reinstatement.[99] Speaking against the 1916 legislation that had increased the power of superintendents over teachers, one citizen protested: "I say the bill must go with Hartwell and with the rest of the silk-stocking gang."[100] In a similar vein, a TEL officer depicted the school board as "members of the 'pink tea' society class, who have no use for teachers because they belong to the *working class*" (emphasis hers).[101] Likewise, the American Federation of Teachers dubbed Hartwell "ultra-conservative," "labor-hater," and "an opponent to any organization of teachers which he could not control."[102] To fortify themselves against the school managers, the demoralized TEL invited Charles R. Stillman, president of the Chicago-based American Federation of Teachers, to speak to their group. After his speech, 1,200 elementary school teachers joined the ranks of unionizing teachers

[95]E.C. Hartwell, "The Greatest Need . . . Leadership," op cit.

[96]*Buffalo School Board Minutes* (11 October 1920): 1685–1686, Buffalo School Board Office.

[97]"Court Action Protects Public School Teachers," *Buffalo Daily Courier*, 23 November 1920, 12.

[98]"School Board Fires Miss O'Connor without Hearing," *Buffalo Daily Courier*, 12 October 1920, 1, 5.

[99]Thomas and Moran, "Centralization and Ethnic Coalition," op cit.

[100]"Demand Dismissal of Hartwell, Removal of School Board Members," *Buffalo Daily Courier* 11 November 1920, 12.

[101]Letter from Mary E. Hinman to Josephine Colby, AFT Field Secretary, 17 August 1921, TEL Collection, Box 20, Series 6 (WPRA).

[102]"Administrative Change in Buffalo," *The American Teacher* 20 (September/October 1935): 20.

throughout the country. Twelve members of TEL signed a charter on October 28, 1920, establishing Local #182 of the AFT in Buffalo.

O'Connor sued the school district in State Supreme Court to regain her post. The Court ruled that the board was within its legal rights to dismiss her as a principal, without a hearing or formal charges; however, she should automatically revert to her position as a teacher, from which she could not be removed without a hearing. When O'Connor called Hartwell asking to be reassigned as principal or teacher in the district, the superintendent, ignoring her rights as a tenured teacher, replied that her connection with the school district had been severed.[103] The board defended publicly its position in suspending the other teachers, charging them with "misbehavior" and "inefficient and incompetent service."[104] Amid protests from champions of TEL, the board president asked the public to consider, "Shall the Board run the department of education, with the aid of the superintendent as executive officer, or shall a coterie of teachers?"[105] Impervious to other public outcries for seating space at the open hearings, another board member shouted, "I don't give a damn about the crowd."[106] Meanwhile, to muster support from fellow Rotarians, Hartwell exclaimed: "Salaries of teachers have been nearly doubled in the past three years, and if there are teachers who cannot cooperate with their superiors, every good citizen should support the action of the Board in dismissing them whether the number be six or six hundred."[107]

On February 14, 1921, the board sustained Hartwell's charges but decided to fire only two of the six TEL officers. In the case of the remaining teachers, the board first concluded that they were guilty and should be dismissed but, in a lenient gesture, granted reinstatement provided that the teachers write letters of apology by March 1, 1921, and agree to cooperate with school authorities. Three of the four teachers capitulated.[108]

As in St. Paul, the school administration in Buffalo appealed to the public's xenophobic attitudes by portraying their own motives as a campaign to "save the country from the socialistic wave." When they had successfully destroyed the teachers' union, they applauded their victory, pointing to "an alarming situation between schoolroom workers and those in administrative charge, designed to undermine the discipline of the schools. The soviet spirit had entered . . . . [but] the disturbers have been squelched and peace has been restored."[109] Reflecting on this severe crisis, Hartwell jokingly confided to his friend back in Michigan: "I respectfully desire to inform you that my scalp is still occupying its normal home and not decorating the wigwam of the enemy."[110]

In effect, a powerful superintendent had taken on a national labor movement and crushed it in body if not in spirit. Union affiliation with the AFT had offered the ousted teachers some ray of hope, but was of little benefit to them in their bids for reinstatement. The superintendent's actions against the teachers in Buffalo had intimidated them. Their dues-paying membership dwindled from a reported 403 in 1920 to

[103]At its 1920 convention, the American Federation of Teachers perceived the Buffalo case as illustrative of attempts by "autocratic boards of education to weaken some of the few tenure provisions now in existence." Convention proceedings, Reports 1–18, 1920, p. 2 (WPRA).

[104]*Buffalo School Board Minutes* (14 February 1921): 1854–1860, Buffalo School Board Office.

[105]"Heads of Teachers' League Let Out by School Board," *Buffalo News*, 11 October 1920, 1.

[106]"Damning the Public," *Buffalo Daily Courier*, 3 December 1920, 6.

[107]E.C. Hartwell, "Speech to Rotary." Personal papers of E.C. Hartwell, Folder No. 1, Buffalo and Eric County Historical Society.

[108]Edwards D. Emerson to the Board of Education, *Buffalo School Board Minutes* (5 March 1921): 1938, Buffalo School Board Office.

[109]E.C. Hartwell, "Hartwell's Vision for Buffalo," *Journal of Education* 88 (1918): 629; and William G. Bruce and William C. Bruce, "The Buffalo School War," *The American School Board Journal* 62 (1921): 60.

[110]Letter from Ernest C. Hartwell to Paul Stetson, 6 January 1921, Hartwell Collection, M77-6. Buffalo and Erie County Historical Society, Buffalo, N.Y.

eight by 1926.[111] Buffalo teacher and union activist Margaret McGee recalled the early accomplishments and demise of TEL in her address to the AFT: "It had a splendid record. It got us the tenure law we are now living under. It got substantial salary raises. That union was smashed in about two months and wiped right out, and is now in pieces and has never been heard of since."[112]

Conclusion

Developments in St. Paul and Buffalo symbolize how conflicts may emerge during periods of reform as one group, seeking to enlarge its powers, enfeebles another group in its simultaneous bid for control. During his superintendencies, Hartwell fired militant teachers and principals when they challenged his authority to implement widely prescribed school reforms that proved most beneficial to his reputation. Adopting a business model of management and applying new state laws to his advantage, this superintendent enlarged the school bureaucracy to increase his supervision over teachers and to isolate himself further from political adversaries. As big businesses had done, he capitalized upon the xenophobic attitudes of the public by linking his opponents to Bolshevism.

Far from being weak and vulnerable, Hartwell found strong support among likeminded, influential career superintendents and conservative business and professional groups. They, along with the Republican press, favored vesting all power in the hands of an oligarchy of school executives. Conversely, the Democratic press, some immigrant groups, working-class citizens, and their labor organizations were suspicious of big business interests and centralization and, therefore, championed the teachers' causes. In their perceptions, the industrial model and the undemocratic ways of its application to schools were characteristic of their workplaces and reminiscent of the repressive regimes that many had left in Europe. To these anti-administration groups, teacher decision making in school affairs meant democratic reform that might benefit pupils.

Hartwell and fellow superintendents claimed the need to depoliticize school governance. He called for a united front between his office and the teachers. Yet, he and many of his administrative cohorts throughout the country seized control of the schools and those who worked in them. Early 20th-century efficiency schemes by superintendents could not have been realized without teacher acquiescence to their superiors.[113] To assure teacher compliance in this power relationship, Hartwell first adopted the efficiency language, applied it to his work to gain more power and status, and then modified it to relegate teachers to subordinate roles in the bureaucracy.[114] He manipulated recently ratified laws on teacher efficiency (meaning obedience) to dismiss educators who resisted his authority.

In the context of a period of reforms, punctuated by managerial efforts to dominate the work force, school superintendents constituted a powerful network of executives. Strengthened by their powerful school boards, they could ignore with impunity diverse interest groups, including teachers and working-class citizens demanding greater participation in the educational decision-making process. Superintendents did not sympathize with the teachers' sense of deprivation when they removed the teachers from the center of power. Following a business model that made few allowances for

[111]Letter from F.C. Hanson, Secretary-Treasurer, AFT, to Owen J. Kavanaugh, 26 October 1926. TEL Collection, Box 20, Series 6 (WPRA).

[112]Margaret McGee to AFT, AFT Local 377, Box 18, Series 12 (WPRA).

[113]David B. Tyack, *The One Best System. A History of American Urban Education* (Cambridge, Mass.: Harvard University Press, 1974), 268.

[114]William B. Thomas and Kevin J. Moran, "The Politicization of Efficiency Concepts in the Progressive Period, 1918–1922," *Journal of Urban History* 17 (1991): 390–409.

democracy in decision-making procedures, superintendents called for stricter disciplinary measures against those who challenged their authority. Superintendents, like corporate executives, were drawn from "old stock, first citizens" and sought stability, normalcy, and control of the social order. These two groups shared the narrow world view that only highly successful and enlightened citizens were best suited to control modern and efficiently operated public schools. Protected by reforms that averted challenges to their authority, superintendents succeeded in perpetuating a structure that sustained their interests and those of their business associates. Using a multitiered bureaucracy to buttress their powers, they were also able to ward off political threats that had mitigated the power of the superintendency in former times.

The events that occurred in early 20th-century St. Paul and Buffalo have important implications for contemporary superintendents. The issues and the actors remain much the same as they were in the period of progressive reforms, when superintendents gained and exercised greater control over school affairs. Some things have changed, however. Special interest groups are now more deeply entrenched. No longer part of a compliant public, they constitute a stronger potential opposition to administrative authority. They are capable of mobilizing to remove school authorities, replacing them with officials more attuned to their particular concerns. In addition, today there is greater state and federal intrusion in local school affairs. These new developments require that the role of the superintendent shift from that of manager to one that highlights an active leadership style. Scholars, such as Crowson, Glass, and Morris, caution that in the current context of grassroots reform movements, the large city superintendency is in deep distress. And in addition to these reform efforts, superintendents across the U.S. consistently face financial, personnel, instructional, and facilities problems. Yet, as these problems become more acute, central office personnel tend to become even more remote, cloaking themselves in the school bureaucracy. If, as Crowson and Morris contend, reducing risk is a key interest of superintendents, then top-down management styles must yield to a bottom-up way of addressing the political and environmental context of the superintendency.[115] Participative and team management is the new coinage of the day in school administration. The new superintendent, whether place- or career-bound, will need to be schooled in effective leadership and community relations that forge consensus rather than divisions. It is certain that teachers and community groups will continue their bids for greater participation in the educational decision-making process. As they become more vocal and more persistent, the top-down leadership model of management common among urban school executives in the progressive period, we predict, will prove increasingly anachronistic.

[115]Robert Crowson and Van Cleve Morris, "The Superintendency and School Leadership," *Advances in Educational Administration* 2(1991): 206; Robert L. Crowson and Thomas E. Glass, "The Changing Role of the Local School District Superintendent in the United States," paper presented at the annual meeting of the American Educational Research Association, Chicago, 6 April 1991.

William B. Thomas is an associate professor in the School of Education at the University of Pittsburgh. 5M38 Forbes Quadrangle, Pittsburgh, PA 15260. He specializes in the history and sociology of education.

Kevin J. Moran is a graduate research associate in the School of Education at the University of Pittsburgh.

The authors gratefully acknowledge the generous financial support of the Henry J. Kaiser Family Foundation at the Walter P. Reuther Archives of Labor and Urban Affairs, Wayne State University; the Ford and the Spencer Foundations; and the University of Pittsburgh's School of Education for portions of this research. We also thank the following colleagues for their helpful comments: Richard J. Altenbaugh, Northern Illinois University; H. Warren Button, SUNY at Buffalo; Robert L. Crowson, University of Illinois at Chicago; and Nicholas DeFigio, Nick J. Staresinic, and Sean Hughes, University of Pittsburgh. We also thank the staff of the Reuther Archives for their assistance.

Appendix B
Data Collection Strategies

❖ **Work Products**

    Selected-response Strategies

      Tests, Examinations, and Inventories

      Rating Strategies

      Ranking Strategies

    Constructed-response Strategies

      Tests, Examinations, and Questionnaires

      Document or Artifact Analyses

❖ **Interviews and Observations**

    Closed-ended Response Interviews

    Standardized Open-ended Interviews

    Interview Guides

    Informal Conversations

    Observation Notes

Data collection strategies can be classified in several ways, depending on the purpose of classification. To simplify this discussion, strategies are categorized here as work products and interviews or observations. Within each category, strategies can be positioned roughly along a continuum, based on the degree of structure within the questions or prompts (see Table B.1)

For example, investigators who use selected-response tests or closed-ended response interviews usually present participants with carefully worded questions in a distinct order. On the other hand, researchers who analyze artifacts or hold informal conversational interviews are not bound by these constraints because they gather data using open-ended techniques.

Quantitative researchers generally prefer the techniques listed in the upper half of Table B.1 because their use permits collection of numerical data, which can be analyzed mathematically. Use of these techniques also permits researchers to remain detached from participants.

The lower half of the table lists strategies generally preferred by qualitative researchers who use them to gather largely verbal data. Open-ended interview techniques, in particular, allow researchers to gather data as participant-observers in research settings.

❖ Work Products

Work products usually fit into one of two major classifications, either as selected-response or constructed-response strategies. As the terms suggest, participants either choose a response from several that are offered or they construct answers to questions asked by the researchers.

Selected-Response Strategies

Selected-response strategies encompass those in which participants choose responses from the options available on tests, examinations, inventories, rating scales, or ranking procedures. Responses are frequently machine-scored and provide numerical data.

TABLE B.1

Classification of Data Collection Strategies

Work Products	Interviews and Observations
More structure	
Selected-response strategies	Closed-ended response interviews
Tests, examinations, inventories	
Rating strategies	
Ranking strategies	
Constructed-response strategies	Standardized open-ended interviews
Tests, examinations, questionnaires	Interview guides
Document or artifact analyses	Observation notes
	Informal conversations
Less structure	

Tests, Examinations, and Inventories

Selected-response tests and examinations use multiple choice, true or false, and matching formats. Data from instruments that use these formats are considered as having interval level measurement.

Included among tests and examinations are actual pencil-and-paper instruments, as well as those in which data are recorded on computer-scorable sheets or processed by computers. Tests can be researcher-made or commercially published, standardized or nonstandardized, norm-referenced or criterion-referenced, and so on. Tests are typically used for the evaluation of cognitive outcomes, including both lower- and higher-level thinking skills.

Usual test procedures assess students' abilities to answer "well-structured, unconditional, knowledge-lean tasks" (Gitomer, 1993, p. 245). The following multiple-choice item exemplifies these characteristics; it requires respondents to abstract meaning from the context to decide which pair of words best completes the statement.

10. The Berlin Wall, constructed between East and West Berlin after World War II, formed a visible political _____; still, on either side of it, people thought and celebrated and dreamed as _____ nation.
    A) barrier..a conquered
    B) boundary..a divided
    C) statement..a separated
    D) partition..a democratic
    E) demarcation..one
       (Carris, 1996, p. 414)

A multiple-choice format is typical in many commercially published tests, including achievement batteries, the *Graduate Record Examination (GRE)*, and the *Scholastic Aptitude Test (SAT)*. Such test data are common in quantitative educational research projects. As an example, Holmes and Keffer (1995) used outdated sections of the *SAT* to measure the effects of a computerized method of teaching Latin and Greek root words (see A4, the end of the Treatment subsection).

Inventories consist of topics or sentences to which research participants respond. Konopak, Readence, and Wilson (1994) used two inventories, each consisting of 15 belief statements about how individuals read and how reading develops. Each inventory consists of five statements representing each of three theoretical orientations. In this project, participants were asked to select five statements from the 15 that best represented their views. Researchers then classified the participants according to the orientation revealed by the preponderance of the views expressed in their selected statements (see A5). These data, therefore, are of nominal measurement level; they were used for classification purposes.

Rating Strategies

These strategies also use pencil and paper or computer-scored instruments to measure either the frequency of behaviors or events or to register agreement or disagreement with statements. Likert and semantic differential formats are used frequently to generate data in surveys or opinnionaires. These data are usually considered to be of interval level measurement.

Likert Format   Instruments using this format often contain four to seven points to represent the response continuum. For example, Wentzel (1997) collects data about the *frequencies* with which middle school students perceive their teachers' support for learning. Students respond to this statement, "My teacher really cares about me" by marking their responses on a scale of 1 to 5, where 1 meant "never" and 5 meant "always" (for more information, see the explanation in the Measures section of A7).

Semantic Differential Format   Instruments using this format contain pairs of bipolar adjectives carefully chosen to provide the data needed by researchers (Osgood, Suci, & Tannenbaum, 1957). With respect to a particular word or topic, respondents mark one of the seven spaces between these adjectives that describes their attitude, interest, or knowledge about the word or topic.

In a scale measuring views of educational research, for example, the adjective pair, *interesting-boring*, provides an evaluation of the stimulus word and is written as follows:

Educational research

interesting:___ : ___ : ___ : ___ : ___ : ___ : ___ : boring

A respondent's mark placed nearest to "interesting" shows a more positive response, scored as 7, than a mark placed nearest "boring," scored as 1. A semantic differential scale usually contains at least twelve adjective pairs for each word. Responses to all the adjective pairs are scored for each word or topic, summed, and averaged as interval level measurement.

As an example, Zevin (1995) used a semantic differential scale to study adolescents' views of national identities of the United States, Canada, and Russia. Students responded to twenty adjective pairs that tapped their perceptions of geographic and political knowledge and their views of the political system, social structure, and economic well-being of the countries. Geographic knowledge was obtained through use of adjective pairs, such as *near* or *far* and *large* or *small;* social structure used adjective pairs, such as *few rights* or *many rights* and *unjust* or *just.* Students marked responses to the same 20 adjective pairs separately for each of the three countries.

Ranking Strategies

Researchers sometimes ask respondents to rank order statements according to their beliefs and values about the statement content. The number of statements to be ranked is usually less than 10 because respondents must keep in mind the meanings for all the statements while they decide on their order. Data from ranking procedures are considered to be of ordinal level measurement.

As an illustration, Olmsted and Lockhard (1995) studied how parents and teachers in the United States, Hong Kong, Nigeria, and Poland ranked in order of importance a list of eight skills categories for 4-year-olds to learn in preschool. The skills to be ranked were language, motor or physical, pre-academic, self-assessment, self-expression, and self-sufficiency skills, as well as social skills with adults and with children.

As either a parent or a teacher, each participant was given a list of the eight skills categories and asked to select and number as 1, 2, and 3 the three most important skills for preschool-aged children to learn. Then they selected and numbered as 6, 7, and 8 the three least important skills. Finally, the participants determined which of the two remaining skills was more important and numbered it as 4; the other skill was numbered as 5. With these data, the researchers could compare most- and least-important rankings among teachers (and parents) in the four surveys.

Constructed-response Strategies

In **constructed-response strategies,** participants must craft their own responses to questions in tests, examinations, or questionnaires. Scoring these responses, of course, requires personnel trained to evaluate responses. In other procedures, researchers study artifacts and documents to obtain data about phenomena of interest. Data from some constructed-response procedures are numerical, but others are verbal descriptions.

Tests, Examinations, and Questionnaires

Researchers sometimes ask respondents to supply their own responses to tests, examinations, or questionnaires. Constructed-responses may have few to many degrees of allowable variation. For example, Gettinger's study

(1993) used two techniques that permit only correct or incorrect responses. First, the third grade students completed weekly tests in which they spelled words they had studied during the week. Then, at the end of each 6-week period, the students wrote stories from dictation that incorporated spelling words studied over that period. In both cases, students were expected to spell accurately the words and sentences as dictated. Each word spelled correctly counted as a datum and the aggregated data were considered to be of interval level measurement (see A1).

Justified multiple-choice questions permit greater variation in answers than do correct or incorrect designations. In addition to selecting an option to the question, respondents must write a brief statement that explains why they chose that particular answer. To score these answers fairly, evaluators use specific holistic scoring guides (Comfort, 1994).

Open-ended questions allow respondents additional variability in their answers. Typically, respondents must think about and solve a problem before attempting to communicate an answer in a paragraph, a picture, or an explanation of data in a chart or graph. Scoring these answers also requires specific holistic scoring rubrics. Figure B.1 provides a sample open-ended question and an answer from a statewide science assessment.

Similarly, open-ended questions may be used in questionnaires. To illustrate, teacher and administrator participants in a statewide study were asked these questions: "What do you use to guide your mathematics curriculum? What is your most pressing need for resources for teaching mathematics?" (Sowell et al., 1995). Open questions, such as these, elicit variable answers phrased in many different ways.

Document or Artifact Analyses

Documents, which include all forms of written testimony, comprise several categories (Gottschalk, 1969). Contemporary records include official guidelines or handbooks, letters of appointment to job positions, minutes of school board meetings, and similar records. Confidential reports, such as journals or diaries and personal letters, may also be useful as data sources if they contain information closely associated with the topic. Public reports include news reports and dispatches intended for the world-at-large. Also included in this category are government publications and official or authorized histories of schools,

---

Open-ended Question: Neesha put snails and plants together in a jar of pond water. She sealed the jar and placed it in a spot where it would receive some light. After several days, Neesha checked the jar and found that the snails and plants were alive and healthy. Explain why the snails and plants stayed alive.

Student Answer: The plants gave off oxygen, and the snails breathed out carbon dioxide. The pond water gave them all the water they needed, and the light that they were under gave them the light they needed to stay healthy along with the other materials.

FIGURE B.1   Example of an open-ended question and answer

From "Authentic Assessment: A Systemic Approach in California" by K. B. Comfort, 1994, *Science and Children, 32*(3), p. 42. Reprinted with permission from NSTA Science Teachers Association, 1840 Wilson Blvd, Arlington, VA 22201-3000.

organizations, or events. Editorials, essays, speeches, pamphlets, and public opinion polls provide valuable data to researchers interested in opinions about particular topics. Literary works, including fiction, poetry, and songs, can provide researchers with understandings about the milieu surrounding a particular topic. Folklore, place names, and proverbs serve similar purposes (Gottschalk, 1969).

Artifacts include objects such as coins, maps, pictures, photographs, and diagrams. For the study of some phenomena or variables, artifacts convey figural or representational information that extends verbal data obtained from other sources. Therefore, the study of artifacts can offer different perspectives on topics. For example, in the historical study on the secondary curricula in the first half of the nineteenth century, Tolley (1996) displays a drawing from which she observed the probable social class of students (see A8 for the context).

To analyze artifacts or documents, researchers frame open-ended questions, then seek their answers through study of the documents and artifacts. Quite clearly, researchers inject their own values and interests into the analysis, because the answers they find are the products of their perceptions and sensitivities. The data are usually verbal descriptions.

❖ Interviews and Observations

Patton (1990) describes four types of interviews: closed-ended response, standardized open-ended, interview guide, and informal conversational interviews. As their names suggest, these interviews differ in degrees of structure from those with carefully worded and sequenced questions to others with open-ended, spontaneous questions. Closed-ended response interviews can generate numerical data, but the other types typically provide verbal data.

Closed-ended Response Interviews

During closed-ended response interviews, the interviewer asks carefully worded questions of the interviewee(s) in a prescribed form and order to assure consistency in response opportunities. The questions contain defined response options from which interviewees select a response (Patton, 1990).

Many questions in the Phi Delta Kappa/Gallup poll of the public's attitudes toward the public schools (Rose & Gallup, 1999) use the closed-ended response technique. The two questions listed in Figure B.2 were asked about the public schools versus other systems. Both of these questions provide only two answer options, but other questions in this poll offer five. Clearly, answers to these questions are quantifiable, and usually are expressed as nominal level measures.

Standardized Open-ended Interviews

Standardized open-ended interviews use questions whose exact wording and sequence are determined in advance. The questions use a completely open-ended format, and interviewers ask the same basic questions in the same

In order to improve public education in America, some people think the focus should be on reforming the existing school system. Others believe the focus should be on finding an alternative to the existing public school system. Which approach do you think is preferable—reforming the existing public school system or finding an alternative to the existing public school system?

Which one of these two plans would you prefer—improving and strengthening the existing public schools or providing vouchers for parents to use in selecting and paying for private and/or church-related schools?

FIGURE B.2   Example of questions in closed-ended interview
From "The 31st Annual Phi Delta Kappa/Gallup Poll of the Public's Attitudes Toward the Public Schools" by L. C. Rose, & A. M. Gallup, 1999, *Phi Delta Kappan*, 81, p. 44. Reprinted by permission.

order to all respondents. A few PDK/Gallup poll questions use this format, as exemplified by this question: "If there was one thing you could change to improve the public schools in your community, what would that be?" (Rose & Gallup, 1999, p. 48).

Standardized open-ended interviews are advantageous in that all interviewees answer the same questions, and data are complete on the topics in the interview. Researchers can compare responses from all participants. The disadvantages to these interviews are the limitations on the interviewer's flexibility to suit the questions to the respondents or the circumstances. Because the questions are standardized, the answers elicited may lack relevance or naturalness for particular research situations (Patton, 1990).

Interview Guides

Interview guides identify the topics and issues, in outline form, to be covered in advance of the interviews. The interviewer decides the wording and sequence of the questions during the interview itself.

An outline helps to assure comprehensiveness in the data gathered and also makes collection somewhat systematic. Interviewers are able to anticipate and close logical gaps in the data. Even with the outline, however, interviewers may inadvertently omit important topics or ask questions in ways that elicit basically different interviewee responses. Attempts to compare responses may be problematic.

Larson and Parker (1996) used two data collection strategies, an interview schedule and a think-aloud task, to collect teachers' perceptions of classroom discussion. Their descriptions suggest that these strategies fit the description of interview guide approaches (see A2). Using the interview schedule or guide permits researchers to ask teacher participants to describe their mental image of "classroom discussion," distinguish between an ideal discussion and an imperfect one, and provide rationales for discussions. In the think-aloud task, participants elaborated on their perceptions of discussion by focusing on the vignettes portraying various types of classroom discussion.

Oral histories use interview guides to record information told to and recorded by interviewers. The information includes both the interviewer's questions and the respondent's answers. For example, Cripps (1995) interviewed filmmaker Ken Burns about the history and significance of documentary film. The transcript of this interview constitutes an oral history, which was published in its entirety. Oral histories may also be recorded within the text of other documents or as parts of collections.

Informal Conversations

In this format, interviewers ask questions that come naturally from the context. These questions are not planned in advance and are not sequenced. This interview form capitalizes on saliency and relevance and allows interviewers to obtain information about observations in the setting.

However, this form of interview is typically less systematic and comprehensive than other forms unless the naturally occurring questions "happen" to be the same. Interviewers usually obtain different information from respondents because they ask different questions. Data analysis and organization can be difficult because of the lack of standardization (Patton, 1990).

Observation Notes

Researchers take notes about what they see and hear within research settings. These notes serve as detailed descriptions of the interactions among people, events, or behaviors observed in particular locations. Notes are arranged chronologically with the date, time, and place on each entry. Insofar as possible, notes are exact recordings of words, phrases, and actions. Concrete details and verbatim comments are included. Nonverbal communication, tone, and gestures are also included. As this description suggests, researchers must be skilled in making observations and in recording them in ways that permit analyses.

Summary

This appendix describes data collection techniques classified as work products or interviews-observations. Strategies that use carefully structured and ordered questions usually result in the numerical data preferred by quantitative researchers. Techniques that provide these data include selected-response tests, examinations, inventories, rating procedures, ranking procedures, some constructed-response tests-examinations-questionnaires, as well as closed-ended response interviews.

On the other hand, strategies with open-ended questions typically result in verbal descriptive data usually used by qualitative researchers. Techniques suited to provide these data include some constructed-response tests, examinations, questionnaires, document or artifact analyses, standardized open-ended interviews, interviews using guides or informal conversations, and observations.

Appendix C
Inferential Statistical Tests

❖ **Parametric Data Analysis Procedures**

    Analysis of Variance (ANOVA) and Related Tests

        One-way ANOVA and Post Hoc Tests

        Planned Comparisons

        t-tests

        Two-way (factorial) ANOVA

        Analysis of covariance (ANCOVA)

        Multivariate Analysis of Variance (MANOVA)

    Correlation and Regression Analyses

        Simple Correlation

        Multiple Regression

        Discriminant Analysis

        Canonical Correlation

        Factor Analysis

        Path Analysis

❖ **Nonparametric Data Analysis Procedures**

    Kruskal-Wallis and Friedman ANOVA Tests

    Mann-Whitney *U* Test

    Chi-square Test

Inferential statistical tests are typically categorized as parametric or nonparametric tests, depending largely on the measurement level of data, the normality of the data distribution(s), and the number of participants. Parametric tests require interval or ratio data, but nonparametric tests can be used with data at all measurement levels, including nominal and ordinal levels. Parametric tests require sample sizes of approximately 30 or more participants, but nonparametric tests can be used with smaller sample sizes. Researchers typically prefer to use parametric tests because they are more powerful for detecting statistical significance than are nonparametric tests.

This appendix briefly describes several popular inferential tests. The intent of these descriptions is to help you make sense of the inferential statistical tests mentioned in the results sections of research reports.

❖ Parametric Data Analysis Procedures

Analysis of variance (ANOVA) and several related tests represent one major approach to testing hypotheses about means or differences among means for groups. As its name says, ANOVA estimates the sources of variance in project data.

Analysis of Variance (ANOVA) and Related Tests

Analysis of variance (ANOVA) can be a simple one-way analysis in which the effect of one independent variable on one dependent variable is examined. However, variations of ANOVA extend to projects in which the effects of more than one independent variable on one or more dependent variables are tested.

One-way ANOVA and Post Hoc Tests

The **one-way analysis of variance** test is appropriately used when several levels of treatment of an independent variable are administered to different groups to determine their effects on a single dependent variable. For example, three *methods of teaching biology* (e.g., laboratory-based, laboratory with discussion, lecture) might be researched to see if they effect change in high school students' *achievement*. Here is the proposed relationship between variables:

INDEPENDENT   DEPENDENT

Methods of teaching ———————————▶ Biology achievement

In one-way ANOVA, the null hypothesis tested is that any difference between groups on measures of the dependent variable is due to chance variation in the population, not the result of treatment. In this example these are appropriate hypotheses:

Alternative: The mean difference in achievement scores in biology of groups taught by laboratory-based, laboratory with discussion, and lecture methods is *not zero.*

Null: The mean difference in achievement scores in biology of groups taught by laboratory-based, laboratory with discussion, and lecture methods *is zero.*

The outcome of one-way analysis of variance is an *F*-ratio or *F*-value. A nonsignificant *F*-ratio indicates that the null hypothesis should be retained and any differences found should be attributed to chance or sampling fluctuations. A significant *F*-ratio, however, suggests that the differences between means (or other statistics) may be due to different levels of treatment of the independent variable.

In tests involving three or more groups, researchers should complete additional statistical tests to determine the source of variation that produces the statistically significant *F*-ratio. These **post hoc multiple comparison tests** pinpoint which effects are responsible for the *F*-value. In the biology project, for example, a significant *F*-ratio indicates that a statistically significant difference is present in the situation.

However, until researchers complete post hoc comparisons, they do not know which of the three instructional methods contributes to the significant *F*. Some commonly used post hoc tests are Scheffe, Tukey Honestly Significant Difference (H.S.D.), Duncan, and Newman-Keuls. Researchers use these tests to locate statistically significant differences between pairs of means in this case.

Planned Comparisons

The most powerful comparison tests available, **planned comparisons** are used in projects in which researchers have carefully thought through their research questions so that they can decide in advance which sets or pairs of group means will be tested. Planned comparisons permit only a limited number of comparisons to guard against the possibility of significant differences where they do not actually exist.

t-tests

A **t-test** may be used to compare a sample mean with a known population mean, a sample correlation coefficient with a known population correlation coefficient, or the means of two groups. If researchers use only two groups, either one-way ANOVA or a t-test can be used to check for significance. (The F-value from ANOVA is equal to the square of the t-test value.)

Two-way (factorial) ANOVA

Two-way analysis of variance is based on the same principles as one-way ANOVA. Used in factorial designs, this test provides analysis of the effects of two independent variables on a dependent variable as well as the possible interaction between the independent variables on the dependent variable. For example, reconsider the biology project. Suppose the researchers want to know if the methods of teaching have the same or different effects according to gender of the participants. Is there any difference in achievement that can be attributed to the combination of method of teaching with gender? If yes, the method of teaching is said to interact with gender.

Here is the proposed relationship among variables. Remember there are three levels of treatment for methods of teaching and two levels of gender, but these are not included in this diagram:

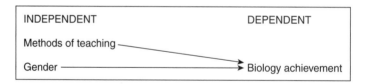

In two-way, or factorial analysis of variance, three null hypotheses must be tested. One hypothesis is for the possible interaction of methods of teaching with gender. The remaining two hypotheses test for the possible effects of method of teaching alone on achievement and the effects of gender alone on achievement. The latter are described as main effects.

Analysis of Covariance (ANCOVA)

In some circumstances, researchers equate groups statistically in terms of an important variable, called the *covariate*. **Analysis of covariance (ANCOVA)** allows the influence of the covariate to be removed from the data. In the biology project, suppose that one group of participants is known to have stronger analytical skills than other groups of participants. By including the analytical skill scores of all students in the analysis as a covariate, researchers can statistically equate the three groups. This enables the results to be interpreted correctly by minimizing the effect of initial group differences.

Multivariate Analysis of Variance (MANOVA)

Analysis of variance can be extended to studies having more than one dependent variable through **multivariate analysis of variance (MANOVA).** This data analysis is appropriate if the biology researchers include attitudes toward biology as a second dependent variable along with achievement. Here are the proposed relationships among variables:

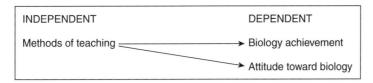

Data from the dependent variables must be analyzed simultaneously, rather than separately, because a strong correlation between achievement and attitude is possible and is detectable using MANOVA. To analyze these data separately is to run the risk of obtaining statistically significant results due to Type II error.

MANOVA can be extended to factorial designs as factorial MANOVA. This holds true when the biology researchers test the effects of methods of teaching and gender on achievement and attitudes toward biology. This situation has two independent and two dependent variables as follows:

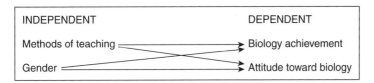

As with factorial ANOVA, the first test is for interaction effects of the independent variables on the dependent variables. Then tests are for main effects of the independent variables alone on the dependent variable. When significant *F*-ratios are obtained, follow-up tests similar to *post hoc* comparisons are used to determine the variables on which the groups differ.

This discussion of analysis of variance and related tests is summarized in Table C.1. The tests are listed according to the number of dependent variables tested, the symbols for test outcomes, and the descriptive statistics tested. Data for use in these tests must be interval or ratio.

Correlation and Regression Analyses

Simple Correlation

Direct reference to appropriate tables of critical values is the test for Pearson product moment- and Spearman rank correlation coefficients. As indicated in

TABLE C.1

Analysis of Variance and Related Tests Summary

Test Name	Symbol for Outcome	Descriptive Statistics Tested
One Dependent Variable		
Analysis of variance (ANOVA)		
One-way (simple)	F	Two or more means
Two-way (factorial)	F	Two or more means or variances and interaction
Post hoc multiple comparisons (Scheffe, Tukey, etc.)	F, Q	Means, interaction after locating significant F with ANOVA
Planned comparisons	F	Pairs of means
t-test	t	One mean, variance, or correlation with a known population parameter *or* two means, variances, or correlation coefficients
Analysis of covariance (ANCOVA)	F	Two or more means with a covariate
Two or More Dependent Variables		
Multivariate analysis of variance (MANOVA)	F	Two or more means
Factorial MANOVA	F	Two or more means in interaction

Chapter 9, if the calculated correlation coefficient meets or exceeds the critical value for the sample size, the coefficient is considered statistically significant. Contingency-, phi-, biserial-, and point-biserial correlation coefficients must be subjected to inferential tests that involve mathematical calculations.

Correlation and regression studies may involve interrelationships among several variables. Tests of hypotheses about these relationships may require multivariate data analyses such as multiple regression, discriminant analysis, canonical correlation, factor analysis, or path analysis.

Multiple Regression

These tests are used in studies with two or more predictor variables and a criterion variable. Predictors, or known variables, must be correlated with the criterion, or unknown variable, in this inferential test. In multiple regression, an equation is used that weights each predictor variable in terms of its ability to predict. The result of using this equation is a squared multiple correlation coefficient, R^2, which can have values between 0 and +1.00.

R^2 values are interpreted in the same way as squares of other correlation coefficients. If $R^2 = .47$, researchers know that about 47% of the variance in the criterion variable is accounted for by the combined predictors. However, the predictors taken singly probably have less common variance with the criterion variable. Therefore, combining the predictors gives more information about the joint variation of variables than single predictors do alone.

Multiple regression is also used as an alternative inferential test for analysis of variance. When this is the case, the posttest or dependent variable scores become the criterion variable and treatment levels and/or pretest scores become predictor variables. The outcome tells whether treatment levels are significantly related to posttest scores, as well as the magnitude of this relationship.

Discriminant Analysis

A variation of multiple regression, **discriminant analysis** is used when a number of predictors are used to classify participants into two or more groups. Groups may be high, middle, or low achievers, completers or noncompleters of programs, and so on. The participant's group membership is the criterion variable.

Canonical Correlation

This test extends multiple regression to projects having more than one criterion variable. **Canonical correlation** is applicable when the purpose of the study is to assess the strength of the overall association between a set of predictor variables and a set of criterion variables, and to determine which specific variables among both groups account for most of the relationship between the two sets.

Factor Analysis

This technique is used to identify the number and nature of broad factors underlying a cluster of correlated variables. Factors are hypothetical constructs believed to underlie psychological measures such as achievement, personality, intelligence, and aptitude. **Factor analysis** effectively reduces a large number of variables to a few factors by combining variables that are moderately or highly correlated with each other.

Path Analysis

When researchers have studied relationships among three or more variables in a correlation study, they sometimes propose a theory about causal relationships among these variables. To test this theory, they use **path analysis** to see if the hypothesized links between variables really exist. Statistical analyses yield path coefficients that show the direct effect of one variable on another variable. These coefficients can range from –1.0 to +1.0 and are interpreted like other coefficients.

❖ Nonparametric Data Analysis Procedures

Nonparametric inferential statistical tests must be used if the data are nominal or ordinal or if the distribution of data is greatly different from a normal distribution. Researchers use these tests sparingly because they are less powerful than parametric tests for detecting statistically significant results.

Kruskal-Wallis and Friedman ANOVA

Kruskal-Wallis and *Friedman analyses of variance* are the nonparametric versions of parametric ANOVA. These tests work on the same principle as ANOVA, except that ranks (ordinal data), rather than interval level data, are used. The Friedman test is selected when the measurements are repeated from the same group; the Kruskal-Wallis test is used with separate comparison groups.

Mann-Whitney *U* Test

The *Mann-Whitney U* is a nonparametric test that is roughly comparable to the parametric *t*-test. Two sets of ranks, ordinal level measures, are analyzed to see if they differ by chance or due to the influence of an independent variable.

Chi-square Tests

Chi-square (χ^2) **tests** are used to determine whether there is an association between categories. Observed frequencies of the items or events in categories are compared with expected frequencies. As is true in other inferential statistical tests, researchers find out whether the result is rare—due to something in the research setting—or if the result occurred due to chance fluctuations in sampling.

For example, suppose that State University researchers poll undergraduate students to determine if there is a relation or association between gender and preference for instructional method in Introduction to Psychology. Choices include live lectures, discussion groups, or videotaped lectures. The actual preferences stated by students constitute the observed frequencies, and the expected frequencies come from a theoretical sampling distribution for chi-square. If the stated preferences are greatly different from chance for the two genders, then researchers may say that their data show significant association between gender and method of instruction.

Chi-square tests are ideal for use with nominal and ordinal data to check on differences. However, these tests are also useful with interval and ratio data if the distribution is normal or if the sample sizes are small.

Summary

This appendix briefly describes the purposes and some main features of popular parametric and nonparametric inferential statistical tests. The information provides background to assist your understanding of tests mentioned in Results sections of research reports.

Through use of analysis of variance, researchers can decide whether the variance they introduced into the research project outweighs other sources of variance sufficiently to say that it did not occur by chance fluctuations in the sample. The many forms of analysis of variance make it a useful parametric test.

Multiple regression allows researchers to analyze data for the magnitude of correlation and to see if correlated variables can be used for prediction purposes. Multiple regression tests can also be substituted for analysis of variance. Related tests permit researchers to test complex hypotheses in correlation and prediction projects.

Nonparametric analysis of variance is possible with Kruskal-Wallis or Friedman tests. The Mann-Whitney U test provides a nonparametric version of the t-test. Chi-square tests enable researchers to determine if differences between observed and expected frequencies are real or are due to chance.

References

Ackerman, M. (1995). Mental testing and the expansion of educational opportunity. *History of Education Quarterly, 35,* 279–300.

Barzun, J., & Graff, H. F. (1992). *The modern researcher,* 5th ed. Fort Worth, TX: Harcourt Brace Jovanovich College Publishers.

Berg, B. L. (1998). *Qualitative research methods for the social sciences* (3rd ed.). Boston: Allyn & Bacon.

Brophy, J. (1998). Introduction. In J. Brophy (Ed.), *Advances in research on teaching: Expectations in the Classroom* (pp. ix–xvii). Greenwich, CT: JAI Press.

Brundage, A. (1997). Teaching research and writing to upper division history majors: Contexts, sources, rhetorical strategies. *The History Teacher, 30,* 451–459.

Buros, O. K. (Ed.). (1999). *The mental measurements yearbook* (9–14th eds.). Online.

Campbell, D. T., & Stanley, J. C. (1979). *Experimental and quasi-experimental designs for research.* Chicago: Rand McNally.

Carris, J., with Crystal, M. R. (1996). *SAT success* (5th ed.). Princeton, NJ: Peterson.

Charters, W. W., & Jones, J. (1973). On the risk of appraising non-events in program evaluation. *Educational Researcher, 2*(11), 5–7.

Chicago manual of style. (1993). Chicago: University of Chicago Press.

Cohen, J. (1988). *Statistical power analysis* (2nd ed.). Hillsdale, NJ: Erlbaum.

Comfort, K. B. (1994). Authentic assessment: A systemic approach in California. *Science and Children, 32*(2), 42–43, 65–66.

Coutts, D. (1996). Are principals computer phobic? *American Secondary Education, 24*(2), 7–13.

Cripps, T. (1995). Historical truth: An interview with Ken Burns. *American Historical Review, 100,* 741–764,

Denzin, N. K., & Lincoln, Y. S. (1994). Introduction: Entering the field of qualitative research. In N. K. Denzin & Y. S. Lincoln (Eds.), *Handbook of qualitative research* (pp. 1–17). Thousand Oaks, CA: Sage.

Educational Resources Information Center. (1999). *All about ERIC.* Washington, DC: U.S. Department of Education.

Eisenhart, M. A., & Howe, K. R. (1992). Validity in educational research. In M. D. LeCompte, W. L. Millroy, & J. Preissle (Eds.), *The handbook of qualitative research in education* (pp. 643–680). San Diego: Academic Press.

Ethical principles in the conduct of research with human participants. (1982). Washington, DC: American Psychological Association.

Ethical standards of the American Educational Research Association. (1992). *Educational Researcher, 21*(7), 23–26.

Fitzgerald, J. (1995). English-as-a-second-language learners' cognitive reading processes: A review of research in the United States. *Review of Educational Research, 65,* 145–190.

Floud, R. (1979). *An introduction to quantitative methods for historians* (2nd ed.). London: Methuen.

Freed, M. N., Ryan, J. M., & Hess, R. K. (1991). *Handbook of statistical procedures and their computer applications to education and the behavioral sciences.* New York: Macmillan.

Gates, J. T. (1989). A historical comparison of public singing by American men and women. *Journal of Research in Music Education, 37,* 32–47.

Genz, M. D. (1993). Looking through a rearview mirror. *Journal of Education for Library and Information Science, 34,* 270–274.

Gettinger, M. (1993). Effects of error correction on third graders' spelling. *Journal of Educational Research, 87,* 39–45.

Gierl, M. J., & Bisanz, J. (1995). Anxieties and attitudes related to mathematics in grades 3 and 6. *Journal of Experimental Education, 63,* 139–158.

Gitomer, D. H. (1993). Performance assessment and educational measurement. In R. E. Bennett & W. C. Ward (Eds.), *Construction versus choice in cognitive measurement* (pp. 241–263). Hillsdale, NJ: Erlbaum.

Glass, G. V., & Smith, M. L. (1979). Meta-analysis of research on class size and achievement. *Educational Evaluation and Policy Analysis, 1,* 2–16.

Gmelch, W. H., & Gates, G. (1998). The impact of personal, professional and organizational characteristics on administrator burnout. *Journal of Educational Administration, 36,* 146–159.

Gold, R. L. (1958). Roles in sociological field observations. *Social Forces, 36,* 217–223.

Gottschalk, L. (1969). *Understanding history: A primer of historical method* (2nd ed.). New York: Knopf.

Hall, G. E., & Loucks, S. (1974). A developmental model for determining whether the treatment is actually implemented. *American Educational Research Journal, 14,* 263–276.

Hartsook, H. J. (1998). Unique resources: Research in archival collections. In C. Kridel (Ed.), *Writing educational biography: Explorations in qualitative research* (pp. 127–137). New York: Garland Publishing.

Hays, W. L. (1994). *Statistics* (5th ed.). Fort Worth, TX: Harcourt Brace.

Henry, G. T. (1990). *Practical sampling.* Newbury Park, CA: Sage.

Hinkle, D. E., Wiersma, W., & Jurs, S. G. (1994). *Applied statistics for the behavioral sciences* (3rd ed.). Boston: Houghton Mifflin.

Holmes, C. T., & Keffer, R. L. (1995). A computerized method to teach Latin and Greek root words: Effect on verbal SAT scores. *Journal of Educational Research, 89,* 47–50.

Huberman, A. M., & Miles, M. B. (1994). Data management and analysis methods. In N. K. Denzin & Y. S. Lincoln (Eds.), *Handbook of qualitative research* (pp. 428–444). Thousand Oaks, CA: Sage.

Jaeger, R. M. (Ed.). (1988). *Complementary methods for research in education.* Washington, DC: American Educational Research Association.

Jussim, L., Smith, A., Madon, S., & Palumbo, P. (1998). Teacher expectations. In J. Brophy (Ed.), *Advances in teaching: Expectations in the classroom* (pp. 1–48). Greenwich, CT: JAI Press.

Kerlinger, F. N. (1986). *Foundations of behavioral research* (3rd ed.). New York: Holt, Rinehart and Winston.

Knowles, T. (1993). A missing piece of heart: Children's perceptions of the Persian Gulf War of 1991. *Social Education, 57,* 19–22.

Konopak, B. C., Readence, J. E., & Wilson, E. K. (1994). Preservice and inservice secondary teachers' orientations toward content area reading. *Journal of Educational Research, 87,* 220–227.

Kulik, C. L. C., & Kulik, J. A. (1991). Effectiveness of computer-based instruction: An updated analysis. *Computers in Human Behavior, 7,* 75–94.

Lancy, D. F. (1993). *Qualitative research in education: An introduction to the major traditions.* New York: Longman.

Larson, B. E., & Parker, W. C. (1996). What is classroom discussion? A look at teachers' conceptions. *Journal of Curriculum and Supervision, 11,* 110–126.

LeCompte,, M. D., & Preissle, J. (1993). *Ethnography and qualitative design in educational research* (2nd ed.). San Diego, CA: Academic Press.

Lightfoot, S. L. (1984). *The good high school: Portraits of character and culture.* New York: Basic Books.

Lincoln, Y. S., & Guba, E. G. (1985). *Naturalistic inquiry.* Beverly Hills, CA: Sage.

Marshall, C., & Rossman, G. B. (1999). *Designing qualitative research* (3rd ed.). Thousand Oaks, CA: Sage.

Martin, R. (1980). *Writing and defending a thesis or dissertation in psychology and education.* Springfield, IL: Charles C. Thomas.

Maykut, P., & Morehouse, R. (1994). *Beginning qualitative research: A philosophic and practical guide.* London: Falmer.

McMillan, J. H., & Schumacher, S. (1997). *Research in education: A conceptual introduction* (4th ed.). New York: Longman.

Miles, M. B., & Huberman, A. M. (1994). *Qualitative data analysis: An expanded sourcebook* (2nd ed.). Thousand Oaks, CA: Sage.

Murphy, L. L. (1999). *Tests in print V.* Lincoln, NE: Buros Institute of Mental Measurements.

Newman, I., & Benz, C. R. (1998). *Qualitative-quantitative research methodology: Exploring the interactive continuum.* Carbondale, IL: Southern Illinois University Press.

Noland, T. K., & Taylor, B. L. (1986). *The effects of ability grouping: A meta-analysis of research findings.* (ERIC Document Reproduction Service No. ED 269 451)

Olmsted, P. P., & Lockhard, S. (1995). *Do parents and teachers agree? What "should" young children be learning?* Ypsilanti, MI: High/Scope Educational Research Foundation. (ERIC Document Reproduction Service No. ED 383 457)

Omizo, M. M., Omizo, S. A., & Honda, M. R. (1997). A phenomenological study with youth gang members: Results and implications for school counselors. *Professional School Counseling, 1*(1), 39–42.

Osgood, C. E., Suci, G. J., & Tannenbaum, P. H. (1957). *The measurement of meaning.* Urbana, IL: University of Illinois Press.

Parker, D. R. (1996). *Emerging uses of computer technology in qualitative research.* (ERIC Document Reproduction Service No. ED 405 349)

Patton, M. Q. (1990). *Qualitative evaluation and research methods* (2nd ed.). Newbury Park, CA: Sage.

Peshkin, A. (1986). *God's choice: The total world of a fundamentalist Christian school.* Chicago: The University of Chicago Press.

Petersen, R. P., Johnson, D. W., & Johnson, R. W. (1991). Effects of cooperative learning on perceived status of male and female pupils. *Journal of Social Psychology, 131,* 717–735.

Publication manual of the American Psychological Association (4th ed.). (1994). Washington, DC: American Psychological Association.

Rose, L. C., & Gallup, A. M. (1999). The 31st annual Phi Delta Kappa/Gallup poll of the public's attitudes toward the public schools. *Phi Delta Kappan, 81,* 41–56.

Rosenshine, B., & Meister, C. (1994). Reciprocal teaching: A review of the research. *Review of Educational Research, 64,* 479–530.

Rury, J. L. (1993). Historical inquiry. In D. F. Lancy, *Qualitative research in education: An introduction to the major traditions* (pp. 247–269). New York: Longman.

Semb, G. B., & Ellis, J. A. (1994). Knowledge taught in school: What is remembered? *Review of Educational Research, 64,* 253–286.

Smitherman, G. (1999). CCCC's role in the struggle for language rights. *College Composition and Communication, 50,* 349–376.

Solomon, R. L. (1949). An extension of control group design. *Psychological Bulletin, 46,* 137–140.

Sowell, E. J., Buss, R. R., Fedock, P., Pryor, B., Wetzel, K., & Zambo, R. (1995). *K–12 Mathematics and science education in Arizona: A status report.*

(Available from Arizona Board of Regents, Eisenhower Program.)

Stake, R. E. (1988). Case study methods in educational research: Seeking sweet water. In R. M. Jaeger (Ed.), *Complementary methods for research in education* (pp. 253–270). Washington DC: American Educational Research Association.

Stevahn, L., Johnson, D. W., Johnson, R. T., & Real, D. (1996). The impact of a cooperative or individualistic context on the effectiveness of conflict resolution training. *American Educational Research Journal, 33,* 801–823.

Strauss, A., & Corbin, J. (1998). *Basics of qualitative research: Techniques and procedures for developing grounded theory* (2nd ed.). Thousand Oaks, CA: Sage.

Tesch, R. (1990). *Qualitative research: Analysis types and software tools.* New York: Falmer.

Thomas, R. M. (1998). *Conducting educational research: A comparative review.* Westport, CT: Bergin & Garvey.

Thomas, W. B., & Moran, K. J. (1992). Reconsidering the power of the superintendent in the progressive period. *American Educational Research Journal, 29,* 22–50.

Tolley, K. (1996). Science for ladies, classics for gentlemen: A comparative analysis of scientific subjects in the curricula of boys' and girls' secondary schools in the United States, 1794–1850. *History of Education Quarterly, 36,* 129–153.

Wentzel, K. R. (1997). Student motivation in middle school: The role of perceived pedagogical caring. *Journal of Educational Psychology, 89,* 411–419.

Wolcott, H. F. (1992). Posturing in qualitative inquiry. In M. D. LeCompte, W. L. Millroy, & J. Priessle (Eds.), *The handbook of qualitative research in education* (pp. 3–52). San Diego, CA: Academic Press.

Zevin, J. (1995). *Perceptions of national identity: How adolescents view their own and other countries.* (ERIC Document Reproduction Service No. ED 380 394)

Zimmerman, J. (1994). The dilemma of Miss Jolly: Scientific temperance and teacher professionalism, 1882–1904. *History of Education Quarterly, 34,* 413–431.

Glossary

A

abstract   Typically the second item in a research report following the title. Report of a research project in miniature; provides major information about the problem, procedures, results, and conclusion.

accessible population   Refers to all of the people having a characteristic in common from which researchers can select samples for research projects.

active variable   Variable whose values are subjected to manipulation by researchers; also known as manipulated, experimental, or independent variable.

alternative hypothesis   Statistical hypothesis derived from research hypothesis, states the negation of the null hypothesis; is the hypothesis used when null hypothesis is rejected.

analysis of covariance (ANCOVA)   Parametric inferential statistical test in which groups are equated with respect to one variable, called the covariate, thought to be correlated with the dependent variable.

analysis of variance (ANOVA)   Parametric inferential statistical test used to assess statistical significance of differences between means or variances; result of this test is an *F*-value, which expresses the ratio of variance that can be accounted for against the total variance.

appendices   Final sections of research reports; contain detailed information about procedures or results; not always included in reports.

assigned variable   Variable whose values are naturally occurring (e.g., gender, birth order); can be managed by researchers through holding the variable constant or taking it into account as part of data analysis; also called attribute variable.

assignment procedures   Refers to the processes by which participants in experiments are placed in groups to receive treatments.

attribute variable   Same as assigned variable.

C

canonical correlation   Statistical procedure used to determine strength of overall association between several predictor and criterion variables; tells which variables account for most of the relationship.

causal comparative studies   Descriptive research design; focuses on comparisons of groups made on the basis of naturally occurring variables (e.g., aggression, gender) in terms of a measured variable; involves no manipulation of variables.

central tendency   The point in a frequency distribution at which scores bunch together; measured as mean, median, or mode.

chi-square test   Nonparametric statistical procedure used to assess statistical significance in comparisons of observed frequencies with theoretical frequencies.

comparative analysis   Type of historical research report that compares two or more phenomena within their educational, social, and/or cultural contexts.

complete observer   Role adopted by qualitative researchers in which participants do not identify them as researchers; researchers may work behind one-way mirrors.

complete participant   Role adopted by qualitative researchers in which they are considered as group members by the participants and are not identified as researchers.

conclusion   Researchers' solution to a research problem; based on careful interpretations of findings.

constant comparative method   Method of data analysis used by qualitative researchers; involves cycles of collection, analysis, and interpretation that feature coding and memo writing as the chief means of data reduction.

construct validity   A type of measurement validity; based on the correspondence between the theory or knowledge about a construct or idea and the data obtained from an instrument used to measure that construct.

constructed-response strategy   Method for data collection in which respondents provide responses on open-ended instruments, such as interviews, or researchers conduct document analyses.

content validity   A type of measurement validity; based on the degree to which an instrument measures the content representative of a knowledge domain; evidence usually established by expert judgment.

control   Goal of research that reveals cause-and-effect relationships among relationships; the ability to direct or influence one variable to bring about change in a related variable.

correlation coefficient   A numerical index expressing the strength and direction of a relationship between variables; written as a decimal number ranging from -1.00 to $+1.00$.

correlation design   Descriptive research design; focuses on locating the magnitude and direction of relationships between two or more variables.

criterion variable   In regression analysis, this variable has an unknown value.

criterion-related validity   A type of measurement validity; based on the correspondence between data from an established instrument and data from an instrument that is undergoing validation, data are collected from the same participants.

critical value   Provides the probability of the occurrence of a significant result (i.e., F, t, χ^2, or z) in the sampling distribution for specified sample sizes.

D

data collection procedures   Refers to the actions taken in gathering data in research studies, including frequency, settings, and expertise of collectors.

data handling procedures   Refers to actions taken in preparing data for analysis, including checks for completeness, decisions about missing data, classification, and transformations of data to lower levels of measurement.

dependent variable   Variable that changes in response to changes in the independent variable; used in studies whose goal is control; also known as the responding variable.

descriptive methods   Methods used in quantitative studies that seek explanation and prediction as their goals; researchers use existing situations for data collection; no manipulation of variables is involved.

descriptive narrative   Type of historical research report that details a single historical event, including an institution, biography, or organization.

descriptive statistics   Procedures for associating and summarizing data from participants to facilitate their communication and interpretation.

discriminant analysis   Statistical procedure similar to multiple regression, except that the criterion variable contains categories (e.g., occupations, gender).

discussion   Section of research report in which researchers provide a conclusion for the project and explain their results.

distribution   Results from a procedure in which a group of observations is arranged to show how many observations fall within specified intervals on a measurement scale.

E

educational research   Application of systematic processes to achieve valid and reliable outcomes that answer problems in education.

educational significance   Practical value; importance attached to research outcomes by the education community.

effect size   Descriptive statistic that provides a common measure of difference between two or more groups across many different research settings.

error variance   Random variance associated with variables in quantitative inquiries.

experimental methods   Methods used in quantitative studies that seek control as their goal; require deliberate effort by researchers to structure situations in which variables can be controlled and investigated; studies involve cause-and-effect relationships among variables.

experimental variable   Variable whose values are subjected to manipulation by researchers; also known as manipulated, active, or independent variable.

explanation   Goal of research that makes understandable the underlying nature of or relationships among variables, includes the description of events and phenomena.

external criticism   Test of the authenticity of data sources in historical research; answers question of whether source is original, forged, or a variation of original.

extraneous variable   Variable whose values can confuse or confound results of quantitative research projects; may mimic effects of manipulated variable and bring about changes in responding variable in experiments.

F

factor analysis   Statistical procedure used to identify the number and nature of broad factors underlying a cluster of variables.

factorial analysis of variance (ANOVA)   Parametric statistical procedure, also known as two-way ANOVA, used to test for significant differences in factorial designs, tests for main effects (independent variables on dependent variable), and interaction effects (interaction of independent variables on dependent variable).

factorial design   Research design that allows for observation of the effects of interaction between (among) variables (factors), used in both experiments and causal comparisons.

field notes   Verbal descriptions of events, intuitions, and feelings about a particular setting, prepared by field researchers.

findings   Results of study, based on data from participants.

G

generalization   Refers to the possibility of making inferences about a population, based on data from a random sample.

goals of research   Provide the purposes for research projects; include explanation, prediction, and control.

H

historical methods   Methods used in historical projects that seek explanation as their goal; require locating and evaluating sources of information, data collection from sources, and creation of narrative to explain relationships between variables.

hypothesis   A conjecture about the answer to a research problem; may be expressed as a research, null, alternate, or statistical statement.

I

independent variable   Variable that is manipulated to see if changes occur in a related variable; used in projects whose goal is control; also known as the manipulated variable.

inferential statistics   Provide the means by which researchers use data from random samples to make inferences about the population from which the samples were drawn.

instrumentation   Preparation for data collection; involves decisions about which data are needed to answer research questions, frequency of data collection, and instruments or strategies to be used.

internal criticism   Test of the credibility of data sources in historical research; answers questions of whether source is accurate and trustworthy.

interpretation   Explanation of the results of a research project with reference to the body of related knowledge or to the design procedures.

interpretive analysis   Type of historical research report that describes and discusses a phenomenon within its educational, social, or cultural context, or any combination of these contexts.

interval measurement   Measures in which differences between numbers assigned to values of variables can be ranked and are considered as having equal intervals; measures can be added and subtracted.

introduction (to a report)   First major section of a research report; provides a context for the problem statement; may contain references to related literature.

introduction to the project   First major section of a research proposal; contains an introduction, purpose of the study, educational significance, definitions, and summary.

J

justification for the project   Statement of the need or rationale for a particular research project; formulated in conjunction with the literature review.

L

levels of measurement   Brought about when researchers assign numbers to objects or events according to rules; levels include nominal, ordinal, interval, and ratio.

level of significance   The probability of rejecting a null hypothesis when it is true; also known as alpha (α) level.

literature review   Provides the context for a research problem; major purpose is to connect a research problem with the body of knowledge related to the problem; typically carries a justification for the project.

M

manipulated variable   Variable whose values are changed by researchers to see their effects on the responding variable; used in projects whose goal is control; also known as experimental, independent, or active variable.

mean   Measure of central tendency, also called the arithmetic mean or average; obtained by summing a set of measures and dividing the sum by the number of measures; requires interval or ratio data.

median   Measure of central tendency that represents the midpoint of a distribution of measures; can be used with ordinal data.

meta-analysis   Descriptive research design; involves statistical reanalysis of data from multiple firsthand research reports on the same variable; provides status of knowledge about the variable.

Method section   Typically second major section of research report following introduction; contains research design information on participants, instrumentation, data collection and handling, and sometimes data analysis; descriptions of treatment included in reports of experiments; also called procedures.

mode   Measure of central tendency that is a score that occurs most frequently in a set of measures.

multiple regression   Statistical procedure in which two or more predictor variables, known to be correlated with a criterion variable, are studied to see if they can predict the criterion variable.

multivariate analysis of variance (MANOVA)   Parametric inferential statistical test used to assess statistical significance of differences between means or variances in designs having more than one dependent variable.

N

nominal measurement   Categorical labels assigned to variables; purpose of labels is to distinguish between values of variables.

nonparametric test   Statistical test used to make inferences about a population based on sample data; uses nominal or ordinal data and higher levels of data if they are not normally distributed.

nonrandom assignment (of participants)   Arbitrary processes by which participants in experiments are placed in groups to receive treatments; processes do not necessarily provide equivalent groups.

nonrandom sample   Sample selected on the basis of the researchers' judgment; includes systematic,

quota, purposeful, and convenience samples; results should not be generalized to ambiguous or unknown population.

normal distribution   Symmetrical frequency distribution in which most of the measures fall near the mean and fewer scores are found near the extremes of the distribution; forms a bell-shaped curve, with the mean, median, and mode at the same point on the curve.

null hypothesis   Statistical hypothesis tested in inferential statistical data analyses; commonly referred to as the no difference (no association) hypothesis.

O

observer-as-participant   Role adopted by qualitative researchers in which they are known to be researchers by the participants; researchers have some contact with participants.

one-way analysis of variance (ANOVA)   Parametric statistical procedure used to test statistical significance of two or more means or variances.

ordinal measurement   Labels assigned to variables; purpose of labels is to rank-order values of variables.

P

parameter   Characteristic of populations.

parametric test   Statistical test used to make inferences about a population based on sample data; uses interval or ratio data that are normally distributed.

participant-as-observer   Role adopted by qualitative researchers in which they are known to be researchers by the participants and are thought of as group members.

path analysis   Statistical procedure that permits researchers to see if hypothesized causal links among correlated variables exist.

planned comparisons   Parametric statistical procedures used to test comparisons between two means or pairs of means, involves advance planning because limited numbers of comparisons are allowed; should not be confused with t-tests.

point of view   The perspective from which a historian tells the story or narrative in historical research.

population   A group that has one or more than one characteristic in common; sizes of populations vary.

post hoc multiple comparison test   Statistical procedure used with results of statistically significant

ANOVA to locate source of variance that produced the significance.

prediction   Goal of research that predicts relationships among variables based on known relationships among related variables.

prediction design   Descriptive research design; focuses on determining whether variables known to be correlated can be used for prediction; known variables are predictors, unknown variables are criteria.

predictor variable   In regression analysis, this variable has a known value.

pre-experiment   Experimental research design in which the effects of manipulating a variable are observed in a responding variable.

primary research report   Account of the processes and outcomes of research projects made by the researcher(s) who actually performed them.

primary source   A firsthand or eyewitness account of information; preferred as data source in historical research.

problems (educational research)   Concern, issue, or question related to education that requires a solution or answer; typically uses systematic procedures.

procedures (section)   *See* method section.

purposeful sample   Sample selected on the basis of how the cases fit the purpose of the study; includes typical case, extreme or deviant case, intensity, maximum variation, homogeneous, and others; results not generalized to other settings.

Q

qualitative inquiry   Characterized by search for understanding of social phenomenon; researchers are intimately involved in setting, inductive approaches to problem solution, and use of results for participants.

qualitative methods   Methods that seek explanation as their goal; characterized by recurring cycles of data collection, analysis, and interpretation.

quantitative inquiry   Characterized by search for understanding of relationships among specific variables, researchers somewhat detached from setting, deductive approaches to problem solution, and intent of results usually to apply in settings other than just the participants.

quasi-experiment   Experimental research design in which the effects of manipulating a variable are observed in a responding variable; characterized by

participants' random assignment as intact groups to treatments.

R

random assignment (of participants)   Systematic processes by which participants in experiments are placed into groups to receive treatments; processes intended to reduce bias and to give equivalent groups.

random sample   Sample for quantitative study, selected on basis that each unit in the population has a known nonzero probability of being included in the sample; includes simple random, stratified, cluster, and multistage samples; results may be generalized to the population.

range   Measure of dispersion around the mode; obtained by subtracting the lowest from the highest measures in a distribution.

ratio measurement   Measures in which differences between numbers assigned to values of variables are considered as having equal intervals and a true zero start point.

recommendation to practitioners   Statement made by researchers to persons who work in educational settings about the possible uses of their findings.

recommendation to researchers   Statement made by researchers to other researchers about the possible uses of their findings, possibly for future research.

references   List of works cited in research reports.

regression analysis   Statistical procedure that allows for the prediction of values of certain variables known to be correlated with other variables in the population.

reliability of measurement   Consistency or dependability of the results or data from an instrument used in data collection; includes internal consistency, stability, and equivalence.

reliability of research   Degree to which research produces dependable or consistent outcomes.

repeated measures designs   Experimental research designs in which participants provide data more than once; changes in these data become the basis for comparison about treatment effects.

research design   Generalized set of research procedures for carrying out a project; same as research plan.

research hypothesis   Researchers' statement of the tentative answer to a research problem or question.

research plan   Generalized set of research procedures for carrying out a project; same as research design.

research proposal   Includes a research problem, literature review that provides a context for the problem, and plans for the collection and analysis of data to solve the research problem.

responding variable   Variable whose values change when researchers alter values of the related manipulated variable; used in studies whose goal is control; also known as the dependent variable.

results   Findings of study, based on data from participants.

S

sample   The people selected for participation in a research project.

secondary research report   Account of research made by someone other than the researchers who actually did the study; may take the form of a review paper.

secondary source   A data source prepared by someone other than an eyewitness; used in historical research to understand the context for a phenomenon under investigation.

selected-response strategy   Method for data collection in which respondents choose responses from options available on closed-ended strategies, such as multiple choice test items or ranking procedures.

selection procedures   The processes by which participants in quantitative projects are chosen to be the sample(s).

social phenomenon   Multiple, closely associated variables found together in complex social relationships.

standard deviation   Measure of dispersion or variation around the mean of a distribution; obtained by summing the squared deviations from the mean, dividing this sum of squares by the number of scores, and taking the square root of the quotient.

standard score   Score whose value is expressed in terms of standard deviations from the mean.

statistical hypothesis   Statement derived from research hypothesis used in inferential statistical data analysis; includes null and alternate hypotheses.

statistical significance   Decision about the worth of results based on the probability of their occurrence by chance; results are declared statistically significant if there is a low probability of their occurrence by chance when the null hypothesis is true.

status studies   Descriptive research design in which researchers gather and analyze data about the condition or standing of variables.

stepwise regression   Variation of multiple regression; statistical procedure in which two or more predictor variables, known to be correlated with a criterion variable, are put into the procedure in a specified order to see if they predict the criterion variable.

survey studies   Descriptive research design in which researchers gather and analyze data about a variety of topics; called sample surveys if participants are part of a population; called census surveys if the entire population is used.

T

t-test   Parametric statistical procedure used to test for significant differences in one descriptive statistic with a known population parameter or between pairs of descriptive statistics.

target population   All the people having a characteristic in common to which researchers want to generalize the results of particular research projects.

title   Initial item in a research report; statement uses phenomena or research variables, expresses their relationship as well as the range of interests represented in project.

treatment (procedures)   Procedures administered to participants in a research project to see if a noticeable effect is produced in preselected variables related to the treatment variable. Sometimes the manipulated variable is called the treatment.

treatment levels   Used interchangeably with treatment.

triangulation   Methods used by qualitative researchers to strengthen research designs by using a variety of data sources, several investigators, multiple perspectives in interpreting a single set of data, multiple methods of study, or a combination of these methods.

true experiment   Experimental research design in which the effects of manipulating a variable are observed in a responding variable; characterized by participants' random assignment to treatments.

two-way analysis of variance (ANOVA)   Parametric statistical procedure, also known as factorial

ANOVA, used to test for significant differences in factorial designs, tests for main effects (independent variables on dependent variable), and interaction effects (interaction of independent variables on dependent variable).

Type I error   Decision to reject the null hypothesis when it is true, implying acceptance of the alternate hypothesis when it is false; probability of Type I error is the level of significance, known as alpha (α).

Type II error   Decision to retain the null hypothesis when it is false, implying rejection of the alternate hypothesis when it is true; probability of Type II error is known as beta (β).

V

validity of measurement   Truthfulness or accuracy of the results or data from an instrument used in data collection; includes construct, content, and criterion-related validity.

validity of research   Degree to which research produces accurate and truthful outcomes.

variable   Property that varies; may have numerical values (e.g., 14, 27) or categorical values (e.g., new method, comparison method).

variance   Measure of variability that takes into account the size and location of each individual score in terms of the mean score; obtained by summing the squared deviations from the mean and dividing by the number of scores; in a more general sense, refers to all the sources of variations in a research study.

variation   Dispersion of scores about measures of central tendency; includes range, quartile deviation, and standard deviation.

Name Index

Ackerman, M., 160, 162

Barzun, J., 159, 162
Benz, C. R., 5
Berg, B. L., 7
Bisanz, J., 33
Brophy, J., 11
Brundage, A., 159
Buros, O. K., 61

Campbell, D. T., 82
Carris, J., 341
Charters, W. W., 79
Cohen, J., 47
Comfort, K. B., 344
Corbin, J., 147, 149
Coutts, D., 48
Cripps, T., 347

Denzin, N. K., 20

Eisenhart, M. A., 4
Ellis, J. A., 182

Fitzgerald, J., 10
Floud, R., 161
Freed, M. N., 134

Gallup, A. M., 97, 345, 346
Gates, G., 104, 222, 273
Gates, J. T., 161
Genz, M. D., 155, 166
Gettinger, M., 3, 30, 31, 39, 66, 67, 72, 115, 123, 135, 173, 175, 176, 178, 201, 222, 223, 343
Gierl, M. J., 33
Gitomer, D. H., 341
Gmelch, W. H., 104, 222, 273
Gold, R. L., 68, 69
Gottschalk, L., 158, 162, 345
Graff, H. F., 159, 162
Guba, E. G., 5, 70, 145

Hall, G. E., 79
Hartsook, H. J., 156
Hays, W. L., 128
Henry, G. T., 44, 45
Hess, R. K., 134
Hinkle, D. E., 128

Holmes, C. T., 3, 49, 61, 67, 170, 171, 173, 178, 201, 222, 253, 342
Honda, M. R., 222, 247
Howe, H. R., 4
Huberman, A. M., 146, 147, 172

Jaeger, R. M., 5
Johnson, D. W., 34, 50, 88
Johnson, J. T., 50
Johnson, R. W., 50, 88
Jones, J., 79
Jurs, S. G., 128
Jussim, L., 182

Keffer, R. L., 3, 49, 61, 67, 170, 171, 173, 178, 201, 222, 253, 342
Kerlinger, F. N., 6, 66
Knowles, T., 33
Konopak, B. C., 30, 35, 51, 66, 178, 222, 260, 342
Kulik, C. L. C., 96
Kulik, J. A., 96

Lancy, D. F., 5
Larson, B. E., 3, 39, 40, 52, 53, 73, 149, 150, 152, 176, 181, 222, 233, 346
LeCompte, M. D., 68, 69
Lightfoot, S. L., 143, 146
Lincoln, Y. S., 5, 20, 70, 145
Lockhard, S., 343
Loucks, S., 79

McMillan, J. H., 160
Madon, S., 182
Marshall, C., 69, 147, 209
Martin, R. 32, 33
Maykut, P., 5
Meister, C., 96
Miles, M. B., 146, 147, 172
Moran, K. J., 156, 178, 222, 319
Morehouse, R., 5
Murphy, L. L., 61

Newman, I., 5

Olmsted, P. P., 343
Omizo, M. M., 222, 247
Omizo, S. A., 222, 247
Osgood, C. E., 342

Palumbo, P., 182
Parker, D. R., 150
Parker, W. C., 3, 39, 40, 52, 53, 73, 149, 150, 152, 176, 181, 222, 233, 346
Patton, M. Q., 3, 46, 52, 53, 345, 346, 347
Peshkin, A., 143
Petersen, R. P., 34, 88
Preissle, J., 68, 69

Readance, J. E., 30, 35, 51, 66, 178, 222, 260, 342
Real, D., 50
Rose, L. C., 97, 345, 346
Rosenshine, B., 96
Rossman, G. B., 69, 147, 209
Rury, J. L., 155
Ryan, J. M., 134

Schumacher, S., 160
Semb, G. B., 182
Smith, A., 182
Smith, M. L., 96
Smitherman, G. 160
Sowell, E. J., 344
Stanley, J. C., 82
Stevahn, L., 50, 51, 84
Strauss, A., 147, 149
Suci, G. J., 342

Tannenbaum, P. H., 342
Tesch, R., 146, 150
Thomas, R. M., 156, 178
Thomas, W. B., 156, 222, 319
Tolley, K., 30, 159, 161, 164, 176, 222, 301, 345

Wentzel, K. R., 3, 30, 32, 49, 51, 62, 100, 101, 137, 170, 171, 172, 178, 181, 196, 222, 285, 342
Wiersma, W., 128
Wilson, E. K., 30, 35, 51, 66, 178, 222, 260, 342
Wolcott, H. F., 68

Zevin, J., 343
Zimmerman, J., 156, 160

Subject Index

Abstract, 9, 10, 36, 37, 177, 192
Accessible population, 43
Active variable, 80
Alternate hypothesis, 128–130
Analysis of covariance (ANCOVA), 350–351, 352
Analysis of variance (ANOVA), 131, 132, 134, 138, 348–351, 352
Appendices (in research reports), 9, 11
Assigned variable, 80, 82
Assignment procedures, 50–52, 82, 84, 85, 202
Attribute variable, 80, 82

Budgets for research proposals, 211

Canonical correlation, 353
Causal comparative design (studies), 96, 98–100
Central tendency, 108–112, 209
    defined, 111
    mean, 108, 111, 112–115, 128
    median, 108, 111, 112, 114
    mode, 108, 111, 112
Chicago Manual of Style, 195
Chi-square test, 131, 132
Comparative analysis, 161
Complete observer role, 69, 206
Complete participant role, 68, 206
Complex experiment designs, 88–89
Computerized Method to Teach Latin and Greek Root Words: Effect on Verbal SAT Scores, 40, 56, 92, 124, 139, 222, 253–259
Conclusion, 167, 171–172, 175
Constant comparative method
    axial coding, 147, 148, 150
    defined, 147
    memos and diagrams, 149
    open coding, 147, 148
    selective coding, 147
Construct validity of measurement, 63, 64
Constructed-response strategies, 206, 341, 343–347
    document or artifact analyses, 206, 344–345
    tests, examinations and questionnaires, 343–344
Content validity of measurement, 62, 64
Control
    as a goal of research, 17–18, 30–31, 78, 200
    examples of research questions for, 18, 30–31
Correlation analyses, 116–119, 351–353
    coefficients, 119, 128, 129, 130, 131, 137
Correlation coefficient, 119, 128, 129, 130, 131, 137
Correlation design (studies), 96, 100–101

Criterion variable, 101, 120
Criterion-related validity of measurement, 63, 64
Critical value, 132, 135
Current Index to Journals in Education, 186

Data analysis procedures
    costs, 201, 209–210
    criteria for evaluation, 122–123, 137–138, 151, 164
    for qualitative analyses, 143–146, 161, 209
    for quantitative analyses, 107–125, 126–140, 209
    personnel, 201, 209–210
    in proposals, 201, 209–210
    relationships with other procedures, 90, 103, 123, 138, 201
    in reports, 137, 151
Data collection procedures
    circumstances, 201, 207
    costs, 201, 207
    criteria for evaluation, 89–90, 103
    defined, 81
    development of strategies, 61–67, 68–70
    personnel, 201, 207
    in proposals, 201, 205–206
    relationships with other procedures, 90, 103, 123, 138, 201
    in reports, 81
    valid and reliable data, 82, 87, 90, 100, 103, 143, 151, 164
Data handling procedures
    costs, 201, 207
    defined, 81
    personnel, 201, 207
    in proposals, 201, 205–206
    relationships with other procedures, 90, 103, 123, 138, 201
    in reports, 81
Dependent variable, 80, 88–89, 90
Descriptive methods
    defined, 21
    examples of research questions, 21–22
Descriptive narrative, 160
Descriptive research
    criteria for evaluation of procedures, 103
    data collection procedures, 95
    data handling procedures, 95
    designs for, 95–101
    goals of research and, 98
    purposes, 96
    systematic application of procedures, 95
Descriptive statistical data analyses
    procedures for analyses of associations among data, 116–121

procedures for group data analyses, 108–116
Descriptive statistics, 107, 137
    central tendency, 108–112
    correlation analyses, 116–119
    distributions, 109–110, 113–114
    effect sizes, 115
    normal distributions, 113–114, 131
    percentages, 109
    regression analyses, 119–121
    standard scores, 115
    variation, 112–113
Discriminant analysis, 353
Discussion section (of research reports), 9, 10, 174–177
    criteria for evaluation, 174–175
Dissertation Abstracts International, 188, 189
Distributions, 109–110, 113–114

EBSCOHost, 188, 189
Education Abstracts Full Text, 186, 189
Education Index, 186, 189
Educational Research Information Center, 186–191
Educational research, nature of, 3–5
Educational significance, 184, 212
Effect size, 115
Effects of Error Correction on Third Graders' Spelling, 12, 39, 56, 72–73, 90–91, 121–124, 138, 175, 222, 223–233
Error variance, 81–82
Ethical Standards of the American Educational Research Association, 3, 7, 27, 169, 213
Ethics in research
    in definition of educational research, 3, 27
    in interpreting outcomes, 169
    in preparation of proposals, 213–215
    in research problems, 29
Experimental methods
    defined, 22
    examples of research questions for, 22
Experimental research
    criteria for evaluation of procedures, 89–90
    data collection procedures, 81
    data handling procedures, 81
    designs for, 82–89
    functions of variables, 79–80
    goals of research and, 78
    systematic application of procedures, 81–82
    treatment procedures, 79–81
Experimental variable, 80
Explanation
    examples of research questions for, 16, 30
    as a goal of research, 15–16, 29–30

External criticism, 158
Extraneous variable, 80, 82

Factor analysis, 353
Factorial analysis of variance
    (ANOVA), 350
Factorial designs, 83–85, 86
Field notes, 144
Findings (in research reports). *See* Results
    section (of research reports)

Generalization, 8, 43, 47, 127, 203
Goals of research. *See also* Control;
    Explanation; Prediction
    importance of understanding, 19
    and inquiry modes, 21
    relationships among, 18
    and research methods, 21
    and research problems, 15–18,
        29–31, 195

Historical methods
    defined, 23
    examples of research questions for,
        23–24
Historical research
    criteria for evaluation of procedures
        and results, 164
    data collection techniques, 159
    data reduction, 161–162
    evaluation of data sources, 158–159
    frame of reference, 160–161
    goals of research and, 155
    location of data sources, 156–157
    narrative construction, 162–163
Hypotheses
    alternate, 128–130
    defined, 5
    null, 128–130, 131–135
    research, 29, 128–130
    statistical, 128–130
Hypothesis testing strategies, 127–136. *See
    also* Inferential statistical tests
    application of tests, 134
    evaluation of test outcomes, 135–136
    selection of inferential tests, 131–132
    selection of significance levels, 132–134
    statement of hypotheses, 128–130

*Impact of Personal, Professional and
    Organizational Characteristics on
    Administrator Burnout,* 36, 104, 136,
    173, 222, 273–285
Independent variable, 80, 90
Inferential statistical data analyses
    hypothesis testing strategies, 127–136
    procedures for inferential statistical
        analyses, 127
Inferential statistical tests
    analysis of variance and related tests,
        131, 132, 134, 138, 348–351, 352
    chi-square test, 131, 132, 354
    correlation analyses, 132, 351–353
    Friedman ANOVA test, 354
    Kruskal–Wallis test, 354
    Mann-Whitney *U* test, 354
    regression analyses, 351–353
    t-test, 131, 132, 350, 352
Inferential statistics
    defined, 127

nonparametric procedures, 354
    parametric procedures, 348–353
Instrumentation procedures. *See also* Data
        collection procedures
    criteria for evaluation, 71–72
    defined, 59
    in proposals, 205–206
    in qualitative studies, 68–70
    in quantitative studies, 61–67
    in reports, 60–61, 70–74
    relationships with other procedures,
        90, 103, 123, 138
    valid and reliable data, 71, 205
Internal criticism, 158
Interpretations, 150–151, 162, 167
    of results in quantitative reports,
        169–171, 174–179
Interpretive analysis, 160
Interval measurement, 67, 112, 131, 209
Interviews, 345–347
    closed-ended response, 345
    informal conversations, 347
    interview guides, 346–347
    standardized open-ended, 206,
        345–346
Introduction (to research projects), 199,
        211–212
    definitions, 212
    educational significance, 212
    introduction, 211
    purpose of the study, 212
    summary, 212
Introduction (to research reports), 9, 10,
        36–40

JSTOR, 188, 189
Justification for a project, 33–34, 193–194

Level of significance, 132–135
Levels of measurement, 205
    defined, 66
    interval, 67, 112, 131
    nominal, 66, 112, 131
    ordinal, 66–67, 112, 131
    ratio, 67
Literature reviews
    content, 32
    creation of, 41, 180, 193–195, 196–197
    criteria for evaluation, 38
    critique statements, 33, 34
    defined, 31
    explanatory statements, 32, 34
    justifications for projects, 33–34, 193
    organization, 32
    purpose, 31, 199
Literature search
    databases for, 186–189
    scope of, 190
    strategies for, 190–191
    use of search results, 192

Manipulated variable, 17, 80, 82
Mean, 108, 111, 112–115, 128
Median, 108, 111, 112, 114
Mental Measurements Yearbook, 61, 208
Meta-analysis, 10, 95–96
Method section (of research reports), 9,
        10, 54–55, 70–71, 89, 102–103
Mode, 108, 111, 112
Multiple regression, 121, 131, 352–353

Multivariate analysis of variance
    (MANOVA), 351, 352

Nominal measurement, 66, 112, 131, 209
Nonparametric test, 131, 354
Nonrandom assignment of participants, 50
Nonrandom samples, 45–47, 49, 203–204
    convenience, 47, 49, 53
    purposeful or purposive, 43–46, 49,
        53, 203
    quota, 45, 49
    systematic, 45, 49
Normal distribution, 113–114, 131
Null hypothesis, 128–130, 131–135

Observation notes, 61, 206, 347
Observer-as-participant role, 68–69, 206
One-way analysis of variance
    (ANOVA), 349
Ordinal measurement, 66–67, 112,
        131, 209
Outcomes of research projects, 4–5,
        167, 169

Parameter, 131
Parametric test, 131
Participant procedures
    assignment, 50–52
    costs, 201, 204
    criteria for evaluation, 55
    defined, 50
    in proposals, 203–204
    relationships with other procedures,
        66, 90, 103, 123, 138
    in reports, 54–55
    sample size in qualitative projects, 52
    sample size in quantitative projects,
        47–48
    selection, 48–49, 52–53
    valid and reliable data, 48, 55
Participant-as-observer role, 68, 206
Path analysis, 353
*Phenomenological Study with Youth Gang
    Members: Results and Implications for
    School Counselors,* 40, 56, 73, 153,
    222, 246–252
Planned comparisons, 349–350, 352
Point of view, 160
Population
    accessible, 43
    defined, 43
    relationship to sample, 43, 137
    target, 43
Post hoc multiple comparison test,
        349, 352
Prediction
    examples of research questions for,
        17, 30
    as a goal of research, 17, 30
Prediction design, 96, 101
Predictor variable, 101, 120
Pre-experiment, 87
*Preservice and Inservice Secondary Teachers'
    Orientations Toward Content Area
    Reading,* 12, 35–36, 73, 104, 124,
    139, 193, 222, 260–272
Primary research report, 9
Primary source, 156, 157
Problem (educational research)
    creation of, 41, 180, 183–185

criteria for evaluation, 38
and literature reviews, 37
revision of, 195
selection criteria, 183–184
sources, 180–182
Procedures section (of research reports), 9, 10, 54–55, 71, 89, 102–103
PsycINFO, 186, 189, 190
Publication Manual of the APA, 194
Purposeful or purposive sample, 45–46, 49, 53, 203

Qualitative inquiry, 5–8, 20
goals of research and, 7
intended uses of results, 8
plans of attack, 7
roles of researchers, 8
settings for projects, 7
Qualitative methods
defined, 22
examples of research questions for, 22–23, 185–186, 195
Qualitative research
computer programs and, 150
criteria for evaluation of procedures and results, 151–152
data analysis and interpretation procedures, 146–151
data collection and handling procedures, 143–145
goals of research and, 142
validity, 150, 151
Quantitative inquiry, 5–8
goals of research, 5–6
intended uses of results, 8
plans of attack, 7
roles of researchers, 8
settings for projects, 7
Quasi-experiment, 85–86, 90

Random assignment (of participants), 50, 82, 84, 202
Random samples, 43–45, 49, 137, 203
cluster, 44–45
multistage, 44–45
simple, 44
stratified, 44
Range, 112
Ratio measurement, 67, 209
Recommendation
to practitioners, 167, 172–173, 175
to researchers, 172
Reconsidering the Power of the Superintendent in the Progressive Period, 12, 165, 222, 319–339
References
development of list, 194–195, 197, 213
in reports, 9, 10
Regression analysis, 119–121, 351–353
criterion variables, 101
multiple regression, 121, 131, 352–353
predictor variables, 101
Reliability of measurement, 64–66, 71–72
defined, 64
equivalence, 65, 66

internal consistency, 64–65, 66
stability, 65, 66
Reliability of research, 5
Repeated measures designs, 86
Research design. *See* Research plan
Research hypothesis, 29, 128–130
Research plan
defined, 24
elements of, 24
Research proposal, 167
defined, 199
development of, 199–216
review board approval, 213–215
Research reports
primary, 9
secondary, 9
sections, 9–10
sources, 11–12
Researcher roles in qualitative research
complete observer, 69, 206
complete participant, 68, 206
observer-as-participant, 68–69, 206
participant-as-observer, 68, 206
Resources in Education, 186
Responding variable, 17, 78, 80, 81
Results section (of research reports), 9, 10, 121–123, 136–137, 151–152
criteria for evaluation, 122–123, 137–138, 152, 164
defined, 10
Review boards, 213–215
Review of Educational Research, 12, 182

Sample, 43
Scholastic Aptitude Test, 17, 49, 61, 67, 170, 171
Science for Ladies, Classics for Gentlemen: A Comparative Analysis of Scientific Subjects in the Curricula of Boys' and Girls' Secondary Schools in the United States, 1794–1850, 157, 159, 164–165, 176, 222, 300–318
Secondary research report, 9–11
Secondary source, 156, 157
Selected-response strategies, 340–343
ranking strategies, 343
rating strategies, 342–343
tests, examinations and inventories, 341–342
Selection procedures (participants), 48–49, 52–53
Social phenomenon, 7, 16, 52, 69, 145, 148, 149
Social Science Citations Index, 186, 189
Social Work Abstracts, 186, 189
Standard deviation, 112–115
Standard score, 115
Statistical hypothesis, 128–130
Statistical significance, 135–136, 137
Status studies, 95
Stepwise regression, 121
Student Motivation in Middle School: The Role of Perceived Pedagogical Caring, 222, 285–299
Survey studies, 96, 97–98
cross-sectional studies, 97

longitudinal studies, 97
sample surveys, 97
Systematic processes, 3–4
analyze and interpret data, 4, 77, 168
collect data about problem, 4, 27, 77
identify problem, 4, 27
relationship to problem solving, 4
review known information, 4, 27
solve the problem, 167, 168

Target population, 43
Tests in Print, 61
Thesaurus of ERIC Descriptors, 183, 190, 191
Time line in proposals, 210–211
Title, 9, 10, 37, 212
criteria for evaluation, 38
Treatment (procedures)
administration, 81
costs, 201, 202
major types of comparisons, 79
personnel, 202
in proposals, 200–202
in reports, 79–81
Treatments (or treatment levels), 18
Triangulation, 70
True experiment, 82–85
t-test, 131, 132, 350, 352
Two-way analysis of variance (ANOVA), 350
Type I error, 133
Type II error, 133–134

UnCover, 188, 189

Validity of measurement, 62–64, 71–72
construct, 63, 64
content, 62, 64
defined, 62
Validity of research, 5
Variables
active, 80
assigned, 80, 82
attribute, 80, 82
categorical values, 6
criterion, 101, 120
defined, 6
dependent, 80, 88–89, 90
experimental, 80
extraneous, 80, 82
independent, 80, 90
manipulated, 17, 80, 82
numerical values, 6
predictor, 101, 120
responding, 17, 78, 80, 81
Variance, 78, 81–82
Variation
defined, 112
quartile deviation, 112
range, 112
standard deviation, 112–115
variance, 78, 81–82

What Is Classroom Discussion? A Look at Teachers' Conceptions, 12, 39–40, 56, 73, 152–153, 176, 222, 233–245
Work products, 340–345